The Artist as Culture Producer

The Artist as Culture Producer

Living and Sustaining a Creative Life

Edited by Sharon Louden

Beth –
You are amazing.
With love,
Sharon

intellect Bristol, UK / Chicago, USA

to the special people in my life who have opened gateways

to allow me to create

and have accepted me for who I am

without reservation

First published in the UK in 2017 by
Intellect, The Mill, Parnall Road, Fishponds, Bristol, BS16 3JG, UK

First published in the USA in 2017 by
Intellect, The University of Chicago Press, 1427 E. 60th Street,
Chicago, IL 60637, USA

A catalogue record for this book is available from the British Library.

Zoë Charlton
Fort Mose
30"x22"
Collage, stickers, graphite, and gouache on paper
2014
Photography by Greg Staley
Courtesy of the artist

Cover design and typesetting by Holly Rose
Copyediting by Susannah Schouweiler
Additional copyediting by Vinson Valega
Production editing by Jessica Mitchell and Jelena Stanovnik

ISBN: 978-1-78320-726-8
ePDF ISBN: 978-1-78320-727-5
epub ISBN 978-1-78320-728-2

Printed in the UK by Gomer Press Ltd on sustainably sourced
Claro Silk paper using vegetable based inks

CONTENTS

PREFACE

From an extensive book tour for my first publication, *Living and Sustaining a Creative Life: Essays by 40 Working Artists*, I learned that visual artists are still widely misunderstood. The old perception remains that artists toil in obscurity, struggling in their studios to heroically reveal the fruit of their labor after much suffering. This traditional viewpoint is still held by the general public, arts enthusiasts, arts professionals, and even fellow artists (both young and old). Over time, I became convinced that this out-of-date characterization—coupled with the stubborn, tired cliché of the starving artist lacking in both personal hygiene and socially acceptable behavior—continues to undermine the true value of the visual arts in our communities. It is time to finally retire the myth of the "Artist Hero" and start embracing the message of the Artist as Culture Producer.

One can easily argue that every artist creates culture simply by making work and sharing it publicly. Although there are plenty of terrific artists who confine art making to their studios, they are not the focus of this book. Instead, I am broadening what it means to produce culture today. For me, the Artist as Culture Producer is someone who reaches outside of the studio to extend creative energies and pursuits into his or her community. It is more than traditional community building, though, since these artists make work and are not, by definition, social workers. They inject creative culture into the cracks of society, where they alter the direction of small towns and large cities, corporate environments and political campaigns, educational institutions and not-for-profit organizations, and within the art world itself. They are on the front lines but hidden in plain sight, informing, educating, inspiring, challenging conventional wisdom, and helping us with their creativity to solve problems and contribute to the well-being of others. Most importantly, these artists exude a spirit of generosity, which was a prerequisite to being included in this book.

The 40 artists that comprise this collection of essays share their exceptional stories, affirming that visual artists of the 21st century are not limited to what many consider traditional art making, but instead oftentimes choose to extend outward in a wide variety of collaborative ways. For instance, Wendy Red Star, raised on the Apsáalooke (Crow) reservation in south-central Montana, has helped re-energize Native culture and imagery in contemporary art dialogue through her work, which is both delightful and humorous, yet serious and profound. Lenka Clayton has led a colorful life, picking up and moving to a city in which she had never before lived. There, she started a free residency for mothers, entitled "Artist Residency in Motherhood." Brothers Billy and Steven Dufala are Philadelphia residents who started a not-for-profit organization located in a demolition waste recycling facility (Recycled Artist in Residency) that challenges traditional notions of how and where we interact with the arts. Andrea Zittel tracks her long running A-Z enterprise, from inception to its current iteration, called A-Z West, located in the California desert. Throughout her career she has focused on building environments that involve community and exchange with other artists. Shinique Smith's collaborative work in the film industry eventually led her back to her roots in the visual arts, where her openness and generosity created pathways for herself and other artists to thrive.

These essays also reinforce the reality that there is nothing romantic about the artist's life. We are just normal, hardworking individuals who are devoted to making the most of our creativity during our short time on this planet. Although it might surprise some, artists are quite similar to the mechanic who services your car, the real estate agent who finds you a house, or the head of your bank down the street. We provide a service to society like every other profession, creating economic value and contributing to the well-being of others on a daily basis. By simply being part of the conversation, our creativity yields freedom, independence, and high productivity. Through our individual efforts and inclination to collaborate, we are committed to sharing and contributing our talents and expression where it can do the most good.

There are 22 women and 18 male artist-contributors in the book. Thirty-six reside in the United States, two in the United Kingdom, one in the Philippines, and one in Australia. Two who appear in my first book — Austin Thomas and Sharon Butler — extend and elaborate on their stories from those previous essays. Many work under the proverbial radar, but all exhibit their work within the commercial art market. Most importantly, these artists are humble, generous, and mindful of others. They are naturally gifted teachers in one form or another. And all stretch their creative output beyond a singular practice, providing services and outreach to many different types of communities the world over.

Unlike my first book, I was not acquainted with many of these artists before I approached them about contributing to this collection. Through the editing process, which sometimes involved many drafts, lengthy conversations, and countless emails, I came to know them all much better. For that, I am grateful to now count them as part of my community. Through these transparent, first-hand accounts, I am confident that you will also feel the same warm and inspiring connection to these exceptional and generous artists.

Hrag Vartanian, Editor-in-Chief and Co-founder of *Hyperallergic*, provides a definitive and inspiring foreword, setting the tone for the essays to follow. Both through his own writing and his daily publication, he is a tireless advocate for artists around the globe. His efforts to show the true value of artists in society are unparalleled.

The three exceptional women who have contributed the concluding statements work on the frontline of the visual arts ecosystem. They are all committed to building bridges between artists and the public, helping to normalize the role of the arts in society. Deana Haggag, Director of The Contemporary, a nomadic museum in Baltimore, Maryland, understands what it takes for an artist to resist and defy chaos in her city. Courtney

Fink, Co-founder of Common Field, devotes her efforts all over the country to bringing experimental work to communities where it is most needed. And Chen Tamir, Curator at the Center for Contemporary Art in Tel Aviv, Israel, addresses the limitations in arts funding today as a form of censorship.

Following the model of my first book, I have chosen to preserve the voice of each contributor by allowing as little editing as possible. I want you to hear their unique voices in your head as you read these stories, each personality demarcated by his or her unique cadence, knowledge, humor, and experience. The length of each essay varies, which was intentional, since I knew that some of the contributors would simply start a conversation, while others would complete an entire story.

Austin Thomas and I often use a phrase to describe selfless artists as those who "plant seeds to grow trees." We consider them "gardeners of creativity" who cultivate generosity by helping artists and other members of our community, thereby yielding more generosity. Visual culture is spread throughout society this way, and the greater good is better served. It is my hope that *The Artist as Culture Producer* will help disseminate, to both the general public and fellow artists alike, the important roles visual artists play in mainstream life. By their everyday actions, artists embrace creativity as a right and show us how freedom leads to a highly valued life.

FOREWORD

At the dawn of the High Renaissance, in 1480 to be exact, the wealthiest artist in Florence was Neri di Bicci, who didn't make his fortune from the altarpieces he's known for today, but from the sale of small tabernacles containing a "painted plaster sacred image (made with a mold), and in an 'antique style' wooden frame." The second richest artist in town was di Bicci's student, Andrea di Giusto Manzini. He's largely unknown today, but during his lifetime Manzini was also a "painter of plaster statues."[1] Artists, it appears, have always been creative at finding ways to sustain their creativity, and their artistic, personal, public, and financial lives have always been more complicated than they seem.

Only recently have we begun to talk about the economic and social realities of being an artist, long hidden under the myths of "genius" or "passion" that can marginalize the serious work of making art. Books like this one are helping those artists trying to shake free of the unrealistic fantasy created by a steady stream of inflated stories about the luxury art market and how it caters only to the richest 1%.

Though the new media spotlight on contemporary art has given the field renewed attention and glamor, there's another type of renaissance taking place in the art world around the evolving relationship of artists to society, and it's one that's largely overlooked. This new wave is being led by creative individuals working to revitalize their communities, often redefining their roles, and challenging the boundaries of art today. Artists are our conscience; they are innovators, healers, chance-takers, and activists. Most importantly, they are a microcosm of society.

Artists excel at generating new models, and their resilience and popularity often come because they respond to the idea of culture as a lived, constantly evolving, and malleable thing that springs from the fount of everyday life. If contemporary art, particularly its newer forms—like performance, new media, street art—has blurred the boundaries of work and life, then all the systems that sustain this type of work are slowly catching up. The lives of artists tell us about our society, and how we do (or more shockingly don't) properly value those who help produce some of the most important aspects of our culture. They are stories we need to hear.

Some may be apprehensive about the idea of artists as cultural producers, but the evolving nature of artistic practice means we have to adapt our language to reflect a new reality. Artists can't be beholden to old stereotypes of inspired acts of creation—or even galleries and museums—to determine their path. They work in culture, but they're also plugged into larger networks of power, finance, identity, and information systems; they create the objects, generate the ideas, and produce the models that allow others to dream, feel, and ponder. Sometimes they reflect our world back at us, and the best of them do it with uncanny precision. Others imagine what we thought impossible and wait while everyone else catches up.

In my dream world, artists would be part of every aspect of our lives. They would help make hospitals more receptive and healing places; they would create street furniture that encourages contemplation and community, and they'd help local governments communicate more effectively with the public. I hope this book will help shatter the old stereotypes of artists as exotic and enigmatic creatures and, in their place, construct a new image using stories of individuals who sustain remarkable artistic lives while nurturing themselves with families, activism, volunteerism, small businesses, hobbies, and politics.

Sharon Louden is one such remarkable individual, who has been a proponent of rethinking artists' roles in society and responding to their needs. When I first met her, I immediately recognized how much compassion she had for her fellow artists—their lives, work, and even their insecurities—but also how contagious her commitment and optimism can be.

How do we create art that challenges capitalism? How can we find new ways to give comfort to those confronted with violence? How do we shed light on those overlooked by society? Why do we make art in a culture that can be antagonistic towards it? Why even continue? The answer to these questions lies in the work of individuals who imagine the future before us, and we call them artists.

Hrag Vartanian
Editor-in-Chief and Co-founder, *Hyperallergic*

1. Guerzoni, Guido. *Apollo & Vulcan: The Art Markets in Italy 1400–1700* (East Lansing, MI: Michigan State University Press, 2011), p. xxiii

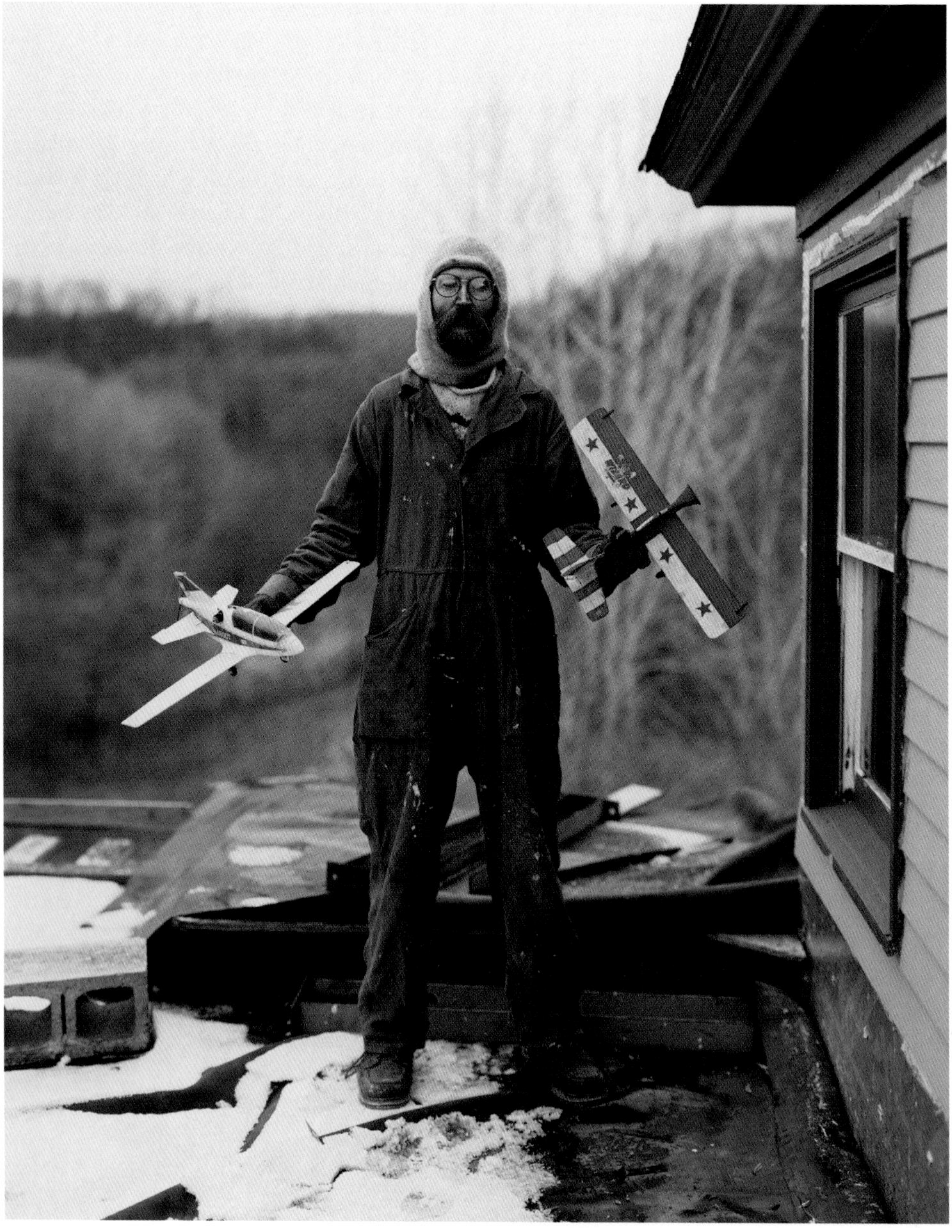

Alec Soth
Charles, Vasa, MN
Chromogenic print
Various dimensions
2002
Courtesy of the artist

I grew up as an introverted kid in a rural area just past the suburbs of Minneapolis. I spent a lot of time in my own imagination, usually in the company of one of my dozens of pretend friends. When I became a teenager, this introversion morphed into social awkwardness. I didn't have a way to express myself, and I lacked confidence. But when I was 16, an art teacher named Bill Hardy saw that something was going on beneath the surface with me. His encouragement to dive back into my own imagination changed my life forever.

Mr. Hardy was a painting teacher, so that was my initial path toward expression. But I felt somehow fraudulent as a painter. Along with my technique lagging behind my creativity, I wasn't comfortable in the studio. In college, I started doing sculptures outdoors. After a while, I started documenting these sculptures with a camera. This led me to a path of becoming a photographer.

One nice thing about being a photographer, at least in the pre-digital era, was that it opened up certain job opportunities. I dabbled in wedding photography and assisted commercial photographers. I also worked for a while as a suburban newspaper photographer. But I found that doing photography as a job killed my love for it. So, I ended up working in darkrooms. These were depressing jobs, but at least they didn't kill my primary love for wandering around taking pictures.

For over a decade, I worked these low-paying jobs in Minnesota and continued to pursue my own photography.

I was tough on myself. If I didn't do work every week, I would get upset. I certainly wasn't making a living doing art, nor did I think I ever would, but my whole identity was nonetheless wrapped up in the activity.

As my work developed, good things started to happen. I had a few small shows in the Twin Cities. After years of rejections, I finally got a grant. That grant seemed to open the doors, and more fellowships followed. As part of one of these grants, I had a studio visit with a notable curator. I didn't think the visit went particularly well, but he ended up recommending me to the Whitney Biennial.

The Biennial was my big opportunity. Fortunately, I had put enough time and energy into developing my work that I was ready to capitalize on this moment. I quit my job and committed myself entirely to my career. I got a gallery in New York and a book deal, and I made the most of things.

My art career was going great, but I was skeptical that this moment would last, mature enough to know that the art world is based on fashion. So, I decided to create a backup plan. Since I didn't have an MFA, teaching wasn't much of an option. Instead, I leveraged my art world success to get magazine jobs. I took every job I was offered. At first, this usually meant photographing Twin Cities executives for business magazines. It was creatively empty work, but I was learning. I figured, if the art career fell apart I could fall back on doing commercial work.

I made a ton of mistakes. But over time I got better, became more connected in the editorial world, and got offered more jobs. I also got better at knowing which kinds of jobs would open things up for me creatively. I applied to Magnum Photos—the legendary international photographic cooperative. It took six years, but eventually I became a full member.

I set up two paths to my career: one in the art world and another as a working photographer. But still, something was missing. When my second child was born, I knew I was going to be staying home a lot. Hungry to exchange creative ideas with others, I started a blog. At first, this blog energized me. But as it became more and more popular, I soon felt it turning into another business. So, eventually I killed it off.

A year later, something else took its place. I was getting interested in self-publishing and decided to create a little DIY outfit, called Little Brown Mushroom (LBM). LBM was a place to experiment and collaborate. I worked with other designers and artists. Our goal was never to make money. It was a place to play and learn. I thought of it as my sandbox. As with the blog, eventually this sandbox became popular, and I could start to feel economic expectations. As I'd done with the blog, I decided to dismantle and then rebuild. In this case, I decided to stop my focus on publishing and move toward an educational venture. I'm currently at the very beginning of our new LBM project, entitled the Winnebago Workshop: a free mobile classroom for teenagers. This project is fundamentally a way to give something back after having had my life changed as a teenager by my art teacher.

My career now has three paths: the art world, the editorial world, and Little Brown Mushroom. All of these paths intersect and diverge at different points, but I find them all necessary. The art world largely pays my bills. The editorial world keeps me in contact with large audiences. Lastly, LBM functions as a non-commercial incubator. At this point, all three of these paths depend on each other for success. Setting up these three outlets has been enormously satisfying, but I wouldn't say it is easy. The biggest challenge is balancing all of these activities with my life at home. I have a wife and two children and travel relentlessly. There is never enough time. In the end, either my family life or one of my career trajectories is always being neglected. I do the best I can to keep all of the plates spinning, but now and then one crashes to the floor.

I've considered alternatives, such as just making work for the art world and being with my family. But I'm fairly certain that streamlining my work would actually be a recipe for stasis. If I were only spinning two plates, I'd likely get bored and drop them both. My creativity thrives on risk of failure.

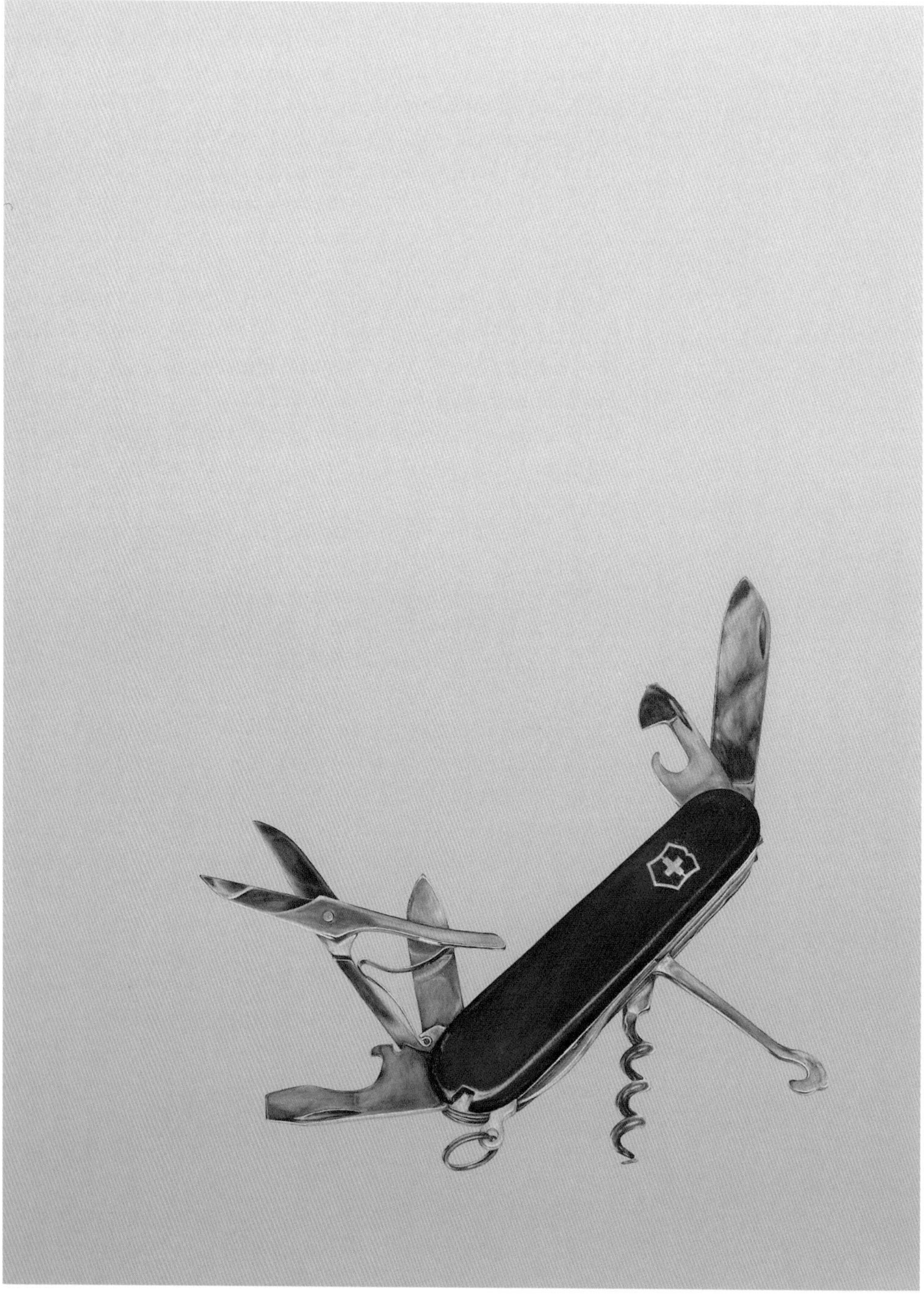

A life in art is something that my parents had never envisioned for me. To be fair, this could be said of most parents whose children chose similar career paths. It was true of my folks especially, though, who immigrated to the States from Hong Kong seeking higher education to build a good life for themselves and, ultimately, for my brother and me. (While they couldn't be prouder of us, ironically, we both ended up as artists.) My parents settled in the suburbs of Chicago and found the best schools for us to enroll. My K-12 education included Catholic school, elite summer schools, and even moving to situate us in a better public school district.

However, I believe my attraction to the arts developed at a small Montessori school, where I have my earliest memories of connecting to the creative process. The philosophy of Montessori schools' hands-on learning through repetition, order, and exactness within long uninterrupted blocks of work time was something that resonated with the sense of discipline and structure that was already instilled at home. I recall sitting at the same station for hours on end, obsessively stitching and unstitching buttons until they were all perfectly mounted to a single piece of cloth. Perhaps it is that early experience working in this type of controlled environment that now drives my attraction to and comfort with working in the deepest middle of the night. With everywhere shut down, everyone fast asleep, and everything still, I feel totally alive, completely independent

Alison Wong
Cure For The Broken Hearted
(detail)
30"x22"
Colored pencil on paper
2015
Courtesy of the artist

and in control, free of judgment and distraction. Even now, it is this time when I flourish in the studio, because it's in these moments that I gain an overwhelming sense of being capable of tackling anything and it's this mindset that carries my practice.

Given the importance that my parents placed on education, going to college was a given, and I knew I had to start thinking about it early. By then, my interest in art was evident, and my parents were supportive of that—for example, allowing me to trade in math camp for art camp. So, at roughly age 13, when I announced that I wanted to go to art school, it didn't come as such a shock, but I did have to work for it. I conducted extensive research on the various programs and possible careers in the fields of art and design to build a case for why art school would be the right decision for me. We visited nearly every art school in the US and an obligatory handful of liberal art schools with strong visual art programs. All this data was used to determine a top ten list of acceptable schools to which I would apply. Even though I had a clear first choice, I prepared and completed applications for all ten, nine of which were never even mailed since I accepted early admission to the Maryland Institute College of Art (MICA), where I would receive my BFA in 2004. Late nights in the studio continued as I began to find my voice, with the support of numerous colleagues and professors along the way. Most memorably, during my freshman year, I had a mentor who taught me the importance of finding personal meaning. Rather than merely executing assignments, I began finding and creating connections through art, learning the joy of doing things for myself and not just for validation or getting good marks.

After MICA, I repeated the application process for graduate schools, only seven this time, and made the decision to attend Cranbrook Academy of Art, completing my MFA in 2006. Having been a student my entire life, from preschool to grad school, I thought it would be a seamless transition, but I had some difficulty adjusting to the nontraditional structure of Cranbrook's "no teachers, no classes, no grades" approach. At the time, the average age of the student population there was nearly ten years my senior, so most had had full-time jobs before and more or less took on a 9-to-5 studio practice. While I tried to fit that mold, it ran counter to my way of working and was hard to manage alongside a work study position assisting the curator of the alumni gallery at the Museum, on top of two part-time positions as a nanny and a clerk at an upscale children's shoe store. Although it was overwhelming, I realized by trusting my natural rhythm (and ditching the retail job) I could, in fact, do it all. Being so overloaded actually became an asset, as it didn't allow any room for dilly-dallying. I was forced to make the absolute most of my time. Toward the end of my two years of graduate study, I was panic-stricken about being spit out in the world as a fully formed adult, no longer able to cling to the safety blanket of being a student.

Luckily, just before commencement, I was offered a temporary position at the Cranbrook Art Museum coordinating an annual fundraiser (a role previously filled by the former curator, who I had assisted). While this wasn't what I imagined doing right out of school, I was happy to stay connected to the institution. I gained experience in planning major events, engaging with benefactors, and overcame the anxiety of making cold calls to solicit donations. There was also the glimmer of hope that the curator position would eventually be offered but, not being one to wait around, I simultaneously pursued and said yes to every additional opportunity that presented itself. Knowing that I am at my best when busy, I filled my plate with sitting on volunteer committees at various arts organizations, teaching an intensive summer arts program for high school students, and taking on several guest curating gigs. Still, my professional future remained an unknown. I didn't have a clear plan, like so many of my peers who aspired for a tenure-track teaching position–quite the opposite, in fact. Even though I had completed the qualifications required to teach at the college level, at 23 years old and with zero experience, I knew teaching was not what I wanted to do at the time. In part, it was the insecurity of my age, knowing I did not yet have the means to live up to the standards set by the influential professors I'd had. But what it boiled down to is that I simply wasn't ready and wasn't willing to do something I didn't have the confidence to do well.

As a result of all my paid and unpaid involvements, I came into my first "permanent" position. Through my work on the museum fundraiser, I gained the attention of Cranbrook's board chair, who recommended me as curator for a traveling exhibition. One of the locations was a local art center, and the exhibition was timed in conjunction with the unveiling of the space following a major renovation. The director of the center was impressed with the show and asked me to join their exhibition committee. I volunteered on that committee for only three months before the center underwent restructuring, and I was asked to take over their exhibition and educational programming, an offer I accepted six months after graduation. This position was pivotal to my professional practice, in all its ups and downs. It was here that I gained understanding and experience organizing programs single-handedly, from development to implementation; I established my curatorial vision and built relationships with artists in the community. It was an incredible experience that pushed the limits of what I thought I was capable of doing. I also learned the very real challenges of nonprofit work. We were a staff of two full-time and one part-time employees. I was in a permanent, part-time, salaried position that amounted to 36 billable hours a week, to save them from having to provide benefits. However, because of my refusing to give any less than 100%, I clocked on average 50-plus hours a week. After five years at the center, I made the difficult decision to leave. It may have been the first time I said no to anything. I drew a line, and that line was drawn on the issue of value. I was hired to elevate the quality and level of exhibitions within the dialogue of contemporary art. While I believe I was successful in doing so by presenting work that brought in new audiences and inspired conversation among existing ones, there remained a majority of the center's constituents that simply wanted things the way they were before. So, more than the value of financial compensation, I came to question the value of what I was both providing and receiving, knowing it could be better served and obtained elsewhere.

Backing up a little bit, during the search to find employment, I had continued to make and show my own work. In 2007, I was invited to join a Detroit artist collective that grew out of the

Museum of New Art. The objective of the group was to create exchanges with galleries outside of our region. We exhibited their artists' work in Detroit and, in turn, showed ours at their spaces in cities such as Chicago, Berlin, Beijing, and Vienna. With all of these exhibition opportunities, I struggled to keep up my studio practice from the living room. So, in 2009, I was ready to move my studio from a coffee table to a dedicated workspace. Given the climate at the time, available space was abundant and affordable. I was fortunate to find the perfect location to house not only a studio but also a venue to further my interest in curation and engagement within the community. This was the birth of Butter Projects, an artist-run studio and exhibition space in a beautiful little storefront that represented everything an artist needs as a place to make, exhibit, and discuss art. The name is a nod to the history of the space, which was originally a market, paired with the concept that butter is an easily accessible ingredient used in the most decadent of dishes—butter, like art, makes everything better!

I founded Butter Projects with another artist as a space dedicated to creating and exhibiting art. We opened our first exhibition, *Something, Everything,* featuring a collaborative installation to mark our new working relationship. This inaugural event was treated more like an open house than a formal exhibition in celebration of our new venture. Thinking we would bring together 50 to 60 of our closest friends, we were blown away by the response: over 300 attendees in our 1,200-square-foot space. It quickly became clear that there was excitement and support for what we were doing. I saw the space as an opportunity to pursue my goals in further engaging and promoting artists in the Metro-Detroit area, serving as a platform for education, dialogue, collaboration, and exchange of contemporary art, literature, and performance. Since our grand opening we have exhibited hundreds of local, national, and international artists. Butter Projects' programming focuses on small group exhibitions to allow us to work closely with artists to realize projects together as well as create connections with each other. In addition to passion and determination, sustaining a project like this takes time and money, two things I think you can never have enough of. Making it all work meant a constant balancing of priorities, scheduling, finances, etc. —all of which I continue to shift and juggle to this day. In our first year, I blew through a majority of my savings getting the space built out and promoting all our programs. To help even things out, I brought on two additional artists to share the load of rent and expenses. While this helped financially, it became a larger job to manage all the parties concerned, with more time spent on conducting meetings and negotiating expectations. At the end of the year, two artists dropped off and soon after, the last one followed. Determined to keep the momentum going, my partner, who had been there supporting the project all along, officially joined me, and the two of us have been keeping it alive since. I approach the space the same way I would a work of art—with lots of tiny adjustments and creative problem solving. Some solutions include taking on additional jobs to help cover expenses, reducing the quantity of programs to keep the quality up, pulling a few pages from my fundraising playbook, and my partner initiated the birth of Butter Press, a publication component to drive sales and extend exposure beyond the duration of exhibitions and the physical gallery space.

The journey I've taken to make ends meet has included an array of jobs, often working three or more simultaneously and, in the thick of it, juggling as many as five. Each position provided me unique opportunities that have all led to where I am today. I was briefly brought on to build a library catalogue for an art foundation where I was surrounded by an incredible collection. I took on freelance work with an architectural consultant, running national competitions and selections, where I got to work with some of the most renowned architects. I accepted a development position as alumni relations manager, where I created lasting connections and networks. Among all the arts-related employment, I also bartended on weekends, which I enjoyed for the social and physical aspects of the work, and because the only part of the job I took home with me was the cash. I was doing so much that I couldn't wait for my shift, because it was like a vacation from taking calls and responding to emails associated with my other responsibilities.

I am so grateful for each and every one of these experiences, and it's hard to believe, none of which I actually applied for.

Who's to say? It could be just a long string of dumb luck, or perhaps a combination of hard work and putting myself out there. I think I'm more successful at having my actions speak louder than my words. I find it so much easier to just put my nose down and do great work than to waste the energy on convincing someone that I'm great. Again, I attribute this to having an artist's mind, with a focus on doing and making. For one of the two jobs I did apply for (and, by the way, did not get), during the interview I was asked about my "technical ability." I confidently and sincerely responded, "Quite good: my paintings are very representational with meticulous attention to detail and craftsmanship." What I completely missed was the fact that, since I wasn't applying for a job as a painter, the panel was asking not about my proficiency as an artist but with computer programs. While thinking like an artist in this situation didn't pan out for me, it usually does. In addition to working hard, I also pay close attention to the details. I'm able to visualize possibilities and am always looking to make personal connections. I'd like to think these qualities are what led to my current positions as adjunct faculty member at the College for Creative Studies (CCS) and director of Wasserman Projects.

Back in 2006, I wasn't prepared to teach, but I started doing so in 2014 after receiving a call from the chair of the fine arts department at CCS asking me to substitute for a painting course for one semester. I was surprised by the offer, in part because I thought the call was about a recent request I sent him to participate in an event for the Museum of Contemporary Art Detroit (where I sit on one of their committees). It turned out he had gotten to know me and my work through Butter Projects, speaking engagements, and exhibiting locally. It was yet another opportunity I couldn't turn down. Despite my early reservations, I had grown more comfortable with the idea of teaching; I realized that's what I'd been doing all along in my role at the art center and Butter. Besides, I wouldn't know unless I tried, and if I failed, it would only be for one semester. On the other hand, if I didn't suck, I would come away with some experience under my belt to pursue teaching later if I wanted. Well, it turns out I didn't suck. I was offered the position, as adjunct faculty, to continue teaching the same course, and I am enjoying it fully.

In the summer of 2015, I assumed my most recent position, as director of Wasserman Projects, an interdisciplinary art space in Detroit's Eastern Market neighborhood. Founder Gary Wasserman and I first met when I was a student at Cranbrook, and our paths continued to cross at various art functions. On one particular visit in 2014 to Butter Projects, we shared our stories of how we came to start these art spaces. We spoke at length about our goals, including all the highs and lows, successes and failures. While operating at different levels, there were many commonalities in our experiences and we connected on countless aspects. At the root, we shared the desire to be part of a dialogue and to make a small contribution to the bourgeoning art scene in Detroit. So, when Wasserman Projects decided to move locations and grow their programming, Gary engaged me in a new discussion—one that further intertwined our two narratives. To work on a project with endless possibility and potential, with someone I respect, was one of the easiest decisions to say yes to. It has been incredibly rewarding to have the ability to do work that draws on all my past experiences, while developing and learning new skills that can be merged together. It is truly a collaborative effort that extends far beyond the gallery walls, with numerous other individuals and organizations doing valuable work.

My choice to stay in Michigan, post-grad school, was at first driven by opportunity and convenience. The reason I wouldn't want to be anywhere else today is my profound respect for the art community in Detroit. I place a lot of emphasis on engaging broad audiences and making connections, many of which I initiate through studio visits. I treasure the relationships that have developed from spending countless hours getting to know the work and the people behind it, not only in studio visits, but because I always make an effort to take the time. The tricky part of giving everything I've got to everything I do is managing it all. Being wired to get crazy focused allows me to marathon through, however the downside is that is it often leaves me blind to the periphery. Realizing and admitting this about myself is difficult but critical to achieving and maintaining a level of balance needed to function, as is knowing when to rely on others. The people I surround myself with, from friends to coworkers and, especially, my partner, are all part of the strong support system that help fuel my fire. Taking the time means making the time and knowing when priorities need shifting; for me, that includes a place for friends and family, snuggles with my dog, and a cocktail (or two, or three) every now and again.

This commitment to having it all doesn't necessarily mean having it all at once. That said, I don't think of it as making a sacrifice. The saying "if you love what you do, you'll never work a day in your life" is one I've never really understood, because I absolutely *LOVE* to work. It's like the best kind of addiction, because I am fortunate to have found work that I'm passionate about, that is fulfilling and meaningful to me. In that work I include my career as a practicing artist. While I may not be in the studio from 9-to-5, I'm mentally there all the time, constantly working, 24/7. I've fought criticism from people who see this level of commitment as masochistic; others have said it just isn't possible to be successful as both a curator and an artist. But, to me, one feeds everything else. I wouldn't be able to curate, teach, or paint the way I do if I wasn't doing it all. It's a conscious effort I put forth to lead the life I want to live. There is nothing more gratifying to me than seeing the smallest details of every single one of these thoughtfully considered parts come together into a thing of beauty.

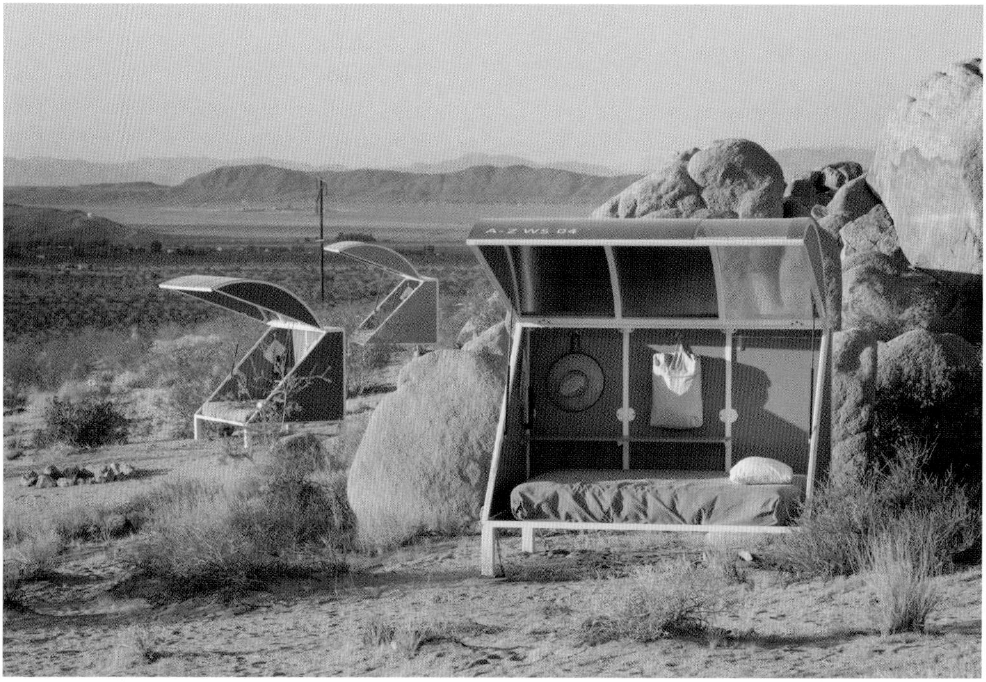
A-Z WS 04

Andrea Zittel
Wagon Station Encampment, A-Z West
2015
Courtesy of the artist and Andrea Rosen Gallery
Photography by Lance Brewer

I grew up in Southern California in the 1960s and '70s, at a time when the entire state felt like it was being developed into an endless suburban sprawl. My parents bought land and built a house in a rural area called Escondido—but by the time I was in high school the entire area had become a suburban neighborhood.

My parents were schoolteachers—liberal, intellectually curious, and interested in travel and culture. But like many people in the larger population, they knew nothing about contemporary art. Art classes weren't encouraged in high school, because they weren't "college prep." In fact, it wasn't until I started college at San Diego State University that I took my first Art 101 class. Instead of teaching us to draw or sculpt, the class introduced more conceptual exercises that no one seemed to understand. There was something about this more abstracted way of thinking that really appealed to me.

After graduating from San Diego State, I was accepted to the MFA program in sculpture at Rhode Island School of Design (RISD). It was 1988, and I did my first cross-country trip over three days in my Volkswagen van, along with my brother and my 80-pound Weimaraner named Jethro. The universal joint in the van broke in Indianapolis, but we managed to get it fixed the same day and got back on the road again. When we got to Providence, Rhode Island, my brother immediately caught a flight home, and I had one of my first, full-on anxiety attacks.

I remember calling my dad from a pay phone (the phone and power hadn't been turned on in my apartment yet) and telling him that I changed my mind and needed to figure out how to get back home. He talked me out of it, but I lived in a state of crisis for several days until Beth Haggart, one of the other MFA students, came over to find out why I hadn't shown up in the office yet, and I finally made my way to campus in time for the first day of school. When I think back about the trajectory of what happened after college, it still seems so unlikely that I would end up going to grad school and, even more, that I would choose a school on the East Coast. I still sometimes wonder: what motivated that bold, ambitious move? Maybe I just wanted something different, and to leave the culture of suburban Southern California, which had always felt stifling and superficial. I think about all the other ways it could have gone—and how significant that one single move ended up being.

One of the first and really hard realizations when I started my MFA was how little I knew about history and contemporary theory. On the academic side, it was hard to catch up in two years. But I think feeling so behind implemented a kind of constructive insecurity, where I feel like I've been working hard to "catch up" ever since. RISD was also a very technical school, and I took advantage of the opportunity to weld, cast metal, and learn furniture making. These skills were all invaluable later on, when I used them both to generate income by working for other artists and to make my own work.

My student work while studying at RISD ranged from formal sculpture to conceptual gestures; by my second year, I was questioning, more and more, what "art" even was, which made it hard to make anything at all. That year was spent in a period of productive inertia, which mostly meant that I worked in my head, rather than making physical objects. My thesis was about "order," and my piece in the thesis show was a very minimal conceptual gesture that consisted of thin tape lines on the ground to demarcate "territories," or regions, of the RISD museum (thinking about the division between natural and political boundaries). This work is surprisingly similar to things I still think about now.

Providence, Rhode Island is a four-hour drive to New York, and, like most of the students in my program, I made it into the city fairly often. I wasn't ready to go back to California after I graduated, so New York was a natural place to gravitate toward at the end of school. In 1990, Manhattan was starting to get expensive, and artists were moving over the bridge into Brooklyn. I settled into a 200-square-foot storefront on South 8th Street in Williamsburg that cost $350 a month. The previous two years of grad school had been paid for by student loans, and this debt limited what I could afford, so the tiny storefront functioned as both a live and work space. I didn't have a phone (this was before computers or the internet) and had to use the payphone a block away to call out. If people wanted to find me, they had to cross the river from Manhattan and come to the storefront. I remember hearing that David Hammonds didn't have a phone either—he was a really important artist by then, and I figured that if he could sustain a career without having a phone, so could I.

Although I rented the storefront out of financial necessity, it influenced so much of my practice. Having a space that was inherently so public was incredibly empowering. Instead of feeling a rush to find a gallery to show my work, I could make work in this space and, when it was ready, all I had to do was open the door and invite people in. Initially, I mostly worked with the large showcase window, but later this thinking would evolve into more direct and immediate forms of public engagement.

Because of my loans, finding steady income was always a top priority; I briefly did a stint casting hydrocal telephone handles for Christian Marclay in his studio near Times Square. Later, Pat Hearn offered me a job at her gallery—my friends who were artists said not to work for a gallery, because I would be pigeonholed as a gallery assistant, but a regular paycheck sounded really good after the tenuousness of freelance work, and I took the job. Alyson Baker was the director. She was around my age, and had grown up with parents who were curators. She was incredibly generous in telling me about the New York art scene—what had happened in the years before I got there and a little bit about each person who came into the gallery. Working at Pat Hearn Gallery demystified the art world. It made things a lot easier when I started to do studio visits and to show my own work.

A few years after I started working for Pat, the recession started to impact the gallery, and the staff got smaller. I found myself taking on jobs that other people had previously done. It was a sobering time. So many galleries had to close, which meant a lot of established artists didn't have galleries or sources of income any more. Even though the art world, in general, was suffering, it was actually a good time to be an emerging artist, since the shrinking art world had really changed people's attitudes toward success and commerce. I know that this recession had a large impact on my practice and the way that I make art. Because I had to work fulltime, my "studio practice" needed to fit into the small crevices of time that I had to myself—literally embedding my practice within the scope of my daily activities. When I started the *Uniform* series, this was something I could do all the time, even when I was working. And the *Living Units* were what I lived in; if I had to spend time and money making furniture, I wanted it to help me evolve my practice at the same time. I also remember thinking that if these pieces weren't successful as art, at least they would still be useful in my own life. One of the most significant impacts of developing a practice during that recession is that I don't think I will ever fully trust the market the way that many artists do now. It's important to me that my work is diverse, self-sustaining, and that it seeks out ways to be independent of any single market or single source of income.

Jack Pierson was one of the artists who showed with Pat Hearn, and I helped him with his installation. I had an old Dodge Dart, and we drove it around town picking up stuff for his show. I think, possibly to return the favor, he told Andrea Rosen about my work. Andrea came to my studio, and it was sort of a crazy studio visit. I can't remember everything we spoke about, but I do remember that lingerie was one of them. Afterward, she asked me to be in a two-person show in her gallery, along with Simon Leung. Andrea said it was important for an artist to take their time and show with different galleries before committing to representation (I always thought of this period as dating). This made sense, so I continued to talk to other galleries until a year or so later, when I finally made the commitment to her as my primary dealer.

Throughout the early 1990s, I was invited to be in more and more shows, and in a few years it seemed like making it as a full-time artist was within reach. Making works for these shows required more time in the studio, so I finally ended up leaving Pat Hearn Gallery and taking on a night shift at a computer output agency. The original plan had been to work at night and sleep in the daytime, but I would always end up working in the studio instead. It was good to have more free time, but it was also intensely exhausting; my body began to break down from the erratic schedule and lack of sleep. My boss miraculously (I believe he did this as a gift) laid me off, so I could collect unemployment for six months. Those six months were the most important "make or break" period of my life—I either had to start supporting myself from my work in that timeframe or go back to working a day job.

Within six months, I was supporting myself (barely) by selling my work. My tiny, 200-square-foot, live/work storefront was virtually impossible to work in, but I couldn't afford to pay more in rent, so I moved into a 1000-square-foot loft in the neighborhood that was still cheap, because it didn't have running water. Living with no water (and almost no heat) was an interesting physical and conceptual exercise; I decided to take that on and to make a body of work informed by this new lifestyle (most of the works that I made while living in the loft were unified, self-contained versions of bathrooms and kitchens).

A year later, my grandmother passed away and my parents were trying to figure out what to do with some modest investments that she had left them. They visited me in my loft, and even though my parents are incredibly hardy and go on long-distance camping expeditions and lived on a 30-foot sailboat for ten years, they thought I should consider an "alternative" living situation that, at the very least, included some basic amenities. No one in my family had ever made a large amount of money, and a huge emphasis was placed on creating security in other ways, such as owning a home. They offered to loan me money from my grandmother's estate at the current going interest rates, if I would buy something with it.

A small row house in the neighborhood came up for sale for $120,000, and I rationalized the debt by figuring that if I couldn't afford the cost of the building, I could live in the basement for free and rent out the three floors above to cover the mortgage. Fortunately, it didn't come to that, but I did rent out the third floor apartment to help cover the mortgage. I used the first and second floors to live and make work in. The building was tiny, but it was a scale that made it easy for me to work with, and I really liked having a storefront again, the direct access that it afforded me to an audience.

Similar to my other storefront and loft space, I used my entire portion of the building for my practice. I called the building The A–Z (later renamed A–Z East after I started A–Z West) and made a different "prototype for living" in each room, which I would live with and then send out to shows when I was done, ready to make a new prototype. Even though this system allowed me to both live with my work and show it in commercial galleries and museum spaces, I never felt like exhibition spaces were the ideal context for my work—often the pieces would feel like caricatures of themselves when I would see them installed in these situations. Because of that, I wanted to find ways to make the work public in its ideal "native" context. So, I opened my space to the friends and people in the neighborhood every Thursday evening, as a way to allow people to see some of these experiments in their original context.

On the second floor of the building, I experimented with different living arrangements—for instance, a series of "fleds," (a cross between a floor and a bed), and a "bofa" (a box/sofa that you would sit inside of). I made a pit bed, which was a large platform with a round pit in the middle of it. When you wanted to go to bed, you would pull two comforters and some pillows out of cubbies that were built into the deck; you could sleep on top of a thick wool comforter and under the down one.

On the ground floor, in the old storefront, we built a bar that was called *Dan's Desk*—Danny, my assistant, also worked as a bartender—and we would serve everyone cocktails out of "A–Z Containers" (since 1994, I have only been using bowls or "containers" for all eating and drinking functions).These Thursday evening open houses turned into cocktail hours; it was the first time in my life I had enough income to afford to buy alcohol, so we enticed people into what was then considered a remote borough by offering free drinks and allowing people to wander through the building and see works-in-progress. One thing I loved about this experience was the diversity of people who came through. The audience ranged from locals in my primarily Polish neighborhood, fellow artists like Ricci Albenda, Wade Guyton, and Judith Eisler, and critics and curators like Jerry Saltz, Roberta Smith, or Klaus Biesenbach, who was just starting out at PS1 back then. I loved A–Z East and my practice right then and felt like I had so much energy for everything that I was taking on. It was sort of a perfect moment, when things really felt like they were coming together.

About a year after moving into A–Z East, I was offered a DAAD residency in Berlin. This was a highly respected residency program usually awarded to more mature artists. While it didn't feel like exactly the right time to take a break from my project in Brooklyn, which was just gaining momentum, the grant paid $1,000 a month as a living stipend. I accepted the residency, viewing it a little like a job, figuring that if I took it, I could live and make work for the year without worrying about having to generate outside income. Despite how public my projects tend to be, I'm actually a total introvert and often extremely socially awkward. Without my project, I felt very isolated. It was one of the hardest years of my life, but I learned several important things about my work and myself. I realized I needed to be living in a space that was my own and that I could manipulate at will. Also, it made me realize how specifically "American" the cultural references in my work are. Both of these understandings, in different ways, motivated my desire to later move back West. I actually started traveling to California from Berlin during my residency in order to start working on a series of conceptual models for recreational vehicles called "Escape Vehicles." Although the year in Berlin was difficult, there were some good moments—for instance, while living there, I was curated into *Documenta X* and *Skulptur Projekte Münster*.

At the end of the year, I was so happy to move back to Brooklyn and pick back up with my practice at A–Z East. The next period was really productive, and I felt like I covered a lot of ground with my work in the years that followed. Often, however, when things become too stable, I find myself wanting to push out further. Maybe it's part of being an experience seeker. Also, I was starting to feel homesick for my home culture of Southern California. In New York, I made work that engaged my day-to-day life, but it was difficult to work within the community itself, because East Coast culture still felt so alien to me. Even though I still felt critical about many things in Southern California, in the end, it was my home culture. I knew it was the one place where I could fully function and feel free. In 1998, I very spontaneously decided to move back to Los Angeles using a new West Coast romance to instigate the move. Finally in the fall of 2000, when my LA relationship ended, I bought a five-acre parcel with a small homestead cabin for $40,000. A few months later, I was living in the desert full-time, starting the project that is now known as A–Z West.

The move to the desert felt like it had been in the works for most of my life—living in the desert was a lifelong desire/goal that actually pre-dated any of my art world ambitions. My grandparents (and great-grandparents) had been ranchers in the Imperial Valley, just south of Joshua Tree National Park, and I had spent my childhood vacations at the El Centro Ranch, riding horses and taking trips out to the surrounding open desert. Their lifestyle, while incredibly challenging, seemed like the best of all possible worlds. I loved how each ranch or homestead in the valley felt like an island, surrounded by acres of open land. This model of a self-contained universe, and the resourcefulness that is required to live this way, was one of my personal ideals.

I started out with my first five-acre homestead cabin and steadily bought more land whenever finances allowed. I also kept A–Z East and rented out the ground floor to a café, which helped fund my new life in the desert. The move to the desert was similar to my move to Williamsburg, in that land was incredibly affordable and the location (at that time) had some separation from the rest of the art world. I was interested in living outside of the scene in order to figure out different kinds of roles that contemporary art could play within society at large. In a sense, A–Z West was my refuge and my think tank. I also know that, after years of having a fairly public life, I was excited about creating some privacy. It is ironic that, over the years, A–Z West has increasingly become a public space, offering residencies to outside visitors and resources to local artists.

High Desert Test Sites (HDTS) was started in 2002, when I had two guests come out during the same week. One was Andy Stillpass, a really wonderful collector from Cincinnati and who owned several pieces of my work; the other was my friend John Connelly, who worked at Andrea Rosen Gallery and later started a gallery of his own. We all crammed into my Toyota truck and drove around the desert for several days, starting to brainstorm a collaborative project where we would buy pieces of land and invite artists out to come do projects on them. We settled on the name High Desert Test Sites, which makes reference to the Nevada (nuclear) Test Sites. The name was, in part, a reference to the understanding that art is not always benign. While I believe in art and its transformative value, I also think, in many cases, the unaltered desert is highly superior to any human conceit that is imposed upon it. Since we planned to impose our projects on the desert anyway, it made sense to us to acknowledge that this was a complicated move by choosing a name that didn't have purely benign references.

While we were driving around, Andy found 100 acres in Pioneertown to buy to contribute to HDTS; over time, I bought 40 acres in Wonder Valley, 20 acres in North Joshua Tree, and ten acres in South Joshua Tree. By putting all of these parcels together, we had a lot of terrain to offer the contemporary artists who we invited out to do projects. Our first big event was in fall of 2002. At that time, Shaun Regen, who was my gallerist in LA, also stepped in to help us, along with my friend Lisa Anne Auerbach, who works with photography, zines, and knitted works. The five of us very loosely ran High Desert Test Sites: each person would visit the desert and contribute something unique to the organization of the program. I was doing most of the on-site and administrative work myself; so, over the years, as the other founding members became busier with their own lives, I've continued to run HDTS, with the help of new people who come into the mix.

One of the primary goals in the HDTS mission is to support and draw attention to works that engage directly with everyday life. It's always seemed odd to me that artists so often wait for permission to put their works out into the world, waiting to be curated into shows or institutions, when some of the most exciting art just happens in the world itself. I wanted HDTS to support the idea that art can exist anywhere, and that often when work is presented out of context, it becomes much more mysterious, interesting, and relevant. I also wanted to show how much it's possible to do with very little money. When we first started HDTS, there was practically no overhead, since I did all of the work myself. (I used to joke that I was both cofounder and the preparator for HDTS.) Shaun would pay for our mailing announcements before everything switched over to email, and Andy would often help by sponsoring costs of some of the more expensive works, such as the time he hired a 35mm projector to screen Piotr Uklansi film *Summer of Love* in Pioneertown. (I'm actually skipping the best part of that story, which is how the massive screen blew over in a gust of wind before the film was supposed to start, and the projector developed a short which was miraculously fixed when someone had the presence of mind to pour beer on the ground wire.) Since then, as our programing has increased and my personal time has decreased, HDTS has now become a nonprofit organization, and we have a minuscule paid staff to help run our programs.

In 2004, all of this was running along fairly smoothly, when once again the unexpected happened: I found out I was pregnant. I had never really imagined that I would have kids, but when my son was born, it was the beginning of a whole new life. People seemed to expect that I would make work about my son, or that I would make living systems for him the same way that I make work about every other part my life situation. But Emmett is the one person who I've consciously kept out of my work, both out of respect for him, and because I think it's still really hard for women in the art world. I haven't felt ready to trade in my identity as a maker for one as a mother.

Raising a son also made me more conscious of my financial situation. In 2006, the art market, which had been very good for some time, was starting to slump, so I did what a lot of other artists were also doing in preparation for the downturn—I took a full-time teaching job at University of Southern California. Full-time, tenure-track teaching positions are difficult to get, and I was lucky to have a job in a really good up-and-coming program. When I teach and become invested in the trajectory of my students' or friends' careers, it makes me realize how much more difficult it is for artists entering the art world now. The economy of having to pay huge sums for an MFA, as well as the higher cost of living and maintaining a studio in urban art centers, makes it so difficult for artists to survive, let alone to make work. I keep thinking that the economy is the one most important underlying issue that needs to be addressed in order to reform art.

In my own career, I manage to sustain a free-ranging and, for the most part, non-commercial practice by showing with a few understanding and supportive galleries. This has been such a gift, but I realize that this isn't the case for most artists. Because of this, I wanted to come up with an enterprise that created a market which could sustain artists outside of the "art market." Originally, "smockshop" was started in Los Angeles with a few former students and other artists who I'd met and responded to. For the project, I created a very simple design for a multifunctional garment, a "smock", that was then reinterpreted by different members in the collective. We did pop-up "smockshop" sales at various art-related venues. The project was a phenomenal success in creating a nurturing supportive community; unfortunately, it was not a long-term financial success. It was difficult to make handmade, one-of-a-kind garments that were affordable for the average consumer. The project made us realize that, as a nation, our low-cost clothing is entirely based on overseas production; before outsourcing, people historically owned only a few garments, rather than entire closets full of them.

I was spending about three or four days in LA each week and would then rush out to the desert to work and do damage control for the rest of the week. There were no days off, and I would commute at nighttime in order not to lose any work hours. After a few years of living like this, I realized that the situation wasn't sustainable and that having time to do my own practice was more important than money or security. Also, by returning to the desert full time, I was able to trim my personal expenses to the point where the job wasn't as necessary as it once seemed. I slowly worked out of the position at USC and used the money from the sale of the house that I had in LA to build my studio out in the desert. I still miss LA, and my students—but sometimes you have to give up things that you love in order to nurture other things that you love.

Moving to A–Z West, full-time, felt glorious, and all of my projects that had been languishing from lack of time came together quickly, now that I was totally focused on them. At first, I was reluctant to build a big studio, because I liked the idea that one should be able to make art anywhere. But as the galleries that I show with have slowly supersized their gallery spaces, it's become a necessity to have a large indoor workspace to produce works. The studio is now 4,000 square feet and includes an office, a large workspace with roll-up doors, a wood shop, and a weaving studio. Another project that has grown over the last few years is the Wagon Station Encampment—a cross between a residency, a retreat, and a campground—where we host people in experimental living structures that I designed called Wagon Stations. The Encampment is open twice a year for four or five weeks each season. A–Z West now consists of over 58 acres, with about 90 more acres scattered across other parts of the high desert. I am now working on plans for a large-scale outdoor sculpture that will traverse several parcels of land between A–Z West and the nearby highway.

I spend a lot of time thinking about the future of A–Z West and High Desert Test Sites. Going nonprofit with HDTS has not been a magic antidote for our money issues, but it has been interesting learning about different models for sustaining projects. For the time being, A–Z West is still the site of my personal residence and studio practice. But after spending so many years buying and connecting the parcels of land and organizing the studio and encampment into a well honed organism, I eventually plan for it to evolve into an entity that will continue to serve a vital function in the community. In the meantime, it's important to find ways to free myself up to have new experiences and explore new and different ways of making art. Our current goal is for A–Z West is to find ways for it to eventually become financially self-sustaining. We are experimenting with a series of *West Works*, which consist of woven panels and ceramic containers. These are produced and sold through the studio in order to create incomes to support the more collective resources at A–Z West, as well as incomes for artists living and working in the high desert.

As an artist, it's important for me to continually re-examine both my personal and professional values. I think it's important to remain flexible and to never take any given way of living for granted. For instance, I love my life at A–Z West, but I could just as easily see myself living in a more remote, or even transient, situation someday. The question is: just what would living like this mean?

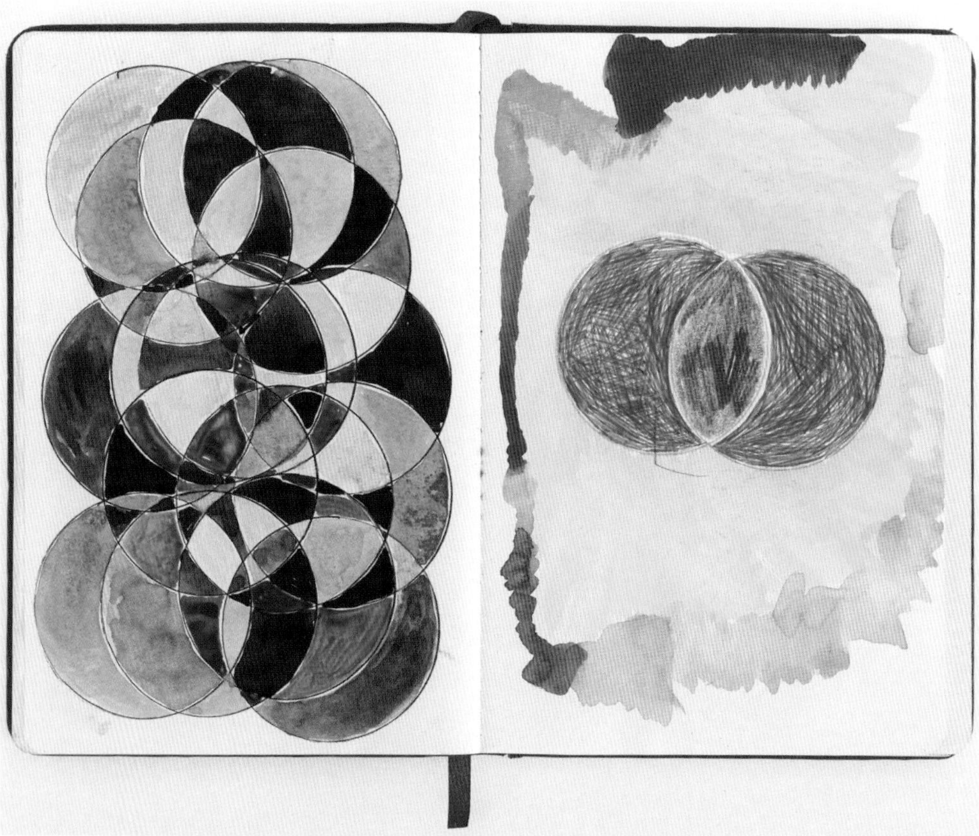

After college, I moved to Washington, DC and worked as a researcher at a socialist think tank called the Institute for Local Self-Reliance. I've always believed they hired me because I was an artist. I organized their database and library and researched environmentally sound and equitable community development.

I moved to New York City in 1994 to finish graduate school at NYU and spent several years working for nonprofits, including Artists Space and *Harper's Magazine*, and for other artists—Betty Woodman and Andrea Zittel (I was the caretaker of her house-as-artwork in Brooklyn). I also worked as an administrative assistant for the president and CEO of a healthcare organization on the Upper East Side of Manhattan. I lived in a couple different places in Manhattan and Brooklyn and was and am still married to my husband Mike, an attorney.

After graduating with my master's degree from NYU, I worked on a particular painting project that had social and anthropological components. Working with poet Suzanne Wise and geologist Kim Knowlton, I made highly detailed portraits of other people's favorite rocks or stones for a project I called *Stones I've Known*. The paintings were coupled with typewritten stories I composed after interviewing the stones' owners to find out where the rock was found, and why it was a keepsake, or special, to its owner. By 1999, I had painted over 200 stone portraits, exhibiting them in my first solo show in New York

Austin Thomas
Two-Paged Painting with Overlapping Imagery
7.7"x10.8"
Watercolor, pen and pencil on paper
2015
Courtesy of the artist

at a little gallery no longer in business, called Sara Meltzer's On View.

My first studio in New York City was located on the fifth floor of a converted warehouse building at 526 West 26th Street in Chelsea, then a burgeoning art neighborhood. Most of the people I saw on the street or in the building on a daily basis were involved in the art world. It was such a small community then that we all knew and tried to support each other. For example, when Carol Green moved into the ninth floor of 526 West 26th Street in 1995 to open the Green Naftali gallery with the backing of building owner Gloria Naftali, I sent a bouquet of flowers. It was a different time.

One day, while riding the elevator to my studio, I ran into Lee Stoetzel, an artist friend who was working for a young collector named Paige West. Lee asked to stop in my studio and have a look at what I was working on. Of course, I said yes. I then asked him to participate in *Stones I've Known,* and he did. He told me about his rock and his personal journey, which I typed up. Lee asked if he could bring Paige to my studio. Paige came and bought several thousand dollars' worth of *Stones I've Known* paintings with their corresponding typewritten stories.

I invested that money back into my work and created something in my studio that I had always wanted to have. It was a freestanding, six-by-six-foot, wooden loft structure for me to climb on and see my work from a different perspective. It also became an attraction for others to climb upon and relax. I called it a "perch." I began inviting a lot of folks to meet on my perch to view my work and share a cup of tea or have a beer. It seemed that I struck a chord with the perch, so I started to build perches for galleries, such as Debs and Co. run by Nick Debs and Mixed Greens, founded and operated by Paige West and for a nonprofit cultural center, Exit Art. I even experimented with making perches for outdoor spaces. In the summer of 2001, I attended a treehouse building workshop at the Yestermorrow Design/Build School in Vermont to further expand my perch-building skills.

On a trip to Home Depot to get supplies for a perch commissioned by the Public Art Fund, I watched a plane hit the World Trade Center. The day after September 11, 2001, I ran into the artist Julian LaVerdiere, who said, "We'll be lucky if we ever make art again." It seemed like I and everyone I knew had post-traumatic stress syndrome. Six months after 9/11, working with a team of architects and artist Paul Myoda, Julian created *A Tribute in Light*, an installation of 88 searchlights placed next to the World Trade Center site, generating two vertical columns of light in remembrance of the September 11 attacks. For me, I had to get far away from New York City.

I found an artist residency run by the Hungarian Multicultural Center and spent three weeks in a small Hungarian town called Balatonfüred. I couldn't even attempt to speak the language, but I did create a whole new body of work. I found my artistic center again by making collages, walking, and looking at the landscape and local architecture of Hungary.

I came back to New York only to spend more time away. I spent a couple of months exhibiting my indoor treehouse perches in Los Angeles at the Chinatown gallery Diane Pruess, run by Joel Mesler. I hosted events in the gallery and was deeply inspired by the art scene there. I spent time in Joshua Tree with Andrea Zittel, and it was there that I fell in love with the Chevrolet El Camino, a half-car, half-pickup truck hybrid.

I came back to New York and, with the help of Wendy Goldberg, a collector and close friend, bought a gold 1973 El Camino on eBay for $2,100. I immediately began planning and constructing a perch with a collapsible table and chairs for the bed of the El Camino. I worked on the project with friends I met at Yestermorrow, architects Kate Harvey, Mark Ericson, and furniture builder Eyrich Stauffer. I called it *Perchance* and thought of it as a float-like scenic overlook.

When my "perch on wheels" was complete, I drove it across country on a carefully planned, Austin to Austin, Texas road trip, thanks to the logistical and programming help of curator Regine Basha. Stopping first at The Bower, an artist-run gallery and living space codirected by Joey Fauerso and Michael Velliquette in San Antonio, Texas, I explained *Perchance* and gave impromptu lectures on the piece, and on my art at schools and other art spaces in Austin.

I hosted lectures, movie screenings, poker games, and picnics in the back of my specially-designed art car. I even spent the month of August, at the invitation of curator Sara Reisman, at

Socrates Sculpture Park in Long Island City, Queens, serving homemade pie out the back of the car. I became an expert on all things pie and vintage cars.

Although I never got a ticket, and the car definitely made the rounds, the El Camino was an expensive art piece to maintain and hard to park on the streets of Manhattan. I managed for a while, but after having a baby, I made the decision to sell the car and *Perchance* on eBay. An El Camino collector in Pennsylvania bought it for $3,500. To this day, I regret handing over the keys.

In 2004, everything changed after having my son, Grant; I had to make art in my head, because I couldn't make it in my studio. Whether changing diapers, wrestling with sleep deprivation, or cuddling my soft, little newborn, I was thinking about art. So, it made sense to sublet my studio. I cleared out my woodworking tools, selling them on Craigslist, and swept up all the sawdust to make room for my first subtenant, Monya Rowe, and her first gallery space in Manhattan. More and more galleries were opening in Chelsea.

Without a studio, I became extremely resourceful: I hung completed works in the hallway of my apartment building for studio visits and worked at empty desk spaces in my friends' offices. I kept track of my experience—in particular, the challenges of working without a dedicated studio space—on a blog called "ATfreespace," writing while Grant napped. I started to read other blogs and slowly began to commune with others writing online, like Barry Hoggard of the now defunct *ArtCal-Guide* and Joy Garnett of *Newsgrist*. Spending nights at home, I became addicted to James Kalm's online videos of gallery openings and exhibition tours.

In 2006, when Grant was two, I took him for a six-week residency at the Contemporary Arts Forum in Santa Barbara (now the Museum for Contemporary Art), thanks to an invitation from the director, Miki Garcia. I built a functional tea room of origami-shaped seats and hosted events for the local arts community. I continued to write about my daily experiences on the blog, and I met many artists, made studio visits, hosted dinners, and organized salons. Years later, I received an email thanking me for helping to organize a small part of the arts community in Santa Barbara. It turns out some of those I met are still meeting monthly for art salons.

Flowing from this community and the way I was making art without a studio, as well from blogging, "saloning," and meeting with other artists, I decided to open an exhibition space. The goal was to create a good place to salon and have a residency program, as well as a gallery space. I convinced my husband and our friend Ted, who helped me build my first perch, to rent me the storefront space in a building we owned together in Bushwick at 1037 Flushing Avenue. I paid $650 a month and called my space Pocket Utopia. I thought of it as a social sculpture. My mom, Sumi-e artist Kay Thomas, gave me a loan for the renovation, and I hired interns, Audra Woloweic and Matthew Miller, to help run the space.

I planned exhibitions and organized events, wrote press releases and editioned affordable prints, but mostly I paid for the space out of my own pocket. I did not set out to create a community of artists, many of whom became very close friends, but that is what happened. I wrote about Bushwick on my second blog, also called Pocket Utopia, and encouraged artists, curators, critics, and collectors to come out for a salon or to see a show. I truly believe I helped kickstart an art neighborhood in Bushwick; soon more galleries opened, and other artists even bought buildings near us, including artist Mary Judge, who now runs Schema Projects out of a storefront in a building she owns.

Seeing Pocket Utopia as a project with a specific beginning, middle, and end, I deliberately closed after two years. After closing Pocket Utopia, I moved into a small studio at the Elizabeth Foundation for the Arts, an organization in the garment district in Manhattan dedicated to providing artists with subsidized working space. I started curating projects with my new neighbors at the Elizabeth Foundation, including Jane Kent, Dorothy Robinson, David Storey, and Karina Aguilera Skvirsky, among others.

At that time, I met Jason Andrew, the founder and director of Norte Maar, a nonprofit arts organization based in Brooklyn and in upstate New York. In the summer of 2010, Jason and I collaborated to create an intergenerational arts camp, Camp

Pocket Utopia (Camp Pocket U.). Jason and his partner, (now husband) Norman, had a house in Rouses Point, New York, a stone's throw from the Canadian border, so that was where Camp Pocket U. was held.

We modeled the camp on the legendary Black Mountain College, a shortlived, experimental art school founded in 1933 in the hills outside Asheville, North Carolina. We offered free art classes to local kids, taught mostly by artists who had either showed, or at least showed up at Pocket Utopia. Some kids commuted an hour each way from Burlington, Vermont to attend camp. We held performances and lectures for adults at night and on the weekend.

We raised enough funds to somehow pay all our teachers. Once there, we provided them housing and worked with a local diner to provide our "camp staff" with breakfast every morning. The local hotel, where we arranged for artists to stay, spelled out "Welcome to Camp Pocket U" on their marquee. Our camp lasted only one summer, but many relationships were formed and seeds were planted for future collaborative projects.

While packing up camp, I got a call from New York City's Percent for Art program informing me that I had been shortlisted to propose a sculpture for a planned outdoor plaza on Humboldt Street in Brooklyn. I was apprehensive at first, as I really didn't want to go back to building perches, but I fell in love with the neighborhood where the plaza was to be located—one subway stop from the original Pocket Utopia. I gave the proposal everything I had, and—after hiring Audra Woloweic, a former Pocket Utopia intern, to assist me in making models for the final presentation—I was awarded the commission.

During the over four years of planning and construction, I watched the Bushwick art scene explode with even more galleries, and I got restless. In 2012, I started having conversations with my network of artists, gallerists, and even other moms about the possibility of opening another Pocket Utopia on the Lower East Side of Manhattan.

Artist and curator Julie Torres hit the pavement for me, meeting with landlords and reviewing rental applications. She found me the perfect storefront space at 191 Henry Street, which was very similar to the first Pocket Utopia, but half the size and more than twice the price at $2,000 a month. I borrowed again from my mom, and when I told them about my plans to reopen Pocket Utopia on the Lower East Side, a couple of artists even approached me, offering to lend me more money, which I accepted.

I started planning exhibitions for my new space and new neighborhood. The shows were to be more commercially-oriented, since the neighborhood around the gallery was more commercial. I decided to experiment with representing only a few artists, including Sharon Butler, Kris Graves, Ellen Letcher, Matthew Miller, and Paul D'Agostino. These artists were like me: they made artwork and contributed to the ebb and flow of the art world, by either writing about art or by running art spaces. Sharon Butler wrote a blog about painting, called "Two Coats of Paint;" Paul D'Agostino ran an apartment gallery called Centotto; and Kris Graves had a gallery in Dumbo, called Kris Graves Projects.

I also made a conscious decision not to show only Bushwick artists. I collaborated with Armin Kunz of C.G. Boerner, an Old Masters print and drawing gallery based on the Upper East Side in New York City and in Düsseldorf, Germany to plan the first show. Armin asked artist Richard Tuttle, who also collected Old Master prints, to curate an exhibition at Pocket Utopia. The exhibition, titled *The Thrill of the Ideal*, included a rare set of landscape etchings of Rome and its surroundings by German painter Johann Christian Reinhart (1761–1847).

In 2013, art critic Roberta Smith wrote in a *New York Times* review of the Tuttle-curated Reinhart exhibition that Pocket Utopia was "one of the more singular bright spots in the Lower East Side firmament." Other galleries opened up on Henry Street, and I witnessed, again, another neighborhood take off.

I also began to exhibit my own work again. In 2014, I had a solo exhibition at Hansel and Gretel Picture Garden, a Chelsea space founded and run by artists Sarah Christian and Jason Vartikar. They suggested that I leave Pocket Utopia empty for the duration of my exhibition at their gallery. I agreed and planned a series of events at Pocket Utopia as part of my exhibition, including potlucks, bingo games, lectures, and workshops. My show of drawings and sculptures, with scheduled "happenings" on Henry Street, was well received, and I began to see Pocket Utopia as an artwork again.

After the show, we decided to merge our two spaces, share certain resources, and grow our audience. I closed the gallery on the Lower East Side and moved to Chelsea. Merging with Sarah and Jason meant a bigger exhibition space for my artists. Our gallery, Hansel and Gretel Picture Garden Pocket Utopia, was located at 511 West 22nd Street. This was the bigtime and, again, the rent increased—this time 350 percent, to $7,000 a month.

Besides organizing shows and shepherding artists' careers, Sarah, Jason, and I started an online art journal called *Art Daily Bread*. We took to the road, first stopping in Washington DC, to speak with museum curators, Klaus Ottmann of the Phillips Collections and Molly Donovan at the National Gallery of Art, about ways to exhibit, look at, and experience art. We explored different ways to function in the art world, be it as a nonprofit space, an artist residency, or even operating without a physical gallery space.

We met and collaborated with Osmos Address in the East Village, working with Cay Sophie Rabinowitz and Christian Rattemeyer. We brewed beer together. I was making a lot of homemade beer at the time, including several batches called "Pocket Hoptopia," while designing the labels and serving it at our openings. We even considered operating a microbrewery in the gallery, but the lease permitted only the exhibiting and selling of art objects.

Ultimately, we decided to close the gallery. Sarah and Jason had a new baby and an hour-long commute from New Jersey to the gallery in Chelsea. In the end, the three of us wanted to shake things up and try different things in the name of art. Our artists wanted us to show and sell their work, but we were trying to keep it interesting for ourselves. The more we did for our artists, the more demands it made on us. We gave our all to the artists by making studio visits, exhibiting and selling their work, publishing their catalogs, and helping them make connections. At the end of the day, we decided to head back to our own studios, whether on a farm in New Jersey (Sarah and Jason) or an empty table at Starbucks (me), and make art.

Although it was inspiring to work with artists, we found it was also liberating to stop working on their careers and focus on our own. We realized that our career aspirations did not include running a gallery and promoting other artists. It is hard enough to make money as an artist; imagine working as a gallerist and not getting paid. We found ourselves working for free. We had to close and rethink what we were doing.

I slowed down, spent more time with my family, read books, and started to research ways art could effect positive change. I educated myself about creative capital and traveled to other cities, like Nashville, Tennessee, meeting with artists and giving lectures.

For a short period of time, I ran a pop-up space called Post Pocket Utopia in Newark, New Jersey, at the Gateway Project Spaces. I brewed beer and organized a crowdsourced photography project, *#seeingnewark*, that anyone using that hashtag could participate in by posting an image of the City of Newark online. I met some incredible artists in Newark, but my attention was elsewhere, as I had to complete my public art piece, *Plaza Perch*.

I recently moved to a tiny studio space in Williamsburg at 84 Withers Street. Located in the shadow of the B.Q.E., an expressway connecting New Jersey, Staten Island, and the Bronx, I read that this building was once home to Flipside, a small artist-run gallery operated out of Tim Spelios and Carolyn Cox's loft. In 1998, Roberta Smith reviewed Flipside, writing that "the neighborhood has long been known in the art world as a place where artists take things into their own hands, opening galleries and running them on shoestrings until energy, money or interest runs out or until their work becomes more consuming." That made me feel at home. In 2000, artist Robin Hill exhibited large, mural-size cyanotypes at Flipside; she was my first studio visit here. So, from this perch on the fourth floor, I will supervise the installation of *Plaza Perch* a few blocks away and contemplate what form the next Pocket Utopia will take.

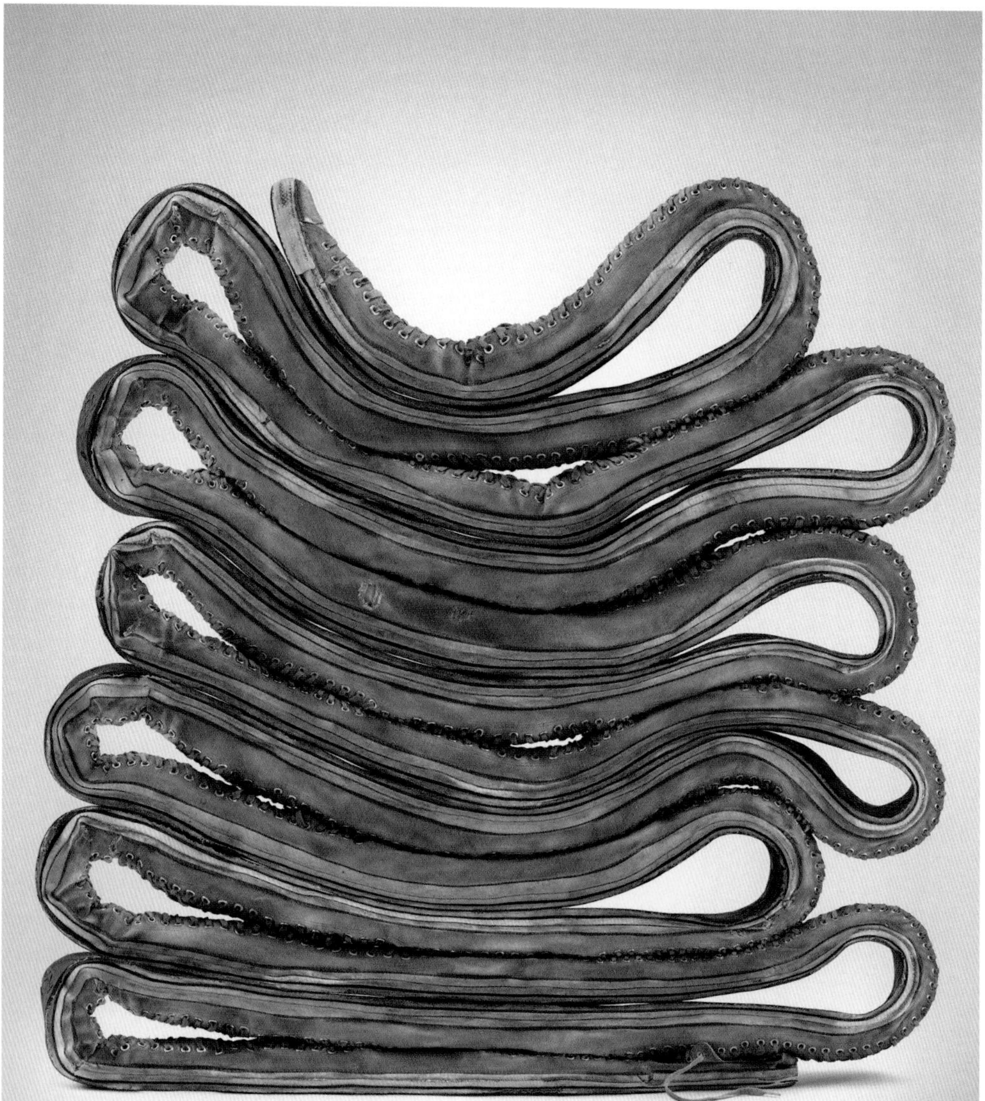

STEVEN: We grew up in a chaotic but very creative household, two of five boys. Both of our parents were trained as pianists, and both taught music. Our father was a zealous do-it-yourselfer, something instilled in us very early on; our mother is a pragmatic and patient woman, something I have tried to emulate my entire life. It is what I see as my *yin* to Billy's *yang*. All of the brothers play music and make art.

Billy and I have always been very close, and we share a basic sensibility about not only the art we now make together, but also about most things in life. Though there are substantial differences in our personalities, it is as if we are moving in parallel lines, near enough to each other in sense of purpose that we have always just taken it as fact that we are collaborators, enablers, friends, and partners. The depth of this relationship is the basis of our practice as artists working together. It is about more than creating artwork; it is mutual trust, a commitment to take the ride together.

I am the middle of the five boys. When I was born in 1976, our parents were operating two day care centers they had recently opened, and our father was in court for an assassination conspiracy to kill the Vice President of the United States after a failed bid for congress in New Jersey. While he was a constant presence, he was an irregular and volatile figure in my life. My care was essentially shared between my mother and my babysitter, who was her good friend who also worked at the

Dufala Brothers
Extra Long Chuck
38"x34"
Archival digital pigment print
2010
Courtesy of the artists and
Fleisher/Ollman Gallery

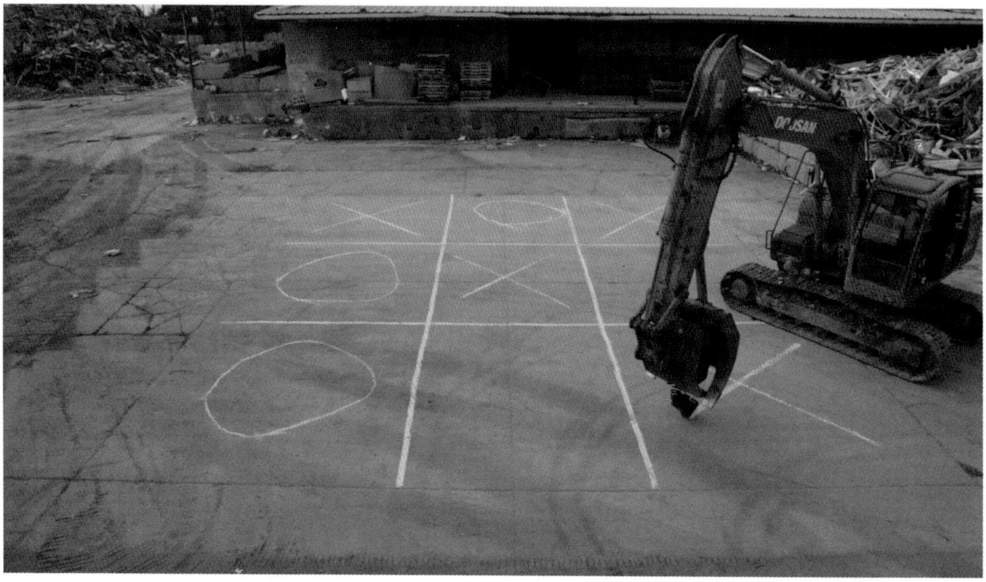

daycare center. So, I kind of had two moms, and I remember spending time with other friends' families, away from home, for a week or more at a time.

Growing up in a daycare center was unique, in that it was an extraordinary social situation. Despite being a relatively shy and quiet person, I learned at a very early age to navigate this complex social world: my siblings, a large circle of friends, and their families, and a general sense of having multiple homes. It is perhaps not surprising that, as an adult, I crave being home, being alone, and being immersed in whatever project I have going, squirreled away in my studio. It takes this respite for me to perform at all in the myriad contexts where Billy and I find ourselves in our creative life.

BILLY: I am the youngest. When I was born, our father was "self-employed," running through what seemed to be a multitude of pyramid schemes and scams, and so he was a stay-at-home father. I was with him all the time until I was seven years old, when our parents divorced. All of a sudden, I was being raised by my older brothers and their friends. I was

Dufala Brothers
Tic Tac Toe
Video still
Duration: 22:05 mins
2015
Courtesy of the artists and
Fleisher/Ollman Gallery

spoiled, got a lot of attention, and sought out attention regularly. Our mother worked four jobs, so my prepubescence was more like adolescence at the same time.

The first musical instrument I played was the drum. The first time I played, I was in second grade, in front of a house party at our childhood home. A heavy metal band had taken a break between sets, and my older brother's friend sat me down behind the drum set, put sticks in my hands, and told me to go for it. Moments later, our mother walked through the door, exhausted from working an 18-hour day, and unfazed proceeded through the crowd of teenagers and twenty-somethings. Somehow, she had faith that it would be okay. She encouraged me to stick to what would make things work for the things that *needed* to work, and that the rest would somehow manage itself.

I am not shy. I am very outgoing and always have been. I gravitate toward situations that put me at the center of whatever is happening. I feed off of this type of experience, albeit I have changed as I understand it better as an adult pursuing a career. It is one of the stark contrasts between me and Steven and, when we work together, it makes the amount of ground we can cover in partnership that much greater. Balance and perseverance is second nature for me. That is one of the similarities between me and Steven…

STEVEN: I moved to Philadelphia from New Jersey in 1994 to study film and animation at the University of the Arts. After two years there, it became clear to me that I wasn't particularly interested in making movies in any traditional sense; I was beginning to make experimental video work, which very few in my cohort really liked. (I was booed at my end of the year show, but very happy with the work I made. This was an important introduction to believing in my work, regardless of whether or not it was well received or accepted by my peers.) Feeling out of place, but energized by what I was learning, I left that program for the Pennsylvania Academy of the Fine Arts (PAFA), a museum school a mere ten blocks north on Broad street.

PAFA at the time was a four-year studio school, its first two years still modeled closely on the traditional European studio school model. It proved to be exactly the thing I was missing, with a depth and rigor that was absent from film school and a student body much more receptive to what I saw as interesting work. My primary interest had become drawing, less as a discipline and more as a type of primary visual language capable of expressing a way of seeing things, a kind of thinking. Keen to avoid the painting department (and its philosophy of drawing tied closely to its service to representational painting), I studied printmaking, where I cultivated this broader understanding of drawing, kept my earlier interest in media arts alive, and gained a real appreciation for printed multiples, complicated and experimental printing techniques, bookmaking, and typesetting. I also began researching nontoxic processes and materials at this time, which in some ways took me out of the print shop on a hunt for information, and began what has become a central aspect of my personal creative practice: research, experimentation, and a unique type of review and critique. Print shops are shared spaces, and so the processes, techniques, and challenges employed there are visible, if not outright shared by all who work there. Make something, and put it in front of people; ask for blunt feedback, and take that feedback standing up.

I was also beginning to sense that my creative life was never going to be rooted in one field, or medium, and was starting to see ideas as mutable things that could stretch across multiple disciplines. I've always loved thinking about things and had come to see drawing as an important language for communication. I also began to understand that *how* a work came to be was integral to my definition of successful work. I was starting down a road of multiple collaborations, and though Billy and I had not yet formally decided to work together, in hindsight, I was laying the foundation for how I would understand collaborative work, in general, and my role in it, specifically. I wanted to be able to work in just about any field, my belief being that, if ideas are important, a broad and multidisciplinary understanding of how this manifests would enable me to do just that.

It was around this time I began working in theater and dance as a designer, more or less as the result of a few serendipitous encounters. My good friend and roommate, the filmmaker

Jeremy Mayhew, and I had been asked to videotape a run of Pig Iron Theater Company's *Gentleman Volunteers,* to document the performance. Our house hosted regular jam sessions, often multiple nights a week. Pig Iron was a relatively young theater company at the time, and after one of the shows, some of us wound up at our place where we played music until very late. James Sugg, the sound designer for Pig Iron and a composer and performer in his own right, invited me to assist him on two new plays they were developing that summer. Once rehearsals started, and it became clear that I was good at a few things in addition to music, I was put to work on all sorts of other aspects of the performance: scenic elements, posters, props. I was hooked, happily exercising so much of my creative self. I guess the main thing it brings back to Dufala Brothers is how much of a team it is, and how the whole team is divided up into specialized areas working together—it's a production, after all, and there is not just one way to do it. I've learned a lot about how to put large projects together so that they allow room for everyone, are enjoyable, and get a good result. With Billy doing so much of the public end of our projects, I feel suited to design the undertaking, so to speak.

Though I had been playing music since a very early age, by high school I had become interested in improvisation, ambient music, and performing. This continued through college, and by the time Billy came to Philly (having already led a group of his own), we were both active in the music scene in Philadelphia. Understanding music as a largely experimental venture, it was simply another tool with which to create and collaborate, for me. Scoring film, creating sound for performance, making recordings on my own—music has been, and continues to be, a central part of my creative life.

I continued experimenting with film and video and, throughout school, continuously found printmaking techniques able mediums for capturing the strange intersections that my work seemed to be exploring. Printmaking is interesting, in part, because it comes from a commercial industry, and so is perfectly suited to translate: going from one form to another, a concept to an image. The print matrix, used to make multiples, seemed a distant cousin to the moving image, and prints can be a relatively affordable artwork to acquire. This was actually very important to me, making affordable art. These ideas would later grow to include ideas about free art, and ways to make things that side-stepped the traditional making of objects for sale, and the process of experiencing art in nontraditional ways, in general: installation, street art, events, etc. Billy and I have always been interested in everything besides working with or showing in a gallery, though we do have, and enjoy, representation by Fleisher/Ollman Gallery.

Philadelphia in the late 1990s and early 2000s was really a very special place. I, and later Billy, found what ultimately felt like an incubator for all sorts of strange projects and collaborations. I used to think of the scene there as made of living rooms and basements, such was the informal and do-it-yourself ethos of the city at that time. It really seemed like everyone knew everyone, and as eager and capable as we felt, we were welcomed into all manner of creative endeavor. The Fringe Festival started a few years prior, and in its early years was a reflection of all of the weird things that were happening; it wasn't long before Billy and I were commissioned to create a work for the festival.

BILLY: I was horrible at school. During my freshmen year in high school, I had 65 days of suspension, which I used as an opportunity to head to Philly and hang with Steven. I was quickly accepted into his community, the novelty of being a little brother who made stuff and played music. There was a point where we tried to convince our mother to let me take up residency in the city, so I could attend the creative and performing arts high school there, but to no avail. I wasn't to join Steven officially until my freshmen year at the Pennsylvania Academy of Fine Arts, where he was in his fourth year. I'm not saying that I hadn't spent many a five-day weekend, due to suspension, hanging out at the coffee shop where he worked and hanging out in the studios at his school, but when I did eventually move to the city, I already had a community that had been cultivated by Steven. That was the start of what would become a lifelong agreement to work creatively together.

I worked as a mover at Mambo Movers for ten years. It was the most flexible job, and I used it to its fullest potential. The company was mostly made up of artists and musicians. Because I had a lot of flexibility in my work schedule, I could work four weeks straight and then take a month off to work in the studio. For the years I worked at Mambo, any time I needed a box truck, I never had to rent one. I think all of the big installations and sculptures we made were influenced by not worrying about how to facilitate the procuring, moving, and the logistical end to big things. And most times, if I needed help, there was always a crew of movers available.

From 2006 to 2013 I played in the band Man Man. This was just after Steven had left the band. As the band became more successful, it offered a similar type of flexibility that the moving company did. When I was not on tour, I eventually didn't have to move furniture any longer because I made enough money being on the road. So, I had lengthy periods of time to focus on making work.

STEVEN: After I graduated from PAFA, I moved to Massachusetts, worked as a carpenter, and helped start a film festival on Martha's Vineyard. I then moved to Brooklyn in 2001, worked odd jobs, and then moved back to Philly. It was just after 9/11, and my friend Scott Kip had just taken a lease on a warehouse space in Chinatown. Scott, his sister Margo, and six others had built out most of the top floor of the building into studio spaces, and when a former storage space opened up, they invited me to join. It was a massive space—extravagant compared to what was available in New York—for very little money. After 15 years, it now costs more than double what it used to, and my studio is still in this building. Over the course of that time, the sewing factories have moved out, and the space has become almost entirely art spaces—galleries and studios. I eventually moved to another floor and, ultimately, took over that lease, rebuilt my space, and am now renting studios to other artists to offset the cost. There must be something to growing up in a very social environment, as Billy and I seem, in one way or another, to always be trying to build environments where people can work—making places for artists, and trying to make opportunities for people.

When I first moved back to Philly, I picked up shifts at the coffee shop where I used to work, and then picked up shifts at another one nearby, and got back into making objects, trying to figure out what was next. I thought a lot about attending graduate school, looking at architecture programs. I had been reading a bit of design criticism and was taken by how clear writing about design was. Compared to writing about art, it just seemed to make much more sense, quite possibly the most lucid assessment of creative work I had read. I felt certain that I did not want to pursue an advanced degree in fine art, already having had quite a bit of experience with it, and I was looking for the next challenge, something that would expand my vocabulary as an artist, not refine or narrow it. Urban planning, the large scale possible in architecture, and the intersection of concepts and technology were most interesting to me. I had also decided, for no reason in particular, that I wanted to start a pop band and asked a coworker at one of the coffee shops if he'd like to play keyboards. He said that he was starting a band of his own, and that maybe I should join his group. This was Ryan Kattner, and it turned out to be the beginning of the band Man Man, a moderately successful indie rock act that became a substantial part of both my and Billy's lives.

The commitments to the band—gigs, recording, and touring—effectively ended the grad school pursuit, and so I figured I should start showing artwork again. Billy had just recently graduated from PAFA and was showing on his own and working collectively with a handful of other Academy alumni. I kind of joined that little team, and we started making and showing work as a group. Though it had a short lifespan, it's out of this experience that I and Billy started formally showing together as the Dufala Brothers.

BILLY: Being in a band that was moderately financially successful is basically what made something like starting an artist residency possible. It just happened to happen all at the same time: band success, being picked up by gallery, selling a bunch of work, and winning a big sculpture prize, more money.

And then, poof, it was back to "how do you do that again?" And, for us, it's not how you do that again; it's how you continue to do exactly what you have always done, regardless of whether you are finding significant monetary rewards in it.

I have always made art a top priority. All of the day jobs that I have ever worked were to make the money that supported making the artwork. I never really dug too much into the details of how to balance work, job, life. I usually just keep the art work up front, and keep the people in my life that need to be happy, happy. And I keep the work for money flexible.

My closest friends and family understand that Steven and I dedicate our entire lives to working on our art all the time. We both pretty much disappear or fall off the map throughout the year as projects get crazy. Without a strong core of family and friends supporting us, it would be difficult to imagine how we would have gotten to where we are now. When things become unbalanced, or things are seemingly falling apart and life takes a dive in a bad direction, making the artwork and playing music keeps me centered.

Initially all of our sculpture was made in a studio I co-founded with friends in a 19th-century trolley depot in west Philadelphia called Traction Company. With 30-foot ceilings and 6000 square feet of clear floor, it includes a wood shop, metal shop, studios, and an open project space. By working collectively, we could facilitate creating our own individual work, larger Dufala Brothers projects, and build a small artist community that could share the burdens of maintaining a large sculpture studio. Traction Company continues to run strong as a 12-member sculpture cooperative.

Having access to a dump/transfer station/recycling center has been something that I have dreamed about for years. A lot of early sculpture work was made out of materials found on the street or pulled from dumpsters. While a student, I remember going through the yellow pages, calling place after place, asking for access, being turned down again and again, but slowly beginning to understand little bits and chunks of what might be possible, and how to approach it better—learning who to talk to and why those people have the ability to do what they do.

I became friends with a few people in the salvage business, one of whom was a man who pretty much knew everyone in Philly and had the ability to access the most coveted of locked-down abandoned buildings. (He was kind of a dreamy idol.) He told us about a load of skyscraper glass being dumped at a recycling center called Revolution Recovery in Northeast Philly; at that time, a fellow studio-mate at Traction Company was looking for a similar material for a project, so we took a ride out there to look into it. This trip turned out to be the beginning of what is now called RAIR, Recycled Artist In Residence, a small nonprofit artist-in-residence that I co-founded and now run, located inside a construction and demolition waste-processing facility.

I now spend most of my time RAIR. It is an art studio embedded in a for-profit construction, demolition, and manufacturing waste-recycling facility. The organization is small at three employees, but we do a lot, taking on a variety of creative projects outside the physical residency space, and are now in our third year of official programming.

What blew my mind, driving into the recycling center with the glass, was that we were ushered right onto the tipping floor where all the dumpsters spill their contents. This is a place that most artists would never see. The foreman was super nice, asked if we were there for the glass, and asked how much we wanted. He had an excavator drop about $30,000 worth of glass into the truck and told us it'd be $150. I met one of the owners, Avi Golen, and we hit it off (or, I should say, I got his card; I now know he thought I was a lunatic at that first meeting). I kept in touch, emailing him a lot of things over the next several months, sending links to cool artists that I thought he could appreciate, like Mierle Ukeles NYC trash truck, or a link to the San Francisco Bay Area artists' residency Recology (also in a dumping site). I kept up with the contact.

As young owners of a recycling center, they used to give presentations about their business model at local universities for sustainable design programs. At Philadelphia University, they met Fern Gookin, who had recently worked with an artist who had done a residency at Recology in San Francisco. She wanted her thesis project to be creating an artist residency at

Revolution Recovery. When Fern pitched this to Jon and Avi, they immediately suggested she reach out to me. That's where it all began. It was quickly apparent that this should go beyond a thesis project and be developed into a real program. I was given incredible access and freedom to explore in the very beginning, and the first project I tackled was making the company's holiday card.

Over a weekend, I fashioned the claw of an excavator with a giant Rudolph the Red-Nosed Reindeer; I showed up on Monday morning dressed like Santa Claus, with Steven and a camera. We drove the excavator around the yard during operating hours for a photo shoot. The workers went wild, everyone loved it, and the owner's clients who received the holiday card were blown away. This now has become an annual tradition.

That first project became a model for the residency, early on. We called this type of project the "Biggie Shortie"—a big project in a short period of time. This was a good example of working towards a document. At the end of documenting a work, the materials are thrown back into the waste stream, to be sorted, and recycled. Working this way cuts out a ton of logistics that often bog down large installations and large-scale sculpture—shipping, crating, and storage are all out of the equation. So, too, is the actual material artwork, but that is part of the idea.

This model was initially piloted by me and Steven, and eventually we invited other artists to try it out in a very informal way. It's through these projects that we learned enough about how to safely work in the recycling facility during and after hours.

This experience has me working with many different artists in a site-specific capacity that is unlike most creative environments, mostly because it's actually a very dangerous place to work if not navigated correctly, and is itself a steady stream of raw material. My role there has allowed me to push the limits of what that environment has to offer different artists, my own individual ambitions, and the work Steven and I make together.

I don't have a "studio" in a traditional sense, and I have not for some time. At the moment, I fit in "making" work around obligations at the residency and in the areas that open up in a calendar that allows me to use the space that is usually occupied by residents. This has put me in a position to understand better how to work outside of a shop/studio and, in turn, utilize the rest of the recycling center as raw material, both in my own vision, Dufala Brothers, and as a broader resource for artistic endeavor. The residency has grown from a pilot phase, with Steven and I figuring out how to make work at the dump, to a full calendar of artists-in-residence and special projects that are being funded with institutional support.

STEVEN: I've long been a believer in the importance and power of capturing a visual record of our work. For larger projects, particularly those that are time- and site-specific (as much of our project-based work is, RAIR included), I feel like what we most need to do, in addition to making the work itself, is to provide evidence of the endeavor, to document it. This thinking has been part of our work almost from the beginning, even making it into our syllabus for the class we teach on found materials and site-specific sculpture; the site-specific assignment we do every semester is critiqued on the students' documentation of it. Part of this is a practical measure: we can't realistically take our students around to every site; the projects may no longer exist if done in public; and (perhaps most importantly) if there's no picture, it's just a story and may as well have never happened. As a teacher, it is also important to me that students understand the difference between a work of art and a picture of that art.

Often, we find in site-specific work that bringing people to the site is great, if we can. But it is important to understand this as a separate endeavor—it's the difference between making and showing, the studio and the exhibition. It is also the space for subverting the importance of the material thing, the object. In creating a document, a stand-in for the actual thing, working digitally gives those documents a potential to become entirely new works themselves. In this context, the creation of a large-scale ephemeral work becomes a point of departure, or raw material for a sort of fiction, and the resulting (possible) confusion over whether or not it is real opens a very important space for us: misdirection, humor, and artifice. At our core, I and Billy are jokesters, as we believe that humor is the very best way to make serious issues accessible. So, we are always on the lookout for clever ways to subvert things, interesting ways to do things *wrong*.

BILLY: I want to say something about humor. We are both sometimes guilty of taking ourselves too seriously at times, and we understand how toxic that can be. Dick jokes, potty humor, irreverence, and/or reverting back to a second grader's mentality is something that I never want to let go of. Making people laugh is something that makes it easier to relate to something that may or may not be understood or comfortable.

Steven is the clean one, and I'm the dirty one. I do a majority of the sculpture. I weld, pour bronze and iron, drive 24-foot box trucks, and I own the chainsaw. I operate forklifts and heavy machinery, and I have the studio that accommodates this type of work: a place where you can grind metal at all hours of the day with no complaints and collect lots of raw material. I do most of the networking; I talk in public to a lot of people, much more than Steven, and I go to more parties and am generally more of an extrovert. I procure materials, make deals, and connect with opportunities that come back to Dufala Brothers central.

Steven is the map-maker, the pragmatist planner, the archivist; he keeps track of all our goings on. He is the designer, the critical thinker, and he turns over every stone after I run across them all, getting from point A to point B.

When we get together about a work, or a body of work, we talk about what we wanna do, how we wanna do it. Then we go our separate ways, getting to work for a while, and then report back, updating and adapting our direction as we go. This back and forth includes emails, text messages, lots of photos and short videos, and when we need to, face-to-face meetings to just hammer stuff out.

STEVEN: Currently, most of my time is spent designing for performance, mostly theater. This is hyper-collaborative work. It puts me in touch with large teams, venues, producers all over the map, and regularly tests my ability to create something and engage a number of other individuals to make it real. It is becoming a larger piece of my financial picture, so I get to keep doing it. And the relationships I build with the artists I'm working with are some of the most important in my life. Though I'm not the biggest fan of what is essentially an itinerant lifestyle, this type of work is a perfect counterpoint to a solitary drawing practice, and it consistently augments the skills I bring to Dufala Brothers, inasmuch as I'm usually the one tasked with implementing strategy when it comes to our larger projects and installations. It also keeps me a challenging and healthy critical voice for Billy's sculpture practice, much in the same way that Billy's work at RAIR, and his *action-first* approach and general fly-by-the-seat-of-his-pants-ness, are an important part of keeping my work grounded. They keep me from getting too clean, hands-off, and conceptual. We both still need and want the other's opinion, because that is the ultimate approval. It is the most constant and, often, truest compass in my creative life.

My personal creative practice is all over the place, but mostly I like to make drawings in watercolor. The work for Dufala Brothers captures a lot of impulses to make things and is a happy home for the pursuit and exploration of drawings. Where Billy may make an actual sculpture, I can render imaginary ones in two dimensions. And it is surprising how these independent works can become seeds for the work of each other. We maintain an unwritten, mutual license to steal from each other—essential sharing, unimpeded give and take. We both take equal credit for the works produced as Dufala Brothers, whatever the medium, and evenly split the money we make.

The actual workload is never quite an even split; our skillsets are offset, and so the actual thought and labor involved is unequally split between us. It wouldn't make sense for us to try and do the same thing, as we are good at different things. I really do think that we would quickly find ourselves in a "this town isn't big enough for the two of us" kind of intractable fight were we to try. The fact is, we are brothers and can fight like only brothers do, so it is vital that our collaboration operate more in terms of departments, where we can both lead. Ours is something of a double practice where we pretend we are a firm, with us each as principals.

BILLY: One of the things Steven and I have always done is make music together. Besides building forts, it is our earliest collaboration. When I was in high school, Steven would often set up opportunities for us to perform as a duo, with me on drums and him usually on guitar or, sometimes, trumpet. Through friends, we played studio parties in NYC, house parties in Philly, and coffee shops and basement shows. For me, it was a chance to play music with my brother, in front of people. There was nothing else I would have rather been doing, and it helped set me up to get my own band going.

Everything Steven and I played was improvised, and this taught us both a lot about unspoken and intuitive ways of communicating, a respect for one another's space, and how to support what we were each trying to do in the moment. This was the beginning of learning how to work together: the music didn't always work; sometimes it needed to be developed further, and it was sometimes just to share between the two of us, not something to be presented. Music continues to be an important part of both of our lives and is key to staying sane when things get tough. Though we maintain separate studios, we have semi-regular meetings at Steven's studio. He has a bunch of different instruments around, and one of the things we'll do to take a break is play together. It's a great way to just step away for a moment and remember that we are brothers first, two guys with a great rapport, who get along, and like playing together more than anything.

Our most recent show at Fleisher Ollman Gallery in September 2015 was, in some ways, one of the most successful shows we have done to date. The artwork came together in an interestingly intuitive and unspoken way. In the months leading up to the exhibition, we were both very busy with other projects, so time to sit face-to-face was extremely limited. We had to simply trust that we were moving in a similar direction and that the work would make sense together once it was all in the same room. We had to be confident that we knew how to support each other, be as present as we could be given the circumstances, and really lean into what we believe to be true: that after ten years of working together, the values we've established are there to rely on. And it worked.

In reflecting on the way we worked most recently, and after moving through all that this essay has made us look at in our past ten years of working together, it seems that an unconscious employment of the core value that we have long ago established is what, in the end, works best, and which we instinctually rely on.

Going forward, it feels good to know that no matter what the other is doing, there will be more work to be done, future projects, separate and together, new things to be learned and shared, and cool things that will excite us both individually and as brothers. It's magic in slow-motion.

We are building more than artwork together. We are building a creative life—the motivations, reasons, ethics, and goals are largely shared. How we balance work and life, curiosity and stress, time and money—we are learning all these things together. Sharing strength and, perhaps more importantly, the burden of weakness, we make each other stronger, fill each other's blind spots, and get each other's backs. We hand off opportunities for each other, independent of the double practice, if one of us feels it's a good thing for the other, or if we ourselves can't do it and it feels like a good opportunity. We enjoy making art as the opportunity arises, not solely out of some blind ambition to make. There is a responsiveness to all of our work, whether material or philosophical or conceptual, that drives us, and this is not limited to the work we make. It is rooted in our relationship to one another.

BRETT WALLACE

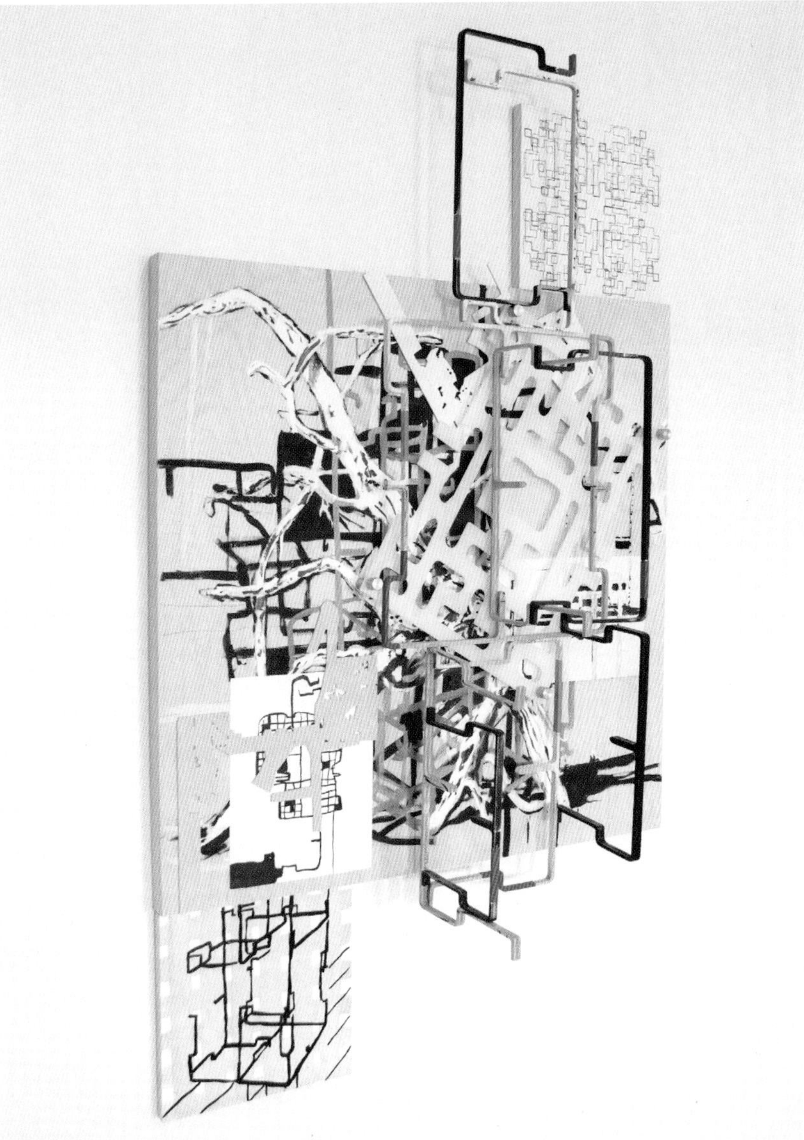

I grew up in a Catholic working-class family in a town just north of Boston, born into the expectations that I would play professional hockey. I was even named after the son of famous Chicago Blackhawk hockey star, Bobby Hull. I played hockey as far back as I can remember, learning how to skate by pushing milk crates across frozen New England ponds.

My family was not overly supportive of my interests in art. As much as they admired individual expression, they struggled to see the practicality of an artistic life. The most artistic thing in our home was a mural of downtown Boston in our dining room made by a graduate school painter. Still, I was very determined to go to art school and convinced my parents to send me by telling them I'd still play hockey outside of school.

I left home, and the Catholic School I was enrolled in, at the age of 14 to attend Walnut Hill School in Natick, Massachusetts. Walnut Hill was well-known for its focus on the arts. There I met talented artists such as Everest Hall, Jonah Freeman, and Cheyney Thompson, who were all slightly older than me. This was a renaissance year for me: I read Aristotle, studied drawing and sculpture, and became an apprentice for my sculpture teacher and dorm parent, Eric Midttun. Eric was a sculptor who studied, first, at the University of Massachusetts Amherst (UMass), and then at Pratt Institute in Brooklyn, New York. Helping out in his studio meant that I got extra art lessons at nights and on the weekends. It also meant that I was able to

Brett Wallace
BS-i1-5.0-2016
60"x36"x12"
Mixed media on wood, paper and lucite with steel standoffs
2016
Courtesy of the artist

escape going back home during summers in exchange for working on commissioned sculptures in his studio.

I'm not quite sure why I made the decision to leave Walnut Hill after that first year. Part of it was that Eric was no longer teaching there; I also got a hockey scholarship to attend Proctor Academy in the Lakes region of New Hampshire. I went on to become the captain of the hockey team and kept making art (but now in a school less focused on artistic excellence). What I left behind in art school, I made up for in life experience, spending a semester studying in Segovia, Spain, a historic city in central Spain, just north of Madrid. I sketched the medieval walls, Romanesque churches and cathedrals, and would take the train to Madrid to visit the Prado and Reina Sofia.

As my senior year wrapped up, my parents wanted me to play collegiate hockey and encouraged me to apply to the big hockey schools in the East. I knew that if I didn't play hockey, I was going to have to pay for art school. I decided to attend the University of Massachusetts Amherst to study art, and during the first semester, I blocked out how I would fund my tuition by focusing on my work. My saving grace was when Paul Berube and Michael Coblyn, both studio art professors at UMass, called me into their office just before Thanksgiving break and asked me if I would like to go to school, tuition-free, for the next four years on a Chancellors' Scholarship. The scholarship alleviated my financial pressures and allowed me to pursue my work, while I covered living expenses by painting houses. The next summer, I studied abroad in a residency in La Napoule, France, accompanied several other professors and a cadre of other art students.

After graduation, I had little idea of what I would do to support myself. One of my friends was an engineer and had a signing bonus and nice salary on the day of graduation. Graduating with a BFA in painting provided more questions than answers as to how I would support myself. So, I moved in with my grandmother in Cambridge, Massachusetts and decided to find work in the art world. I had very few connections and did not think, at the time, to ask for advice from my professors.

To find work, I put on a suit, printed out a resume, and visited all the galleries I cared about in Boston. My first job, which paid a small hourly wage, was installing shows at the Judi Rotenberg Gallery. I convinced Judi to hire me part-time after I swiftly transported 30 or so large paintings back from an exhibition nearby by soliciting the help of a truck driver for $80. At first, I worked part-time at the gallery and had to hold odd jobs, such as valeting cars, to get by. I handled and installed work, and I also parked Judi's car and fed the meter, while conducting performance reviews with her then husband (Richard), who was an advisor to CEOs. The job became full-time when the director moved on, and I was slotted in to oversee operations. I am grateful to Judi for believing in me, since I was so naive about running a business at the time. Working there taught me the basic operations of running a gallery (which was invaluable experience) by being thrown into the fire. During this time, I met a young woman, Laura, through mutual friends who visited the gallery, and we started dating. Eventually, we moved into my apartment together in South Boston.

One of my clients opened up a gallery in the Boston suburbs and offered to show some of my work. I began to show a series of expressionistic paintings I'd recently finished and had a lot of financial success early on. The first two-person shows I had sold out, and I cashed the biggest check I had seen at the time. Despite the early success, after rent, living expenses, and art supplies, I still struggled to find long-term financial stability. I was not making enough money working in the gallery, and while it was a great experience, there were still other things I wanted to do. As an artist with some gallery success, the gallery director where I was showing encouraged me not to change my work, wanting me instead to focus on particular commissions. But this is not why I became an artist. I realized that building a life to support the work I wanted to do was going to require me to adapt my skills into more specialized work that was both sustainable and that paid me more (and didn't zap all of my energy, so I could still paint at nights).

Like most artists, I was entrepreneurial, self-motivated, and determined. And I figured that I could find a job that simultaneously paid well and where I could also learn and inform my artwork. The biggest questions in my mind were "how could I apply my creative skills?" and "what new skills would I need to learn to find and excel in a job?" I threw out any envy I had about not coming from money or the right artistic family and, instead, opened myself up to transformation.

When I left the gallery business in the early 2000s, I joined a company called Forrester Research, a firm that analyzed the impact of technology on society. I was attracted to technology—its ubiquity and growing presence in our lives. The hiring manager at the time dabbled in making art, and during the interview process, I talked about my broad worldview as an artist, and how I would be a good fit for an entry-level job there supporting customers. Shortly after I started, the US fell into its first recession in ten years. I saw this as an opportunity to retool my skills by taking a role in new business sales (known in the industry as "hunting new business"). It was arguably the hardest job in the company, because it came with a steep target to hit every month from scratch. I figured that if I could do this job in a downturn, I could make a lot of money when the economy improved and develop a specialized and employable set of skills. I learned quickly that I could be really successful at this job by doing three things: 1) securing meetings with senior executives who were hard to reach and had no time; 2) building shared vision between what I was selling (advice on the future of technology) and how I could help them reach their goals; and 3) rinsing and repeating this process more often than anyone around me. I picked New York as a big part of my territory, which allowed me to continue to visit galleries a few times every month. So, here I was: an artist with little prior sales experience, at the top of a leaderboard of about 200 people. People with ten times more experience than me would call and ask what I was doing. It did not seem like rocket science to me—as an artist, I was already a self-starter and comfortable simplifying complex narratives into a story. Our CEO would pull me aside for lunch each quarter to get my perspective on various matters. He eventually asked me to build a team to replicate what I was doing, and I spent the next few years building and transforming teams.

After a few years of leadership success, I decided to pursue a program at Harvard Business School (HBS) designed for high-potential leaders rather than an MFA, to continue to take myself out of my comfort zone and to broaden my understanding of the world. To apply to HBS, I needed sponsorship from Forrester. I wrote a business plan of what I wanted to do in three to five years and discussed with my manager, who was running the biggest business in the company, how this program would transform me and what I could do for the company. I also tried to convince her to pay for me to attend HBS out of the company budget; even though I was not successful with that proposal, I ended up getting a portion of my tuition sponsored by the company, which made it a no-brainer decision.

Before attending the program at Harvard, I took summer prep classes in finance and economics. I felt that I could hold my own in a business conversation or solve my way through a problem, but when it came to finance and accounting, I knew very little, so there was a steep learning curve. Failing the first finance exam might have meant I could not attend in the fall, so I made sure I nailed it. The test was untimed, and it was suggested to take four hours to complete it; that test took me an entire weekend, but I got every answer correct.

After arriving on campus in the fall, the next thing I knew, I was the only artist in a class of 150 talented professionals, debating HBS case studies (often real world accounts of leadership challenges). Soon, I learned there was a method to the madness, a way to zero in on the problem to be solved. The classes were as intense as any board meeting, and we worked in study groups late into the night. There was little else to do besides study and go to class—it was like the intensity that artists feel the week before a show. I got really good at using data, a skill I lacked going into HBS. I found time to paint sporadically during 2008 to 2009, balancing my work at Forrester and HBS, but it was too time-consuming to move my work forward in any serious way. While it was a short-term sacrifice, I left HBS with a framework of how to think about sustaining my work long-term.

After I finished up at HBS in 2009, I decided to try my hand as an executive at a start-up, ZoomInfo in Waltham, Massachusetts. Laura and I now had a two-year-old daughter, and our son was soon to be born. I was recruited into the company to help transform their go-to-market strategy. This turned out to be a hard grind, due to a variety of challenges inside the company and the fact that the economy was still recovering from the 2008 financial crisis. I stuck with it for about two-and-a-half years, and we were able to pivot the business into new markets and grow significantly by growth standards. But it was draining.

I knew I needed to find a new job, but I did not want just *any* job. I wanted a great job at a great company. It dawned on me that, while I was using LinkedIn to conduct research to find a new position, I should also consider opportunities at LinkedIn. That same week, I also saw President Obama on TV speaking at a LinkedIn event at the Computer History Museum in Mountain View, California, so the company was top of mind. I found Pat Cronin, a senior LinkedIn recruiter, and sent him a tailored message on the platform. Pat called me back in ten minutes and, after a series of phone screens, I flew out to New York for an interview with the hiring manager. While I came to the meeting with questions about the position and company, I also came with a detailed plan of the creative things I could accomplish in the role: how I could lead and inspire people through creativity, how I could build a go-to-market strategy, how I could break down processes with art and science. I then flew out to LinkedIn's Mountain View, California campus for more interviews. I showed up in a suit, but quickly realized I was overdressed and folded my tie into my suit pocket. The senior executive of the company's biggest business unit, Dan Shapero, walked into the room in the signature Silicon Valley dress code of a t-shirt and jeans, and the first question he asked was: "How does one sell art?" It was a perfect opening for me to discuss how selling (and also making) an intangible product like art was similar to that of telling the story of a consumer network like LinkedIn. Culture is hugely important at LinkedIn, and the most important part of LinkedIn's culture is transformation (transformation of the employee, the company, and eventually the world). I talked to

Dan about how artists constantly transform in public all the time. And I think the company was also very open to diversity. Having someone who was an artist on the team was unique (and LinkedIn knows diverse teams win).

LinkedIn made me an offer to move to Silicon Valley (and to pay for relocation). LinkedIn was a company I wanted to work for, in terms of culture, and I now had a pass to the West coast. I poured myself into the business that first year, regained balance with my family, and set up a studio in the Dogpatch neighborhood of San Francisco. It was a stressful move, but the rich outdoor life (hiking and running) in Northern California soon set it in and made things really enjoyable for our young family.

After my first year, I spent a weekend hand-sketching a series of drawings about what I learned about LinkedIn and the culture inside the company. The next Monday morning, I uploaded the visual story onto Slideshare (a platform LinkedIn owned). The story went viral, and this really put my artistic work on the map at the company. In January 2013, Jeff Weiner, our CEO, asked if I would collaborate with him on an upcoming all-hands meeting sharing the strategic vision with our thousands of our employees around the world. (LinkedIn now has 10,000 employees.)

Later that year, I met Nancy Duarte, a storytelling guru in the valley. Nancy helped me with some early feedback on my storytelling work. I went on to collaborate on visual stories with other LinkedIn leaders inside the company, on topics such as how LinkedIn's consumer network creates opportunity (with Mike Gamson), how to build billion-dollar startups (with Dan Shapero), and the alliance between employers and employees (in collaboration with Ben Casnocha, who co-authored the book, *The Alliance,* along with Reid Hoffman and Chris Yeh). My most recent project was with Fred Kofman, a world-renowned philosopher who works at LinkedIn, on compassion and mindfulness. These collaborations have contributed to my identity inside the company as an artist. They also led LinkedIn to purchase a few of my installations for the offices in Mountain View and San Francisco.

After a few years in Silicon Valley, I asked LinkedIn if I could move to New York, since I was managing a team spread across multiple offices. The company supported this move. I have a strong relationship and alliance, both with my manager and with LinkedIn, that is mutually beneficial and measured in multiyear project milestones. I have discussions with my manager about the artistic life I lead (and the commitments to exhibitions and residencies it requires). And I commit to the company that I am not going to leave for greener pastures while I am working on specific projects. It's a two-way street: while LinkedIn is committed to my growth and artistic life, I am also committed to focusing on specific projects, such as building go-to-market strategies and teams, to help the company achieve its mission.

In 2013, LinkedIn launched *Influencers*, and 500 of the world's luminaries began writing content for the platform. I thought it would be cool to adapt the idea to the art world, and I also started a conversation series on LinkedIn with artists, curators, and critics. It was shortly after this time, after I landed in New York, that I started *The Conversation Project* in order to cultivate a community of artists and cultural producers that inspired me.

The Conversation Project commenced with an interview with Michelle Grabner after I reached out to her over LinkedIn. I had absolutely no idea what I was doing when I started. I would pull LinkedIn's executive editor (who launched the *Influencers* program) aside, asking for interview tips and publishing advice. LinkedIn has been gracious to lend resources and equipment to turn some of those interviews into videos. I have been fascinated by how each interview illuminates a unique story of someone in the art world making it in his or her own way. Looking back, I am proud that over half of the interviews are with women, who are still far too underrepresented in the art world.

When I landed in New York, I rented a studio at Hot Wood Arts, located in a waterfront warehouse in Red Hook, Brooklyn. It was a quiet space, and I spent the first year heavily entrenched in the studio, rethinking my work. I also got out and saw as many shows as I could, starting to get familiar with the New York landscape.

Once fully entrenched in new and interdisciplinary work, I moved to a studio in East Williamsburg with more light and space. This has led to a regular cadence of studio visits from curators, gallerists, artists, and writers and allowed me to engage in more dialogue around my work. I now have achieved the balance in my life, to support our family and to make the work I want to, without daily financial pressures. At the time I am writing this essay, our kids are in second grade and kindergarten, Laura is taking coding classes to re-enter the workforce, and I am preparing to attend Maryland Institute of Art's (MICA) MFA program to develop my work and advance my progress. I am also looking forward to my first solo show in New York at This Friday Or Next Friday Gallery in Dumbo.

My life may be atypical. I may veer off the traditional parenting script from time to time to make things work by dragging our kids to the studio or an opening or two. Someday, they will learn that they have been provided with a unique and alternative perspective on living. My path has not been simple, but, looking back, it has taken relentless energy, a bias towards action (getting stuff done), and the cultivation of relationships beyond the studio walls to help me build and sustain a creative life.

CAITLIN MASLEY

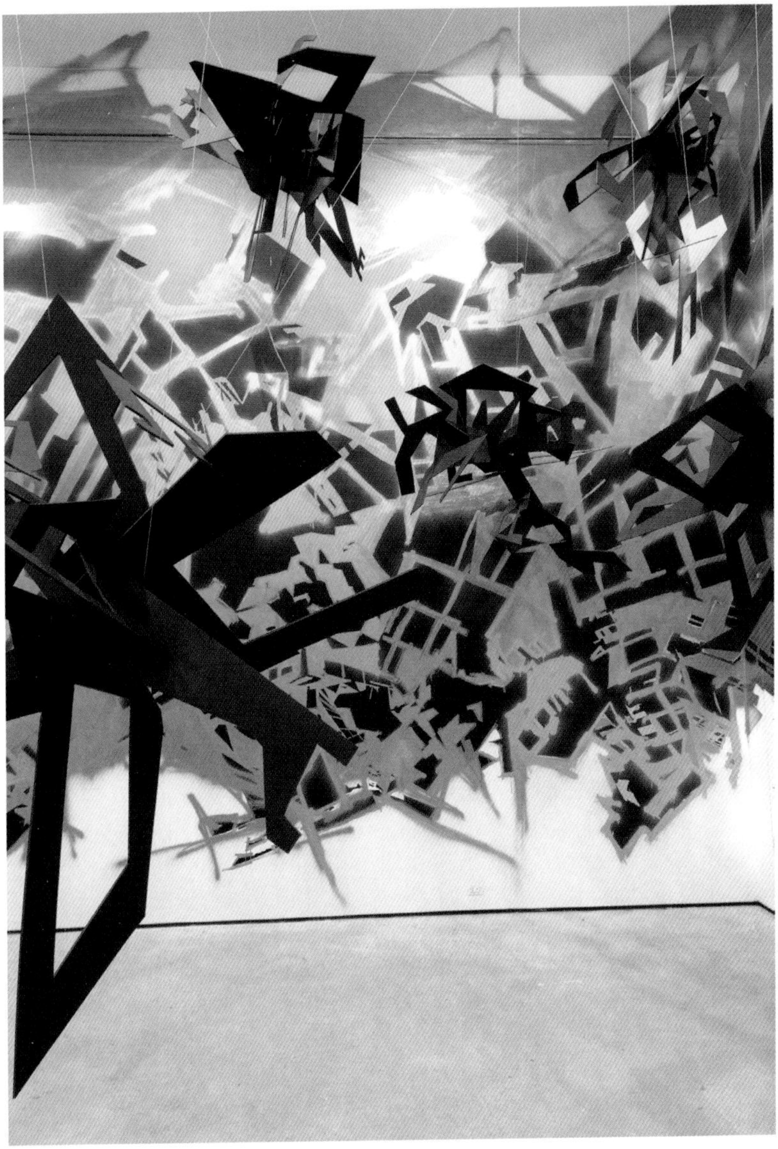

Since I was a teenager, I have carried with me a series of old photos from the '70s.The photos show my grandfather's brown shoes and pants, while he is bending down, handing me more pencils to draw with. I have no real memories of these moments, but being in his studio etched an impression on my life even before I got started. His own life and career as an artist from an immigrant family is story of determination and success, and it is a continuous reminder throughout my own creative life.

From my beginnings of being raised in a creative household, it seemed appropriate to go to college and study art in a more focused way. Becoming an artist meant so much to me, that I moved myself into the basement during high school to make it my own studio. I also realized I needed to go to college to find a community of like-minded artists. But my parents couldn't afford it, with three kids, full-time jobs, and freelancing as well, my college expenses weren't something that they could manage. Nonetheless, it seemed that there had to be a way to make it happen. I ended up enrolling in the College of Creative Arts at West Virginia University in Morgantown, West Virginia, where I received financial aid and found a part-time job to make it all work.

The art studios and fellow art students in college became my home and family, as they did for many there. A small group of us began to organize art exhibitions, curating and occupying various spaces throughout the college, to have more

Caitlin Masley
Abandonment of the Solid
Dimensions variable
Multimedia
2013
Courtesy of the artist
Photography by Etienne Frossard

opportunities for projects and experimentations. These spaces included parts of unused buildings, bathrooms—just about anywhere we could find space. During the summer, after my third year of undergraduate studies, I had an opportunity to collaborate with a group of American and Italian art students on a series of public art works and performance projects for a month in Venice, associated with the Venice Biennale. This month of daily meetings, sharing ideas, active discussions, making objects, and performances together with 20 people, as well as trying to breach a language barrier, was the beginning of my understanding of the importance of working with artists in the public realm. I had such a narrow idea of what art was before then, and I realized that it was time to vastly expand my definitions of what art is, and what it does.

A couple of years later, after a failed attempt to join the Peace Corps with an art degree, I began to apply to graduate school. This time, I was not just looking for an art school, but for a program that matched my desire for diversity and vastly expanded ideas of art. After applying to many schools, I decided to enroll into the University of Arizona's MFA program. I did so not only because they offered a full tuition waiver and a large dedicated studio, but also because it was a three-year program and part of an expansive university campus that could be tapped. During my time in Arizona, I was given physical space to create large-scale installations, and also the mental space to contemplate subject matters that would formulate the base of my MFA. These manifested themselves in concepts of planned utopias and future societies; this involved not just digging into my own personal history of growing up in a planned community, but also that of the Biodome that was situated in Tucson.

Much like during my undergrad years, I began to organize with other grad students to curate pop-up projects, performances, and exhibitions in rundown buildings and massive old drainage pipes in downtown Tucson.

Toward the end of my three years, I met an older, established artist who I began a relationship with. After I graduated, we moved to New York City. Being in New York City expanded my idea of what it meant to be an artist—not just the creative side, but also the very intense business side. But as much as I learned the basics about how to be an artist in New York, it seemed like there were some crucial links missing. I was looking for community, not just critic groups or artists associated with a gallery but a network of artists who truly supported other artists.

The work I was making at the time pushed a continuation of my MFA thesis on future cities and utopias into an expansion of public artworks and installations. Two years later, the relationship that brought me to New York ended, and I began to travel consistently to artists' residencies, a result of many months of researching and applying for international opportunities. And that was the beginning of years of on-and-off travel throughout Europe. While living and working abroad, I developed lasting relationships, created new work, and continued to have an open engagement with professionals in the art world, which was in direct contrast to my experience in New York.

As my work continued to evolve towards large-scale, site specific wall drawings and installations, my precarious financial situation prompted me to work with cheap or found materials, such as foam core and glass sheets. I found new ways to make work, and for a time my freelance job at an outdoor billboard company sponsored a project of large images of my work in Manhattan. During the same time, the fall of 2001, I had my first solo exhibition in an established Chelsea gallery, but the events of 9/11 halted everything throughout New York City. And as the economy stalled, my financial situation did as well. I sublet my room in my shared apartment and, this time, went straight to Berlin, then to Copenhagen. Then, I traveled further around Europe for a couple months, crashing on friends' sofas to rethink my practice and life as an artist.

After I returned from traveling, I found that I couldn't sustain an apartment and studio just freelancing in New York on my own for long. My parents sent me money; sometimes I would sell an artwork, get a grant, or another residency allowing me to continue for a little longer. During this time, I encountered so many artists who had also been rethinking their practices, trying to find alternative ways of paying the bills when so many galleries had closed and collectors took a step back.

Meanwhile, I had come to a point where I met someone, and I wanted to pursue this relationship seriously. Therefore I altered my practice by changing the hours I worked in my studio and freelancing to be able to spend dedicated time with this person. During the following years, I cobbled together a precarious life: a studio share, gallery representation, limited amount of residencies, freelancing, teaching, continuous applying for opportunities. And because it was all so loosely sewn together, parts began to fall off.

Plus, the future of my relationship was becoming a larger commitment. My partner and I had a lot of dialogue and questions about what and how we wanted our future life to be like together. We also questioned how that life may or may not work in New York City. What would we lose and gain as a couple by staying? What would we lose and gain professionally? How would it change as we got older? Would we feel like we had too many regrets? We made some basic changes, which included moving our home and studio to lessen the financial burden and open the possibilities of life with steady employment outside of the five boroughs of New York City, while trying to start a family.

In the years before getting pregnant, I continued traveling for residencies as I had done previously. Three years later, when I was pregnant, I was awarded a very generous Pollock-Krasner grant that would support my life as an artist for one year. To extend that funding, I found a smaller studio closer to our apartment, so that traveling would not be a barrier to making work and less expensive. I also began to build a community of other women artists who were mothers—some were introduced through friends, some were from online social platforms, and some were based in my own neighborhood. We began to swap playdates and babysat for each other, so that there was time for seeing shows and making work. The exchanges with this community were what truly helped me through the first year of parenthood.

Soon after our first child was born, I began to research and apply for family residencies and places that would provide full financial, living, and studio support for a small family. It was a new idea to me as an American but had been going on in Europe for quite some time. I happily received three or four invitations. We decided to accept an offer from Künstlerwohnung Chretzeturm, Stein am Rhein, Switzerland and Action Art Actuel, Centre d'Artistes Autogere Residency, Quebec. Both of these residencies offered housing, studio, and monthly stipends, plus some money for travel and materials.

As my husband was granted a sabbatical from the architectural firm where he worked, and because we used our savings to travel as a family, we were able to do this. I was able to focus and make work for exhibitions in America, Europe, and the Middle East, while my husband was the primary childcare giver. As the year was coming to an end, and our planned return became closer, our conversations turned to why and how we could stay in Europe. The work/life balance that we had experienced seemed priceless to us, but, in the end, there were not any options for employment that would work for him.

Upon returning to New York, I was lucky enough to receive the Abrons Art Center Artist-in-Residence award and continue my goals to connect with other artists who are parents. I strove to create another community and form a support system of creatives that let us all have extra time in our studios and not pay for extra babysitting. We swapped drop-offs and pick-ups during the school week and arranged for longer after school playdates, so that we each had a couple of extra-long days in the studio or writing during the week. Through this community, I found that I wasn't alone in wanting to redefine creative career trajectories. I helped organize an online resource for artists who were mothers, but also parents in need of similar stories and a place to find information on family residencies. Often I was contacted by parent artists with questions of how one can make it work with family, studio, and employment. There is no one answer to this, but rather a series of building blocks that change and evolve to each situation. For example, there were times where I was on a cherry picker, eight months pregnant, installing a show; or the week after giving birth to my second child, back in the studio, nursing and rocking a sleeping baby in a car seat, while finishing large, detailed drawings at the Triangle Arts studio residency. I did all these things, because I was inspired by so many women preceding me, who did so much more. It wasn't easy or ideal, and there were plenty of frustrations and tears. The lack of a steady and secure income made a huge impact on the type of work I made, or even whether I had a studio. But by being able to give and receive support from others in the community, I was able to continue making work, while also being a parent to two children.

When it became obvious that I was choosing to make the kind of work that was not easily salable, I made another conscious decision to go back to school and harness all the skills I learned over the years to contribute to a larger vision of stability for our family. Going back to school full-time for a Master of Science in Design in Urban Ecology at Parsons didn't seem too far off base. However, to make ends meet and connect all the dots, I had to add in a part-time job with two kids in full-time care, a new student loan, and while still actively exhibiting a few times a year. Life became very busy on a level that challenged my true motives. But in this new program, I was completely humbled by the amazing work of many others dedicated to cultural production and social justice. From my fellow students, I learned and realized what I could do to push forward my definition of how I think of my artistic practice, from decades of experiences and accumulated knowledge. I found that I could lean into and expand these new ideas of what it means to live one's life as an artist.

After I graduated, I spent months seeking a steady form of employment. Through many conversations with a good friend who was in need of information, knowledge, and direction to grow a new arts organization and build out the operations and programing for a new artist residency, I negotiated and offered to act as deputy director. For this organization which hosts an artist in residence, I can finally share my accumulated knowledge and experiences of decades of participating in residencies and create a solid foundation for it to grow. For me, what could be better than hanging out with other artists, helping them to have sustainable careers and learning from them as well? The details of my position center on programing and operations, which ranges in its needs depending on where the organization is at any given time. This includes grant writing, core programing, workshops, organizing panels, board building, community outreach, and building membership, among many other things. My degree from Parsons has been a complete asset for this position, but it is pairing that education with my own experiences in my career that has offered the best solutions, ideas, and the day-to-day know-how.

On a daily basis, I ask artists what I can do for them. What do they need to push their work, and who would they like to connect with? I don't make promises of success, but I try to do what I can for artists and for the organization as a whole. I am happy to work behind the scenes with the other staff and the larger community that surrounds us to build a series of smaller movements and building blocks so that we can strive to have a solid foundation and lasting impact.

This position also enables me to have flexible hours, so I can take my kids to school and pick them up, do homework with them, and have amazing conversations where they make me see things in wholly different ways. My colleagues understand and fully support me having an art career, being a parent, and an employee. They understand I'm also an artist who needs to spend time producing my own work for exhibitions and projects, and they make room for that.

My own personal practice has also evolved quite a bit over the years, from a very solitary photographic and drawing process, to large-scale wall drawings and installations that depend on groups of volunteers to execute. These volunteers are essential to making large-scale drawings and to reconstruct various building materials into possibilities of architectural topographies. In this installation process, the conversations we have are a multitude of sharing stories, experiences, laughter, eating together, and new friendships, and they are all crucial aspects to my practice.

All of these ways and methods of making work that I have explored over the years not only survive outside of the global economy, but also thrive beyond it. For me, there is no one category of being an artist because the foundation of all of this is continuation of the producing of work.

As an end note to this essay: as I write this, I have been informed that I have been awarded two family residencies for this year, as well as a long-term subsidized studio space from Spaceworks. This means that my practice will change yet again, and the foundation for a new way of producing is still being forged.

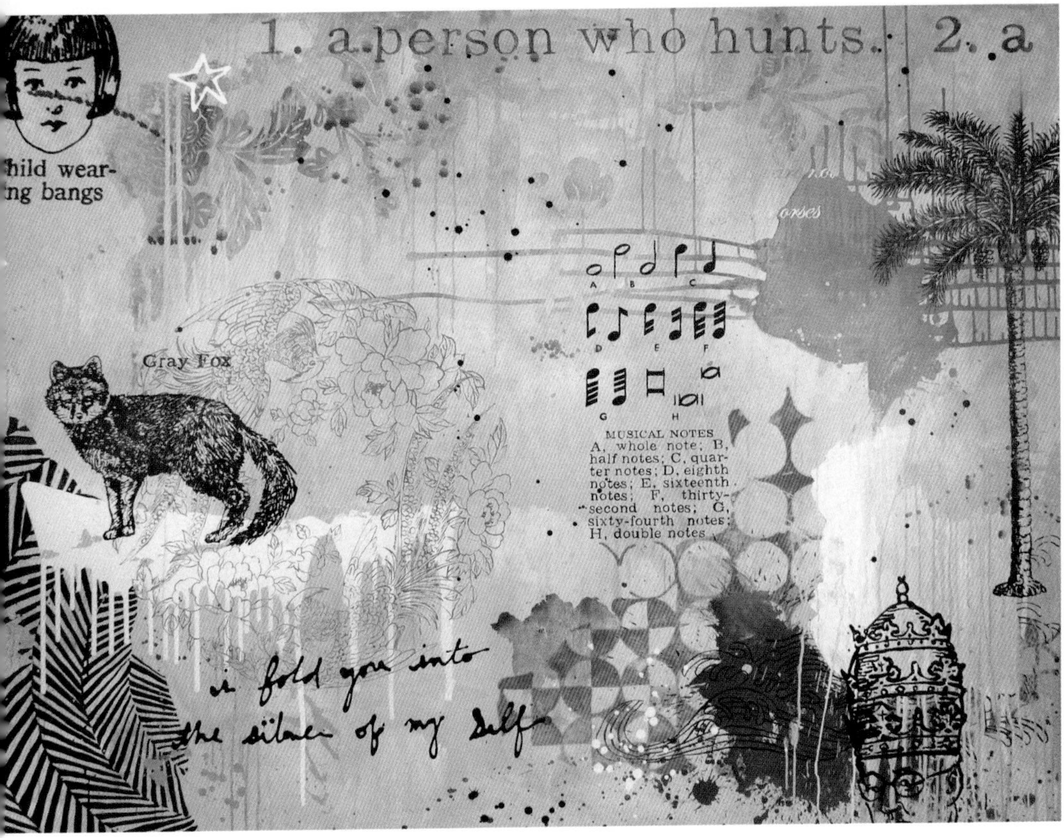
1. a person who hunts. 2. a
hild wear-
ng bangs
Gray Fox
MUSICAL NOTES
A, whole note; B, half notes; C, quarter notes; D, eighth notes; E, sixteenth notes; F, thirty-second notes; G, sixty-fourth notes; H, double notes

Over the past two decades, I have made paintings, blog posts, exhibitions, essays, college classes, decadent meals, a print magazine, and even a tiny human. Although my medium of choice is continually shifting, I find nothing more satisfying than the process of creating. The thrill of the challenge, the camaraderie of collaboration, and the terror of failure all shape me into a braver, smarter version of myself.

That I have transitioned from a visual artist who writes to a publisher who also makes art should come as no surprise, but I will admit that my current position as Founding Editor and Publisher of BmoreArt, Baltimore's daily online and new print art magazine, is still a great surprise to me. However, when looking back at my personal history, my career might seem preset.

In 1982, at age nine, I was the highly successful co-author of a series of illustrated children's books. At Westminster Elementary School, my friend, Kasim McLain, and I wrote a whole series of stories told from the perspective of a witty and sarcastic family dog. I can still remember the unselfconscious joy I felt, working with our heads together over paper and crayons, cracking up over plot lines and dialogue. We did this work when all the other kids were out on the playground. Instead of playing dodgeball and kissing boys, my friend and I stayed inside with no supervision. We were so passionate about our work that our teachers just got out of the way.

Cara Ober
Forgotten Bestsellers
96"x72"
Mixed media on canvas
2010
Courtesy of the artist

Looking back, this collaborative, narrative, visual process is so similar to the writing, editing, and publishing I am doing now, that my path seems obvious. But as I transitioned out of childhood, I became very confused about what to do with my life. I attended a liberal arts college and studied art. I learned how to paint still lifes, but I was given no direction in pursuing the life of an artist after graduation. Between my professors and the small town where I grew up, I had few mentors and found little encouragement in pursuing my goals. I knew I wanted to be an artist and live a creative life, but I didn't know what that meant. When I asked questions about how to build this life, I was told by well-meaning adults that being an artist wasn't a real career, that the life I envisioned for myself was a fantasy.

I was always a good student, and my parents are both teachers. I decided to apply for an MFA after college, because school was a safe way to sidestep my career questions. Although I was accepted to a few graduate programs, I was rejected by those at the top of my list and I took this to heart. For me, it confirmed my own doubts that I wasn't a viable artist.

I took a creative U-turn and became an art teacher, following the safe path of my parents. I got a great job teaching Advanced Placement art in a small town in Maryland, with good benefits and decent pay, but I was incredibly, senselessly, frustrated. This "good job" was not a good fit for me. I liked my students, but my ambition and creative work, in and outside the classroom, was not appreciated. I didn't have a community that understood the art that I wanted to make. Outwardly, I had found a live/work balance that should have been satisfying, but it wasn't. Most frustrating was that I didn't know how to construct the life that I envisioned.

The only thing that propelled me forward was the desire to make my own work better. I began taking adult education classes at the Maryland Institute College of Art (MICA) and eventually moved to Baltimore. I rented a studio with other artists and began making larger paintings, and also showing my work and writing about art in local publications. A few years later, I was accepted to MICA's low residency MFA program. This was a compromise, because I was desperate to quit my teaching job, but the program allowed me to work full-time and pay tuition in increments. I was able to avoid taking out student loans and continued to produce and show my work in the region.

At the end of the four-year MFA program, I had a much better sense of who I was and what I wanted professionally. I was finally ready to quit my full-time teaching job to be an adjunct professor, curator, artist, and multi-faceted creative professional. After exposure in a few national magazines and juried shows, I started showing my paintings in galleries all over the country, and this was validating. More importantly, I was regularly connecting with colleagues and creative partners, the people I could work with and learn from who appreciated what I had to share with them.

At one point, I was so busy with shows in Brooklyn, DC, Baltimore, Atlanta, Raleigh, and Dallas that I felt a tangible sense of success. But I was so exhausted. My feverish pace was fueled by a desperate need to prove to myself that I was a viable artist, and this desire was insatiable. No surprise, my studio life and insane schedule started to take a toll on my creative output. My art career began to feel more like a job than my life's work. After all the making, shipping, PR, travel, and pressure to perform, I was burnt out and unable to replenish my creative energy. Also, I naturally tend to rebel against rules and systems, even a system that I created myself, so I allowed myself another creative U-turn.

In 2009, I decided I wanted to become a parent. Those months of pregnancy and expectation were exciting and terrifying. How would this new responsibility affect me as an artist? How would I be able to make the time to be considered a professional by an art world that is constantly, frenetically, competitively busy? During these months of incubation, my creative focus shifted from creative production to research: how did other artists build a sustainable career and survive? How did female artists who were mothers continue to make their work?

I had started BmoreArt as a community art blog in 2007 as a side project to my art career, and it had become an addictive hobby with a rotating cast of collaborators. I also wrote art criticism for a number of local and national publications, but BmoreArt gave me control over my own critical voice and generated countless opportunities to work with other artists.

This publication took on a much more significant role in my creative practice at a time in my life when I was simultaneously looking inward and out to a larger art community for inspiration and strategies for my life as a parent. Sharing my research and observations with a larger audience was inspiring, and I could feel my creative energy increasing through the process.

The main reason I created the publication was to let people know what was going on in Baltimore, to encourage more participation and attendance at events and openings. There were so many amazing artists and exhibits and very few reliable sources of information about them. I also wanted to document the best work being made in Baltimore; to share it, celebrate it, and critique it. With BmoreArt I was able to create a collective archive, so that ephemeral exhibitions could be remembered and learned from.

My professional transition from being "an artist who writes" to "arts writer who makes art" has continued organically. I found that writing engages my mind in the same way that making art does and deeply satisfies me. I continue to self-identify as an artist, but my definition of an artist has evolved. Working as an arts writer and editor has helped me to get to know myself better, as a maker and thinker. For most of my life, I have been an introvert and a successful student, so writing about art allows me to have purposeful conversations with the artists who interest me. It gives me a reason to show up, the power to ask nosy questions, and a motive for others to answer them.

In 2010, just before my son was born, I was offered a job at *The Urbanite*, a monthly print magazine based in Baltimore that focused on city life and social justice. My position as Arts Editor included weekly deadlines, and I was able to work mostly from home. Despite having a new baby, my writing assignments got me out of the house, and I wrote in energetic bursts during his naps or when I could schedule a babysitter. I didn't get rich from this job, but I learned a lot. I worked with editors who were very tough on me and made my writing stronger. The magazine ceased to exist in 2012, but the experience taught me that my city was hungry for coverage of its art and culture.

I decided to build BmoreArt into a robust daily online publication, determined to fill the media void left by my former employer. I planned to sell ads to fund the "webzine" and recruited a team of contributors. We worked together for a year to publish something original every day, and we all worked for free. I edited everything and did all the back-end blogging. At the end of a year, I had sold very few ads, applied unsuccessfully for many grants, and received no funding. I had created the endlessly interesting and dynamic job I had always wanted for myself but was unable to attract the financial resources to sustain it.

Now that I was a mom, I had a responsibility to my family. I couldn't keep working full-time for free. I decided to give it another month and, if I couldn't find funding for the publication, I would have to quit and do something else.

I said it out loud once or twice to colleagues I trusted, that I needed to quit blogging to do something more financially responsible. What I didn't realize was how many people were reading BmoreArt, that an audience was growing, and that there were people who had begun to value the work I was doing. I'm still not sure if my willingness to admit failure had anything to do with it, but a month later something magical happened: I was invited to lunch by the president of a local foundation. We had a great conversation about the work that I was doing, about the issues we both felt passionate about, and the potential for the art community in Baltimore to enact meaningful change. It turned out that, in addition to funding individual artists and small art nonprofits, this foundation was starting a media portfolio and wanted to invest in a local, independent art publication with integrity that was both professional and ethical.

The fall of 2012 was the first time I was able to pay myself for my work at BmoreArt and to pay our contributors. The funding has led to amazing changes for me, for the publication, and for Baltimore's creative community at large. Our readership has grown regionally and nationally and we have received grants, launched a podcast series, attracted national advertisers, organized well-attended lectures, sponsored events, and built strong relationships across the region. We publish original content at least five times a week online, and it gives me so much pleasure to publish essays and reviews that are smart, challenging, and unique.

BmoreArt's newest, and most ambitious, project to date is a print journal, just released in November 2015. I had always wanted to create a physical publication and, when I received funding, I was able to put together a team of artists, writers, and designers to make it a reality. While I am thrilled to put this beautiful magazine out into the world, to see people reading and enjoying it, this has been the most difficult, stressful, and challenging project I have ever done. I am completely in love with it, but the process has given me gray hair and zits and, at the height of its production, my stress level was out of control. I drove myself, and my family, crazy.

One reason creating a print magazine has been such an emotional journey for me is that the medium so succinctly puts together all of my interests: aesthetics, conversation, community, politics, design, language, and accessibility into an ideal method of communication. In many ways, it is a dream come true, but it's also a new frontier. I have returned to a place where I don't have the answers, where I have to rely on collaborative partners and my own intuition, and many of my earliest insecurities have returned. What if I do it all wrong? What if it is a failure? The stakes are higher in creating a print publication than anything I've attempted before, because so many people have participated in its inception and so many resources have been invested in it. There's so much pressure, largely self-initiated, to cultivate the success around it that it deserves, and I am still developing the skills to do that.

When I am feeling terrified by all the things I need to do that I don't know how to do, my only way forward is to remind myself that this is a learning process, and success is collective. If I can focus on collaboration and forget about my ego, the energy from a larger community propels me forward. Like our online site, the new print journal celebrates the power of artists in Baltimore and presents a range of diverse and meaningful projects. I have to remind myself that this publication is the sole showcase and chronicle of the thriving Baltimore art scene and it's not about me.

And what is success anyway? Success is ephemeral. It's constantly changing. For me, success occurs in the learning. Success happens when I'm exhilarated, exhausted, and terrified. Success happens when I get a big, expensive, crazy idea and then bring it into existence so it can catalyze energy and excite others. I have learned that the idea can be an event, a new art medium, a collaborative project, or even the creation of a new person in my family.

Five years in, I would describe parenting as creative, collaborative work. It is frustration and satisfaction. It is constant learning. Despite all the misogynistic comments I have received as a woman in the art world, suggesting that I am not a serious artist since I am also a mother, I believe that parenthood has made me more ambitious in my career and a better artist. It forces me to prioritize the time I spend with my work and my family and to be efficient, and even ruthless, in getting my work done.

As the editor and publisher of an art publication based in Baltimore, my life is full of these brief moments of brilliant excitement. Sometimes I feel it while reading an inspired review by a contributing author, and I'm so proud to publish it that I get tears in my eyes. Sometimes it's when I'm attending art events, conducting interviews and studio visits, meeting with potential funders, or drafting an unpopular opinion. My creative process needs variety, challenge, collaboration, image and text, and a conviction that I am making a difference in my community.

In addition to publishing BmoreArt online on a daily basis, teaching classes at MICA and at Johns Hopkins University, and working to publish the *BmoreArt Journal of Art + Ideas* twice a year, I see my art practice expanding. For the first time in my career, I am intrigued by performance art, video, sculpture, and animation and am exploring ways to incorporate these new approaches with my ideas. I don't know exactly what I'll be doing in the future and this is how I like it. My creative process is constantly evolving.

CARRIE MOYER

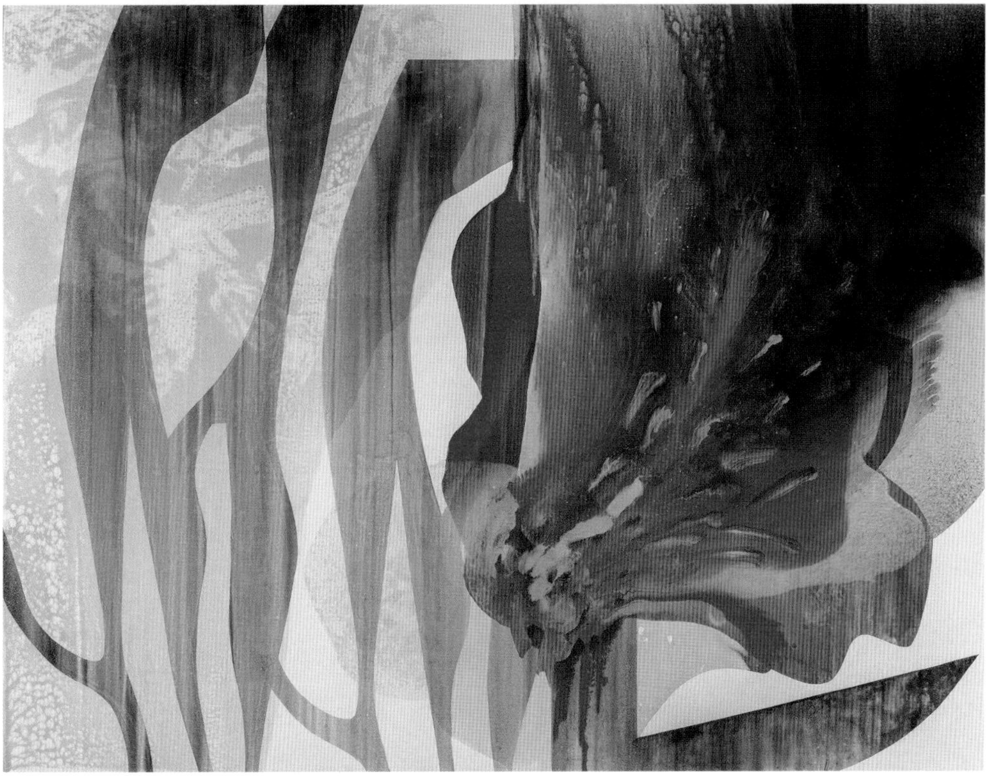

Before I came along, there weren't any artists in my family. I was born in 1960 to teenage parents who were just out of high school. My mother and father came from working people in Detroit, Michigan—bank tellers, church deacons, policemen, waitresses. Many of our male relatives had done a stint at the Ford Motor plant at some point in their lives. Completely alienated from the suburban dreams of their families, my parents became immersed in the political and cultural unrest that took hold of America in the mid-1960s. At that point, they were in their mid-20s, with dead-end jobs and two small children whom they took with them to anti-war demonstrations and the like. My mother also brought the revolution home, incorporating ideas drawn from feminism, environmentalism ("ecology" as it was called in those days), and alternative education into our everyday lives. She even turned her bedroom into a place for me and my sister to draw and paint; my parents slept on a pull-out couch in the living room. So began my mother's steady encouragement of her children's artistic interests and talents.

In 1969, my parents sold everything, bought an old Bell Telephone van, and drove across the country from Detroit to Berkeley, California. We moved into a collective household, all four of us sleeping in a single bedroom with our dog, Bob. Throughout the 1970s, our family moved sporadically up and down the West Coast, living in small towns, from the Bay Area to Puget Sound. With each new school, my interest in art

Carrie Moyer
In a Cool Blaze
96"x72"
Acrylic and glitter on canvas
2015
Courtesy of the artist and DC Moore Gallery

morphed and expanded—from dance to theater to visual art. I also gradually realized that I was a lesbian, and that I needed to be around people like me. As a voracious reader, I figured out that New York City was where all the artists and gay people lived, and I couldn't graduate from high school fast enough. I wanted to be one of those mythic Americans who "immigrated" to New York City in search of the kind of freedom, energy, and creative enterprise that can be found nowhere else in this country. I drank the Kool-Aid.

I moved to New York in 1980 and, soon after, was enrolled at Pratt Institute, majoring in painting. Going to art school was like going to heaven. However, when you're a penniless student, living in New York City is both intoxicating and grueling. Somehow, my homesickness manifested itself in the big biomorphic, abstract paintings I began to make. Metaphysical abstraction rooted in American landscape painting (Georgia O'Keeffe, Morris Graves, Mark Tobey, etc.) became a long-lasting passion. At the same time, I was stealing moves from the likes of Elizabeth Murray and Carroll Dunham in attempt to create something of my own.

During this time, I was also confronted with how much sexism and homophobia were interfering with nearly every aspect of my life. New York City in the 1980s was a precarious place for young women and out lesbians, especially after dark. At Pratt, they were still handing out prizes and fellowships designated for male students only. My last year at school I became increasingly active, both at school and out in the world. Recognizing this, my teacher Amy Snider found me an internship at *Heresies*, one of the first feminist art magazines. *Heresies: A Feminist Publication on Art and Politics* was published intermittently from 1977 to 1993. Each issue was produced by a different collective of artists and focused on a single topic, such as sexuality, racism, women and violence, the environment, etc. For a young lesbian artist experiencing a growing sense of injustice, *Heresies* was a thrilling introduction to the possibility of using art to make change. My time at the journal also introduced me to a generation of women artists and feminist activists who I continue to learn from.

In 1985, I graduated from Pratt with a BFA in painting. My head filled with my teachers' admonitions about what it took to be a "real" artist, I spent the next several years struggling to earn enough money to keep my work going. At a certain point, it was clear that housecleaning wasn't going to pay my studio rent, and so I learned how to type. Computer graphics—"desktop publishing," as it was called at the time—was a brand new field. Unlike the Macs in use today, these were standalone systems that required specialized training. Because I had gone to art school, I was selected from the typing pool to learn the new equipment. Eventually, I became a designer and worked for many different advertising agencies throughout the city.

At the same time, I was also becoming involved with the burgeoning LBGT civil rights movement. The public panic surrounding the AIDS epidemic had suddenly put gay men in the spotlight, and the need to confront entrenched homophobia and societal neglect gained a new urgency. In 1987, ACT UP (AIDS Coalition to Unleash Power) was formed; soon after, Queer Nation coalesced to combat the escalation of anti-gay and lesbian violence on the streets and prejudice in the arts and media. Both ACT UP and Queer Nation included many artists in their ranks and became well-known for their highly performative, confrontational tactics as well as their powerful graphics and slogans.

Putting aside my brushes completely, I threw myself into queer activist art. I wanted to use my design skills to produce posters and agitprop that made lesbian concerns visible to the rest of society. For the queer artists and design professionals of my generation, the lack of images of lesbians and gay men in mainstream culture just didn't compute. During this period of time, one of the goals of the gay civil rights movement was to come out and make ourselves "visible" to the world at large. In 1991, I met Sue Schaffner, a commercial photographer, at a Queer Nation meeting. We quickly discovered a shared desire to design activist posters that would subvert the kind of heteronormative advertisements produced at our day jobs. So, we joined forces to form Dyke Action Machine! (DAM!).

From 1991 until 2004, DAM! evolved into a kind of "advertising agency" for lesbian identity. We created over 17 different projects that used the tools and design sensibility of mainstream media to address the social and political condition of lesbians. A typical campaign consisted of 5,000 posters wheat-pasted all over the streets of New York City. Other projects appeared any and everywhere the public gets its information. Print publications, websites, postcards, bumper stickers, matchbooks, buttons, and removable tattoos were all used as delivery systems for DAM!'s message. Our campaigns inserted images of lesbians into the visual framework of popular culture. DAM! took on the role of the advertiser, promising the lesbian viewer all the things she'd been implicitly denied through her visual absence: power, inclusion, and the public recognition of her identity.

Because DAM! poster campaigns appeared on the street for only a few weeks at a time, their subjects always spoke to the moment. *Straight To Hell* (1994) envisioned the repercussions of President Bill Clinton's misguided "Don't Ask, Don't Tell" policy, which permitted gay people to serve in the military as long as they stayed firmly in the closet. In our poster, a trio of bad-ass dykes, expelled from the army, return to wreak havoc and revenge. *She came out. So the Army kicked her out. Now she's out for blood: Straight To Hell.* Our 1997 project, *Gay Marriage: You Might As Well Be Straight,* articulated the grassroots sentiments felt by many lesbians about the drive toward legalized gay marriage. The poster took the glossy *Wedding* magazine fantasy to its psychotic limits by showing one ecstatic bride dragging her mate through a landscape of matrimonial booty. *Lesbian Americans: Don't Sell Out!* (1998) combined the earnest tone and formal elements of 1940s war effort posters with the opportunistic patriotism peddled by brands like Tommy Hilfiger and Ralph Lauren. Our campaign positioned the butch lesbian as the embodiment of the revolutionary, independent American spirit who resists the marketing of the gay "lifestyle."

By the mid-1990s, I missed working alone, pulling images out from an indescribable place in my head. I missed making art that surprised me. I missed painting. The 40-hour-a-week job at a pharmaceutical advertising agency was replaced with freelance production. Going freelance meant I could alternate between an intense month of painting at an artists' residency and a few months of design jobs to pay the bills. After collaborating on work that required computers, photography, text, and outside printers, being alone again in my studio was quite a challenge.

I continued to work with Sue on Dyke Action Machine! until 2004, but restricted my other agitprop efforts to special "guest appearances."

One of the "residencies" I attended was Skowhegan School of Painting and Sculpture in the summer of 1995. As someone who was still finding her way back to painting, it was both terrifying and exhilarating to be surrounded by so many talented, accomplished peers. One afternoon, I met the sculptor and installation artist Sheila Pepe while trying to dog paddle in Wesserunsett Lake. Later that day, she rolled into my studio and started talking to me about my paintings (an absolute no-no at Skowhegan, where the privacy of studio is sacrosanct). As offended as I was by her casual audacity, I was secretly intrigued to meet another working-class lesbian artist my age. There weren't many of us out in the art world at that time. So began a friendship that evolved into a long-term relationship and, eventually, a marriage in 2015. At this point, I can't imagine being involved with anyone other than a visual artist... What would we talk about? It has been critical, to my wellbeing and my success, to have a partner who shares the same level of commitment to developing her own work.

After Skowhegan I realized that, to fully reclaim painting, I needed to be part of an academic community. At age 37, I decided to go back to school and enrolled in the Milton Avery Graduate School of the Arts at Bard College, an unusual program where students earned their MFA over three consecutive summers. This structure allowed me to fit school into my life, not the other way around. Through freelancing, I'd figured out an effective way to support myself and my studio, and I wasn't about to give it up. At Bard, I began developing a painting language inspired by the immediacy and formal strategies of graphic design and activist art. I spent a lot of time studying utopian imagery of both Modernist art and 20th-century protest movements, including the revolutionary graphics of Constructivism, the Situationist agitprop of Atelier Populaire and Mai '68, as well as the "artifacts" of Herstory conjured by Feminist artists in the 1970s. Hard-edged fragments protest graphics were overlaid with washes of fluid acrylic paint and the iconography of color-field painting, to create a kind of ill-fitting frame around our utopian desires. While still in grad school, I had my first solo show, *God's Army*, at Debs & Co. Gallery in Chelsea.

I began moving away from didactic iconography around 2005, looking to return to a kind of abstraction that relied on both movement (pouring) and suggestive form (intimations of a hand, foot, breast, or eye). I began to look again at art and texts from the Feminist Art Movement in the 1970s and the empowered vision of mid-century women surrealists, made manifest in the paintings of Remedios Varo and Kay Sage and the soft sculpture of Dorothea Tanning. I was in search of nearly recognizable forms that could generate the preliterate force of the Venus of Willendorf and looking for technical processes that could offer complex readings of painting history. The graphic allusions to recognizable iconography have given way to a set of fugitive painterly signs "caught" momentarily in ever-changing compositions. Nearly a decade later, this dance between movement and form continues to be the dynamic center of my painting.

As my painting began to flourish and receive some recognition, I started to pay attention to other aspects of my life. I was getting increasingly bored with working in the basement of a big advertising agency (the basement is always where they put the production department). Somehow, I just couldn't see myself designing for AT&T or the Christian Music Club when I was 60, no matter how flexible the work schedule was. Teaching would allow me to talk all day about what I loved and knew best. As a life-long introvert, it would also force me to overcome my terror of speaking in public. Around 2004, I gradually transitioned from design work to adjunct teaching, greatly reducing my income. I was showing regularly, which helped me secure classes at a wide variety of institutions, including Rutgers, Tyler School of Art, Yale School of Art, Cooper Union, and many others. Invitations to lecture around the country helped fill in the financial gap. I held my first full-time teaching position at the Rhode Island School of Design from 2007–10; since that time, I have been an Associate Professor at Hunter College in New York City.

Around the time I began teaching, I also started writing art reviews. A desire to publicly articulate what I knew about art was an underlying factor in both endeavors. Critical writing provided a framework for research and connecting with the work of other artists, particularly those of earlier generations. It has been a particular goal of mine to write about artists who have been historically marginalized. For me, the social, political, and historical context in which art is made is inextricably woven into the content of any work. Over the years, I have written on a wide range of painters, including Jo Baer, Rochelle Feinstein, Maria Lassnig, Pat Steir, Charline Von Heyl, and many others. Recent projects include catalogue essays for the museum retrospectives of Louise Fishman and Nancy Grossman. I have also written extensively and continue to lecture on Dyke Action Machine!, chronicling my own participation in the LGBT civil rights movement and queer activist art-making.

At a panel discussion, I once heard the painter Joan Snyder declare: "It takes ten years to make a good painting." My painting has begun to garner significant recognition during the past six years, including the Joan Mitchell Foundation Painters and Sculptors Grant, the Anonymous Was A Woman Award (both 2009), and a Guggenheim Fellowship in Painting (2013). It's been a gratifying affirmation of this demanding, exhilarating avocation I've chosen. Although I went to art school during the heyday of Post-Modernism, I'm very interested in notions of mastery and originality, especially as it pertains to painting. At the same time, I'm looking to develop a kind of generous abstract language that comes directly from my own hybrid identity as a serious scholar of painting and art history, a woman, a lesbian, an activist, and a child of a white working-class family.

My current paintings explore and extend the legacy of American abstraction, while paying homage to many of its innovative female figures, among them Georgia O'Keeffe, Helen Frankenthaler, and Elizabeth Murray. The work overflows with visual precedents, inviting references to Color Field, Pop Art and 1970s Feminist art through its interplay of poured paint, graphic shapes, and tantalizing glimpses of recognizable imagery. My work has reached a new plateau, where the craft of painting and material itself trigger seemingly endless invention, and the studio is really the only place I want to be these days. I've barely made a dent in what I'm capable of.

Over the years, I have been involved with so many different aspects of the art world, from agitprop, printmaking, and painting to writing criticism, lecturing, and teaching. Consequently, my inbox overflows with requests for my time. When I moved to New York as an ambitious 20-year-old, I was so hungry for opportunity that my automatic response to any offer or request was always "yes." After all, you never knew who you might meet! This is one of those Big City platitudes that proved to be both true and useful, especially as I started building a network for my work. I'm starting to break those knee-jerk habits, so that I can narrow my focus to painting and an occasional piece of criticism. A teacher of mine at Pratt used to say: to be a really good artist, one has to be in their studio every day. For years, as I struggled to support myself and my work, I saw this as untenable, an almost cruel thing to say to art students. I'm starting to understand what he meant: an amazing sense of freedom and unknowing opens up as I spend more time immersed in my painting. The next goal is to spend all my time in the studio.

During much of the learning curve outlined above, I've been fortunate to be in a relationship with my wife, Sheila Pepe. Throughout, she has been critical to my development as a person *and* an artist. Perhaps most importantly, we are happily matched in our intense commitment to art-making. A perfect day for Sheila and Carrie looks something like this: long hours spent alone in our respective studios, followed by a delicious, late-night meal together.

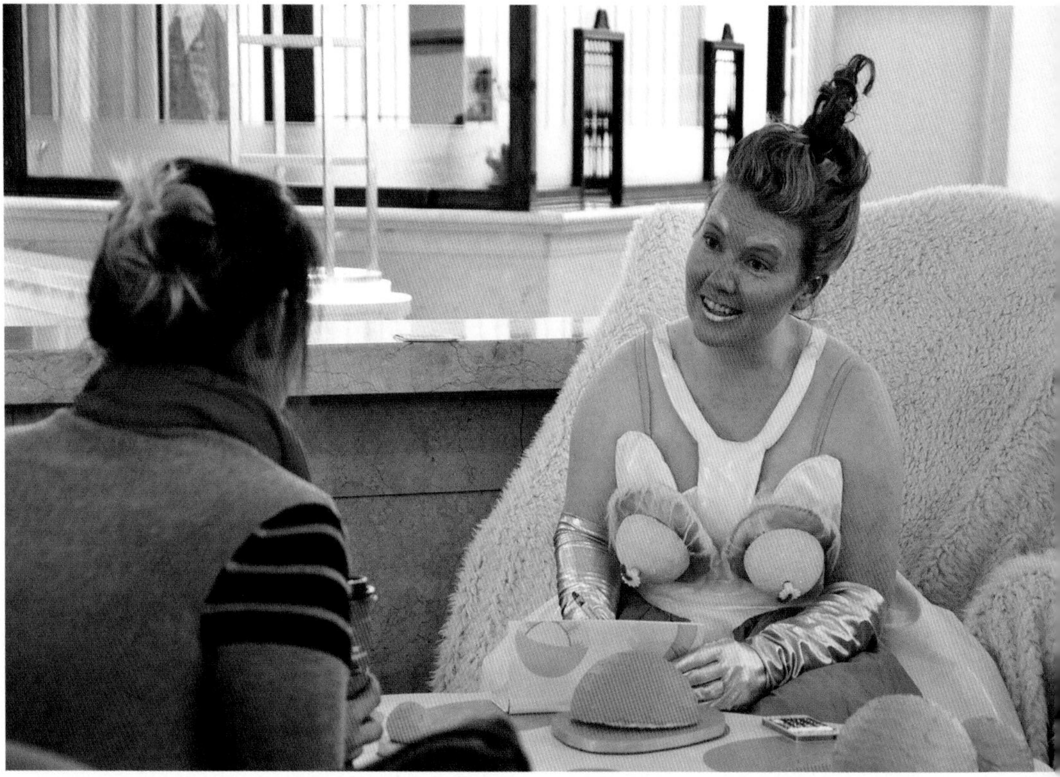

I grew up in a socially conscious household, where both my parents were actively involved in the peace movement and second wave Women's Liberation Movement. My parents were part of Iona Community in Scotland, which believed in applying the Bible to real life situations. The community would send families to live in impoverished neighborhoods in inner cities throughout Scotland. I was born in the U.S., but my earliest memories are living in Easterhouse in Glasgow. This firsthand knowledge of how difficult life is for parts of the population made an imprint on me at an early age. As an adult, I haven't belonged to a specific religious practice, but I do think my earliest experiences instilled the belief that I have a responsibility to make the world a better place. After two formative years in Easterhouse we moved to Plymouth, Devon, a city on the southwest coast of England.

My art foundation teachers strongly encouraged me to apply to Goldsmiths College. I had no idea how influential Goldsmiths was back then, but I took their advice and was accepted. I was the only student in my year group to receive a first class honors. The education I received at Goldsmiths was vital to my training as an artist. It taught me how to have a rigorous creative practice and how to navigate the professional world. It was at Goldsmiths that I discovered my creative trajectory. I find myself always referring back to the many valuable lessons I learned there. Goldsmiths provided me the ticket to get into the

Carron Little
Unto Each Their Own Safe + More by The Queen of Luxuria
Performance at Bridgeview Bank, 2pm to 4pm each day, October 19 & 20
Performers: Meghan Moe Beitiks, Natalia Nicholson, Olive Stefanski and Carron Little
2013
Curated by Eden Unluata
Courtesy of the artist
Photography by Jamie Gannon

master's program at the School of the Art Institute of Chicago, where I now teach. My educational experience, from both sides of the pond, gave me the tools to live a creative life. It hasn't always been easy, but I have lived with determination. When I'm despondent, I often look at the statistics for women in solo shows and museum exhibitions—the disparity provides me the motivation that I need to continue!

After graduating with an MFA, I moved back to London. I had recently seen a retrospective exhibition at the Museum of Modern Art of Jackson Pollock's work. I learned that, as a young artist, he had copied the masters and, in doing so, developed his own unique visual vocabulary. I wasn't a painter and was not planning to go down that path, but I appreciated Pollock's creative invention. To further my artistic practice, I landed a job teaching art and earned enough money to start traveling. It was my goal to immerse myself in the history of art and culture. Up until that point, I had predominantly studied contemporary art. I traveled throughout Italy and France, and went to Dali's home in Spain to witness his golden eggs. Throughout this time, I was also able to study how things were changing in my own hometown of London. The European Union began selecting Cities of Culture in the mid-80s, in large part to provide resources to enhance economic development. Glasgow was one of the first cities to be awarded the City of Culture, and what a remarkable difference it made. Upon my return to Glasgow I barely recognized it—the dark buildings had been cleaned, and it looked beautiful. The city had reclaimed a sense of pride in itself and its history.

I remained in contact with Pennina Barnett, one of my professors from Goldsmiths. One day, she called me at home and said she had a free ticket for me to attend a conference organized by the Freud Museum, called *Sex, Shame and Sexuality*. I was invited to lunch with the panelists, Grizelda Pollock, Director of the Courtauld Institute, the Director of the Freud Museum, and Pennina Barnett. It was one of those seminal moments where I thought to myself: I have been educated by these phenomenal women, I am the next generation, I need to go and do something with my education. As I was walking home that day across the

Millennium Bridge, there was a public art projection on St Paul's Cathedral. I later found out the piece was by Jenny Holzer. She had projected words onto the Dome in different languages. I think the first word was "breasts," then "Allah," and then "peace" in Urdu. I was elated and made a commitment to change my life and focus, full-time, on my work. I had already started saving up money to move to Chicago. So, in 2009, I shipped everything I loved to the city I love.

Art has always been my first priority. In the early years of my career I focused on my work and didn't think much about this. For me, focusing on art has not been without its challenges, and I've made certain choices: one choice was not to marry and another was not to have children. I've had three long-term relationships throughout my adult life, and in each one I stuck with the Virginia Woolf idea of keeping "a room of one's own" by maintaining my own space and freedom to live as I choose. A great friend gave me the advice her mother had given to her: "It's a women's prerogative to change her mind." Being independent gives me the freedom to avoid oppressive relationships and prioritize my practice above domestic responsibilities. I grew up with strong and powerful female role models. My mum was part of the Nuffield Institute that worked with the British Government to organize long term health planning, and at Goldsmiths I had the good fortune to be educated by more amazing women—most notably, Janet Anderson, who was my personal advisor, and Katy Deepwell, who was my critical theory professor. Janet's wise words still ring in my ears to this day. I grew up with the idea that I could do anything I wanted—gender was of no consequence.

When I first arrived back to Chicago in 2009, I got a job writing reviews for a local newspaper, and although it was unpaid, I got to know artists and galleries very quickly. I had learned from the professional practice course at Goldsmiths that I needed to make the connections, so I set out to embed myself in the local art world. An important turning point was writing an article, entitled "Make Believe," about the funding of a local public art project by the SSA (Special Service Area) #33 and the Wicker Park Chamber of Commerce. I discovered a consulting firm was paid $75,000, and each artist was paid $1,000, to produce an art installation in unoccupied shop windows. "Make Believe" was a great idea, but the art wasn't as good as it could have been, precisely due to the budget invested in the installations. It was at that time I saw the need for more funding to be directed to artists, so that they could realize their ambitious ideas. As artists, we all know that we need a reasonable budget to spend on materials for a project and cover the cost of living expenses while we are doing it. This was the argument I made in the article published in the local newspaper. The following year, I was invited to sit on the arts committee for my local neighborhood as a direct result of writing the criticism.

The arts committee had a budget of $70,000 to fund public art projects. I knew I needed like-minded allies, so I invited Whitney Tassie, who was then assistant director to gallery owner Monique Meloche. In the early months, I focused on gaining an understanding of the politics involved. We decided on a long-term funding program and a short-term funding program. The first year, we funded six murals around the neighborhood. One of the gallery owners thought we should give each artist $2000. I argued for $5000. I outlined a realistic budget and explained the real costs: $1000 for paint supplies, $1000 for rented scaffolding and prepping of the wall, and the balance for living expenses and hours on the job. I went around to each person individually prior to the voting meeting and had a discussion on the importance of providing a living wage for artists. When it came time to cast our votes, I didn't have to say a thing. One person made a motion for $5000, someone seconded it, and the project was funded.

Working as an artist, I always start with listening and observing. I began to think about what defined my neighborhood culturally. I had learned this from my time in London observing the development of Cities of Culture, Brit Art and the expansion of the Tate Modern. I kept witnessing unexpected surprises that would happen in the neighborhood. One day, in a creative brainstorming meeting, I suggested we organize an out of the ordinary orchestra, or a dance company to perform in a public area as people come home from work every Friday night. Whitney Tassie's response was: "Do it." And so, *Out of*

Site (OoS)—Unexpected Encounters of Public Performance was launched in 2011.

OoS happens in public space and is nomadic throughout the city. Artists choose specific sites in the neighborhood and, three months prior to the start of the festival, I submit permits for the use of the public space and contact local business owners that it might affect. People have referred to the city as our studio. I was tired of seeing my friends in the performance community never earn a penny for their work. In building *OoS,* I worked with Joseph Ravens, of Defibrillator Performance Art Gallery, to create a funding structure for solo artists, duo artists, and groups. One of the early performances for *OoS* was socially active, and the performers were intentionally engaging the public. A member of the public brandished a pocket knife, and I had to intervene so that he'd put it away. I realized that if we were going to create a more peaceful city in Chicago, we needed to bring culture that altered and shifted the paradigm of aggressive behavior. I trained a steward team to actively engage the public and coached them in dealing with difficult situations utilizing non-violence training techniques. I had learned these techniques from my early days in the youth peace movement and youth Quaker training sessions.

OoS has become a successful, albeit modest, public performance program—we have an annual budget of $20,000, with support from Propeller Fund and Chicago Department of Special Events and Cultural Affairs. One of the audience members who comes to nearly every performance insists that it reduces crime. We've prioritized creating performances in neglected areas of the neighborhood, where violent crime is a problem, in the hope that we might alter the dynamic of the public space. I also realize the importance of programming into the festival a diversity of artists. If we are going to engage the diverse make-up of the public body, we need to mirror them in the representation of the work.

We just completed our fifth year of *OoS,* and it's been an invaluable learning experience. I've learned that artists applying must have a comprehensive, well-designed website and well-written proposals that clearly describe their intentions. From working on the Jury panel, I've learned what to do and what not to do. I've been able to improve my own practice by witnessing others' mistakes. *OoS* has expanded my own professional network, and I'm fortunate to have been able to work with amazing people from all over the world and engage in conversations about public performance art in an international context. *OoS* has played a vital role in supporting the local performance community and their practices. Through the series, we've been able to cultivate a public performance practice that is unique to the Chicago context. Numerous artists have performed with us first and, subsequently, have gone on to do work with the Museum of Contemporary Art, High Concept Laboratory, and Arts Incubator. I think a lot about the need to create ecosystems that are healthy and provide sustenance for our practice. The most important thing has been to witness the way we have altered or shifted the public perspective and to see moments of joy and wonder created for people. I believe I've created a model for how public performance artists should be supported in the early stages of their career, and I'm excited to work on larger city-wide projects in the future.

My own work has expanded as well. I've had the opportunity to develop projects showing work nationally and internationally. These opportunities have allowed me to listen to the local communities and create work that is relevant to the local population. This goes back to my early training at Goldsmiths, when I made a commitment to create work for everyone. *OoS* is about the magic that happens as you come across something when you least suspect it.

In 2014, I was an artist in residence for Chicago Department of Cultural Affairs and Special Events (DCASE). I worked on a performance project that was to happen in different locations around the city. I wrote a paper outlining the arts-related policies we had created in my own neighborhood. One evening, I had a rehearsal at the Cultural Center and bumped into one of the people who create policy for the City of Chicago. She asked me if I could write down everything I had done locally related to policy. Magically, I'd already written the rough draft! I edited the paper and emailed it off to her later that night. Within a couple of months they had implemented some of my suggestions. I think about the importance of the ebb and flow of creating a culture where people mutually help each other. This ethic really goes back to my upbringing. But the question goes further, in terms of creative practice and cultural policy-making. For me, the question is: how can we help each other to do better work as artists, so the public gets to experience more mind-blowing culture? It takes an ecosystem, and a press that shares the ideas and inspires a dialogue, and it takes institutions that support artists to make big, ambitious projects. It takes the village that surrounds the artist to make the work.

OoS functions nomadically, so we make an extra effort to bring people together during the festival. We arrange talks, screenings, host dinner parties, and partner with other organizations in an effort to connect people. When *OoS* is happening, I divide my time into studio days and *OoS* days. The winter tends to be my most generative time in terms of creative development and applying for funding. I may not receive the residencies or awards I apply for, but after writing them, these ideas become seeds for future opportunities. An idea I had proposed three years ago and submitted for a residency in Switzerland just got accepted this past year for the Beverly neighborhood. My mantra is "never give up," and I teach that to my students as well.

In addition to directing *OoS*, pursuing my personal art practice, or finding public funding, I teach part-time to supplement my income. Last year 50% of my earnings were made through my art practice, and the other half through teaching at the School of the Art Institute of Chicago and as an artist-in-residence in Chicago Public Schools. I love solo time, but I'm always elated after working on a collaborative video or group performance. I love both, and need to do both, but there is something so rewarding for me when I'm working in collaboration. I know that art can make a difference in people's lives and art has definitely saved me at points when I was struggling. In making public performance and curating, I can be a part of producing many unique experiences for the public. The most rewarding moments for me are hearing the public discussing art and contemplating the broader meanings of the work. *OoS* often has people stop in their busy tracks and moved to joy while watching a performance. These are the precious moments that I live for.

PLEASE STAND.
FACE A STRANGER.
RAISE YOUR CUP.
HOLD EYE CONTACT.
DRINK.
MOVE ON.

I sometimes say that I'm in the art world by accident.

I don't mean this to be flip. Nor is it a case of extreme Imposter Syndrome, although I've suffered from that at times. I'm not the first person to state that what we set out to do often leads us down a funny path towards something else. I graduated from college with a strong inclination that I was a theater-maker. A director, definitely. An actor, occasionally. A writer, perhaps.

I was wrong.

There are a lot of very long stories I could tell about why it didn't work out for me and theater, but I'll boil them down to their essence:

There is no better collaborative process in the creative world, at least the world I've experienced so far, than making a play. Truly, the process of making theater teaches a great deal that all other art forms (and many businesses) could learn from. However, this doesn't resolve the issue of product. Working intensively for four months (or more) to make a product that goes before an audience for four days (or sometimes only four hours) is a bad pay-off, and one that becomes exponentially worse if the maker is dissatisfied with what's been produced.

The theater world, like any creative field, is full of no. And no is something that every artist, of any kind, needs to get used to. But it became more and more difficult for me to accept theater's "no" when there was another creative world that said "yes" to the type of work I wanted to make.

Chloë Bass
Linger Longer Napkin
4.5"x4.5" folded
Hand-stamped ink on cocktail
napkin, edition of 50
2014
Courtesy of the artist

Many artists, including myself, have been in one field as a masquerade, while we danced around another in our own self-images. I was speaking with a friend the other night at a raucous holiday party for an organization we both love. She used a phrase that caught my ear, and I commented on its beauty. "Well yes," she replied, "I'm a writer." She's a well-regarded associate director at a museum, a woman who does not consider herself a curator, but wonders if being a writer means that at all times she must be writing. That is, at what point does not writing, due to the constraints of her other commitments, make her not a writer?

In the ten years from 2006 to 2016, I've called myself any and all of the following: student, director, actor, performer, maker of devised theater, playwright, performing artist, performance artist, interdisciplinary/multidisciplinary/transdisciplinary artist, post-studio artist, research-based artist, situation artist, social practice artist, conceptual artist, and public practitioner—not to mention all of the job titles I accrued in order to get paid properly. (As an aside, the artist Julia Cole gives a wonderful presentation that she begins with a list of everything she's done in order to get paid; "horse groomer" stands out from my memory of her hilarious yet honest talk on this subject.) My father likes to tell the story of how I came home from school at age eight and told him I wanted to be a director. He didn't even think I knew what a director was. My statement was wrong, but the impulse was right: like a director, I'm making a world, and shifting the pieces within to match that world aesthetically, linguistically, and dramaturgically. The major difference is that, now, I call it art.

So, what happened? I graduated from college with a BA in Theater Studies in 2006 and scampered right back to New York City, my hometown, where I house-sat for a few months in Chelsea and interned (for pay!) at the Department of Sanitation's Waste Prevention, Reuse, and Recycling office. I'd had two work-study jobs during college: the first as a box office girl at the campus theater and the second as an educator for our campus recycling program. This sum total of reasonable work experience left me unprepared for a job fair where no theaters were tabling. Thankfully, the Department of Sanitation was, and

I took the internship they offered without a second thought. A few months later, I scrapped everything. I got an internship at the Wooster Group (no pay!), where I found two potential roommates and a connection for an apartment in Bushwick. I started making theater with said roommates in the aforementioned Bushwick apartment, became an SAT tutor for the wealthy, and not-so-eventually, but completely accidentally, fell in with the group of artists and community organizers who were becoming Arts in Bushwick, best known for producing Bushwick Open Studios. My priorities at age nearly-23 were simple: I had just moved to a new neighborhood, and I wanted friends. When my roommate and I were asked to host a cabaret at the Bushwick Starr theater on the first night of June 2007, I imagined fun. I did not imagine that I would somewhat drunkenly meet the people who would become my closest collaborators.

Arts in Bushwick (AIB), in its inception, imagined artists not just as creative people, but as good neighbors. This inclination towards open friendliness, rather than the competitive environments I so often faced (and, frankly, feared), made it easy for me to stick around and see what the group was up to. I quickly learned that sticking around, doing the work that needs to be done, is actually the fastest path towards leadership in a fledgling all-volunteer organization. I was nearly three years into co-lead organizing what became three festivals per year (Bushwick Open Studios, which persists, along with BETA Spaces, a festival to highlight local curators, and SITE Fest, a festival to highlight local performance of all sorts), when I became aware that Arts in Bushwick was my identity. Although I had been making some theatrical work, the vast majority of my labor, social experiences, public engagements, and invitations to do consulting on the side were as a result of my involvement with and leadership in AIB. In other words, I was not known as an artist (theatrical or otherwise). I was known as a community organizer, sometimes mistitled as a curator, and as a local, Bushwick voice. I had made a great deal of progress, but not with my own creative work. As an artist, I was invisible.

This was equal parts freeing and frustrating. In the aftermath of the 2008 recession, I applied to graduate school, in a program that I thought would have me: Brooklyn College's interdisciplinary

MFA program in Performance and Interactive Media Arts. This was my chance to start the switch from theater to art. I wasn't sure quite what I wanted to make, but I hoped school would allow me to shift how I saw myself, and how others saw me. In the meantime, Bushwick was changing, and I felt less and less satisfied by producing a major annual event for a neighborhood in which I no longer felt truly engaged or comfortable. In 2011, I graduated with my MFA, left Arts in Bushwick, moved to Bed-Stuy, and dedicated myself to the unclear but determined path of "just" being an artist.

After the tricky Arts in Bushwick experience, I actually don't think of myself as a culture producer. In my current artistic life, I am, perhaps, a cultural noticer. Very much of my work—both my artwork and my daily-life work—comes out of noticing what's already in the world and figuring out ways to reinterpret, repurpose, or re-view it. There's a great deal of power and privilege in being the one who gets to point and name. I only know that what I offer now as an artist, even when it's public-facing or socially engaged, is much smaller, more intimate, and more crafted than what I offered as a creative community organizer.

However, there are elements of the Arts in Bushwick experience that I hope never to lose. First, it's a lot easier to manage my own artistic career than when I was previously trying to manage a team. Second, I learned a great deal about direct and clear communication through AIB, as well as about the necessity to speak to people in a way that's compelling to them—not just compelling to you. Being in business for a few years primed me well for the elements of what I now call "public practice:" writing, guest lecturing, facilitating workshops and panels, and teaching at all levels. This flexibility of practice (what constitutes work, rather than distraction), alongside an ongoing curiosity about what it means to be a community, has been invaluable as I travel with art projects throughout the country and internationally. Without Arts in Bushwick, I don't think I would have any sense of how to share my work with people in a way that works for them and responds to their circumstances, rather than to my own assumptions.

Finally, Arts in Bushwick gave me access to a tremendous range of people in all levels of the art world: the other amazing artists, curators, critics, educators, publishers, gallery directors, and so on, without whom I would never have started to make strides in my own independent artistic career—even though I was never a "Bushwick artist."

As an artist, I can meet with people one on one or in small groups, at my studio and beyond, rather than spending my days coordinating dozens to thousands of people at a time. I have more time to be curious about things, which means I write more, spending time every day working on words as part of my practice. I clarify my thoughts and questions about artistic practice through teaching, both during visiting artist appointments and as a professor. And instead of staying home and focusing all of my efforts on two square miles of Brooklyn, I now base my life in New York but have the flexibility to allow my work to take me to other places.

As a native New Yorker, the amount of travel I now do surprises me. The first time I left town to do a project, it was at the invitation of a collaborator who was going to Germany for a year. The chance was hers, not mine, but I was willing to share it. This willingness is key: now that I'm "on the map" as interested to go anywhere, I've been fortunate to have a plethora of conversations with curators doing projects outside of New York's particular cultural center. Some of this also has to do with the type of work I make: I'm known for working directly with live people in a particular way, which, in part, inspires far-flung organizations (residency programs, fellowships, and exhibition spaces) to express interest in hosting my type of practice in their communities. I've done this at home, through the Laundromat Project most particularly, but also throughout the country, through organizations like Cleveland's SPACES Gallery, Greensboro's Elsewhere, and Omaha's Bemis Center for Contemporary Arts. Travel has offered amazing, well-funded opportunities to develop and present my work, which allows me to maintain a practice focused on genuine inquiry rather than sales.

I'm a thirtysomething now, and I'm happy to be making more informed, and less accidental, choices for myself and my career.

But suddenly my desires are face to face with some real life facts. My parents are getting older—and my grandparents, who I'm lucky to still have, even older than that. At the same time, my financial stability has not increased at a rate that can possibly meet these looming familial challenges. It is a fact that some of the highest honors in the art world really only provide their winners with an amount of money akin to an annual middle-class salary. The money and opportunities that we compete for award more cultural capital than financial. Although cultural capital can offer many invitations to drinks and parties, it does not put food on the table, pay for dental bills, or support family members in need. If anything, it makes me less likely to answer the phone when my family calls. Cultural capital is emotionally exhausting.

The question is not whether to keep going, or even precisely *how* to keep going, but what kind of reasonable expectations I can have for my current and future life? Getting into the art world through the side door (familiarity, location, organizational labor, and happenstance) has been fun. I'm here because I feel I consistently have permission: the permission to change, at least on paper, what kind of artist I am, as long as my work continues to tell a clear and developing story. I feel I can continue to make my work fluidly, without the obstacles of "no." The question now is how to use that fluidity to increase stability. I may have come here by accident but, by hook or by crook, I'm planning to stay.

DUNCAN MACKENZIE

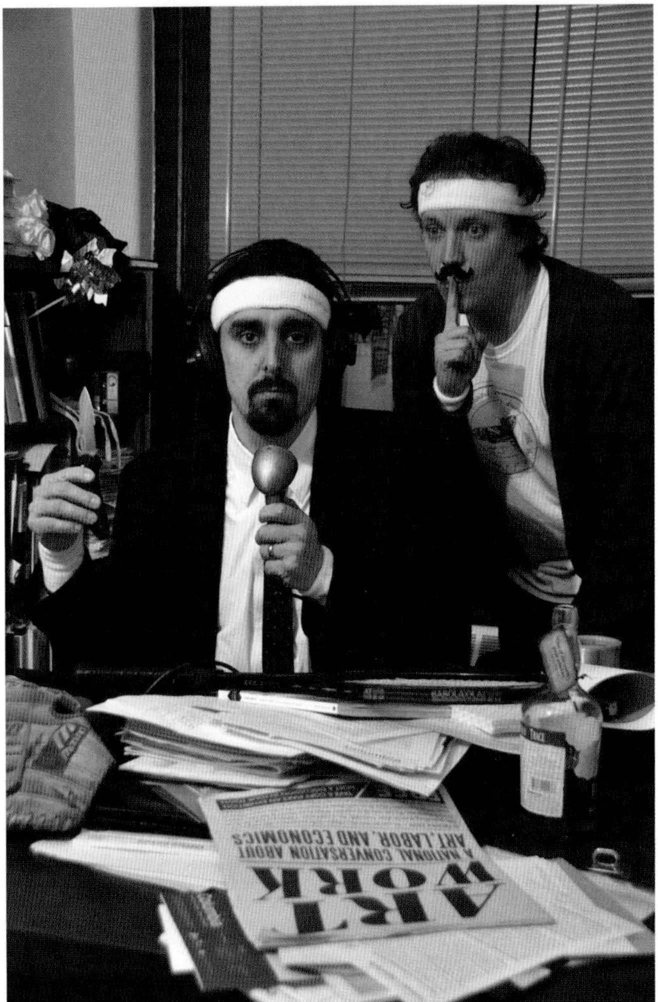

Umm. Stuff...

The two questions that always haunt me at the beginning of every project are: Is this useful? And is this fun? In a nutshell, my approach has been to put myself in situations I think could be potentially enjoyable and to create the things that will make the greatest contribution to the other people in that space.

It should be obvious that the percentages of those two things shift very considerably in any given project, but both are major factors in my willingness to pursue it. These days, most of my efforts are spread across five different spaces: my work as a professor in the Department of Art and Art History at Columbia College Chicago; the art discourse of our collaborative, *Bad at Sports*; my artistic collaboration with Christian Kuras; the adult-themed "not quite LEGO" toy manufacturer Citizen Brick; my children, and marriage.

I grew up in middle-class, suburban Calgary, in Alberta, Canada. It was as fine a place to grow up as any other, and I was reluctant to leave it at 17, and so, ended up studying at the University of Calgary. There were great people there, and some of them were willing to work for you, if you seemed like the kind of student who was willing to work for them. Through three principal mentors, I learned the important things. I learned perseverance through the model of a graduate student, named Les Thomas, who had rebuilt in his life and practice after a decade-long derailment. From William Laing, I learned the

Duncan MacKenzie
Richard Holland and Duncan MacKenzie as Bad at Sports
Poster for Apexart, New York, NY
12"x18"
2010
Courtesy of the artist

value of work and presence. Maybe most notably, I learned a permissive intellectual curiosity and never-ending wonder from Paul Woodrow, who constantly reminded us of the mysteries to be solved in hybridization and cross-pollination.

On the west side of Canada, it was very difficult to find models of engaged intellectual and rigorous artistic practice that was not based out of a university. In fact, it was almost impossible. At the time, two of the most obvious Western Canadian artists were Jeff Wall and Ken Lum, both based out of the University of British Columbia; it was very difficult to look beyond the foothills of the Rocky Mountains for examples of artists who figured out other economic routes. So, by the age of 19, I was doing everything I could to position myself well for a teaching job.

A lot of my initial impulse to be a teacher had fallen away by the time I left graduate school at the School of the Art Institute of Chicago in 2002. At the time, I was watching many of my close friends and colleagues pick up adjunct work, which seemed to be making it hard for them to find other full-time employment, which, in turn, made it hard to pay back their student loans. So, my principal concern became finding full-time work, and I became a model builder for a fabrication company.

At the same time, I was a very active artist in two different ways. I was showing big photographs of staged, proposed environments very regularly across Canada and the United States, and I was curating with another ex-pat, Canadian artist-cum-curator who was living in Chicago, Shannon Stratton. We curated under the name Middle Management, which I still think is a snide/funny name that carries the awkward flippancy that marks my daily life.

In 2003, I was part of a three-person show in Montréal with Christian Kuras and Valerie LaMontagne. Kuras and I had been in school together from 1994 to 1996, and we both showed up a little early for the install; we spent six days arguing and chatting. The show redefined how I approached art making. Kuras and I had almost the exact same set of concerns but approached them in very different but complementary ways. The week ended with me learning hard lessons about drinking at one's own opening. I'll skip the story and summarize it in this way: if you are expected to speak at any point during your opening, do not have more than two drinks. If you are not expected to speak at any time during your opening, do not have more than three drinks. And, more generally, try and act like you respect yourself when humans are visiting the things you have made. Rules I still try and live by.

Kuras and I cooked up this cockamamie idea: we would exchange sculptures and essentially evolve an exhibition in which the pieces were built in direct response to one another, so that any viewer could see a "call and response" logic working through a chain of object events, all echoing from one nonsensical starting place. What was super dumb about this idea was that we actually thought we could make sculptures and ship them across the Atlantic Ocean (Kuras = London, MacKenzie = Chicago) and that it would be no problem. It turns out, sculptures are often heavy and expensive to ship, and they also take a really long time to produce. So, our answer to this was that we would start shipping back and forth sketches of the objects we were building, communicating through a series of MP3 monologues, so that we would have a complete record of our conversation. This went pretty well for a short period but, before long, we were offering each other suggestions and trying to fix the other's pieces or augment their ideas. By 2005, it was clear that we were slowly entering into a transcontinental collaboration.

At the same time, my work with Shannon Stratton was ending, as she took a job as the first full-time curator (shortly after, she became the Executive Director) at Threewalls in Chicago, and I was leaving fabrication to join a dodgy, for-profit, post-secondary education company/college that was then setting up a downtown Chicago campus. One night at a bar, a former graduate school classmate offered me a full-time teaching job in their graphic design program. It was the best recruiting meeting I have ever had. He explained that he needed someone he knew he could trust, that we would teach on the same schedule, and get drinks together every Monday, Wednesday, and Friday. Tuesday and Thursdays I would have as prep time or studio time. Why would I say no?

During that same period, I married my college sweetheart, Joanna Topor (MacKenzie), and shortly afterward had to explain to her my brilliant plan to cut my salary in half and teach for a living.

The balance of the work has always been crucial. It was never enough just to curate or write or make. I depend upon a multivalent engagement. In curating, you get to access many different ways of thinking and speaking through the work of other artists, but while I'm doing it, I often find myself dreaming of the pieces *I* want to be making. Writing or talking about work is deeply inspiring and transformative. It allows me to luxuriate in an explanation or interrogation of something. But by the time I am through the grind of the editing process, I am always hungry to return to my own studio. Then in my own studio, things either click so that I'm there for 12 to 16 hours, or I'm constantly trying to claw my way out.

As luck would have it, the building my dodgy college was in also housed a law firm—a law firm at which my lawyer and *Bad at Sports* co-founder, Richard Holland, was employed. Aside from being a lawyer/artist, Holland had been, in his past life, an audio engineer and a talk radio junkie. In the eight months I worked in the building, he and I would often get together to swap audiobooks and exchange rumors about this new phenomenon, podcasting. Then we started meeting more regularly, in advance of us pitching an exhibition at the Michelle Grabner and Brad Killam project, The Suburban. The three things we talked most about were the end (and perpetual underserving) of Chicago-based art criticism, radio shows, and what our shared piece would be for the show. As it turned out, *Bad at Sports* (*B@S*) was essentially our shared piece for the exhibition. It just happened to take root and develop from that into a much bigger project.

In retrospect, it feels like I was searching for a new way to make a contribution to my scene. Working and showing just didn't feel like enough of an engagement. And the idea of creating a contemporary art chat show that was a little bit Howard Stern, a little bit *Frieze* magazine, and a little bit BBC radio seemed like a way I could add something. I remember thinking: "At worst, we are going to say horrible things about our friends' artworks, and they will hate us, but at least there will be a public record of what we collectively did here." What I learned was no one hates you for saying horrible things about their work, although they might not like you very much. Their friends, on the other hand, do actually hate you.

One fateful night in August, when it was 100-plus degrees outside and 110 inside our recording studio (Holland's apartment attic), we recorded an interview with curator Chris Cook. It set us up for what has now been a 540-week audio exploration of the art world. Very early on, Amanda Browder joined us, and we became the founding Chicago team; Brian Andrews joined us to become our San Francisco founder. As we grew, we expanded our blog to have 20 to 30 regular contributors, with writers and audio producers in San Francisco, Portland, Minneapolis, St. Louis, Chicago, Detroit, and New York City, amongst others. *Bad at Sports* is a collaborative devoted to talking about art in the ways artists live and experience it. So, we talk about it in a semi-reckless but devoted way, and we let the passionate and poetic people of the art world swear. We focus around the pulse of the contemporary conversation, and we work to emblemize what the artists of the contemporary world mean and then share or expand the dialogue.

We have done *B@S* for a little more than ten years as volunteers, and it is an unusual labor of love. It was pretty clear early on that there was never going to be enough money to pay everyone what their time and intellect was worth, so we decided not to worry about it. It's a funny decision because, on one hand, it means that there's no economic stability to the project; instead of paying people something very token, we pay everyone nothing. But it also means that our primary allegiance is to each other and the work, not to our advertisers and our paychecks. No one's ever been paid, and until the collaborative makes some radically different decisions, no one ever will be.

Everything was pretty outstanding. I had switched schools twice, *B@S* was growing, and Kuras and I kept finding new avenues to explore. So, in 2009 my wife and I decided we should have a baby. I found out as I sat down with Amanda Browder in Miami to interview the artist Chris Duncan in the middle of the NADA art fair. They were the first two people to know we were pregnant. I told no one else for four months. Baxter was born in the summer of 2010, and Wylie followed in the summer of 2013.

As an act of defiance to common sense or reasonability, upon having a child I became a partner in another creative endeavor. This time, for obvious reasons, it included a profit motive. While I had been off forming *B@S*, another artist friend of mine, Joe Trupia, had been wrestling with the question of how LEGO prints on LEGO. In 2010, he figured it out and formed a little company called Citizen Brick, and then he needed a partner. What we figured out and then perfected was that we could make a kind of Lego minifig that LEGO would never make. We could acquire blank LEGO stock, sometimes from LEGO themselves, and print our own designs on them. This allowed us to make the less family-friendly denizens of Legoland. We started with a range of five or so custom figures: a leather daddy, a gimp, a fully tattooed figure, a metal head, and a pot smoker. Each was named as an enthusiast. So, our pot smoker is labeled a "botany enthusiast," or our metal head was a "Norwegian black metal enthusiast." This set the tone for the kinds of minifigs and sets we went on to produce over the next five years, most notably the "Super Lab Playset" and "Center for the Performing Arts." It has also provided the opportunity to work for and with major media outlets like Sony, HBO, and DC Comics.

I suppose that's when things got a little crazy. Trying to maintain my working life and family life has proven to be a little challenging. I often feel grateful that my collaborators are deeply understanding and willing to put up with my shenanigans. I have struggled to make sure that I am as useful as I can be to all of these projects, while knowing that no matter where I am, I am stealing time from somewhere else. I often try and keep it out of my mind and just be 100% present, wherever I am. But whether I'm in my classroom lecturing, in a Skype conversation with Kuras, editing audio for *B@S*, sorting LEGO at Citizen Brick, or at home trying to parent my two boys and be a passable husband to my wife, I am constantly aware that I am needed or committed to being somewhere else.

These days, I feel like I am chasing the work. It's as though I'm struggling through mountains of clutter, administrative chaos, and emotional uncertainty to create those few moments where everything just seems to work, where things come together, one after another, and I find myself perfectly in harmony with whatever is happening. It's weird to talk about. I feel like a ridiculous New Age surfer saying it, but I do think about it like "chasing." It is in the work that I find my connection to life, to other people, to being. It is in those times when it all comes together that I feel like I am not subject to the world, but helping to author it. It is tough to find those things elsewhere, and admitting my commitment to the (often silly) things I do as work makes me feel a little like a bad parent.

Parenting is hard, and I find it difficult to be 100% *with* my kids when I am with them. I am often distracted and ill-tempered, because I feel like I am not doing something else I am clearly obligated to. The feeling of that obligation is very difficult to put away. My children are amazing to me, really amazing and delightful, but they require a lot; they are entitled to it. They have changed the way pressure is allocated in my life; they devastate the amount of time I am able to devote to my colleagues, students, and fellow travelers in my interconnected and collaborator-dependent life. I have no answers about the relationship between parenting and art making. It is something that I wrestle with a lot. How do I not give up on something I find valuable in order to be more present in my children's lives? Especially when that question sometimes reads: "Why are my children trying to take my life away from me?"

The major problem is that a creative life is a stupid-fun adventure, and I never want to give any part of it up. I imagine the challenge is the same for many. You start out with something you love doing, and you're pushing to develop a world you want to be a part of, but then once you have a handle on that, you start thinking there must be a way that you can make a greater contribution. So, you stretch to provide a wider value. Then there is the siren song calling toward family. Each step requires rebalancing, but as soon as you hit equilibrium, you start looking for the next adventure. For me, no matter how it turns out, it is ridiculously fun. And there are two young men sworn to avenge me.

EDGAR ARCENEAUX

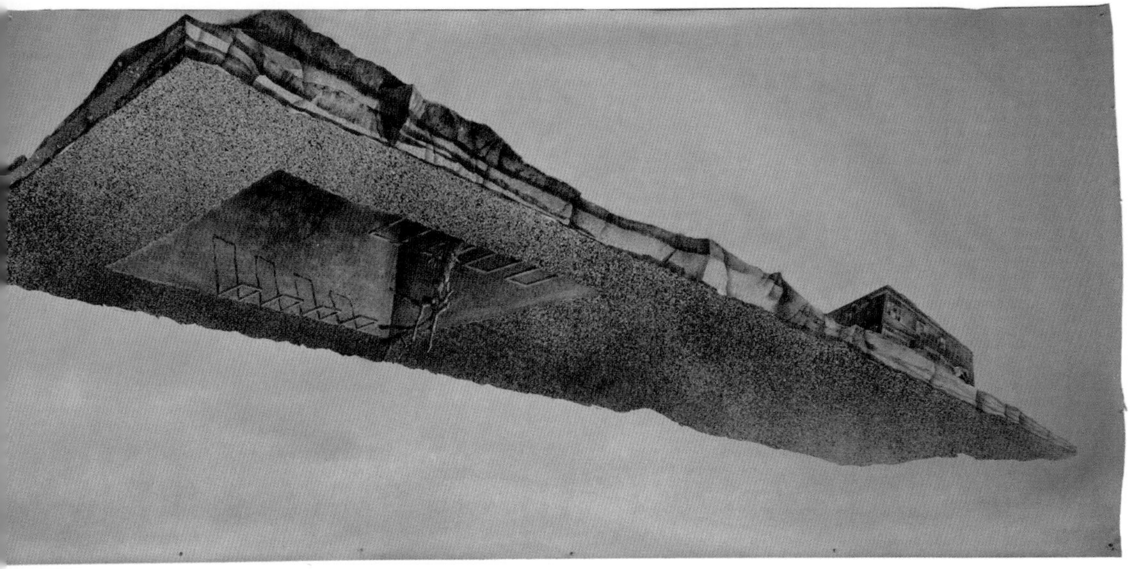

When my daughter Zora was born in 2006, I began to have the nightmares from my childhood again. The specific fears surrounded the dark and dangerous Shadow Man. As the middle child of six, I found myself in the unenviable position of sleeping in a full bed with my two younger brothers. This meant it was incumbent upon me to protect my littlest brother from the Shadow Man by placing him in the middle spot in the bed. This left me dangerously exposed on the far edges of the bed to the worst fear of my young imagination—being snatched into the darkness.

There were other things to worry about as a kid as well. I grew up in South Central Los Angeles in a big house with lots of young families in the neighborhood. Playing with the kids from my neighborhood was fine, but the older kids from the junior high at the corner, that was another story. It wouldn't be long before many of these kids, the very ones we grew up with, would become part of the gangs that populated the area.

Before all that, while we were a family having fun, I thought the worst thing was the Shadow Man. There are two generations of kids in the Arceneaux family. I'm the fourth of six children and I was always a little different from the rest. I had three older siblings who I could learn from, but I was also the oldest of the younger children. My knowledge that power can be a fleeting thing started at a young age. Being somewhere in between having

Edgar Arceneaux
Blind Pig #3
72"x168"
Acrylic, graphite on paper
2010
Courtesy of the artist and
Susanne Vielmetter Los Angeles
Projects
Photography by Robert
Wedemeyer

authority and at the mercy of the older siblings is probably the foundation of my political awareness.

For as long as I could remember, my mother would tell us stories of how great a man my grandfather Edgar was. He lived in our home after my grandma died, so my three older siblings got to relish in his presence, being spoiled by him daily. They'd recall how life changed when he died, retelling so many stories of him that it produced an absence in my life, a dense fog that only imagination could attempt to fill. From my mother's stories, I began to conjure glimpses of my worldview that were forming well before I was born.

Edgar Young migrated from Greenville, Mississippi to Los Angeles in the 1920s for a better life. He was part of that first great wave of migrants who fled the southern US to escape the institutionalized dangers of Jim Crow laws. (My family would later be part of the great exodus of Blacks out of Los Angeles in the 1980s, but that's later in the story.) He was able to marry, purchase a home, raise five children, and was a self-taught painter and inventor. He did all of this with only a fifth-grade education—something almost impossible to do in Los Angeles today. Before trash trucks, city employees like my grandfather would push a broom and waste can on wheels, cleaning the neighborhood streets. His story, in many ways, has formed the foundation of my interests.

As I grew older, people would tell me that I looked like my grandfather. Not only that, but that I walked like him, talked like him, had a similar sense of humor. We both loved working with our hands, and we loved making art. I grew up looking at his paintings on our walls, wondering what could have made us so similar. I was searching for a definitive answer, but instead encountered a paradox. Could I be him? If so, how can I be myself at the same time?

Eventually, the gangs and drugs ran us out of the neighborhood we loved and out into West Covina, a rural community in the San Gabriel Valley. We had a nice house and great neighbors, but we were one of only two black families in what was now our new home. The year was 1984. I was 11 going on 12, and the particular area we found ourselves in was going through tremendous growth. My parents could only afford to send one of us to Catholic school, so the youngest three had our first introduction to public education. But it was good in many ways; most important was that it was safe. That meant we could ride our bikes everywhere. And we did.

All of my new friends were roughneck outcasts who came from troubled homes. We had the greatest adventures, because they had no curfews, but they also had no parents to speak of. The group of us, about eight in total, remained close through high school and into college. West Covina is just far enough away from Los Angeles to seem like a different universe, but the same cycles of loss, financial hardship and family discord were present there, too. But all the victims of it that I knew in West Covina were white. I didn't have any white friends before this, and they didn't have any black friends before me. My attributing whiteness with wealth, something I learned from TV, was upended.

Less than ten years after moving there, it would also be on TV that I would see Los Angeles go up in flames during the 1992 Uprising. Our house sat up on a small hill, where we could see the unnatural fog of smoke plumes consume the city during those six days. This uprising, like its predecessor, the Watts Rebellion of 1965, tore open the contradictions in the American Dream that my grandparents fled from the South to find, that my parents taught us to believe in, and that my siblings and I dutifully pursued. In the aftermath, I needed to be involved in the rebuilding of Los Angeles somehow but was uncertain as to how. What role could an artist play, and what could art do that other approaches could not? I set out, determined to figure out how.

Two years later, I was living in Pasadena as a full-time student at Art Center College of Design (ACCD). I was getting this amazing education, with access to unbelievable resources, but I constantly sought opportunities to learn and meet new mentors outside of school. I felt a strong desire to teach, but the school wouldn't allow me to as a first-year student. It was a chance meeting, though, that led me back to South LA, just a few miles from the neighborhood I grew up in. I joined the "Art on Saturday" program as a volunteer, to teach everything that I was learning at ACCD, for free, to youth from across the city. I was initially invited by "Art on Saturday" founder and graphic designer George Evans to come check out the old fire house building they were in, and I wound up staying there for more than three years.

I could have never predicted that the beginning of my entire art career would be a succession of events from the time I was teaching at the Fire Station on Hobart Street and attending ACCD. In this confluence of moving across this spectrum of communities, I came to know artists and thinkers like John Outterbridge, Rick Lowe, Eugenia Butler, and Charles Gaines. The circles of influence expanded to institutions that merge art, design, and community-building, like St Elmo's Village, Tricia Wards' Culabra Art Park in Highland Park, Project Row Houses in Houston, and Sci-Arc (Southern California Institute of Architecture). I got my first paid teaching job because of the experience I gained volunteer-teaching on Hobart St. Because of the work I did at the Museum of Contemporary Art, LA in the groundbreaking exhibition *Uncommon Sense*, in 1997, a German collector saw my photos in the catalogue and invited me to a residency in Aachen, Germany. This led to several long-lasting relationships with curators, galleries, museums, and artists across Europe that last to this day. Reaching outside of my relationships in school, I followed my passion to give back somehow, not suspecting that I would be introduced to the great influencers of my practice, philosophy, and life.

It was Charles Gaines who was the first artist that I met who was interested in the same type of questions that inspired me. He offered both a philosophical and aesthetic language that critiqued power and explored representation that did not rely upon the conventions of figurative painting. He helped me understand that duality was a trap that could produce faulty pictures of the world, linking identity not to what something is, but to what it isn't. I am black as long as you are convinced that you are white, to paraphrase James Baldwin.

Recognizing the contributions of my peers and mentors, I needed to build a path for my own work that would contribute to the discourse with artwork and ideas I felt were needed. The communities I was a part of and the subjects I was attracted to were often exclusionary of each other, so how could I make work that could engage with them all?

During my last term at Art Center, anger and disappointment followed my encountering illustration students having job interviews in the art office. Seemed like, every nine weeks, the entire school would rally around transportation designers giving presentations for jobs to major auto manufacturers. Deducing that all the other majors had job placement opportunities as well, it seemed unjust that we ART students were left to sink or swim with the very same student debts. I used to sell shoes, games, and rifles at Big 5 Sporting Goods in West Covina, before starting my degree at Art Center. This was the worst of the Big 5 stores in the region, but it was better than working at McDonald's, which was my first job. (It was not nearly as much fun as my summer gig, though, playing a zombie prisoner at Knott's Berry Farms, Halloween Haunt theme park.) It was honest work, but I promised myself that I would never go back to those jobs again. After five months of borrowing from my parents, taking freelance gigs, paying rent late, and scraping by where I could, I applied for welfare.

Standing in the unemployment line had a grim irony. I went from public college to private school to public subsidy in just four years. My first adult engagement with the social safety net would be a formative experience in life. I couldn't go to the bank, because my account was overdrawn with late fees, so when I got my first payment, I went to the check-cashing store near my barbershop. The long lines were filled with working-class people like myself, students, moms and dads, immigrants wiring money back to Mexico, the elderly, disabled, and a mix of down and outs. Along with money, you'd get food stamps for the supermarket. I was both excited to have some cash for groceries and also wondered if those other black folks who chose to major in law and medicine were wiser than I had first suspected. Standing in the check-out line, I looked around me, embarrassed, fearing the social stagnation people project towards the needy. Then, my earliest memories of relying on the government merged with my current situation. Having five brothers and sisters, when my father was out of work, my mother shopped with food stamps. As a kid, I wasn't sure what that strange looking money was but knew we were fortunate to have it. "Oh yeah," I thought. "We've been here before and… I'm doing okay." This just wasn't the start I foresaw, being the first in my family to graduate from college.

With no job in sight, I was going to take advantage of the time and make a complete body of work using a process of my own creation. At that time, in 1997, one of the main issues I had with my education was how I was asked to articulate a clear picture of my project first, before I had made it. I felt that, when you place ideas so squarely into words, it cuts the edges off their amorphous nature. I wanted to make a body of work that would carve itself out through time, where the process would determine the outcome. I continued to push my drawings further, from the page to immersive, room-sized installations where people could participate in my explorations along with me.

Markets work by turning culture into reproducible units, so I knew being pigeonholed into a given style or look would doom me. So, early on, I strove to build a practice that would allow me the flexibility to make whatever I wanted and become whatever that project needed me to be. Part strategy and part recognition of a personal need for change, this path led me to a very diverse practice. Artist, draftsman, installation artist, community developer, filmmaker, theater director, researcher, author, teacher, and mentor. These are the many different disciplines that I could be working in at any given moment, but I could never do all of this alone. I show with some great commercial galleries and consider Susanne Vielmetter, my Los Angeles gallerist, as family. We've both grown and expanded together over the 14 years we've been partners, and she supports my various efforts, many of which she cannot sell. We don't always agree, but she believes in me, and the feeling is mutual. She does remind me that she is a commercial gallery when we do a show. There need to be things that can make money. She doesn't tell me what to make and respects my process—though at times, it can drive her crazy.

There is no balance to be found between commercial and non-commercial interests for me. It's a conflicted ebb and flow, with deep peaks and valleys, where at times opportunities can be rich and other times not. I am never certain what's coming; that can be exciting for some and make others flee the field entirely.

The concern that, "if I changed my work, I might lose my supporters" wasn't entirely unfounded. The exchange was that these varied approaches to art-making enabled me to see new pictures and potentials where I might not have seen them otherwise. How far could I take this? I debated: "Could it work in Watts? Could I take this way of making art and apply it to Watts House Project?"

I visited the Watts Towers for the first time in 1996, which I hesitate to confess, having grown up only seven miles away from them. In elementary school, I learned about Simon Rodia, the Italian immigrant who built these spiraling Towers in his backyard. But like many Angelenos, I never made the journey to see them in person. As a kid, I imagined they were the size of the Eiffel Tower; they appeared larger in my memory, because most photos exclude the houses around them. This bit of editing makes the Towers appear framed by ideal blue sky and denies that they are in a historically poor neighborhood. Erasure of the homes from the frame is a subtle statement that the families and their traditions did not matter.

The Watts Towers are on a triangular lot carved by the Pacific Electric Railroad. Rodia would use the train tracks as a tool to build his masterpiece. Standing nearly 100 feet tall, they were begun in 1933, and Rodia walked away from them in 1954. Rodia had a grand ambition, and it was to build monuments that stand as a testament to the will of the individual. During the 33 years he built the towers, jazz legend Charles Mingus walked by them to school, and he would describe how some towers went up and some came down, and it was always a work in progress.

I met artist Rick Lowe by chance in 1996, when I was visiting my mentor, John Outterbridge, in his studio. Rick was invited to Los Angeles as part of show called *Uncommon Sense* at MOCA Los Angeles. The theme of the exhibition was social engagement—work that existed between exhibition and social service. Rick was going around the city, meeting artists and inviting them to participate in this project he was trying to do.

I knew this was the connection I had been looking for and told him I'd love to be involved. I cannot recall if the project had a name at that point, but I jumped in with both feet, believing it would deepen my efforts to do something to rebuild the city after the '92 LA Uprising.

I became Rick's on-the-ground person in Watts, running errands, fielding meetings, passing out flyers, and acquiring the confidence to make personal connections with strangers around an idea. This is when the first vision for Watts House Project (WHP) was conceived, on the city-side of the street. The Watts Tower Art Center was built to support and preserve the Watts Towers by being a hub for the surrounding neighborhood, and it had been there since the mid-1960s. The art center had had an ambition to start an artist-in-residence by its founding director Noah Purifoy and, later, by John Outterbridge. The residency idea never fully took root, so Rick was attempting to renew the effort. Working on city property in LA can be a bureaucratic trap for artists and left the project's wheels spinning in the mud for more than two years. That, combined with a renovation plan that was too expensive to build, and the project stalled. Though I was focused on WHP, I was still making my drawings, which allowed me to do two artist residencies, at Project Row Houses in Houston, Texas and at the Banff Center for the Arts in Alberta, Canada. It was during this time period that I began putting my thinking into writing about the tensions and connections between drawing and socially engaged art. At that time, I wasn't able to find any synthesis between the two endeavors, other than the obvious fact that I was doing them both.

Over those first three years of WHP, from 1997 to 1999, we had visioning meetings with residents from the neighborhood about what changes they'd like to see on the block. But this was Watts. They had been at this party before—in fact, they'd been at the party for over 30 years and had been promised things repeatedly. Since the 1965 Watts Rebellion, the City of Los Angeles had promised, without much action, economic, educational, and entertainment reinvestment in the area.

I took over as director of WHP in 1999. The dual role of project director in both LA and Houston proved too much for

Rick to manage. Project Row Houses, the model which inspired WHP, was beginning to expand exponentially, and Rick was never able to build the traction in LA that his plan needed to take root. There was a small amount of money left over from his efforts, and over the phone he said to me, "Do something with it." So, I did. I began by shifting the focus of the project away from the city-side of the street and towards the families.

The Towers have always found advocates and protectors among artists, architects, and activists, yet the Towers' improvements present a stark contrast to the neglected homes that surround them. If the Towers are what Simon Rodia could do as an individual, imagine what great things we could do as team.

Our first project was going to be with the Madrigal family, one of the most beloved families in the area. Felix Madrigal would tell me stories about how he and his family would get parking tickets in their own driveway, because it was unpaved and made of dirt. He couldn't park in the street overnight, so they would get tickets, accumulating up to a $1000 in penalties per year. So, we worked on the drawings for a new driveway together; Felix graded the soil and hired a group of his friends to lay the concrete. In three days, we had a new driveway, at a third of the time and a third of the cost. Afterwards, we all celebrated with carne asade BBQ and cerveza to thank everyone for their beautiful work. With that small amount of funds, we now had a team, and organically, like that, our process began spilling over the fence to other houses. Genaro and Rosario Alvarez lived two houses down, and, unlike Felix, they did not own their home. When I met Genaro, he already had an idea for a project: a new fence with a radial sunburst motif. We had a brief planning meeting, and the next day, we went out and bought the materials. Three days later, I came back and half the fence was built. I said, "Genaro, I didn't know you knew how to weld."

"I don't" he responded. "I taught myself how to do it."

For a project like WHP to work, it required four things to take root: it had to extend from the values that already existed in the neighborhood; an individual or family had to vouch for it; it needed some institutional support; and, if possible, be in a location that people recognize, like the Watts Towers. The team was growing with each project, but the funds were beginning to run out. After Rick departed from WHP, there was no passing of the torch, no walking down the street and letting folks know I was taking over the efforts, like Felix had done for me when we did our first project together. Tensions between WHP with the Watts Towers Art Center had begun but wouldn't come to critical mass for another decade. I wasn't exactly certain why, and no one would explain it to me. That would happen much later, after it was too late to reconcile. I was young and focused on the getting the work done at the expense of political strategy, not really taking in the gravity of how those 30 years of unrealized promises from the city had left people raw and wary of anyone's promises. With the Watts Towers Art Center unwilling to help us, having limited resources of its own, I reached out to a local landlord I met in hopes of finding some support to keep working in the neighborhood. It would be the last project for another eight years.

I chose not to be paid for the work I did with WHP. It was important to me that all the money I raised was going directly back to the families and the neighborhood. So, to support myself, I had a part-time job teaching, and I continued making my drawings and getting into higher profile exhibitions. My girlfriend Sascha and I were soon to be married, and this allowed for me to get health insurance through her job and expand our income base. This level of security was transformative, as I could take greater risks with my work without concern of immediate financial peril. Since I was not able to raise any more support for WHP, it was becoming clear that, because I had no reputation to stand on, no one was going to financially back this project. When politicians heard I was an artist, they'd move away across the room; foundations wouldn't take the risk to give any real money, because I was an individual artist, unaffiliated with an organization. So, after 2001, I decided I was going to focus my energy on building my career and speak about WHP every opportunity I could. From Dusseldorf, Germany to Basel, Switzerland to New York and Minneapolis, every time I'd present my drawings, I'd talk about WHP.

In 1997, I estimated it would take about ten years to build a following and support for my work. So, in 2008, when I was invited to be in both the Whitney Biennial and the California Biannual, bringing national exposure, I began exploring restarting Watts House Project. One conversation gave birth to another and another, which led to a pivotal moment for me and the project. It was in Minneapolis, at the Walker Art Center, that I met then-curatorial intern Aimee Chang. She was later a curator in Los Angeles at the Hammer Museum, where they had just started a socially-engaged art initiative through the Irvine Foundation. WHP became one of its pilot projects. Back when I was questioning the relationship between drawing and socially-engaged practices, I never imagined that they would merge in this way. With a grant for $30,000 from the Hammer Museum, WHP would become recognized as an important model for art and community engagement across the country.

Sue Bell Yank, who was a past student of mine at the University of Southern California, was my new collaborator, and with her, we formed a new mission for WHP. Bringing our shared interest together, around socially-engaged art, WHP's new mission described it as an ongoing collaborative artwork in the shape of a neighborhood redevelopment. Because of my experiences with the Madrigal and Alvarez families, I knew that, through cooperation between residents, artists, and architects, we could all work together to find creative solutions to everyday problems facing the neighborhood. We worked with families on an individual level but also had to address overarching neighborhood concerns. Leveraging local skill-sets to renovate the homes around the Watts Towers neighborhood evolved WHP into a vehicle for self-empowerment, as well as a way to utilize the arts as an economic engine for the neighborhood. Genaro Alvarez was now a professional welder, which he does for a living, and he built most of the colorful fences you see up and down 107th Street today. His wife, Rosario, loved to cook, and in 2009 we incubated her business as well by having her cater all of WHP's events, building her capacity.

As an art project, WHP was nimble. When we had an idea, the family and artists involved would design it and build it together, completing each effort in a week's time. We didn't concern ourselves with insurance or liability; we were just focusing on the work and having fun doing it. Getting support from the Hammer Museum made us competitive for even greater funding. The contradiction being, of course, when I really needed the money, no one wanted to give it to me. But when others were giving me money, I got even more support from those that rejected me the first time. But the larger foundations would only support us if we became a nonprofit organization ourselves. WHP now had a small committed team of artists, administrators, and curators on board, so, as a group, we greatly debated this next step. Could you still be a fluid art project and an organization at the same time? The environmental movement had become a green economy, and social networks had transformed socialism from an ideology into communication platforms. Emerging in the shadow of despair coming from the crashing housing market were new incubator models popping up in every field around us. Obama had just been elected, and "hope and change" made anything seem possible. Amongst all the optimism, none of us realized just how fateful a decision it would be to become a formalized organization in a neighborhood ruled by informal economies. The nonprofit model is a child of the industrial age, an out-of-date tool not well-suited for the post-industrial information age. Yet the ethos of the nonprofit is still beautiful. No one person can own it; it exists to bring value to the social body. With few choices available to us, I cofounded WHP as an organization with Sue Bell Yank in 2009. Could we still be a fluid art project and an organization at the same time? When the IRS got involved, everything changed.

We built a board of directors and began growing in ways we could only imagine. Our annual budget went from a few thousand dollars to raising $750,000 in three years, including another $250,000 in donated hours from a vast range of volunteers. In 1999, it was just the Madrigals and me. In 2012, there were 85 participants involved with WHP, from every walk of life, class, race, and skill-set. We were building the airplane while it was taking off from the runway, so I was never fully in control of its direction. At first, the changes were subtle. For example, WHP's board of directors concluded that our mission statement was confusing, changing its language to reflect redevelopment as not just an effect of art but its primary goal. When you have a board of directors, you are no longer the author of your project; the board is the boss. After we incorporated and became an organization, those same conflicts that plagued the Watts Towers politics had infected the inner workings of WHP.

The families of the neighborhood were never able to fully interface with the board leadership, and their opinions were no longer steering the ship in the way they did when we were just an art project. Going into people's homes to do work became a legal liability, exposing the board to potential lawsuits, and so, all the work we decided to do, in the future, would have to be done by licensed contractors. This alienated the workers in the neighborhood, many of whom were qualified to do the work but were unlicensed. This wasn't an issue in the past, when we were working from the edges of legality but guided by trust, in collaboration, amongst the artists and families. The very same building laws meant to protect homeowners were now strangling us, bringing almost all of our home improvement work to a halt. The cumulative effect was the slow transformation of the families from collaborators into clients.

Relationships with the neighbors became increasingly strained, and word of their discontent was being relentlessly spread by our detractors, the landlord and the Watts Towers Art Center. I believed that good work would rise above the slander, and indeed this was true. The neighborhood improvement work did withstand the contempt, but my ability to outlast it, personally, was waning. My candle was burning out at both ends. Not taking a salary for my work at WHP meant I was relying on my art sales, which were slowing because I was spending less time in the studio. The financial frustrations negatively affected my life at home, and the passion that fueled my efforts in Watts, being with the families and building together, was mired with bureaucratic tape. A core group of families continued to work with me and were my constant reminder of why we were there in the first place. But the negative has a way of overshadowing the positive. The tensions that were coming from the Art Center and the landlord were reflective of a much older ideological divide within the neighborhood. Working with the landlord turned out to be a mistake ten years before, as her motives were political, using WHP for territorial gain, to benefit from the tax dollars that had been promised 30 years before. The landlord saw us as competition, and so would publicly misrepresent our work so that it appeared exploitive of the neighborhood.

Unfortunately, a writer from the *Los Angeles Times* took these growing pains and wrote a front-page story about it. The article was harsh and full of innuendo, lacking any hard facts about improprieties. The writer of the article set out to blame someone, and she found me. Was she right? Did I let the community down by turning WHP into a nonprofit? In the beginning, I saw the forming of a nonprofit as a tool, a vehicle to do the work we were already doing, but better. But the WHP board, which I helped create, saw the organization as an end in itself. To protect the organization, the board concluded that removing me from the leadership was the best way to remedy the controversy. In response, I resigned from WHP, leaving behind a project that I had spent a third of my life building. So many ideas and projects that we dreamed up together, that I would never get to realize with the families, have left a deep longing, a deep darkness, that remains with me. The most difficult part was the feeling of abandoning my friends on the block who had become part of my family. I watched children grow up, participated in quinceañeras, attended funerals, watched children start their own families, witnessed joy and pain and all its cycles. The sense of public shame for falling down, and of being unsure if I would get up the same, lasted for months.

A few years later, when I was offered a chance to participate in a new medium, performance art, in the Performa Biannual in New York, I realized a way to seize the light.

Years ago, I watched a documentary on African-American artists and saw a performance by Ben Vereen that I've never been able to forget. It was Ronald Reagan's inaugural gala in 1981, and Ben performed a moving tribute to the legendary vaudevillian actor Bert Williams. At that time, Ben Vereen was one of the one of the biggest stars in America. The TV mini-series *Roots* had just changed the discourse on slavery in a way that the nation had never experienced before, and his portrayal of "Chicken George" in the final episode had earned him an Emmy nomination. He was known as a triple threat:

he could act, sing, and dance, and he had a Tony Award to prove it from his starring role in Pippen on Broadway. In the video, Ben Vereen's performance, *Nobody*, brought down the house, receiving a roaring ovation from the tens of thousands of white conservatives that filled the convention hall. What made it stick with me, as well, was that the entire performance was done in blackface makeup. What surreal number of events could have produced this bizarre world, where Vereen would be in blackface in front of an all-white audience in the 20th century? The song and dance number was moving, and I got to see the performance's beginning and heartbreaking ending. I didn't realize, at the time, that I was one of the few who had seen both parts.

"UNTIL, UNTIL, UNTIL..."

A few months after Performa commissioned me to do a performance, I still had no solid idea as to what I was going to do, but that was about to change. I was fortunate to have a chance meeting with Vereen at a children's birthday party that I crashed with a group of friends. I seized that opportunity to talk with him about his performance of *Nobody* at the Reagan inauguration. His body language changed immediately; his shoulder sunk a bit and, for a moment, he just stared at me. I told him that I'd love to chat with him more about it, if he'd have me. As it turned out, he was the grandfather of the boy whose party it was; his daughter and son-in-law, artists Koran and Noah Davis, were throwing the party. She vouched for me, convincing him I could be trusted, and a month later, I was at his home, where he filled me in on the story.

Nobody was a portrayal of the legacy of black performers and the sacrifices that were made by them. Ronald Reagan, himself a veteran actor, was elected President of the United States because of his political notoriety as a Republican activist fighting against socialism, unions, and activism on college campuses. With the performance, Vereen had hoped to remind Reagan of his early commitments to progressive politics and help shape his presidential policies.

A tragic aftermath reframed the performance, its popular reception, and Vereen's life. *Nobody* had two acts: the first was a true-to-life minstrel show, but it was the second act that made it transcendent. The local cable company omitted the second half of the performance that contained the critique. As a result, audiences at home would only see a minstrel show lampooning black Americans, misperceiving it as the entire artwork. Two days later, Ben would be attacked in the press from across the country, by the very same community he was there to represent. He was never given the opportunity to tell his side of the story. He was blackballed by the media, and his friends turned their backs on him. Frank Sinatra, Johnny Carson, Jesse Jackson, and Sammy Davis Jr., just to name a few, forgot he even existed. As we sat in his living room, I could see that Ben was still carrying the scars, some 30 years later.

I loved the performance of *Nobody*. It was, in my opinion, one of the most important performances in the 20th century, and one that almost no one could remember. Hearing about how it affected his life connected with the pain and longing I still carried with me from Watts House Project.

There are no words to describe the feeling of working to help others and having your efforts misunderstood and turned against you in a way that's tragically unjust. Listening to Vereen talk about the time after his performance made me realize something about myself, something I had to do to correct the wrongs of the past. Much like my fear of the Shadow Man, my job was to explore the darkness I was carrying inside me. It was time to face it, own it, and find a way to make it useful to me and to others.

I asked for his permission to tell his story of what he went through and show the world the full performance he had intended. Reluctantly, he said "yes," but he made me promise to protect him, that I wouldn't ever let that type of attack happen to him again. I promised that I would and made the same promise to myself, too.

Ben and I continued to meet over the next year as I was developing the script; we grew closer, and the material grew richer for it. Having a commissioned play meant that I didn't have to raise any money. I could focus on the work. Performa was hands-off most of the way, encouraging me to push my boundaries and yet to try and bring my aesthetic from my films and drawings into the work. This type of encouragement was paramount to the success of the play, though the first draft of the script wasn't immediately well received. The subject matter of doing a performance around blackface could be a polarizing experience, and they were concerned that my approach to the material would be too literal. But through intense dialogue, I was able to incorporate their concerns into the script and move on with the show.

I realized early in the process that I needed to be as honest with myself as Ben was being with me. What were my strengths going into this new medium? What had I learned at WHP that would benefit me as I moved forward with a crew made up mostly of students? And, most important, what were the things I learned at WHP that I should not repeat? These questions helped me to realize just how much my political awareness had become intertwined with my creative choices.

This project was being produced by the Center for New Performance at CalArts in the theater school, thus the reason for my student crew. Universities, like boards, are political animals. Keeping the students engaged in the process would be paramount. Listening to and incorporating the concerns expressed by all the people from all these involved entities would be fundamental to the project coming together smoothly and on time.

Entitled *Until, Until, Until…*, the play was to open in New York as the very final event of the Performa Biannual. After Calarts, we were in New York for three weeks. We rehearsed and built a show, which up until that point didn't have a completed script. Most of it was still in my head, and many of the elements were still waiting to make sense to me. I worked to keep my promise to Ben: to tell the whole story of *Nobody*, the injustice he had gone through, and to protect him from it happening again. The story in the play was complex; it was written from the perspective that everyone and everything in my dreams is me. Though there is a real Ronald and Nancy Reagan, in our memories those people become projections for our traumas. So, instead of writing the play from a historical perspective, I wrote the show from how Ben remembered it.

The show was a solid success, selling out every show in its initial run. There were more than 40 performances during the Performa Biannual, but *Until, Until, Until...* went on to win the Malcolm McLaren "Best in Show" Award. The *Los Angeles Times* wrote a front-page article about Ben's 1981 performance of *Nobody*, telling the full story of his intentions and how its misrepresentation had affected his life. The story was out there, and the record was clear. I'm grateful that he trusted me, and that I could keep my promises. Future plans for the play include a US and world tour.

Until, Until, Until... gave me the opportunity to explore the shadow of another and to reflect upon my own. The re-emergence of the Shadow Man after my daughter Zora was born was no coincidence. The Shadow Man, representative of fear itself, rises at our most vulnerable moments—young kids scared in the night, the birth of a first child, the loss of control in adulthood, trying to live up to the grand image of a man you never knew. Though it can be dark, I was wrong to fear the shadow, because it is the very well of creativity itself. As Zora grew, I began to see parallels between the life of a child and the control of my fears. I found that, as I grew into being a father, I became more confident, more in control of this life that scared me so often. I learned that fear would get me nowhere if my wife and I wanted to be successful in raising our child to be a strong, self-assured adult and successful, as well, in my work as an artist.

Realizing the pain of failure, as I did at WHP, caused me to question, again, what my art should be about. As much as I had resisted putting words to my work, it was John Steinbeck that reminded me that it is the ancient commission of the writer, who is charged with exposing our grievous faults and failures, with dredging up to the light our dark and dangerous dreams for the purpose of improvement.

In so many ways, working within the social body is about understanding the soul of oneself. The rapid growth and slow decline of WHP was a coming to terms with the more primal parts of my own shadow, discovering a profound tension between my beliefs. Is building loving and trustful relationships an illusion; are people inescapably suppressive and brutal, as a society? I came to reconcile those conflicts by concluding that, if we were not creating a more trusting environment for the relationships in the neighborhood, it did not matter how many homes we improved or fences we painted. We had not gone far enough. Building rapport—where strangers can become friends, and friends can become family—must be a part of any collective effort to merge with the shadow, from the darkness into the light.

EUAN GRAY

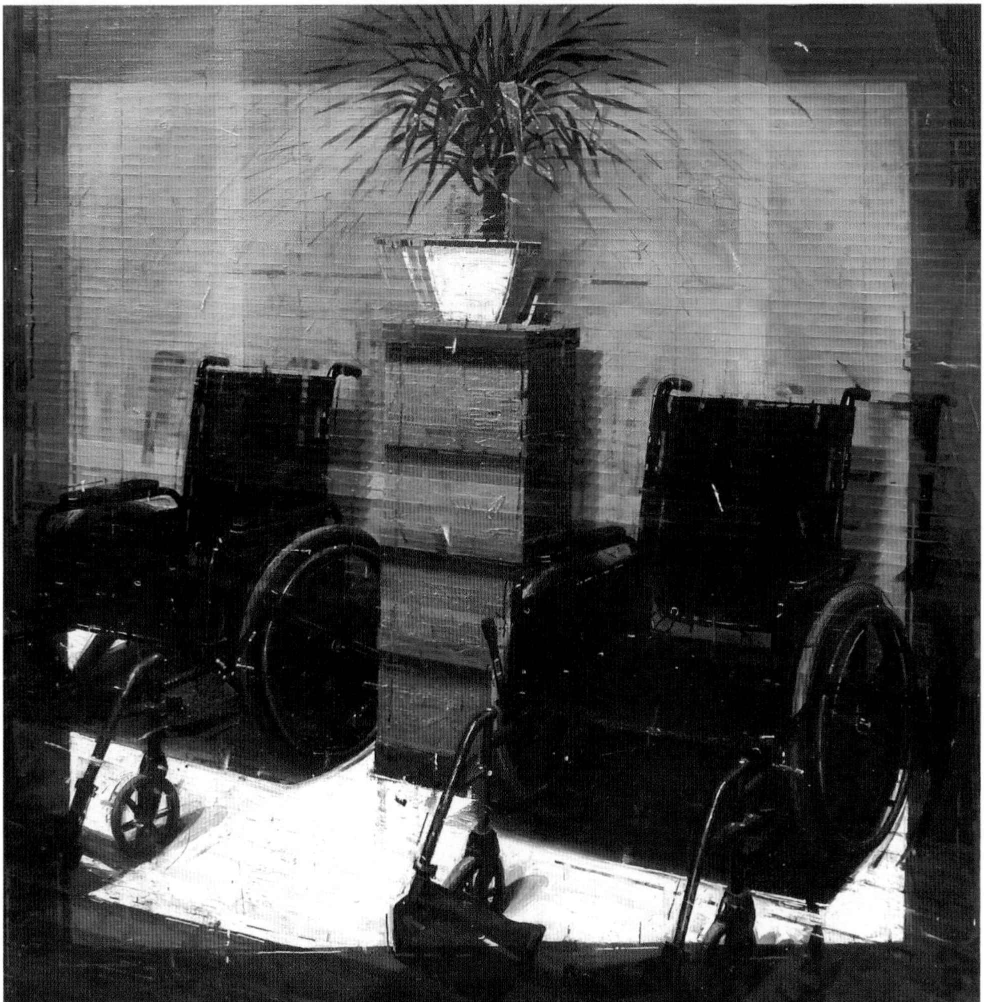

As a teenager, I had no idea what I wanted to do for a living. I grew up in an artistic environment with a father who was working every day as an artist. Art was accepted in the family—as it was not for many of my friends. To rebel would have been to become an accountant or a bank manager. Luckily, for once, I followed the advice I was given. I enrolled at Edinburgh College of Art when I had finished school, and despite a relative degree of financial hardship throughout my life, I have never regretted it.

I enjoyed art school at Edinburgh and, later, the MFA course at the Slade School of Fine Art in London. They were periods of hard work, and I took full advantage of my time in both institutions. Edinburgh, itself, is a culturally vibrant city, steeped in history. Although at times overwhelming, London, too, offers the possibility of heightened exposure and invaluable access to various networks, collectors and galleries. I won a number of national awards and, like many young, ambitious students, I believed somewhat naively that the initial success I gained at college would translate into immediate success in the art world when I left school. Despite being fortunate enough, as a student, to sell work to a number of collectors, I soon realized that it was considerably harder to succeed than my initial expectations had led me to believe. I would need to establish other ways to finance a life in the arts.

Euan Gray
Hotel Lobby (Lourdes)
67"x67"
Oil on canvas
2009
Courtesy of the artist

I accepted a year-long tutoring post at a school in the North of England on completion of my master's degree. At the time, I had an aversion to teaching which, in retrospect, I find perplexing. Perhaps it was because my parents taught and I was always determined to follow a different path; or, perhaps I was drawn to the romantic notion of the struggling artist leading a hand-to-mouth existence. But I turned down a second teaching contract and endeavoured to survive on part-time jobs, supplemented by the sale of paintings. I am fortunate that I own a flat in the centre of Edinburgh, which I purchased a number of years ago with the proceeds from the sale of paintings when house prices were low. Over the years, having a flat of my own considerably reduced living costs while I was living there.

When I was at the Slade School of Fine Art, London, the artist Ian McKeever told me that he became a refuse collector when he finished his degree in philosophy, which led him to start painting when he finished his shift at 11 a.m. every morning. The idea of finishing work early enough in the morning to paint appealed to me. And, for the past ten years, I have been lucky enough to survive on specific part-time jobs which seem to pay disproportionately well for the exertion applied, allowing me most of the day free to pursue my artistic endeavours. I am currently employed part-time selling tickets on the railway.

These jobs provide a level of daily social interaction important for maintaining a healthy psychological balance. I usually produce work alone in my studio, cut off from contact with other people, and having a degree of interaction is important if one is to achieve a level of happiness.

Over the years, I have been fortunate that my salary has been supplemented by numerous grants and scholarships. A series of travel awards, in particular, have provided opportunities of invaluable experience and some of the most enjoyable times I have had in my life. The awards have enabled me to spend, in total, over four years abroad, moving from country to country, observing the global art world from different perspectives, which in turn has informed my practice as a curator. Artists have obviously always travelled. Rome in the 17th century was a favoured destination of Velasquez, Lorrain, and Poussin. Over the proceeding centuries, cities including Paris, Berlin, and New York have all witnessed an influx of artists seeking financial gain, inspiration, or sanctuary from political oppression. In the 21st century, migration and leisure travel are still increasing, with reduced transport costs making destinations ever more accessible. My own itinerant experiences have formed the thematic framework for much of the work that I have executed over the past ten years.

In 2004, the Royal Scottish Academy gave me significant funding to embark on a nine-month journey following the route that the Scottish writer Robert Louis Stevenson took when he crossed the Pacific at the end of the 1880s. Being handed a large sum of money to visit a series of tropical islands dotted across the South Seas may seem like the ideal chance for an extended holiday, but I did not squander the opportunity. Stevenson was a prolific writer and an adventurer who sailed across the South Seas in search of warmer climates to stem the onset of a debilitating illness which eventually killed him in Samoa. My 21st century experience differed, in that I could reach my destinations with relative ease by air, but the remote islands remain largely unchanged. His determination to keep producing work, regardless of the obstacles, has been inspirational. I painted every day in these distant locations, and the resulting work led to my first solo museum exhibition, which was a financial success.

Throughout my career, I have consciously tried to exploit moments of serendipity and opportunities when they arise. An unexpected result of the travel scholarship was that it reconnected me with an ex-governor of Edinburgh College of Art who came to the opening of the culminating exhibition. She invited me to become a member of the Alumni Council at Edinburgh College of Art. I was delighted to become involved, and it proved fortuitous. Many influential figures were on the council, and following a brief period on the committee, I was asked to co-curate an exhibition to celebrate the 250th anniversary of the formation of Edinburgh College of Art. The show was well received, and producing it led to the curation of subsequent exhibitions.

Curation was never a path I had considered, but the benefits have been numerous. Trying to make sense of contemporary art world infrastructures is not easy, and broadening my activity beyond solely making artworks has led to a much deeper understanding of the creative process, in general.

On one level, I would rather work in the studio than spend evenings at openings, but developing contacts and establishing networks is a crucial aspect of developing a career as an artist. Curation involves collaboration, and the exhibitions I have worked on have connected me with an array of artists, dealers, and museum curators. The required focus on other artists' work has stimulated a variety of new approaches in my own work, as I engage with the other artists' concepts and ideas. Exhibition opportunities have come forth indirectly through submitting proposals to museums and being introduced to museum staff with whom I am already working. My profile has risen through significant media exposure connected to the exhibitions.

Since 2008, Britain has been living in an age of austerity. Many galleries and project spaces have closed during this period. Self-motivation is crucial, and finding a life/work balance is not easy when you are working for yourself at something you love. The impulse is to work all the time, which has implications for the people around you.

I am fortunate that I have a very supportive family and an understanding partner backing my career. Edinburgh was my home for most of the previous 15 years, until we recently bought a house in the countryside about a 40-minute drive from the city centre. The property has a large stable attached, which I am currently converting into a studio. We are adjusting well to life in the country, and I am confident that the move will lead to a very productive period in my life.

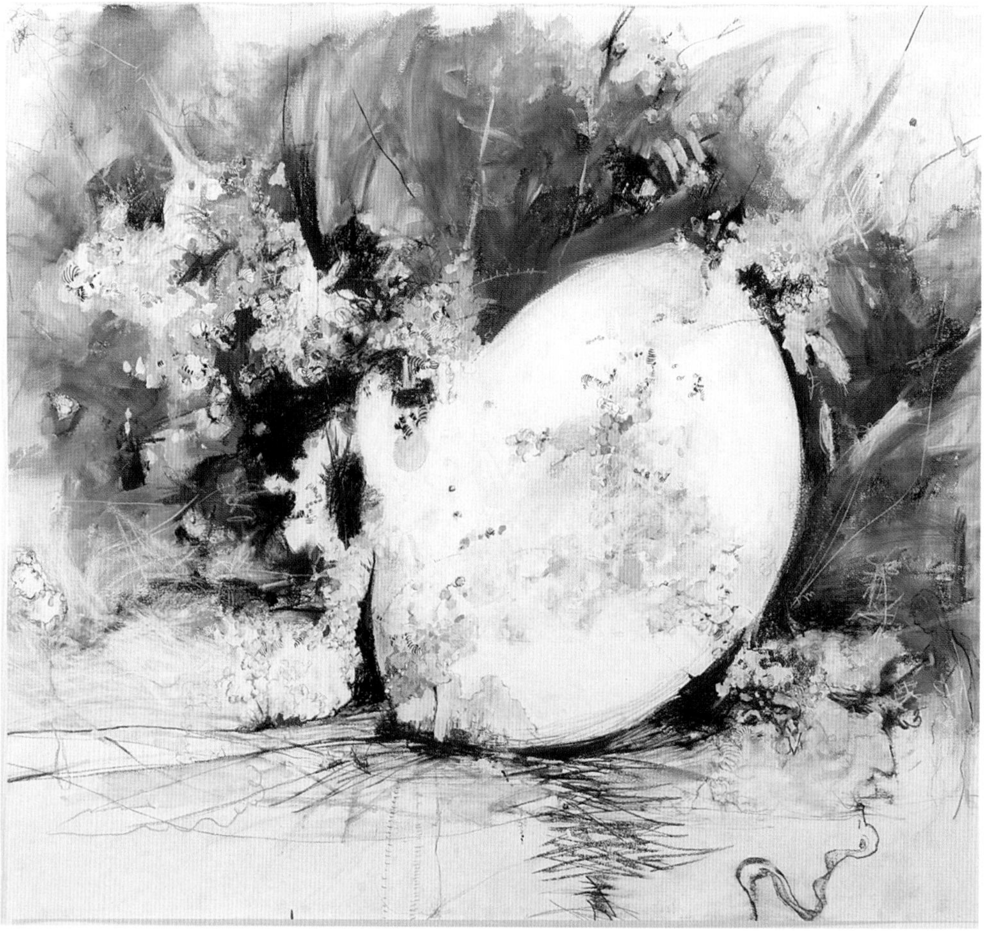

Faina Lerman
Cell Clumps
46"x48"
Acrylic, ink, pencil, and charcoal on paper
2013
Courtesy of the artist

FAINA: When I met Graem in 2001, he was already deeply embedded in the Detroit art community. He was living at the Bohemian Home, a former Czech social hall that was slowly being converted into an artist space, with rough live/work spaces, a huge stage, and studios. Raves, group castings, and weird art parties would happen on a regular basis. I was into my first year of undergrad at the College for Creative Studies (CCS), waiting tables at Cass Cafe in the Cass Corridor and just starting to tap into my visual language. My work at the time was very personal, intuitive, and emotional, inspired greatly by abstract expressionism and "outsider art." I didn't think much about content or concept. I was more interested in raw emotion, intuition, and tapping into something universal through gesture, color, and form. I loved process, and I loved getting messy. At CCS, I settled into the foundry, exploring casting in metals, rubber, and plaster. I began combining painting and drawing into one—smearing charcoals with gesso, drawing into paintings, and painting into drawings—just soaking everything in and exploring as much as possible. I was a bit older than my peers and, in some cases, was closer in age to some of my professors. My studio was in the living room/kitchen of the house I was renting in Hamtramck until my senior year, when I got a small studio space at school. Meeting Graem, and seeing the way he worked and lived in this crazy space in a community

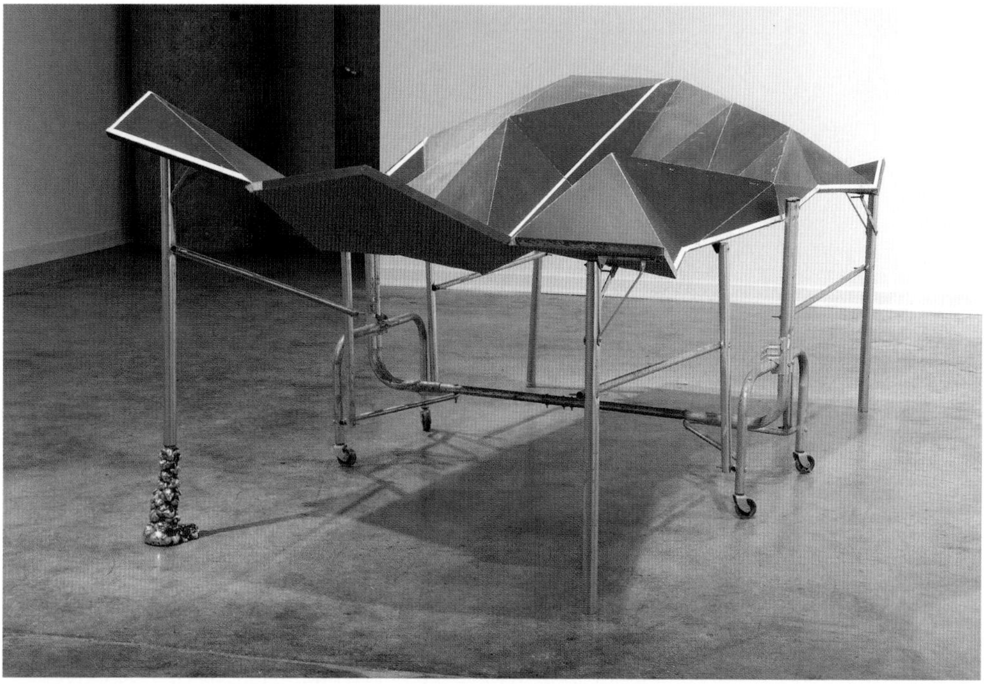

of other artists and musicians was super inspiring, and I began to reimagine how my life as an artist might look.

GRAEM: I guess, when I was living at the Bohemian was the first time I had found my own artist community. I had gone to art school, but only for a year, so I didn't really have that network of art friends. I was also a bartender for 14 years, and that had a built-in community of creative types, too, but it was more about hanging out, as opposed to actual creation. In late 2004, I started a series of weekly, one-night art shows, called "This Week in Art," at Motor City Brewing Works. At that time, the Detroit art scene was steady but scattered, and there weren't too many galleries in the city proper. I gave a show to anyone who asked, so it really gave an opportunity to students and emerging artists, and to more established artists looking to test some stuff out. Works tended to be smaller, because of the space, which put some quick cash into the artists' hands, and I benefited from increased bar traffic. "This Week in Art" took off and became a real hotspot for artists to get together to hang out and talk art every week over a beer or three. I ran that night for the first four years (and it continues to this day), with shows every week, until I quit bartending, and we started doing programming at Popps.

FAINA: Over the years, we lived all over the city in different warehouse spaces, lofts, and, once, even a house. After getting married in 2005, we started looking into buying a space where we could live and work.

GRAEM: We were actually looking at houses, and close to putting an offer on a large 1890s Victorian, when a friend told us about this building for sale in Hamtramck. We weren't exactly sure what we would do with it, but it had a flat upstairs and a large, raw warehouse space that was more than enough space for our studios and a ping-pong table. It was a bit of a blank slate that gave us the opportunity to experiment with both the physicality and functionality of the space. We were a little cautious about the neighborhood at first, as it was considered the "bad corner" of Hamtramck, but a friend encouraged us by

Graem Whyte
Venue for Advanced Conflict Resolution
102"x50"x44"
Modified ping pong table, cast bronze, paint
2011
Courtesy of the artist

saying our presence would make things better and potentially affect those around us.

We bought the building from a couple who had a t-shirt shop; before that it was a cookie factory, and, originally, it was used for meat packing. We liked the notion of paying homage to that history and adopted the building's original name, Popps Packing. Plus, it has a nice ring to it. That was right before the market crashed in 2007, and a mortgage was hard to come by, for us. Luckily, we were able to work out a land contract with the owners and borrowed money from family. (A land contract is a form of seller financing. It is similar to a mortgage, but rather than borrowing money from a bank, the buyer makes payments to the owner, or seller, until the purchase price is paid in full.) We moved into the apartment upstairs and began renovating the 4500-square-foot building as needed, one project at a time. By 2009, we had carved a second living space out of the warehouse and moved down there, so we could get some rental income from the upper.

FAINA: We were both still bartending part-time; Graem was also a technician in the foundry at CCS, and I was teaching afterschool art programs and summer art camps. We were living month to month, but when money got tight, a commission or random art sale would pull us through. That year, we were awarded a large commission for *Memory Field*, a public artwork in Calimera Park in northeast Detroit. It was our first significant collaboration and helped keep us afloat for a while.

GRAEM: We've never had the money to be able to hire things done. Faina has been awesome with taking on most of the administrative duties, like coordinating the residency program and leading our efforts toward nonprofit status, taking care of our newsletter, and other PR. I've done most of the physical work myself, learning new skills like electrical or plumbing, as needed. Even with some recent grants, I'm still doing most of that kind of work to be able to stretch the grant dollars further. I've also been fortunate that I've been able to work on the necessary infrastructural components of Popps, while framing it as an extension of my art practice. Many of the doors, stairs, cabinets, and such have my visual language built in, which I think adds to the overall charm of the place. And my work has definitely changed as a result of Popps. I had been more of an object maker, but now my work is much more about place and the creation of spaces.

FAINA: There has always been a fluidity and versatility to Popps. Openings would turn into wig parties, jam sessions in the shop, large bonfires in the yard, and impromptu ping-pong matches. Initially, my studio was in the front of the building where the gallery is now. (Graem builds or modifies most everything to have wheels, so it was easy to move stuff out of the way when we had shows and happenings there.) After our daughter was born in 2011, I spent less time in the studio, as it was harder for me to find large chunks of time to work. So, we decided to turn that space into the full-time gallery, with exhibitions about every six weeks. Around that time, my practice shifted to focus more on performance art, which I had been dabbling with for a few years with my friend Bridget. She had just bought the house across the street and was helping us with the various projects and the new baby. We would bounce ideas off each other while I was breastfeeding or cooking. Bridget and I would work on music composition, choreography, and costume-making at her house, and we rehearsed in the gallery or the shop after the baby was asleep. Graem and I are currently working on building a dedicated painting studio for me, so that I can pick up my painting practice again.

Also in 2011, we purchased two properties at the Wayne County tax foreclosure auction for $500 each. One was a house with attached storefront and the other a single-family home, both across the street from us, on the Detroit side. (Popps Packing is on the border of Hamtramck and Detroit, Hamtramck being a dense and diverse neighborhood, while this section of Detroit is fairly rural, with clusters of houses.) We purchased the buildings for a few reasons: to stabilize our neighborhood, to potentially expand our programming, because we could afford them, and because nobody else wanted them. Both buildings were barebones, not completely stripped, but in need of complete, systemic overhauls. One had been empty since we moved here, and the other used to be occupied but had since become more of a source of bad activity.

GRAEM: In hindsight, acquiring these houses was instrumental in helping to develop our current, immediate community. Once the guesthouse was livable, our good friend (and writer/musician) Bill moved in, helping provide a presence on that side of the street while adding to our overall creative clan. Soon after that was when Bridget bought her house across the street from us, on the Hamtramck side. The next year saw four more artist friends buy nearby houses. And that trend continues—most recently, a couple of artists from New York (one a former Detroit resident) bought houses down the block. I think that's an important aspect of what we're trying to do here, the communal nature of things. We got a great taste of the value of community when we lived on Farnsworth Street, on Detroit's near east side, before buying Popps. Our landlord at the time, Paul Weertz (an educator and small scale farmer), initiated things years ago by buying vacant properties on the block he lived on, fixing them up, and either renting or selling them to like-minded folks over a period of years. Neighbors look out for and support each other, communal gardens are prominent, fences have been removed, and everyone on the block is invested. It makes it easier to get things done, it makes day to day activities more fun, and it makes it a better place to raise kids with a bunch of nurturing influences. That's something that we're trying to build toward.

FAINA: For me having an extended family around was always important. I grew up in a very tight immigrant community, just outside the city. My family came here when I was five from Soviet-occupied Latvia. Having little money and resources, they relied heavily on their network of friends, also recent immigrants, for support. I remember the amazing gatherings they would have every weekend: large tables crammed into tiny two bedroom apartments and filled with Russian salads, cold cuts, and lots of vodka. My friends, family, and school were just a stone's throw away. I still think of the accessibility of everything back then. I need my family to be a part of what we do here. Mother sometimes makes flower arrangements for our openings, and my dad randomly drops off windows, cabinets, and whatever else might be left over from his construction jobs, knowing that Graem may be able to use it for something down the road. Only recently have I begun to realize how much my family has influenced how we live and what we've created here at Popps.

GRAEM: Our residency program expands a bit upon that: our community isn't limited by geographic location. Many of our former residents feel like family and stay in touch, and we are looking forward to visiting many of them in the future. The program began with a loose notion and a conversation between us and friends from LA who expressed interest in returning to Detroit for a collaborative project. Michael and Christian lived and worked with us for six weeks in the summer of 2012. They cleared out the storefront/house that we had recently purchased, using materials from within for their installation. At the same time, Erik, a Dutch artist we had befriended the year before, was living on the compound to help out with various projects. Ownership lines were blurred, and a real collaborative spirit was in the air. Shortly after that, a friend and colleague at Wayne State University reached out to us about a German painter who had been looking for a residency in Detroit. At the time, there really weren't any in the area. We liked his work and had space open, so we invited him to Popps. That summer was pivotal in the direction that Popps would take for the coming years. We formalized things a bit with a website the next winter and instantly began to get inquiries from around the world about the residency program.

Detroit was just starting to get international attention for the $100 house and the city's devastating foreclosure crisis, as well as a little buzz about the art community and cheap living. Foundations and corporations started to invest in parts of the city, creating new funding opportunities for artists and arts organizations. We have been fortunate to partner with some awesome artist-run organizations operating in our neighborhood in an effort to secure grants, share resources, and to better support each other's projects. For many of the artists who live and work in this neighborhood, it's important to have a say in what our community looks like, and taking advantage of some of these opportunities is a way to get a seat at the table.

FAINA: The new spaces, especially Popps Emporium (the storefront) and the empty lots, have made us more visible to our neighbors. We want them to know who we are and what we do, and we think about the type of events and activities we host with them in mind. Last summer, we started hosting monthly Barter Bazaars—skill-sharing swaps on the empty lots on the corner—and saw more of our neighbors come out and participate in those events. And thanks to a couple of recent grants, we are planning a tool-lending library, a community gallery in Popps Emporium, and a family residency space for parent-artists like us.

GRAEM: And we're starting to place a focus on sustainable living for us and our immediate community. Through this next round of development, we are planning things like a greenhouse, chicken coops, and water collection systems, to name a few. By adding these environmentally sustainable projects to our overall fabric, we can ease our monetary burden in the future, while increasing our quality of life. We will also be adding several communal studios (clay, print, woodshop, etc.) to make it easier for all of us to supplement incomes or provide day to day necessities. We will develop these in collaboration with neighbors and resident artists to make them all as inclusive as possible.

FAINA: As the scope of our projects expands, we are considering reworking some program schedules, with more space in between shows and residencies, in order to give ourselves an occasional breather. With two small children, it's harder for us to manage so many different programs on our own. I still struggle with the balancing act of managing Popps, the family, and everything in between. I often feel defeated by QuickBooks, budgets, or other administrative logistics, and I have to remind myself that I'm doing the best I can. We both get overwhelmed at times, and we ease that a bit by giving each other personal work days or designated "administrative days," so that there is a little structure within the chaos.

As we try to simplify life, we are always confronted with opportunities to expand and complicate it further. Because of the timing and where we live, there are lots of opportunities to reimagine our immediate environment. As artists, we think of solutions or applications for the empty land or structures around us. For example, the 20 empty lots across the street could be a great park, but do we want to be the ones to initiate it? Maybe we should, because we have kids, and our kids play with the other ten kids on the block, and there is no park around. Then we have to step back and ask: How deep into this do we want to go? Is this our responsibility? Should we focus more on our individual practices? How do we balance all of it and two kids? We understand our limitations better now and think about those opportunities more cautiously. While we try to "go forth boldly," we are still figuring out how everything fits together for the future.

GRAEM: We've been lucky to be in the right place at the right time. Detroit is a good place to be right now for exactly what we want to be doing. We had a space, the desire, and a community that has allowed us more opportunities to be able to do what we would be doing anyway.

Our sustainability is directly tied to our artist community and to Detroit's ability to sustain itself with its newfound status as a city of the arts. We've been lucky to have so many great artists who want to show here, who want to come here and support what we do. Ultimately, we strive to keep things loose, too, giving ourselves and artists a place to experiment—a laboratory of sorts. We try not to be afraid to fail, and we encourage the same in the artists who show here and the residents who stay here: explore, have fun, don't worry, keep it greasy. It's as much about the processes as it is about the outcomes.

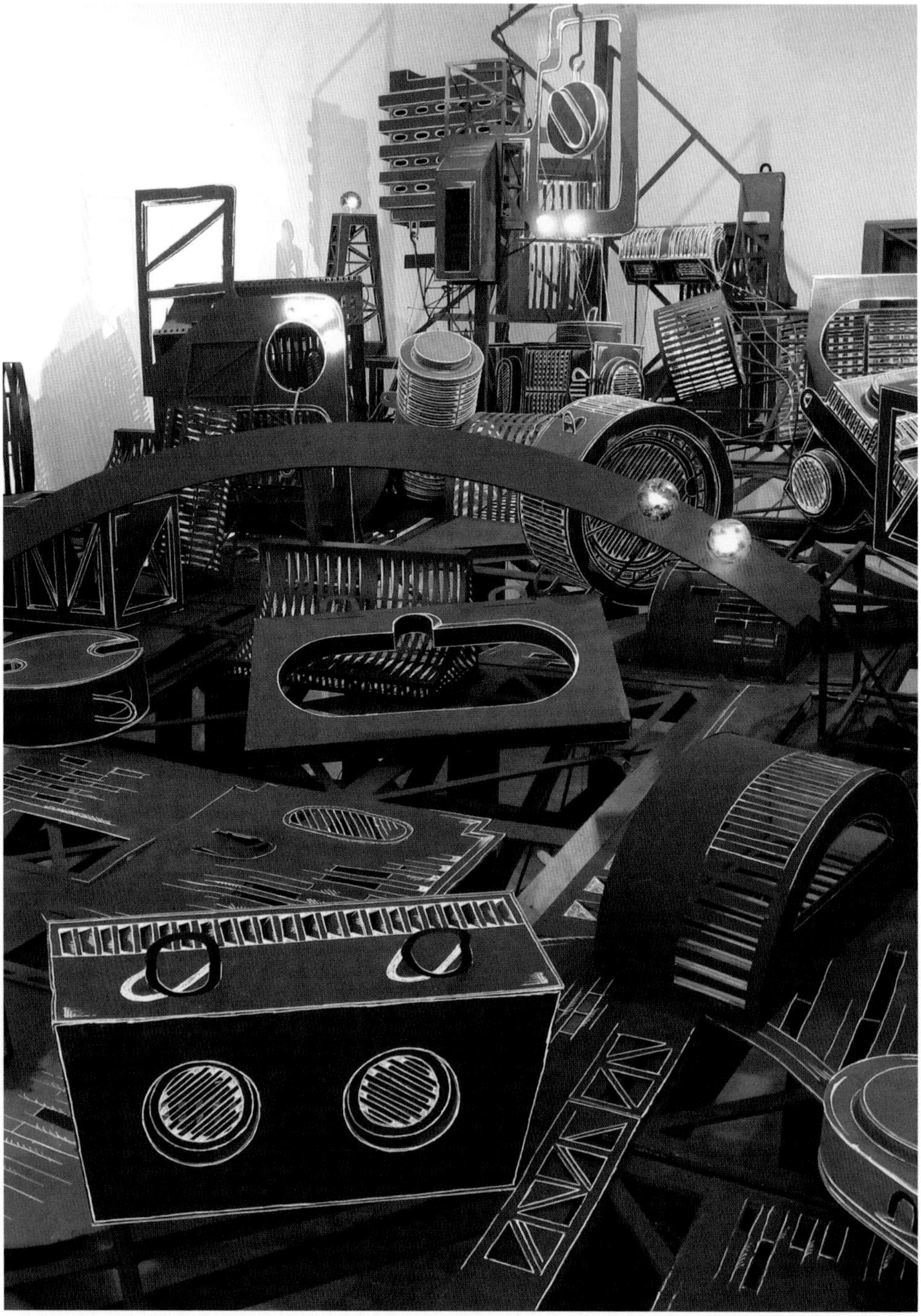

Jane South
Raked (detail)
9.5'x12.5'x16.5'
Hand-cut paper, ink, acrylic; structure of wood, MDF, cable; electrical cords, bulbs, hardware
2014
Site-specific installation at Spencer Brownstone Gallery, New York
Courtesy of the artist and Spencer Brownstone Gallery

In 1989, I moved from London to New York with no particular plan in mind. I had studied Theatre Design at Central (now Central Saint Martins) School of Art and was part of a small company working on experimental productions of Beckett plays in rooms above pubs. A brief visit to New York in December 1988 got me hooked on the idea of living in a city where the pubs did not shut at 11 pm, and you could still run into the likes of Quentin Crisp on the Lower East Side.

Fresh from Thatcher's Britain, New York felt alive to me with creative communities of all sorts; the rent was not crippling and there were many ad hoc artist groups meeting for discussion, to draw, perform, play music, or show work. None of these activities seemed driven by anything other than the impetus to congregate, share, experiment, and see what happened—to be involved in a space of creative incubation, all contributing to the feeling that one lived and worked in a city that was supportive of individual and collective creativity. I spent a wonderful six years engaged in varying combinations of waitressing, communal living, mediocre art-making, narcissistic navel-gazing, and hedonistic abandon.

After six years in New York, it was clear that the ratio of day job(s) to studio time was reaching an imbalance beyond justification. Moreover, my navel had been thoroughly gazed, and the joys of hedonism were wearing thin. The self-designed art school I'd constructed from classes at the Art Students

League and life-drawing sessions hosted by friends in Williamsburg lofts was not helping to elevate my work beyond the mediocre. I was stuck. I decided to go graduate school. Coming from the (then) free higher education system in Great Britain, the notion of paying for this experience was a non-starter, along with the feeling that it might be good to be away from the distractions of a big city. So, I settled upon Greensboro, North Carolina, where I had been offered a full scholarship. The experience of being in post-industrial, small-town America was entirely new to me, and that, along with having the time to work and investigate ideas with feedback from faculty, proved to be invaluable.

In 1998, soon after graduate school, I went to my first residency at the Roswell Artist in Residence program (RAIR) in New Mexico. With no internet, TV, or cell phone (at the time, internet access was not ubiquitous), my experience of time was deliciously oceanic, albeit at times unnervingly so. It was also in Roswell that I met people who were further along in their lives as artists than I. Not only did they become good friends, but many have subsequently referred me to jobs, grants, and residencies and provided crucial perspective and advice on everything from shipping and insurance to negotiations with gallerists and curators. At that time, I was making large concrete and steel constructions that required space and equipment. I was interested in outdoor rather than gallery venues, so I applied to Socrates Sculpture Park in New York for an emerging artist residency. I'm sure I applied for other things, too, and if I had got any of those, the trajectory of everything since may well have been different. But Socrates it was, and I took time out from Roswell to drive to New York and spend a month building my first on-site public sculpture. This was truly terrifying. I had never built on this scale, and if I failed it would be in public. Perhaps it was a lesson in leaping before looking—if I had thought it through beforehand, I might have been scared off. But the camaraderie of the Socrates group kept me steady, the long hours of on-site work paid off, and all turned out fine.

The end of the Roswell residency marked a transition from several years of funded art-making to the reality of having to find a way to pay the bills and continue to make work. It was the serendipitous availability of a live/work sublet in Red Hook, Brooklyn (cheap because it included the caretaking of three cats, one of whom needed twice daily injections for diabetes) that made me decide to move back to New York.

The next couple of years were fairly solitary. I had a part-time job managing the office of a sculpture-fabrication company, which paid the bills. As my work was in transition (from the large scale steel-and-concrete work to constructions made from paper), the remainder of my time was spent in the studio trying to develop it, with no intention of looking for exhibition opportunities. I tend to know when my work is not ready—much as I may try to convince myself otherwise! Many of the folks I had known before I left New York for graduate school were no longer around, and because I missed the community of peers that I'd had in Roswell, I spent time researching and applying for grants and residencies. When I was accepted for a two-month residency at Yaddo, I quit my job and hit a streak of good fortune. The Drawing Center invited me to be in a group show (curated from their slide registry); the Pollock Krasner Foundation awarded me a grant; and I was offered a temporary teaching position at Williams College.

The Williams College position was both an artist-in-residence and a teaching position, but there was no studio provided. Acting on the advice of the Roswell friend who had recommended me for the position, I negotiated funding for a studio from the Williams College Art Department. Then, I had to find one. In a complete reversal of the New York problem, in the Berkshires the challenge was to find somewhere *small* enough; most spaces being enormous open-plan floors in disused warehouses. I had phoned MASS MoCA, figuring that they might have space to rent, and been told that they did not, but after numerous fruitless attempts elsewhere I thought it was worth another try. And so, I wandered into the lead curator's office. It turned out that this curator was a Williams College graduate. She immediately took me on a tour of the yet-to-be renovated buildings, offered me a studio space, and a year later, commissioned a site-specific installation for the museum.

The group show at The Drawing Center introduced my work to Spencer Brownstone Gallery, with whom I had my first solo show in 2004 and my most recent one, in 2014. This was sheer good fortune as, at that time, Spencer Brownstone was right next door to the Drawing Center, and it was there that the gallery director had seen my work. Having witnessed the New York gallery world expand and contract over the last 15 years, I am grateful to have a steady relationship with a gallery that is based on mutual loyalty and respect rather than commerce. I never imagined that I would make a living selling my work, but there was a period when I was doing so, and it began to feel uncomfortably like generating product. Fortunately, it didn't last!

When the Williams College position ended, I moved back to New York to a live/work space in DUMBO, Brooklyn that I still occupy. In 2003, it was a different neighborhood. Like many people, I bemoaned the changes, on the one hand, but have benefited from them, on the other. What I do know is, if it were not for the NYC Loft Law that has protected and secured my tenancy for the future, I would likely have had to leave the city. Not having a full-time job has meant I have had the flexibility to travel for visiting artist positions and residencies, but it has not been easy. At times, I accumulated debt, struggled to pay the rent, and worried about having no health insurance.

My third solo exhibition opened at Spencer Brownstone Gallery in 2009, after which I began a three-month residency at the Brown Foundation's Dora Maar House in Ménerbes, France. This led to another residency at the Camargo Foundation in Cassis, which meant a total of six months in Europe, with funding to make work and no rent to pay. It was easy not to consider the future, so it came as a bit of a shock when, five months in, I realized I would shortly be returning to New York City, with no job and one month's rent in my bank account. Perhaps this also coincided with a dim awareness that I had hit middle age, as I felt a sense of urgency about this fact that I don't remember having experienced before! For whatever reason, I leapt into action and started scouring online resources for opportunities. The strange thing was, not only did I find a posting within a couple of minutes, but also my initial suspicions about that position (it sounded too good to be true, must be a scam, etc.) proved to be so completely wrong.

The posting was for a US-based artist to assist in establishing a nonprofit art school and residency program in Siena, Italy. Within ten days, I'd had a Skype interview and, two weeks later, I was in Siena. I have been working with the Siena Art Institute (SART) ever since, helping to build a school and a residency program that has hosted numerous artists on funded residencies and students from all over the world in studio art programs. SART has also taken me to colleges and non-profit arts organizations in India, Palestine, and Greece—all while working alongside people of immense creativity, integrity, and generosity. Working with SART does not pay all the bills, and I have continued to teach part-time. I supplement my income with lectures, visiting artist positions, exhibitions, and grants. However, working with SART has given me the opportunity to collaborate with people on ideas for artist projects, new programs, and curricular initiatives, which in turn feeds into my teaching and has introduced me to fresh, collaborative ways of working.

At the same time, my work was evolving out of a studio based practice into a site-specific one, driven by a resurgence of my interest in the theater and, most especially, in performative spaces. It's been interesting to me how teaching has informed my work, and I'm not sure that without this context my work would have evolved in the way it has. Alongside my work with SART, I teach part-time in Sculpture at the Rhode Island School of Design (RISD), which has put me in regular contact with younger generations and is a great way to keep in touch with emerging creative voices. Teaching seminar and performance classes has allowed me to research and communicate ideas that feed into my studio work and to test them out within a diverse disciplinary environment. Of course, teaching can be draining and frustrating, but I have also frequently found it to be energizing and generative of alternate ways to experience and think about contemporary art.

I commute to Rhode Island weekly and spend several weeks a year in Italy, but New York City is my home. In my opinion,

New York has shifted from a place of experimentation to one of professionalization. This is an oversimplification, of course, and too large a subject to get into here, but part of what I feel to be missing is a collective space for sharing ideas and interests outside of formally structured events like panels, symposia, and artist talks. About ten years ago, I began to ponder how to orchestrate an informal forum beyond the professional sphere, where ideas tangential to, but not focused upon the work itself could be shared. These thoughts are at the root of Flat 46, an event and platform for conversation that I started in 2007.

I host Flat 46 in my Brooklyn loft about every four months. Weirdly, it was Facebook that helped to shape it. Through Facebook, I became aware of the wealth of curious "peripheral" interests that my friends and acquaintances had. People whom I had casually known for years revealed themselves to be amateur experts in a range of subjects as multifarious as digital hoarding, pyrotechnics, and Balinese music. It seemed a good idea to ask these people to share these other strata of knowledge/exploration with the rest of us.

The first event was organized by a core group of six creative individuals: myself, along with a poet, an artist, a journalist, a novelist, and a critic. We decided the structure of these events would be to invite two people to present for about 40 minutes each. Their topics might feed into their work as artists/writers/scientists etc. but, importantly, speakers *could not present their own work*. The initial idea of having a core group orchestrating the event was to ensure that those invited were not always the same people, or people who were already good friends. Each of the six was to invite two new people to each event, and only former presenters would always be invited. As my space is an old-school Brooklyn loft—with one dodgy loo that's prone to malfunctioning and a buzzer that does not work (requiring the front door key to be thrown out a third floor window)—these could not be large gatherings. To keep numbers manageable and the atmosphere intimate, invitations would be individual—meaning no spouses, partners, or plus-ones. Sometimes that rule has not gone down well with people who perhaps misinterpret the motivation behind it, although a few have expressed relief to, at last, have a good excuse *not* to invite their partner/spouse!

Beyond these aforementioned practical considerations, Flat 46 is also about connecting individuals, which is really the way I see my role as host—making sure that person X meets person Y, etc. Compiling a guest list with synchronicity in mind is therefore important, and if the numbers are potentially doubled by unknown plus-ones, it all becomes too unwieldy.

One of the first presentations was "Porn and Porcelain," where an artist/critic and collector of Sèvres porcelain and 1970s gay porn gave a wonderfully witty, playful, and illuminating talk about this seemingly unlikely pair of interests, drawing a sociopolitical and aesthetic connection between the moment Sèvres went from soft- to hard-paste porcelain, and gay porn moved from celluloid to video. Some presenters use Flat 46 as a place to test drive and get feedback on specific threads of inquiry that feed into their work or to try out ideas about the work of others. Though many are slide talks, some have focused on food or music. A talk about Alice B. Toklas was accompanied by food made from the recipes in her eponymous cookbook. "Depending on what you believe Punk was, you get the Postpunk you deserve" was a journey through the evolution of the Rough Trade record label via selected LP tracks. "Don't open that jar!" was a tour of fermented foods, with tastings of homemade kimchi (delicious) and Ancient Egyptian beer (disgusting), and simultaneous viewing of their bacterial images captured on a microscope.

There are two questions I'm often asked. The first is whether the presentations are recorded. It seems important that these evenings are ephemeral; to document them would change the atmosphere and, maybe, make the exchanges self-conscious. (There is no respectful silence during presentations! Instead, frequent interruptions and spontaneous contributions—welcome or otherwise—are made.) Many of the presentations are not fully formed, they're a first draft, and some fail miserably. This space for experimentation and failure is key, as is true for any creative endeavor. When something is too resolved, it can be sort of dead. Conversely, while still being figured out, it feels alive, and perhaps it's this liveness that invites an active encounter between the listener and the ideas, just as an artwork lives in the zone of connection between artwork and viewer.

In this open space, something might be generated, but it's not always possible (or necessary) to articulate the specifics of what that "something" is.

The second question I often get is related, but more specifically about "outcomes," as in: "Were any collaborations/publications/works initiated at Flat 46 that resulted in something beyond the event?" The answer is yes. For example, Suzanne Bocanegra's "When a Priest Marries a Witch" was presented at the Museum of Modern Art, New York in 2010, and Alexi Worth's "Misunderstanding Manet" evolved into an article in *Cabinet* magazine, titled "The Invention of Clumsiness," in 2014. It's important to stress, however, that this is not the goal—there is no notion that this gathering should lead to some form of tangible cultural impact, or any specific new work or idea. The event itself is the thing, because just as opportunities to produce are necessary, so is a space in which not to produce in measurable terms—most especially in a cultural climate seemingly fixated on quantification and assessed outcomes. Hopefully, over the last nine years Flat 46 has provided an opportunity for some of the above.

My life now is a blend of all of these things: working at SART and RISD, hosting Flat 46 when possible, writing grants/proposals for site-specific installation works, and, of course, my studio work. I don't try to balance all this evenly. I just take care of what needs to be taken care of and don't worry too much if, at any time, one thing is demanding more attention than others. I love to be busy and have been surprised at how much I enjoy collaborating with people on ideas for artist projects and programs, or developing curricula, and organizing events. The installation works I make have many parallels with these activities, involving site visits, collaborative negotiations with curators, and logistical/budget planning. However, there is a large part of this work that cannot be planned and has to emerge in the studio through making, as this is the only way I can make something that I cannot imagine. My studio work is the core of everything, and it requires discipline to ensure that time is made that work, despite whatever else is going on.

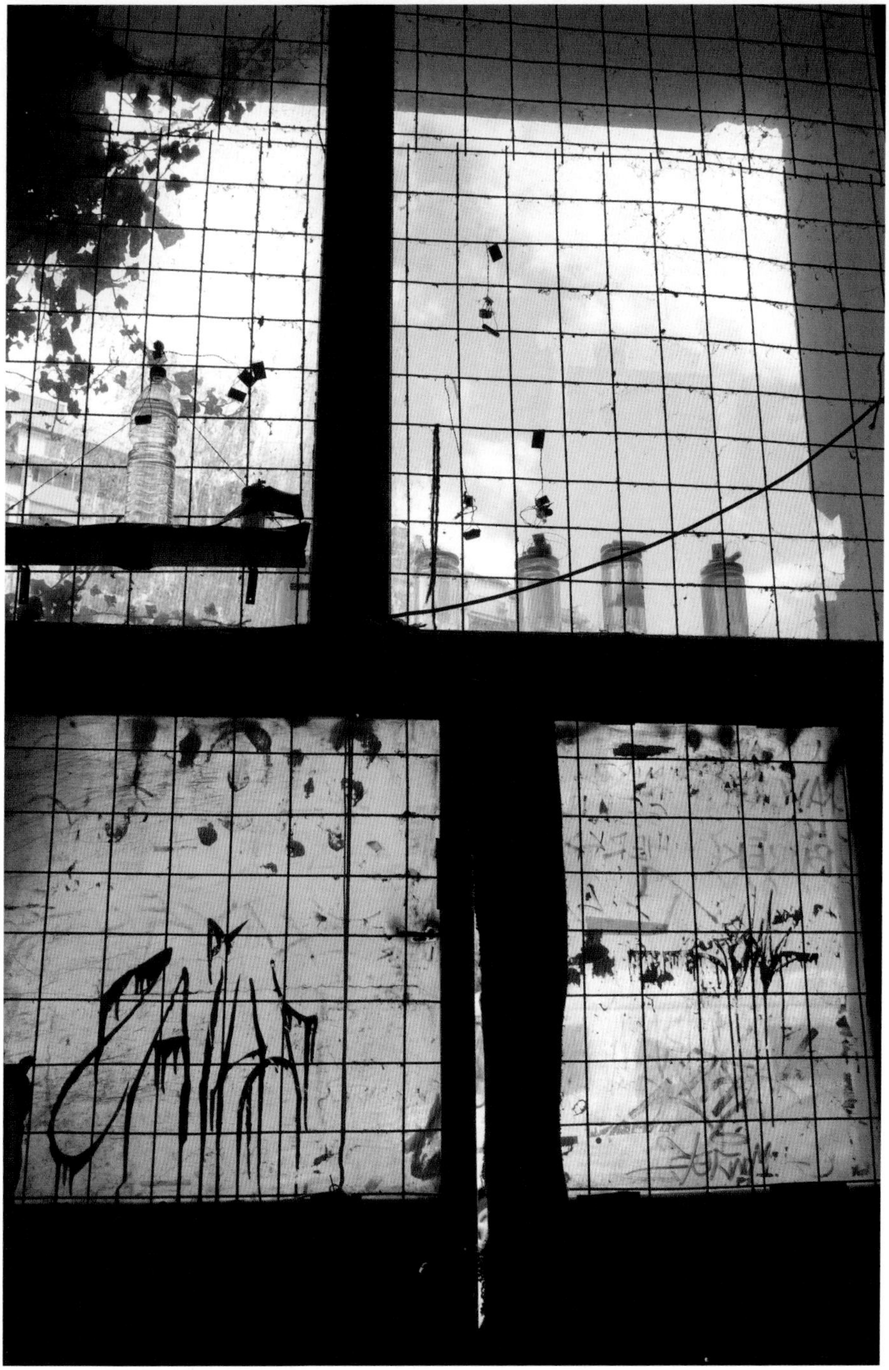

I was born in Washington, DC and raised in Maryland. I graduated from St. Mary's College of Maryland with a Bachelor of Arts degree. I was an English major, focusing on poetry, creative writing, and photography. My mentors were professors Lucille Clifton, Michael Glaser, Grace Cavalieri, and Hilton Braithwaite.

After school, I moved to New Orleans for a brief time to focus on photography. I set up a darkroom in my bathroom, developing film and prints at night and shooting by day. I soon moved back to Maryland, and then to DC, where I have lived since 1996. My first solo exhibition, *Washington in Black and White*, was held at the US Botanic Garden Conservatory in February of that year.

In 1997, I attended a really inspiring group exhibition organized by the Washington Project for the Arts, called *Options*. Afterwards, I wanted to take a stab at organizing an exhibition of my work and that of my friends. It seemed possible, and being new to the scene, I wasn't yet connected with the art community. An exhibition in my house seemed doable, practical, and something I could put on my resume. I talked with an artist friend and decided to host the exhibition in the group house where I was living. It was big, with tall ceilings and good light. Why not? One of the artists had an enormous following, so it was a very successful event. People came, ideas were shared,

Jayme McLellan
Cirkulacija 2, Slovenia (from the series "Signs")
Dimensions variable
C-print
2013
Courtesy of the artist

and work was sold. We had a lot of energy to do another event, but we never worked together again. I did, however, organize several more do-it-yourself type exhibitions. In a way, all of my later work is an extension of this practice.

My first paying jobs in DC were at bars, until I started working at the café at a Borders bookstore downtown. It was through one of these jobs that I met the director of DC Arts Center (DCAC), B. Stanley. He really took me under his wing as a mentor. Trained in theater and a disciple of Alfred Jarry and Antonin Artaud, he taught me much about avant garde theater and what it means to have a dedicated practice to one's craft.

DCAC is both a theater and a gallery. While volunteering and, later, creating a fundraising position for myself there, I was exposed to multiple genres of art including contemporary visual art, theater, poetry, and more. I also witnessed rehearsals and exhibition installations. I learned about the challenges of working with artists, funding an arts organization, and the physical maintenance needed to keep an old building functioning. The first time I set foot in DCAC, I told B. that I wanted to raise money for the arts center. He said, "great," and handed me a broom to sweep the floor. But I was persistent and consistent. I showed up when I said I would.

B. eventually let me curate a weekend show of artist friends called *Masters of Art*. The name was a tongue-in-cheek play on the '80s cartoon *Masters of the Universe*. They were a peer group of about eight artists who had loosely organized to do pop-up exhibitions around town. I wanted them to exhibit at the arts center, so I pushed hard to make it happen. I'm not sure I totally fulfilled the role, but it was my first curatorial experience in a gallery.

This group gave me confidence, and I continued to create opportunities for myself and other friend-artists. It seemed this inspired others to do the same. We were taking turns organizing exhibitions and including each other in them. We did about five shows this way, anywhere we could from 1999 to 2001, while I was learning from more senior arts people at DCAC "how the pros do it." I could then apply that learning to our raw enthusiasm, and it worked well. I was making and showing work, connecting with my peers, and growing a network of support.

Fortunately for me, B. Stanley also green-lit the Tandem Project: a huge idea where I'd go to the countries of the former Yugoslavia to meet with artists and curators and bring some of them to DC for a residency and exhibition. I teamed up with independent curator Katherine Carl, who was a fundraiser at the Dia Center in Chelsea. She had managed a residency program for artists from the region, called ArtsLink, and she was also working on her PhD in southeastern European contemporary art. In a short period of time, we raised $36,000 for the project from two private foundations, allowing us to travel to Ljubljana, Zagreb, and Sarajevo just four years after the end of the Bosnian war and in the dead of winter. We met with artists in each city, thanks to introductions from the curators at the former Soros Centers for Contemporary Art, and I was able to spend some alone time walking the city streets with my camera.

We selected five artists and created two incredible exhibitions—one at DCAC, the other at the now defunct Signal 66 art space. I used the research trip, where we were meeting with artists we would exhibit in DC, as an opportunity to expand my understanding of war and struggled to find a meaningful way to photograph it as an artist, not a photojournalist. I shot a ton of work that still, to this day, has not seen the light of day. The remnants of war, in the depth of winter, proved very depressing. I have gone back to the negatives many times and may eventually do a project with the images. I have a very big organizing project for that photo archive calling my name right now.

Through the Tandem Project, I met Victoria Reis, an independent curator who was organizing exhibitions in her home and for the Washington Project for the Arts. She hosted one of the Tandem Project artists, Vesna Pavolvic, in her apartment, and I organized a crew of artists, including Colby Caldwell, Casey Smith, and Bill McKenna, to serve as Vesna's DC support team. All of the visiting artists were partnered with DC artists for help, advisement, and coaching.

Victoria also asked to curate an exhibition of my work and that of my friends, Lisa Garfield and Mica Scalin, at a project space in Mt. Pleasant called La Casa. I Xeroxed photographs and made a slow-motion video of birds in flight from the Hitchcock film. The images were all of birds, or motion, or swirling. Things were really moving in my life at the time. It was through this exhibition that I met fellow photographers and musicians. The artists and I continued to work together and reached for spaces outside of DC to exhibit. Mica had contacts in Richmond, where she grew up, and we organized a four-person show of women artists, called *Conspiracy of Vitrines,* at a gallery called ArtSpace. I was continuing a passionate experiment with film, where I played around a lot with filters and cross-processing film. I also took a stab at working with and making some textile pieces.

In addition to managing the Tandem Project, working at DCAC, and showing my own work, I also instigated a peer mentorship and critique program, called The Exercises, which was held in the common room at a co-op studio space downtown. The Exercises was a meeting for a group of artists who gathered to discuss work created in the past week. I designed the program to support artists out of school and in need of critique and community. I needed it and so did my friends.

Meetings took place at the defunct art studio, called The Hosiery, or Gold Leaf, where several of the artists in the group had studio space. That place had many names over the years and served as a studio space for hundreds of artists for decades. I also organized the first and only exhibition of the first incarnation of The Exercises. It was called *E4: Jump in the Fire*. It was our only exhibition, because I would soon start my own arts organization, for which I would make The Exercises a formal program.

The combination of this ad-hoc artist-to-artist program, the experience of managing the Tandem Project, and finding a partner who shared my desire to create a more permanent support system for artists led Victoria and I to create Transformer, a nonprofit arts organization that continues to thrive as an anchor of support for artists. I didn't know at the time that starting this organization was basically going to put my art career on pause for ten years. I learned that the hard way, but when I look back now, it was worth it. I learned so much about leadership and discipline and navigating personalities.

In 2002, Victoria and I didn't really mean to get a space for Transformer so soon, but we did so because of Sarah Finlay from Fusebox gallery, who was a consummate mentor to us. The now closed Fusebox, run by Sarah and her husband Patrick Murica, raised the bar on contemporary art in the DC community. It was inspiring to witness their hard work. The gallery was beautiful, with tall ceilings, great light and an amazing, freestanding pivot wall. Fusebox was designed by architect and collector Peter Hapstak, and by Sarah and Patrick, to instill collectors with confidence as well as to give artists the professional exhibition space they needed. There was a severe lack of such space in DC at the time, and the gallery opened in a part of town where there were no galleries at the time. And then more galleries, like Transformer, followed; Transformer is still in this space today.

The story of how we got the space goes something like this: Sarah called me one day, three times, until I picked up the phone. She urged me to call this guy, Mike Benson, who was starting a restaurant, called Café St. Ex, and was giving up his small studio space around the corner from Fusebox. I called him, and Victoria and I immediately met with him to talk about the cost of rent and the nature of the landlord. Rent was only $800 and, after some convincing, Victoria and I both felt comfortable with taking on the responsibility. Worst case scenario, we could wait tables to pay the rent.

After getting fiscally sponsored as a nonprofit by friends Vivienne Lassman and Richard Dana, and then raising $3500 from friends via an email request, Victoria and I began Transformer in 2002 and ran it together as co-directors for four years. We organized many exhibitions and added programs like The Exercises and the Framework panel series, which were discussions about the basic framework of support needed for artists in a community.

Transformer's first year budget was something like $35,000. We received donations from friends and got a few grants. In our second year, the Warhol Foundation awarded us a three-year project grant. We were ecstatic! But we had to get our own nonprofit status to be awarded funding. We worked with the Washington Area Lawyers for the Arts, particularly Paige Totaro, who was our first board member, to apply to the IRS for 501(c)3 status. We were approved in just three months.

Near the end of our third year of operations, in addition to funding from local arts agencies and individual donors, we also became a part of the Warhol Initiative and received a $135,000 capacity-building grant. The foundation partnered us with a consultant who worked with us as co-directors, and with our board of directors, to create a capacity-building plan. Since we'd both been working part-time at Transformer while holding down a second job, we decided hiring both of us full-time and creating a cash reserve would be immediate steps toward becoming a more sustainable organization. We worked together until May 2006, when I felt a pull to create my own gallery—one that would exhibit the same group of artists again and again and allow them to grow and experiment. I wanted to help artists create a more stable support base than our programming at Transformer, alone, could do. I felt that developing artists' careers through solo exhibitions and the many other benefits of commercial gallery representation was the way to do that. And although I never stopped photographing, I was not actively working on growing my career as an artist at this time. I had a lot of energy for the curatorial work, and as long as I was still carrying my camera around, I felt okay about not pushing my own career. It felt right to push that of others.

With Fusebox as an inspiration, I set out to create my own gallery. Less than six months after leaving Transformer, I opened Civilian Art Projects as a spaceless and roving gallery project representing ten artists, many of whom are still with the gallery. I had been making my own work and showing it some, but for the next four years, I would primarily focus on building this next-level step for the community of artists around me. I launched the gallery with a small group of painters, photographers, a sculptor, and two very conceptual artists working in a variety of media. Some of the artists I knew well. The others I found by word of mouth or suggestion.

With a line of credit, a credit card, and no business plan, Civilian was born with a group show at the Warehouse Gallery run by the Ruppert Family in December 2006. The exhibition was a huge success, but no artwork sold. I began to see the importance of space to identity. No one knew this was an exhibition designed to encourage Washingtonians to buy the artwork of the artists living and working around them.

It was during our second "roving" exhibition, at G Fine Art, where I was approached by Nikki Sorg, who was managing storage in a professional gallery space. Her job was to find a sub-letter for the former Numark gallery at 7th & D Streets; it was a third floor walk-up in a building with creaky stairs and no elevator, but I could afford the rent. Never mind the terrible HVAC system and no hot water, it was a beautiful space with high ceilings, a stand-alone wall, and beautiful, hardwood floors. It looked very professional. After a good paint job, some tears, and a wad of money spent, we were off and running with our first exhibition, a two-person show with Jason Zimmerman and Jason Falchook.

The artists I have selected for representation, two of which were represented by Fusebox, each push his or her practice conceptually, or through innovation, or expertise in process. As a fine art photographer, I may have subconsciously selected photographers who are the best at their craft, so that I can learn from them.

Whether it is through painting, photography, experimental technologies, or ideas about activism and challenging power structures realized in a variety of media, the artists I gravitate toward all work incredibly hard. They are articulate and compassionate. I work with nice people, and that is by design. Life is too short to work with jerks.

Civilian has and will always be about doing things for the community. The gallery has supported emerging and established artists through group exhibitions and solo shows. We've hosted dozens of talks, poetry readings, dinners, dances, private parties, and more—so much, it's a blur. I just counted, and I have organized 120 some exhibitions alone! (Plus scores of art happenings, parties, and band nights.) Once, I hosted a 1 am Red Bull and vodka party—bad idea. The gallery was graffiti-ed, and we finally had to throw everyone out at around 4 am.

Despite all of the action, early on, I realized that I should not count on the gallery to sustain me financially. I focused on paying the artists, the bills, and the taxes. If there was anything left over, and there rarely was, that was my paycheck. I needed to take on other projects to make ends meet, including waiting tables at a local restaurant and hosting events in the space in between exhibitions. The events turned out to be decent money-makers and excellent tools to create community, because they brought together diverse audiences and made it look as if the gallery was super dynamic by doing all sorts of things all the time. But they were a lot of work and tore up the space, and I was working way too many hours. Yet I said yes to all curatorial gigs and anything to do with supporting artists—partly because I wanted to do the work, and partly because I needed the cash.

Through contacts in the activist world, I was asked by a mutual friend to come on board as a curatorial assistant for a project to tour images, taken by photojournalists and one Marine, of the genocide happening in Darfur, Sudan. The images were projected on the facades of 27 museums around the world in just 24 months. Leslie Thomas was the force behind this project, and I got to help her put together a few shows. Coincidentally, I was able to organize the exhibition in Ljubljana, Slovenia, where I reconnected with colleagues from the Tandem Project. And I was able to quit my job waiting tables.

For the next few years, I continued to plan and open exhibitions at the gallery and to seek employment opportunities in line with my career goals. Sales were intermittent, but I was making enough for the rent and, living in a group house, my home rent was really affordable. I didn't own a car or have a mortgage, but I was starting to accumulate a lot of credit card debt. I was also longing to make work again, but there wasn't the time or the money. Photography can be expensive. Something in me started to feel uneasy about getting pigeonholed as a gallery director or a curator, and my attention started to shift once again to my art ideas. But I still found it hard to say no to really compelling curatorial projects.

It was around this time (2007) that I teamed up with Lucian Perkins, Lely Constantinople, and Alec MacKaye to put together an exhibition and, eventually, a book about the birth of the DC punk scene. The project, called HARD ART DC 1979, is a labor of love and does not result in high sales or big revenue. But it has allowed me to curate at the Center for Documentary Studies at Duke University, at Good Children Gallery in New Orleans, and Agnes B in Paris.

HARD ART also allowed me to dust off my fundraising cap. We have raised money through a very successful Kickstarter campaign, where we met our goal in 48 hours. We asked and received support from an individual donor. I wrote and secured a Sister Cities grant from the DC Commission on the Arts and Humanities for $12,000 to take the project to Paris. We sell some of the work sometimes. And we all receive royalties from our amazing publisher, Akashic Books. While we don't get paid, the funds raised have been enough to keep the project going, and we have been able to travel to some great places. And we have a gorgeous, *airtight* book. HARD ART and the gallery itself have been my best teachers. Literally, art is hard. No one is going to step in your shoes and do the work for you. Intention and perseverance are key.

Later in 2007, that same year, Civilian Art Projects participated in its first art fair, Scope Miami, which was happening during Art Basel-Miami Beach. Super excited, yet way too green, I brought the work of too many artists, and they all wanted to come down and hang out in the booth. I also tried to rehang the booth every day, which was stupid. I didn't account for the climate change of Florida, and our mounted photography started to bubble at the vernissage. I remember taking a nap in my rented car outside of the fair, wondering why I had punished myself in this way.

On the bright side, we did a little better than breaking even financially. and I got to work with the great artist Jen Stark, I was able to show off the gallery program. When I had a spare moment to myself, I noticed a sharpening of focus in myself, as an artist, and I was starting to commit, however loosely, to some themes that had been fomenting in me for years.

So, I licked my wounds and decided to try another art fair. This would begin a series of fairs—New York in March and Miami in December—that would last until 2011. Art fairs can be fun and exciting when all is going well. But when you are in that booth for hours, with nothing selling, and then some calamity strikes, fairs can turn from okay to bad really quickly. They can be really expensive and exhausting ways to advertise.

In 2009, due to my work in supporting artists in the community, I was recruited by artist and professor Dennis O'Neil to teach an adjunct professional practices class at the Corcoran College of Art and Design. I had a lot of freedom there. He encouraged me to design the class how I wished. I was also contracted by the Soap Factory, that same year, to curate an exhibition of artists from New Orleans. We filled the 40,000-square-foot space with site-specific installations and mini-projects about loss, memory, the energy of New Orleans, and the transition and connections from one location to another. It was a great experience, and I was again being paid as an independent curator. I worked closely with Dan Tague during that exhibition and decided to offer him a solo exhibition at Civilian. We have been working together ever since.

A major bump in the road of running a gallery came just after the Soap Factory gig, when the building that housed my gallery was being sold and turned into a giant BBQ restaurant and offices. I had to find a new space quickly. The gallery would go on to find a more secure home in a space run by the Ruppert family, and for four years, we didn't worry about getting kicked out. But eventually, that building would be sold, too. DC real estate has sky rocketed since we started the gallery, and the downtown area, in particular, has largely pushed out artists. There are very few galleries there now.

After moving to the new space, I started working with an artist who had a growing collector base. We had a very good year selling artwork, and we sold out our booth in Miami. Finally, I'm selling enough work to pay all of the bills. I'm enjoying teaching, the art fairs are challenging, but mostly worth it. I'm doing too much and not taking enough time to rest, yet I continue to say "yes" to projects. But I'm working again, seriously, on my own work, and I'm starting to make some real space and time for it.

Then came a series of disasters. My dear cat, Tommy Lee, died. A mentor artist died from Lou Gehrig's disease; an artist's brother, who I knew very well, died. My relationship of 14 years ended. It was also the time the DC community learned that the board of the Corcoran Gallery of Art and College of Art and Design was considering a massive change, including selling its flagship building. I was already over-burdened, but I called a few colleagues who were also shocked and appalled by the move, and we created the Save the Corcoran coalition in June 2012.

To try to save the Corcoran, I quickly organized a meeting in the gallery to discuss what we could do, and everyone showed up—press, former staff, the provost, students, faculty, current staff, and members of the wider community. From this meeting, a group of activists came together to create a marketing campaign, including a Change.org petition to urge the board not to sell the building. We also met with lawyers, the DC City Council, and our congressman to see what we could do. At this point, I was teaching two classes at the Corcoran and considering a third, but walking into the classroom was becoming very difficult. Students were very upset at the potential loss of the school and the building, and they looked to me for answers. I didn't really have any for them, but I knew if I wanted to fight, I had to put everything I had into it. I continued to organize exhibitions at the gallery, but I resigned as a teacher at the Corcoran and went full steam into advocacy to try to challenge the powers that be from doing the worst to the place.

It was during this tumult that we received a publishing deal for HARD ART and that I received a grant through a curator friend in Slovenia to do a workshop and residency in Ljubljana. I remember getting the news of the residency on a really hard day when I felt like nothing was working. The residency was an opportunity to share my knowledge of the US-based arts system with local artists and arts professionals. And I got to spend ten days in Ljubljana, after which I headed to the countryside and Venice and Florence to photograph. I had a show coming up, and I needed to focus on my own work.

I was also recruited to teach professional practices for MFA students at the Maryland Institute College of Art (MICA) and an art history class at St. Mary's College at this time. And I was once again letting myself get too busy. But the MICA gig was just in the summer, for the low-residency sessions, and St. Mary's would allow me to condense my course to go to Ljubljana for the residency. Although I had been teaching undergraduates for several years, I was nervous about teaching MFA students in the condensed six-week format of MICA's MFA in Studio Art program. I was eager to get back to making my own work. Things were tenuous, and the Corcoran battle didn't help.

By early 2013, it was past time for me to have a solo exhibition. I was aching for it. For over ten years, I had been giving all I had to support the work of others, happily doing so most of the time, but I was ready to be as much of a full-time artist as possible. I put together a photographic series and video of primarily new work and called it *Jealousy of Clouds*. I pitched it to Margaret Heiner of Heiner Contemporary, and she agreed to exhibit the work at her gallery in Georgetown.

That exhibition was where I realized I had to make myself and my work more of a priority. I had been letting the gallery, students, and other artists drive everything. My relationship ending, and all of that death—it was the hardest time of my life. I had built the gallery around the love of art, but the rock of it was my partner's artwork. He was in that collective, the Masters of Art, and he was the first artist I believed in wholeheartedly. The break-up was really difficult, but as the cliché goes, sometimes things have to come apart or end for something new to happen. This was and continues to be the hardest lesson.

We fought very hard but lost the battle to save the Corcoran. In August 2014, a judge voted to dissolve the institution into the sum of its parts, with the National Gallery taking the majority of the collection and George Washington University taking over the school. Losing that battle was another death. In the years since, I find myself still processing the implications of losing one of the oldest museums in the nation. And as I'm still working there, I feel the transition from an independent institution to a large, research university acutely.

Fortunately—and here's another cliché—when something bad happens, something good usually follows behind it. I was asked to do another solo exhibition at a different venue downtown. And I was soon recruited to teach in the curatorial program at MICA. Although a super-early morning commute in the winter to Baltimore from DC sucks, I really enjoyed sharing my knowledge and learning from a roomful of emerging curators. The energy and enthusiasm with which the students approached their projects breathed new life into mine.

My class coincided with the murder of Freddie Gray and the resultant uprising and protest. One of the last classes of the semester was spent in having a very honest discussion about race and prejudice. I'll never forget it. I learned so much about the pain people were feeling and the need for real and honest dialogue. I continue to work through some of these issues with the students who were in my class. They are now curators working in the field.

There have been many times, too many to count, when I have questioned the intensity of my career and whether I can keep up. But I always figure out a way—I always find the money, some way to survive. This reality continues to inspire an intense feeling of gratitude for the community around me—my friends, family, artists, collectors, the DC art community. I could not do this work without them, especially a few core and diehard supporters. You know who you are.

JEAN SHIN

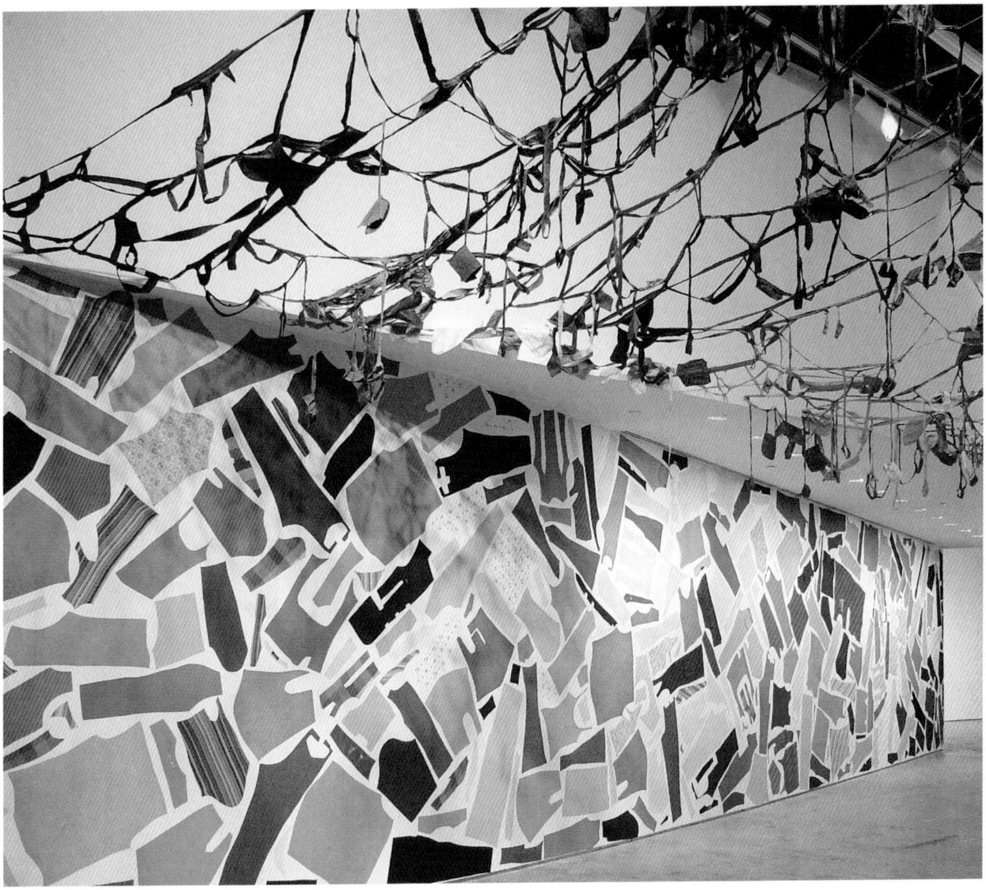

My family's immigrant experience in America has shaped my life's perspective in many ways, personally and as an artist. My parents, who were professors in South Korea, moved to the United States in 1978 and struggled with discrimination. They owned a corner convenience store and, later, a small liquor business in a poor neighborhood of Washington DC. Despite their hard work, they faced cultural inequity and the daily brutality of racism. As first generation Korean immigrants, striving to build something greater for their children, they did little else but work in order to pursue their American dream. On weekends, when not in school, my older brother and I also worked at the store, helping out at the cashier and restocking inventory. I learned to be fiercely independent and self-sufficient at an early age, taking care of myself and doing the house chores, while surviving on TV dinners most nights.

Growing up, I experienced two very different realities simultaneously: the intense hardship my parents faced daily as immigrants and, in contrast, the comforts of a middle-class suburban community that their labors afforded me. Having the opportunity to attend excellent local public schools in Bethesda, Maryland, I excelled in both my academic studies and the arts. With my high school art teacher's guidance, I pursued painting seriously and developed a strong art portfolio that earned me early national recognition from foundations advocating for young artists. Receiving these prizes and awards for my art

Jean Shin
Cut Outs and Suspended Seams
19'x60'x15'
Cut fabric (clothes from MoMA employees), thread and starch
2004
Installation at MoMA QNS, commissioned by The Museum of Modern Art, New York
Courtesy of the artist
Photography by Masahiro Noguchi

provided me with the validation that I needed to convince my worried Korean parents to support my decision to pursue a future in the arts. Equally importantly, Pratt Institute offered me a full-tuition merit scholarship to attend their college. This level of financial support made it possible for me to make the most pivotal decision in my life, to follow my childhood dream of becoming an artist.

In 1990, I moved to New York City to study painting at Pratt Institute. I've been living and working in Brooklyn ever since. My fine arts education developed my skills and discipline, as well as providing me access to art history and a wonderful peer group. More than the education, the school gave me the freedom of being debt free. Without the burden of college debt, I was guided by my own interests and personal attraction to materials, forms, and ideas. Trying to unlearn my early training as a painter, I gravitated towards crafts and things I did in my childhood before I was taught how to make art in school. Not having been formally taught how to make installation art, I felt free to trust my own creative instincts in assembling everyday objects around me.

After graduating, I needed to support myself with a full-time day job. I applied to museum jobs, because I wanted to better understand how these powerful cultural institutions worked to define how we view art. My own experiences spending so much time regularly seeing art at museum exhibitions and permanent collections in Washington DC and, later, New York City were formative. Wanting to be part of this influential and stimulating environment, I set out to find meaningful work where my day-to-day responsibilities could have larger, cultural impact. Responding to a *New York Times* classified ad, I applied for an entry level position at the Whitney Museum of American Art. At the interview, it was clear that my passions were not in the finance department where the position was listed. But I got a foot in the door, and the Human Resources personnel kept my resume afterwards and called me back when an assistant position eventually opened up in the Curatorial Department, months later. Working as a curatorial assistant in the Whitney Museum's permanent collection was a phenomenal experience. Not only did the position provide behind-the-scenes understanding of the curatorial process and how museums shape our contemporary culture, but I was also directly contributing to this cultural production. Working closely with the top curators, I researched and helped organize major, landmark exhibitions on American and contemporary art. I was also part of this incredible community of curators and museum professionals that would become an important asset in my career, as well as a source of life-long personal friendships. Learning how curators and museum educators articulate the importance of art in culture had a great influence on my studio practice. I began to look at my work, not only from the point of view of the maker, but also considering the audience who would experience it.

Many of my materials in my early works came from the street, inspired by the detritus encountered during walks to my studio. In collecting these mass-produced remnants, my work archives consumer waste while reflecting cultural identity. I would pick up losing "scratch 'n win" lottery tickets that litter the sidewalk outside a corner bodega and transform them into a large house of cards. With no adhesive used to make these towers, they appeared precariously balanced and vulnerable, yet the careful labor in building one relationship with the next creates surprising strong foundation, where each card depends on the others for its strength. I recognized that this resilience in the face of inherent risk and uncertainty was very similar to the realities of my life, and how I sustain myself as an artist.

Repurposing goods and giving these castoffs a second life in my installations is connected to my belief in environmental stewardship and the urgent need to address the consequences of our material consumption. Discards are often considered ephemera; however, I believe their accumulated abundance in the world has become a permanent reality in the Anthropocene era. While redirecting materials from landfills, my use of free, salvaged materials at hand has the added benefit of keeping my material costs to a minimum. For similar economic reasons, I also work in small units that are assembled off-site, which helps me avoid expensive storage and shipment needs.

Early in my career, the opportunity to place my installations outdoors presented me with new challenges and unexpected rewards. First, it forced me to take risks by working outside the comforts of my studio. Secondly, it pushed me to make works at a very large scale, big enough to have presence within immense outdoor environments. When I installed *Penumbra* at a sculpture park, the wind would lift the umbrella fabric up in the air and slowly float it back down, repeating this gentle movement as if the work was breathing. I was pleasantly surprised by the visitors' interaction with the work: couples and families took refuge resting under its shade, watching the playful dance of light and shadow cast from the work onto the grass beneath. Because the source of my found materials came from the street, placing my work outdoors in public spaces where people would continue to encounter these materials in transformed situations seemed very fitting.

Years later, one of the young aspiring curators, who I met during my museum job, became a curator at the Museum of Modern Art. She invited me to have my first museum exhibition. With her initiative, the museum commissioned me to create a new site-specific installation. Instead of accumulating found objects from the street, this time I decided to select specific materials from the museum that would speak to their collective identity. I wanted the exhibition to highlight the presence of museum workers, whose labors are often invisible. I, thus, invited everyone, from the director to the janitor, to donate their work clothes. The curator became my "in-house" liaison, communicating with her museum colleagues and reaching out to various departments and other employees she hadn't worked with before. In the process of representing the variety and diversity of museum's staff, we found an institution both fractured and hierarchical. This realization ultimately structured the piece. In the studio, I deconstructed the donated work clothes by cutting around the seams, creating flat patterns of fabric for the walls, and sewing the remaining seams together as a canopy above. During the weeks installing the work at the museum, staff members visited me, proudly pointing out their shirt or pants among the myriad of professional dress code pieces on display, and sharing with me their perspectives of being part of the institution. Through this process, I generated an abstract portrait of the staff in the workplace.

Inviting participation from a community through a request for materials did a few key things for my work: it activated a social interaction with people unknown to me (and often unfamiliar with art), while creating an audience invested in the exhibition. It also meant that the museum or other commissioning venue would facilitate material acquisition and become an active part of my art-making. This collaborative process allows individuals to share personal stories behind the objects that they donate, generating a richer narrative around the work.

I met my husband, Brian, in college. A brilliant, talented architect, he's my strongest ally in life and in art. His care and commitment extends beyond the personal, crossing over into formal collaborations when we've created artworks together for several exhibitions. Often times, he's behind the scenes consulting me and troubleshooting my projects. I depend on our ongoing conversations to provide honest and critical feedback on my work. Going from one project to the next, constantly putting myself out there as an artist, can be extremely exhausting. To balance this, my home life with Brian is a place of comfort, security, and unconditional support, allowing me to recharge. I take strength in our relationship. When we're not consumed by the demands of our professional practices, on weekends we're renovating our home and studio. Even with all the time we spend together day to day, there's never enough time to get done all that we envision and want to accomplish and enjoy in our lifetime. In our willingness to be there for each other through the professional challenges that confront us in our uphill journey, our mutual determination grows and brings us even closer.

With the birth of my son in 2005, being a parent became a big part of my existence, along with childcare duties. Although I was physically tired, sleep-deprived, and often distracted, I reveled in the pure joy of connecting with our lovely newborn son, Tyler. The demands of motherhood and wanting to maintain a close relationship as my son developed necessitated different approaches to my art-making.

During my residency at the Fabric Workshop and Museum in Philadelphia, the opportunity to work with project managers, interactive designers, and fabricators opened up a new working method for me. Up to this point, I had been working predominately with my own labor in my studio, in part because I couldn't afford assistants, but mostly due to my own attachment to my hand in the work. The work ethic and devotion to labor that I inherited from my parents were always strengths in my work, but I now recognized that holding on too tightly to this could also be a burden, not allowing my practice to be enhanced and empowered by others. Through this new experience at the residency, seeing an ambitious project that was managed and accomplished remotely with great effectiveness, I became comfortable with letting go of some of the control and trusting others to make the work for me. This was big learning curve. The director encouraged me to explore utilizing their extensive resources. In the beginning, there were lots of questions and doubts, trials and errors. My project managers patiently produced countless samples for my consideration. I was no longer limited by my own skillset, labor, or time. I could instead see how all these variations and options opened up endless possibilities. *TEXTile,* the sculpture that came out of this residency, documented the process of producing a work remotely. Using over 22,000 recycled computer keycaps to spell out our emails in an endless scroll, the work not only credits my collaboration with the Fabric Workshop and Museum, but also archives the correspondence between the various individuals involved in creating the sculpture. Instead of being only a producer of objects, I saw that I was a catalyst in a chain of relationships between people, generating dialogues, activating ideas, and collaborations. I wanted to make the hidden processes in the work's creation visible, as well as transform virtual communication into a physical, tactile experience for the viewer. Creating this ambitious, labor intensive, interactive work would have been impossible to make as solo practitioner.

I also found myself energized by the unique collaborative relationships that are formed from working so closely on a project together. I recall my own experience as a young artist, being hired for a month to be one of the many assistants producing Sol Lewitt's retrospective exhibition in New York. Creating Sol's large-scale wall paintings and drawings was an insightful, hands-on way of learning about the artist's process, while developing close bonds with a network of like-minded peers. In the same generous spirit of Sol, I share my art-making and community-building process with others. Each project invitation brings me in contact with a team of new local assistants, who I would never have had an opportunity to work with otherwise. They make it site-specific in an entirely new and special way. Through their time, labor, and thoughtfulness, participants become intimately aware of their roles in generating these projects and willingly give more of themselves in order to meet the demands of the work. I believe this experience fosters a genuine connection between individuals. When they see how their contributions are vital to the work's existence, there is a shared ownership and care for the work.

Another turning point in my career occurred when the federal government's Art in Architecture Percent for Art Program asked me to give a proposal to create a permanent public work to be installed in a US General Services Administration Building in Baltimore, Maryland. I was nervous about the commission, because all my public installations to date had been created using ephemeral materials. Perhaps having a child and imagining his life in the future, I began questioning my artwork's long-term impact. With this opportunity, I consulted conservators and fabricators to figure out the best ways to translate my material choices for permanent placement and longevity.

As fate would have it, the same federal building that my commission was destined for housed the very office of Citizenship and Naturalization where my parents, brother, and I became US citizens, 23 years prior. My family's journey, from Korea to finding a permanent life in America, gave me insights into the current wave of immigrants. The Immigration Office shared a building with the Veterans Administration, generating an interesting dialogue for my future work. For *Dress Code*, I celebrated these two groups that embody the spectrum of American identity. With the government agencies' assistance, we convinced a diverse group of veterans and immigrants alike to give me their clothes and military uniforms as artifacts from their life's journey, to be part of the permanent public work. I solicited contributions at a swearing-in ceremony, inviting immigrants from Peru, Nigeria, Honduras, Mexico, China, Sir Lanka, among 25 different countries to participate on the day of their citizenship. One man I met was so enthusiastic about the invitation to mark this special occasion, he gave me the actual white oxford shirt he was wearing, right off his back. Others who signed up mailed me distinctive garments that were linked with the customs and cultural heritage of their countries of origin. These garments were juxtaposed with the veterans' uniforms, representing military service from World War II to the recent conflicts in the Middle East and from many branches of service, including the Army, Navy, National Guard, Marines, Coast Guard, and Air Forces. In most cases, these camouflaged uniforms were personalized by use, evident in the worn-away fabric and the military badges earned by their original owners. Listening to these soldiers and officers speak about their time in service was illuminating and moving. Their willingness to trust me with their uniforms was another small sacrifice they were proud to make. In turn, I wanted to honor and humanize the men and women in uniform.

The challenges of creating public art are many: navigating very long process, from generating proposals and presentations; competing in the selection process; investing time in countless meetings and conference calls; the elaborate contracts, paperwork, and multiyear schedules that go into collaborating with various government agencies, fabricators, architects, engineers, and contractors each step of the way. Because of my previous professional skills gained working full-time at the museum, this type of administrative-heavy work that public art requires seemed second nature to me. I was also familiar with multitiered, collaborative processes in planning, because of my close proximity to my husband's architectural practice. I've shared a work space and even worked collaboratively on art installations with Brian for many years, which has generated a unique studio environment for me. Although the administrative work of public art commissions often consumes my studio time, I remind myself that, in the lifetime of the permanent works, this elaborate process is only a small percentage.

While previous projects explored American identity, when I was selected to create a MTA public art commission in Flushing, Queens, a predominantly Korean-American community, I took the opportunity to travel to my birthplace in Korea. I was inspired by the elegant and fragile beauty of Korean celadon pottery found in most Korean homes. Visiting the workshops where these vases are made, I was struck by the vast landscapes of broken shards surrounding the kilns, discarded because of their imperfections. Working with a fabricator to create my first mosaic project, *Celadon Remnants,* literally and metaphorically reunites something broken in Korea into new form in America, a portrait of the diaspora I was a part of.

My work also returned me to Washington DC, near my childhood home, for a solo exhibition at the Smithsonian American Art Museum. Visiting this familiar city with a new perspective, I saw the capitol as a place that is entangled with the nation's memory, but also with my personal history. It is a city of buildings and public monuments embodying ideals, yet the National Mall, its most powerful image, is a void left empty in the middle. Recognizing the site's potential for people to come together in celebration and protest, this place felt akin to my work.

For this installation, *Everyday Monuments*, I chose trophies as intimate monuments to one's personal achievement. I wanted to create a monument to the unsung heroes of our society, whose everyday labors go unrecognized, including the often invisible immigrant or undocumented populations. We transformed over 2,000 donated sports trophies, making each miniature figure's pose into the unsensational, yet distinctive gestures of work, such as typing, cleaning, cooking, etc. Tapping into my high school community in suburban Maryland, many local parents cleared out their children's trophies which were collecting dust in their basements. One local PTA parent became my community liaison, connecting with families and collecting the trophies in her home. I recognized that her commitment to the project and each trophy that materialized were gifts from my hometown. The exchange with donors that followed was particularly meaningful. One family had donated several large martial arts trophies earned by their deceased son. I was struck by their generosity in the face of loss. Letting go of these trophies, in some way, helped them process their past tragedy. Their participation deepened the project's significance for me: I recognized that trophies weren't just about competition and glory; sometimes they can also symbolize unfulfilled hopes and dreams.

I find a great sense of purpose knowing that I am contributing to the experience of art as part of people's everyday life. My public artworks will be on view for generations of people who rarely visit museums or buy art; instead, they will encounter my artworks in the lobby of a government building, a hospital, a public elementary school, on the sidewalk near a bus stop, a park, a plaza, train station, and the subway. In creating public works, both permanent and temporary, I am continually rewarded by the possibility of engaging a community in the transformative powers of art-making. With each new project, I work with the conditions of a particular place: its history, people, and identity. When it's successful, it's like a great adventure. Each new challenge gives me the chance to discover something new about myself, even if it brings me back to places in my own personal history. In my early years, I thought that my life experiences shaped my art. However, more recently, I believe it goes the other way around: art shapes life.

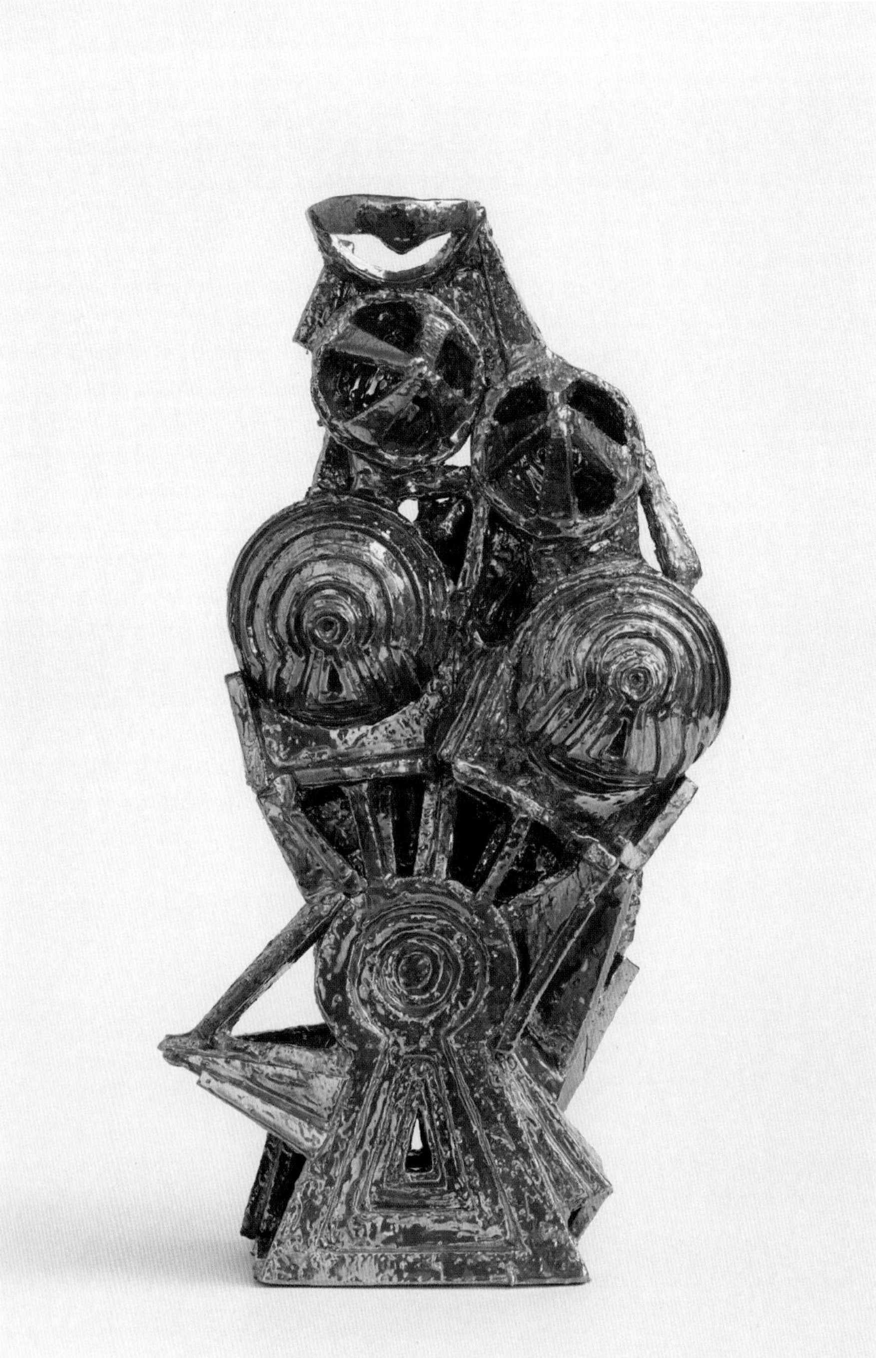

When was a teenager, I would wander into the pottery shop at the University of Vermont and sit, mesmerized, watching the potters at work. Hideo Okino, head of the shop, saw me make some pieces in exchange for babysitting for one of the potters, and he offered to let me work there for free. As a result, I made pots and sculptures every day for three summers. Hideo was instrumental in helping many studio potters get their start in the 1970s. When I was looking at colleges, I asked him for advice. He imparted to me that I should only become an artist if I was absolutely sure that I couldn't do anything else. That phrase has always haunted me, because I knew that I was interested in and capable of doing a lot of other things. But it turns out that all of my skills and interests—including literature, politics, writing, research, languages, and community building—have been vital to my life as an artist.

Around age 13, I read Lillian Hellman's memoirs, and her exciting life (whether true or not) impressed upon me that I had something to say, even if I wasn't sure what that was yet. But I had no idea how to get there. I thank my mother for having great books around the house, and I am grateful that I was able to sneak into the library at the University of Vermont. I came out to myself at age 14 and wrote the word "lesbian" on a scrap of paper, put it on my forehead, and xeroxed my face. I then hid the document. I can't help but think that I became an artist

Julia Kunin
Woman at Keyhole
21"x13"x7"
Ceramic
2014
Courtesy of the artist and Sandra Gering Inc.
Photography by Jeffrey Scott French

largely due to the combination of needing both a lesbian culture to identify with and a means to express my sentiments about being gay. The impulse to encode my identity within an object or image has remained a key element of my work.

I have been driven by the desire not only to be an artist, but to be involved in social change. Occasionally, the two have overlapped in my life. Politics is in my blood. In 1961, the year I was born, my uncle Edgar May won the Pulitzer Prize for local reporting, exposing problems in the welfare system in New York State. He later worked on the "war on poverty" in the Johnson administration and served in the Vermont state senate. He and my mother came to the United States as immigrants in 1940, escaping the threat of Nazism in Europe. In 1972, my mother gave her maiden speech in the Vermont state legislature in support of the Equal Rights Amendment. In 1985, she became the governor of Vermont, and she is still active in politics to this day. My father, my three younger brothers, and I all campaigned for her, knocking on doors, giving out brochures, and going to rallies. In 1982, I took time off from college to work on her first bid for governor. My grandfather on my father's side was a kosher butcher in Brooklyn, a socialist, and a member of the Workmen's Circle; he painted in his spare time. My father made every effort to escape Brooklyn, attending Columbia University on the G.I. Bill. I ended up returning to Brooklyn—a very different Brooklyn, but Brooklyn nonetheless.

I've been a sporadic activist, helping to start a lesbian group on campus at Wellesley College in 1979 (later called WLF, Wellesley Lesbians and Friends) and participating in WAC (The Women's Action Coalition) in New York in the early '90s. I went to graduate school at the Mason Gross School of the Arts at Rutgers University from 1991 to 1993, at the height of identity politics. During that time, I made videos that were in lesbian, gay, bisexual, and transgender festivals and showed in some queer group shows. I was thrilled to see my sculpture, *Red Suede Saddles,* on the cover of *Damn Fine Art by New Lesbian Artists* (1996) and displayed in the window of a gay and lesbian bookstore in New York City.

Ever since completing my undergraduate education, I have structured my life in order to be an artist. I have always worked a "day job" fewer than five days week, reserving the summers for complete immersion in the studio, whether that be through a residency or something I have organized on my own. I thank my good education for the invaluable skill of being able to write grant proposals and fill out applications. I create my work as much as possible during teaching breaks and in the summertime, and then continue to develop ideas during the year, while having studio visits and conducting the business aspects of art. I have waitressed, worked for artists, temped as a word processor, worked as a secretarial assistant, and taught as an adjunct and part-time at several institutions. I have recently enjoyed writing about art and have created some design projects. I often juggled three jobs before becoming the head of the art department at the Allen-Stevenson School in 1997, a private school based in Manhattan where I presently teach grades K through 9. I credit this job for giving me the stability I needed to develop my art career. My art sales support my studio and enable me to leave New York every summer.

I received an extraordinary liberal arts education at Wellesley College, and I spent my junior year in art school at Carnegie Mellon University, experiencing the best of both worlds. After graduating from Wellesley College in 1984, I had no idea how I was going to support myself as an artist. I only knew that I was going to the Skowhegan School for Painting and Sculpture. It was my first introduction to the art world, and I met artists there who remain close friends today. I created a huge body of work but had no sense to save it, and absolutely no business sense. Luckily, I had the work photographed, which proved helpful in future applications. I spent that following year as a babysitter and artist's assistant, working for a former professor. I then waitressed and, in 1985, was accepted into the Alfred G. Glassell School of Art Core Residency Program, at the Museum of Fine Arts Houston. The residency was unknown at the time but provided a small stipend, studio space, a visiting artist program, and an opportunity to teach. I supported myself in Houston, first, through waitressing, and then by working as an assistant at *Newsweek* magazine (a job my roommate passed on to me). I made strong friendships, created several bodies of work, began exhibiting, and started teaching art classes. I had never taught before, so I learned on the job.

I was in my second year there when Lynda Benglis, a frequent visiting artist at the Core Program, overheard me saying that I was considering a move to New York. She asked if I wanted to be her assistant, and I agreed. In 1987, I shared a loft in Greenpoint, Brooklyn with two other sculptors, one of whom was a friend from the Core Program, who I'd also gone to Skowhegan with. It turned out that many of my Skowhegan and Houston friends were also then in Brooklyn, and I found myself in a great community of artists. I worked for Lynda Benglis for nine months, running lots of errands for her, including shopping at Dean and Deluca and going back and forth to Paula Cooper Gallery in Soho. Lynda was a great role model for me. I concurrently did temp work and was a part-time secretarial assistant for the top editors at *Newsweek* magazine in New York, from about 1987 to 1996. In Williamsburg, Brooklyn in the late '80s early '90s, I was involved in an alternative art space called Epoche, where I ran a feminist discussion group and co-curated an exhibition. Being part of an artist community is paramount for me. Not only is art-making about the studio, it's about relationships: cultivating them and sustaining them.

In 1989, inspired by a friend that I met at Skowhegan who was making a living teaching art to children, I began teaching at the Little Red School House, all the while keeping my *Newsweek* job and juggling some word processing work. Teaching serves as important ballast for me. I often think back on the mentoring I received at the University of Vermont pottery shop, and it continues to inspire me to mentor others. I taught in the early childhood program at Studio in a School from 1994 to 1996, where I also evaluated art teachers and conducted research. In addition, I have given lectures and done stints as an adjunct at colleges and universities, including a graduate ceramic sculpture class at Pratt. One of my favorite classes that I teach at the Allen-Stevenson School is "Facing History and Ourselves," an interdisciplinary course in which 9th grade students research and then make art about a social justice issue of their choice.

In 1999, I received a fellowship from CEC ArtsLink to go to the Republic of Georgia to learn how to make handmade felt. I had been inspired by a trip to visit my brother Daniel, who was working there, and was determined to find a way to go back. This marked the beginning of leaving my narrow art world of New York and realizing that I was passionately interested in learning about the former Soviet Union. It also reminded me of my love of languages, and I attempted to learn some Georgian. In addition, this is when I began to dip my toe in the world of design.

In 2000, I collaborated with a friend who owned Brooklyn Handknit, where I helped coordinate the felt part of the business. We designed and sold bags, hats, skirts, slippers, and felt flowers. The felt was made by a group of women in the Republic of Georgia, where I went back and forth to help with product design. I also received a grant to enable a group of Georgian women to build a small felt-making studio. This was a very challenging project in terms of logistics, such as transporting the felt from a small village to the airport in Tbilisi to be shipped to New York where the bags and slippers could be sewn. It was also a labor of love in which family and friends helped with all aspects of the business. In the end, we broke even. In 2002, I had to decide whether to fully commit to the business or return to being an artist. I chose to stick with being an artist.

Learning languages and traveling in order to conduct research for my work are both passions of mine. In 2000, I had a residency for four months in Wiesbaden, Germany at the Bellevue-Saal, where I honed my German. In 2007, I had the good fortune of receiving a John Michael Kohler Arts Industry Fellowship; it was a life-changing experience, making my work in a factory environment. In 2009, I went to Hungary to work with porcelain and explored working in a factory there, something my experience at Kohler made me realize was possible. Since then, I've been studying Hungarian and have returned numerous times to create my sculptures, subletting my apartment in the summers and living off of art sales and my teaching salary for the two months I'm there.

In the summer of 2010, in Hungary, I was welcomed to work in the studio of the porcelain expert Sandor Dobany, who refused to charge me rent. I asked him what he most wanted, and he replied: "Exhibitions." As a result, I included his pottery in a Hungarian ceramics exhibition that I co-curated at Iliad Gallery in New York, and I received a grant from the Trust For Mutual Understanding to bring a group of the artists to New York for the exhibition. In 2013, I received a Fulbright to go to Hungary, which provided me with seven months to make my artwork in a ceramics manufactory, do research, and teach a graduate class at the University of Pecs. It was heaven.

Ever since arriving in New York in 1987, I have exhibited in group shows, but my big break happened in 2007, when I was officially represented by Greenberg Van Doren Gallery. In 2012, I had my first solo exhibition there. In 2014, I began working with Sandra Gering Gallery. Both experiences have been highly professional, personal, and meaningful, and I have felt very much supported as an artist. I am currently exploring design once again, having created a series of vases and a ceramic lamp prototype. I am passionate about everything I now do to support myself as an artist, and I most value the relationships that I have been able to forge in doing so.

KAT KIERNAN

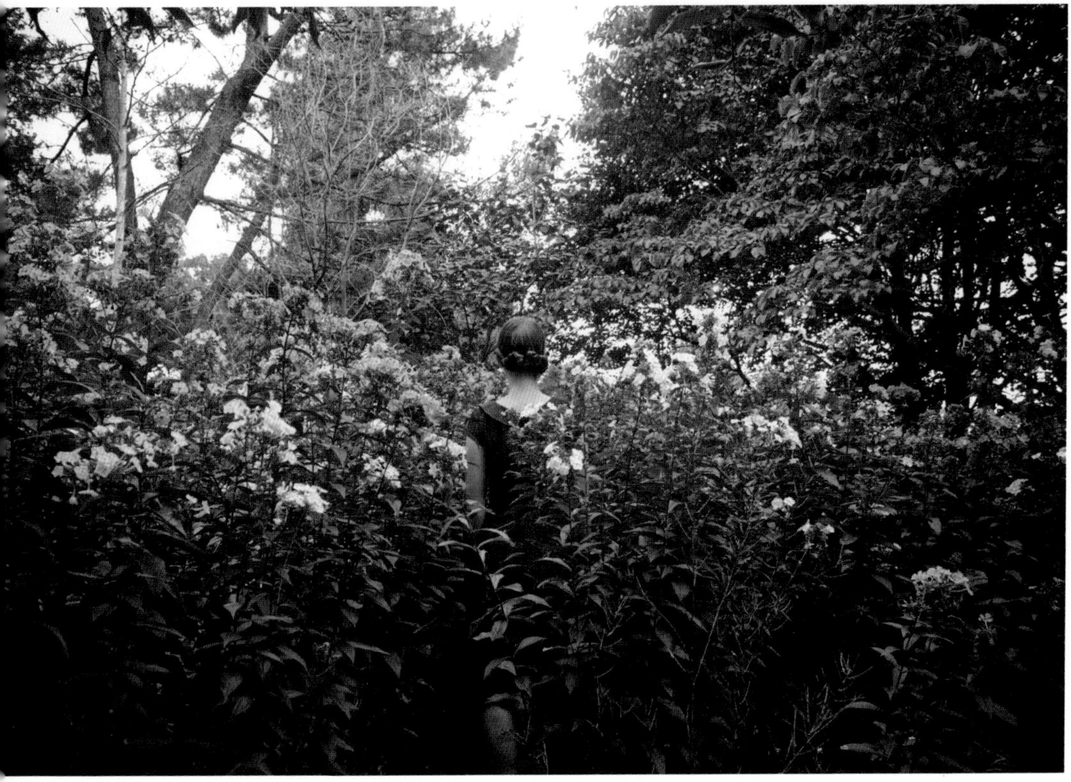

When he asked if I was an artist, I said "no." I answered almost reflexively, but still the word felt heavy in my mouth, as if I were telling a lie. The gallerist went back to his booth at the art fair as my boyfriend shot me an incredulous look. I have a BFA in photography and had a decent exhibition history for an emerging photographer, yet I had declined to identify myself as an art-maker. Those in the arts can and do debate about what it means be an artist, but it is a given that to earn the title one must make art. Busy with other creative projects, at the time of the art fair I had not done so in over a year. I had owned and operated a successful photography gallery for three years and had launched a photography magazine, but somewhere in all of that, I had let go of the "artist" label in favor of "curator," "dealer," "critic," and other more prestigious-sounding titles. Though I would like to be equally artist and arts promoter, the reality is that creating opportunities for other photographers often impedes my own art practice. This is not to say that I do not live a creative life. In my "business hours" position as the Assistant Director of the Louis K. Meisel Gallery in New York City, I design advertisements and catalogues, manage inventory, write press releases, and curate the occasional exhibition. After hours, I manage and write for my photography magazine, *Don't Take Pictures*. I also curate independently, write for other publications, and attend portfolio review events. These jobs are

Kat Kiernan
Untitled
8"x10"
Photograph
2015
Courtesy of the artist

themselves creative and constant sources of inspiration for my photography. Some of them also help to pay the bills.

Admittedly, it is unusual for someone my age to have moved relatively seamlessly into a career in the arts. Young people often struggle to be taken seriously, and at times my lack of years has been a hurdle. However, youth comes with certain advantages that are often overlooked. For example, just out of college and without any job prospects, I was able to make a long-distance move from Boston to Virginia with minimal hesitation. I put my meager savings into opening a photography gallery and hoped that everything would work out, reasoning that if it didn't, losing my own money was better than losing the bank's. When you don't have much to lose, you don't worry as much about losing it. Looking back, I see how naïve I was about small business operations, but perhaps if I had had more experience, I would have been too wary to take the plunge into art dealing.

The Kiernan Gallery opened its doors in November 2011, six months after I graduated from the Art Institute of Boston at Lesley University. As I was making plans to open the gallery, while simultaneously careening toward graduation, I was surprised at how many recent graduates with art degrees were entering the world with sparse résumés, if they had one at all. I myself had had only a handful of juried shows and my thesis exhibition. Of course, timing is everything, and it was at this time that I met a boy. After a whirlwind romance, he asked me to move with him to Virginia while he attended law school (we are still together five years and three states later). Opening a gallery had always seemed like something that I might do later in life, but intrigued by the idea of moving somewhere new, I researched the area. The low cost of living and disproportionally large arts community suggested that I could make this dream a reality sooner than expected. My goal with the Kiernan Gallery was to create a venue where emerging photographers, like myself, could exhibit their work. Had I stayed in Boston, there is no way I would have been able to afford to rent an apartment, let alone an exhibition space. In the name of romance, I packed my things and moved south.

I signed the lease on the gallery space two weeks after my boyfriend and I unloaded our U-Haul at the apartment that we had rented, sight-unseen. The former sporting goods store that would become my photography gallery had original pine floors and exposed brick, providing just the right amount of charm to help potential collectors envision hanging the art shown there in their homes. The gallery consisted of two rooms, one for group exhibitions and the other for solo shows. Each month's group exhibition was curated from a pool of submissions by a gallerist, editor, curator, or photographer interested in discovering new artists; I curated the solo shows. The juried show model helped photographers expand their professional contacts, something that I benefited from as well, developing relationships with the jurors as well as the artists I had shown. Located on the same street as five other art galleries and situated between two colleges, my gallery quickly found a place among Lexington, Virginia's art lovers and the larger photographic community.

Over the next three years, I mounted more than 30 exhibitions with corresponding catalogues and expanded the gallery's activities to include off-site pop-up shows and other events. Located in the rural Shenandoah Valley, I relied heavily on the internet to present work and reach people beyond the borders of my small town. As a photographer, my love for a finely crafted print runs deep, and as an art dealer, I appreciate collectors who purchase original art online instead of buying only what is geographically convenient. Experiencing art as reproduction is not a new concept, but it has become more prevalent with the rise of digital technology. For that reason, the gallery's website, social media presence, and newsletter were designed with the understanding that most of the people on our mailing list might never experience the Kiernan Gallery as a brick-and-mortar space.

As is often the case with projects and career paths, one thing leads to another in unexpected ways. So it went with my own shift, from gallerist to writer and publisher. From the outset, I knew my time in Virginia was finite. Knowing that I would move again (destination unknown) upon my boyfriend's graduation from law school, I wanted to find a way to continue the work that I had started there, regardless of where I lived. I felt invested in a number of the photographers I had exhibited, and though we did not have a representation arrangement, I wanted to maintain these relationships. A printed publication seemed like an excellent way to present a portfolio and accompany it with writing that was more in-depth than an artist or curator's statement. Deliverable directly to doorsteps, neither the readers' proximity to the art nor my proximity to the reader would matter. Now more experienced and more connected to the photographic community, I called on friends and colleagues for help with writing, design, and promotion. Showing excellent photography is important, but having something to say about it elevates both the artist's work and the medium itself to a new level. The magazine's title references the shift in vocabulary from "taking" pictures to "making" them, while also serving as an attention-grabbing name. *Don't Take Pictures* connects a global audience with photographers who engage in the considered act of making photographs.

While the work I was doing with the Kiernan Gallery had garnered some press, *Don't Take Pictures* opened the door for me as a voice in the larger photographic community. During my last year in Lexington, the gallery, the magazine, and my own photography were all competing for my attention. Aside from a very part-time student intern and the occasional assistance from my boyfriend, most of the time I was a one-woman operation. As copies of the magazine made their way around the country, and the online articles travelled from Twitter feeds to Facebook posts, I also started to receive invitations to critique at portfolio review events and jury exhibitions. Having an official moving date on the calendar helped me to make the most of my time—without it, I do not know how much longer I could have continued going at such a frantic pace. At this time, the gallery was my only income-generating venture, and here I was preparing to close it down, making our impending move all the more daunting.

After my boyfriend graduated, we decided to move to New York City for its large art and legal communities. A few months before the move, I interviewed Lou Meisel for a *Don't Take*

Pictures article about the camera's role in photorealist painting. Over the course of our three-hour conversation about art, business, and collecting, I mentioned that I was planning to relocate to the city. He mentioned that he was looking to hire someone for a newly available Assistant Director position. It soon became apparent that we were interviewing each other. After the article was published, I received a phone call from Louis offering me the job. Though not a photography gallery, my position at the Louis K. Meisel Gallery requires many of the skills I developed at my own space, and it has helped me find a foothold in the New York art scene.

There is a misconception that those who turn to curating or criticism are failed artists. I have heard it said enough times to know that it is a popular theory, especially among artists. Perhaps if I spent less time helping other photographers and more time on my own work, I would have a more developed art career. Nonetheless, I enjoy watching the successes of my peers and am happy when I can share in their experiences. It has taken a few years, but I have slowly started to forgive myself for the weeks in which I don't pick up my camera.

Although I did not have any new work to shop around when I arrived in New York, I did have a new perspective on art-making. Only after leaving Boston did I begin to understand the importance of an artistic community. As a student, community comes prepackaged, with peers, faculty, and lab techs. Without regular critiques and discussions, I felt isolated in Lexington, as though I were making work in a void. In New York, I found myself once again in a new place. I was determined not to let this transition distract from my art practice, so I signed up for a photographic workshop in Maine. Immersed in the workshop's creative environment, I was able to put aside my other projects and dedicate myself to making pictures. Photographers of a wide range of ages and experience levels provided a diverse and fresh array of perspectives on my photography as it evolved. At the end of the workshop, three photographs, collectively entitled *The First Lesson*, found a place on my wall as a reminder of what I can accomplish when motivated and inspired.

Graduating from college had freed me from the project-per-semester model. At first I resisted, then embraced the added time for exploration. I quietly learned historic photographic processes, documented Virginia's fox-hunting traditions, and even took on a few commercial assignments. By moving outside of my usual canon and not worrying about when to release a series, I embarked on a new way of art-making, one that embraces the long-term. I have recently begun to view my artistic career in terms of decades rather than years. Thinking on this timeline helps me to set goals for myself and takes the pressure off of me to chase accolades and other fleeting measures of success.

I find owning the label "artist" difficult. In my experience, people in the art world will apply their own definitions of the word, deciding whether or not those around them check all of the necessary boxes. People outside of the arts ask me to define my work, seeking a way to connect it to something that they understand. This is usually followed by, "But what's your real job?" I did, and still do, feel uncomfortable responding that art-making is my "real" job, preferring to talk about the Louis K. Meisel Gallery or my magazine. Does this mean that I am not committed to my art? I don't think so; it just means that I don't wear the "artist" nametag as easily as others.

KHALED SABSABI

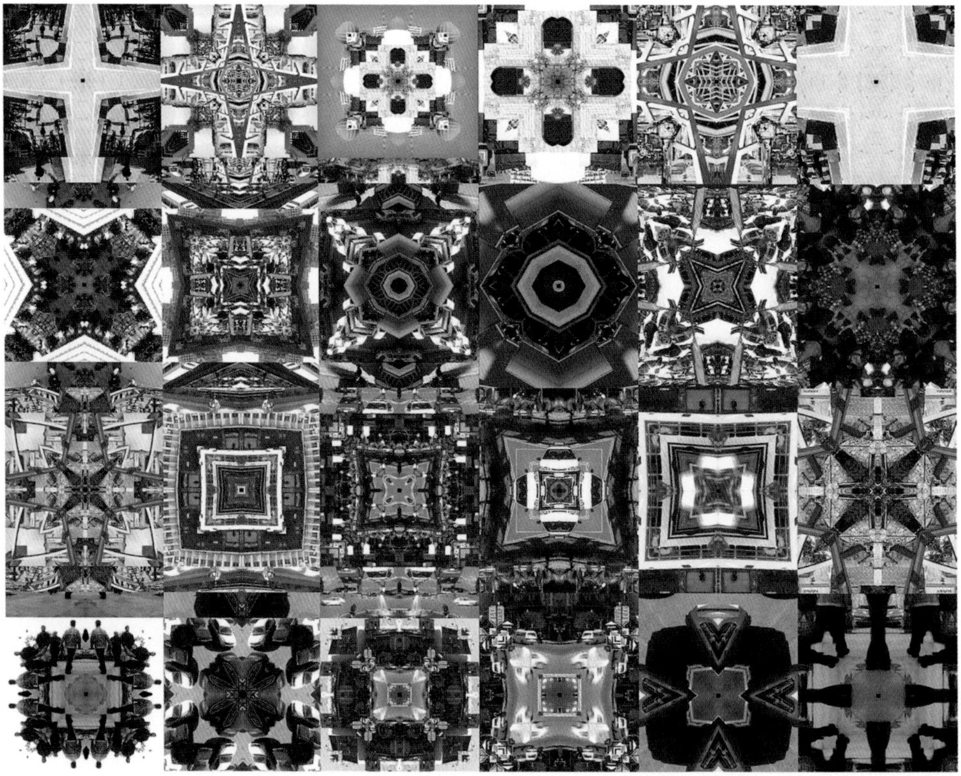

One of the earliest memories I have is of falling. Later in life, I found out that, in fact, I did fall down a flight of stairs as a baby at eight months old. I was born in 1965 in Tripoli, Lebanon and spent my early childhood years growing up in that coastal city. My family immigrated to Australia in late 1977, due to the Lebanese civil war, and settled in western Sydney, Australia's most multicultural area. I was 12 years old. For 30 years, I've made work that questions the rationales and complexities of nationhood, identity, and social change in various media. I personally regard art-making as my view of a true reflection of society, attempting to produce a constant movement toward expanding limits and perceptions to contribute to an open and more just world.

During my childhood, I witnessed much suffering and hardship, living in an uncertain, violent, and terrifying place. These times were the early years of the Lebanese militia and civil wars. My story, in brief, is that my father, Walid, migrated to Australia in 1969 to work, and my mother, Wafa, followed him in 1971. I and my younger brother, Hussam, stayed with my grandmother, Khadijah Al Kurdi. One thing led to another, and we got trapped in Tripoli during the war.

I have two memories to share from this experience. The first concerns the militia factions butchering each other in and around the olive groves just outside Tripoli at the edge of the mountains. It's ironic because, in the first instance, the olive

Khaled Sabsabi
Syria
Two channel video installation with sound
2.4mx2.7m
2012
Courtesy of the artist and Milani Gallery, Brisbane, Australia

branch is a symbol of peace and, in the second, I remember my grandmother telling me and my younger brother, while sitting to eat dinner, that if you ate 15 olives, it would be like eating an ounce of meat. I remember a truck that sat parked opposite my grandmother's apartments; it was full of dead bodies, piled on top of each other in its open rear tray like a mound. I recall the smell, but most of all I remember the mothers, fathers, and families looking for their dead, like searching for lost items in the sand. This was the first time I had seen death.

The other memory is from the civil war, when our neighbourhood was heavily shelled and bombarded by factions and the Syrian army in the surrounding areas of Tripoli. These were extreme hostilities, and I recollect living for days in the basement of our building, with little food or water. After a while, we had to leave the building because it was getting unstable and was at risk of collapsing. I clearly remember we had to run across a street which was targeted by snipers; much caution was required. As I was making the crossing, I was fired on and could feel the wind and hear the sound of the bullets passing in front of my face—everything shifting into slow-motion. After completing that stretch and crossing, at the shelter space between the next sections of crossing, I suddenly fell to the ground. No matter how hard I tried, I couldn't get back up. I couldn't feel or control my legs. In the panic, everyone had moved to the next crossing to safety, but I was left there on my own. I screamed and yelled, and I could hear people telling me to get up and run, but I couldn't move. After some time, a man ran to where I was; he carried me on his back and took me to the shelter.

Besides these memories of war, violence, and hopelessness, there are other, more pleasant memories and experiences of play, love, and creativity—learning to make do with what we had in order to create games using found and common objects, such as sticks, rocks, and the discarded stones of apricot fruits. The last memory I have of my early life is standing in front of my grandmother and not wanting to say goodbye or to let her go before being taken out of Lebanon.

Coming to a new land I felt out of the ordinary—everything was different and unfamiliar. People didn't understand me, and

I didn't understand them. In the first three months on arrival, fellow school students mocked and teased me, and I'd wonder why. I was bashed in the playground and was once abducted by a group of older Anglo-Australian boys, who tortured me by putting out their lit cigarettes on my arms, shouting at me: "You fucking wog, go back to where you came from." After a while, I started to make friends with other children, who were mainly from migrant ethnicities also.

In 1979, I started attending an all-boys high school. Here things became somewhat normal. I learned how to speak English and was starting to fit in. I played sports, mainly rugby league and cricket, because I noticed the deputy principal liked both. I quickly became good at these sports, to the point where the deputy principal would no longer discipline and cane me when I was sent to his office; instead, he would sit me down and speak about the game we played last week, how the team could improve. In regards to inspirational people and moments of change during high school time, there was an art teacher that saw a sketch I did; she asked me if I had made much art before. I said no, and she took me to speak with the head teacher of the school's art department, Mr Roulston. He looked at the drawing and asked me if I liked art, to which I replied, yes, and he said: "I want you to take art as an elective subject next term." This was rare, because students were not allowed to change subjects during the school year. But he spoke to my teachers and made it happen. I ended up dropping economics and picking-up art instead. Mr Roulston supported me greatly for the next three years: he gave me unrestricted access to the art workshop and introduced me to many artists and their work.

My discovery of hip hop, in the early 1980s, had a major influence on me and changed my outlook on life. Accepting music was easy, because I've always been exposed to it: as a child, mainly through the classical Arabic music which was played in our home. But when I heard hip hop for the first time, it was something else altogether. Hip hop was fresh, and I could associate with it easily because it was rhythmic—as everyone knows, rhythm and the beat of the drum are primal and universal. What also attracted me to hip hop was that it was an alternative to the mainstream Australian rock scene of the time, which I couldn't connect with or understand whatsoever, maybe because the lyrics didn't reflect what I felt and who I was. I started to attempt making beats and trying to be a DJ, while also writing rhymes, but I didn't quite know how to make hip hop music. At the time, the only references I had were a few video clips and movies. I couldn't just Google "how to make hip hop;" it was all about trial and error, learning and sharing information from other hip hoppers doing the same. Soon after these early experiences, things changed again: I clearly remember listening to the first Def Jam compilation album and, in particular, to a group called Public Enemy. This was a revelation. From that moment, it was clear to me what I needed to do.

I rented a large house with a garage space for a studio and asked another rhymer, Ilhan Goktas, to move in with me. We formed a crew, which included a few other young rhymers from our local area in western Sydney. For several years, through to the early 1990s, our crew, which we named COD, grew in local support and performance attendance, to the point where the garage studio became a hangout for young people like us to sit, listen, and get educated about hip hop. There were many complaints from racist neighbours, and the police were regular visitors. Although I had a full-time job, all my existence throughout those years was about producing, performing, and recording. We achieved very little headway in making it into the mainstream music scene, but this didn't matter, because it wasn't about the fame. It was about lyrical content, phat beats, and performing anywhere and everywhere. However, it's important to mention that we also experienced some hate—our house was fire-bombed in the middle of the night while we were asleep, causing us to flee for our lives. The police said they don't know who did it, and no charges were laid.

My introduction into community art was in 1991, when I had a visit from Mouna Zaylah, a local girl who was working for a community theatre company, Death Defying Theatre (DDT), based in the nearby suburb of Auburn. She asked me if I would be interested in meeting with the company's artistic director, regarding a production they were putting together for schools. I agreed to the meeting and met with the artistic director (Fiona

Winning) and the actors involved in the production. I was asked about the pre-existing music used in the production; the title of the play was *Rap it Up*, and it was a production for young people in schools and explored issues around consumer rights. I was honest and told them that the music had nothing to do with hip hop, and I offered to remix it. Fiona agreed, and the following day, I showed up to their office with a new remix of the music. They loved it.

We kept in contact and, nine months later, they asked me if I would be interested in facilitating hip hop workshops with young people. At the time, I didn't understand what a workshop was and, besides, hip hop to me was about being hardcore and real. DDT organised a two-week creative development workshop with other experienced theatre practitioners, actors, and performance poet John Komninos. Here I learned how art could be used as a tool for participation. After this two-week period, a comprehensive six-month workshop was designed and scheduled by DDT in various locations to harvest stories. The content collected was used for another touring production, *Eye of the Law*, in 1993. The workshops were held in youth centres, youth prisons, detention centres, women's refuges, men and women's adult prisons, as well as in community gatherings and schools. The importance of these workshops to my practice is that they taught me the power of art and of collaboration. I went on to perform and tour *Eye of the Law* at 70 schools, while also working and performing in DDT's major multimedia production, *Hiphopera*, in late 1995.

In 1993, I decided to work as a youth worker and to focus on working with so-called disadvantaged, or at-risk youth from diverse cultural backgrounds. The idea for me was simple: use hip hop as the language and entry point and, from there, refer these young people into support programs and services that could assist them with the complex issues in their lives. I was offered a position at an NGO, called Bankstown Multicultural Youth Service; I was Australia's first non-English-speaking youth street worker. The irony of the situation is that I was a young person as well. The highlight for me during this time was a project that came about as a result of young people being involved in riots with police at an annual multicultural festival which attracted over of 80,000 people. I was consulted and appointed to find ways to address issues of youth violence. I coordinated a pilot youth music performance stage, as part of the 1994 Arabic Day Carnival, which was highly effective.

After nearly two years in this job, I began working with the Central Sydney Area Health Services, a state institution that operated on a larger scale. The first few years were great, because there were like-minded people and staff who believed in taking a holistic approach, with youth health and art at the core of well-being. I initiated art projects that addressed various important, and sometimes taboo, subjects such as youth suicide, youth crime prevention, HIV and Hepatitis C education, drug and alcohol education. Also, during this time, I was able to realise a full recording studio, dedicated to training young people in recording hip hop and other forms of music. In 1997, a restructure happened which forced the people who supported me out of the organisation. Work situations became difficult, as my priority was on the youth using the centre, but due to new procedures and policies put in place, funding for artistic programs were cut. I got depressed, as I was spending most of my time in management, supervision, and mediation. I resorted to substance abuse, at this point, and resigned in 1998. This period was the lowest point of my life. This lifestyle and condition continued until the birth of my first child, Walid, in 1999. At this point I decided to clean up, in order to see beyond my self-imposed darkness and to broaden my opportunities in life. I think we are all in some sort of exile and torment, whether physical and or psychological. All along this period, I continued to make music, sound, and site-specific installation artwork where possible.

I returned to work at the end of 1999 for another NGO, this time the Liverpool Migrant Resource Centre (LMRC). As an information officer, I facilitated a program for newly arrived migrants and refugees, as well as for broader non-English speaking communities. During my time at the LMRC, many art and community projects were designed and delivered. The highlight for me was the establishment of an outreach multimedia van for creative training and teaching. It was early

2000, and the digital revolution had arrived. Video, audio, and other digital media production technologies started to become accessible and affordable. The project idea for the multimedia van was to refit and custom design a domestic caravan for the propose of making it into a portable digital production training facility, which could be moved across different suburbs and neighbourhoods to give access to people who wouldn't usually have access to such technologies and tools. For realising this project, I want to give thanks to Gorkem Acaroglu, the LMRC art worker at that time, for her shared vision, commitment, and support.

In 2001, the world changed. And in late 2002, I decided to return to Lebanon, after 24 years living in a foreign country. My rationale for travelling back was both professional and personal: professional, as I was exploring Arabic hip hop through an Australia Council for the Arts Fellowship I received in 2001, and personal, because I was overwhelmed with the portrait of Australian Muslims in local media and needed to face these demons elsewhere.

On arrival in Beirut, I felt a strange duality of familiarity and uncertainty. I recall being in a taxi, on my way to Tripoli, gazing through its windows at the scenery of landscape and people that quickly brought the realities of this place back to me. I saw a large image, a mural of a militia faction leader, which jolted my memories. I sarcastically asked the driver, "Are these people still here?" And he responded, "They never left." From that moment, I felt that coming back to this place would challenge all my ideologies on my identity.

There was another instance in a taxi, in Beirut: I received a remark from a frustrated but honest driver, who added a few extra sentences to the usual small talk you receive. I'll never forget, he said to me: "Well, if you like it here so much, why don't you live here and try to earn a living, then come back and tell me if you still like it here." His remarks at the time made me confused and angry, because I was directly confronted with the reality that I was just another privileged tourist, high on romantic notions of belonging and childhood memories. Here I was, working my life away in another place and land for art, social awareness, and justice, forgetting my people's situations and their suffered hardships. So, over the duration of my visit, I extended and exhausted myself in order to reconnect with my land, people, and forgotten family members. I visited Damascus and reconciled my troubled childhood memories of the Syrian army's invasion of Tripoli during the civil war.

After my stay of three months in Lebanon, I left for Turkey. In that month away, I had time to seriously reflect on the motherland and its people. I felt a void that was much deeper than before. But I questioned my own ability to be effective and functional, if I had stayed in Lebanon and hadn't migrated in the '70s. Also, I wondered if I would have been able to achieve the work I'd done in Australia in Lebanon. I decided that I needed to return back to Australia to try to find what I was looking for.

In 2003, I was determined to work and strive locally. I think, at that time, this was the only way to deal with my struggles with belonging and being misplaced. With this focus, my situations and emotions now became different, sometimes difficult, always amplified. Regardless, all were important experiences, as they constitute what and who I am—as an artist, as a human being. The art work I was personally making at the time was a cross between sound art, performance, and video installations. While working in Lebanon and Syria, I connected with various NGOs, thinkers, and teachers to learn and, where possible, train and collaborate with like-minded artists working specifically around audio and video production possibilities.

I utilized and adopted what I had learned in my Australian community cultural development experience to create a multimedia training and documentation studio room in Beirut, with the aim of engaging Lebanese and Palestinian people and their communities. I wanted to help them document their own stories and histories, while building their skills and mentoring others in multimedia production technologies. These experiences had an enormous impact on the kind of work I would go on to make in my western Sydney studio, as I came to the realisation that there is no separation from the self and the identity it carries—like hooks entrenched in memories, land, and people.

What's also notable during this time was meeting my wife-to-be and the love of my life, Yamane Fayed. I'm forever grateful to her, as she instilled in me the important role education and cultural institutions play in society, especially as viewed through an historical perspective. From her I learned not to take these opportunities for granted. Yamane gave me the strength to confront my own definition of who I was and to redefine my practice; prior to meeting her I had always operated on the outside, or on the fringes, of these institutions. In 2004, we married, and the following year, I completed a postgraduate degree in Arts at the University of New South Wales. Soon after, we were blessed with two daughters—Haneen, born in 2006, and Yasma, in 2010. My three children are a major source of influence and gentleness on my physical, creative, and spiritual well-being. They've taught me how to live life simply and have helped me to see what life can offer in its many faces. I remember on two separate occasions—once with Walid, my eldest some years ago, and more recently with my youngest, Yasma—occasions where I would be lying next to them as I was putting them to sleep, gazing into their wide and bright eyes. In a moment of enlightenment, I could see the entire universe in those eyes, something truly remarkable and beyond comprehension.

For us, as a family, there is no separation from art and the everyday. We attend art openings together and regularly collectively travel while I'm exhibiting around Australia or overseas. Our home is in the culturally diverse western suburbs of Sydney, and my studio and workspace is a single garage attached to our home—an unglamorous, yet practical and purposeful work space in which I have realised many works that have shown in museums and galleries, from Sharjah to Shanghai. The important thing is this: a long time ago, I made a conscious decision to remain, live, and work within the cultural richness of western Sydney, a choice that I believe has truly enriched my work as an artist.

On that note, from 2006 until the present day, I've worked full-time as the Community Cultural Engagement creative producer at Casula Powerhouse Arts Centre, a public institution established in 1994 within a grand, formerly industrial building owned by the State Electricity Commission. Throughout this period, I've continued extending my practice between a multidisciplinary and interdisciplinary flow of ideas and outcomes, which includes community cultural partnerships, music, video, film, theatre, sound, media, installation, and curating. I'm an artist and cultural producer who fluidly but respectfully draws on the experiences of the communities around me to inform what I do. The social platform has always been my natural habitat. What keeps me motivated is a deep commitment to voices being heard and to raise awareness of the often unappreciated and undervalued worth of cultural expression and creative freedoms.

LENKA CLAYTON

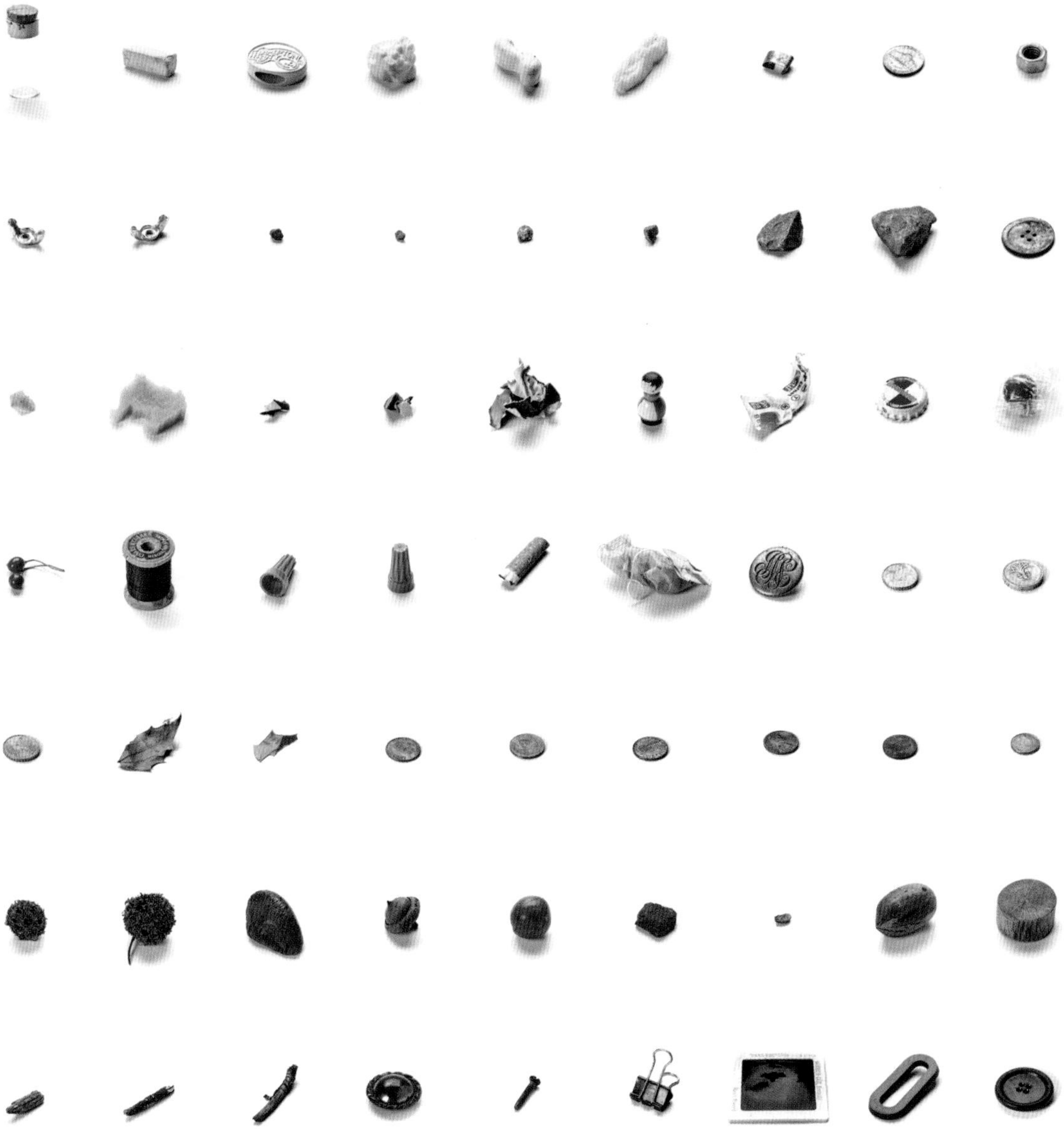

I was born in 1977, in Derbyshire, England. One of my earliest memories from teenagehood is being part of a photography group in my tiny Cornish seaside town; the group was run by a dynamic young photographer called Steve Tanner. Aside from copying the paintings of Salvador Dali in pencil onto A3 paper at school, this was my first real taste of making art. I remember making a life-size composite portrait of an 80-year-old man, called Alf, who I'd met in the street. I photographed every part of his body up close, printed each shot onto 10 x 8 photo paper, and then glued them all together. Steve and the other staff asked after our ideas and our lives and spoke to us as if we were already artists.

When I was age 16 and 17, art lessons at school were handed-out photocopies of ovals with pencil marks halfway down them, showing where the ears definitely go when drawing a face. We were asked to do a project about an artist. I chose Derek Jarman: a radical film director, gardener, gay rights activist, writer, and artist who had then recently died of AIDS. I'd seen his extraordinary, angry, and beautiful paintings in an exhibition. He used melted tar, feathers, and smashed mirror on huge canvases. I made terrible copies of them using a can of coal tar from the hardware store that had to be opened in a well-ventilated place; I mixed the tar with feathers from the pillow off my bed.

Lenka Clayton
63 Objects Taken From My Son's Mouth
Dimensions variable
Acorn, bolt, bubblegum, buttons, carbon paper, chalk, Christmas decoration, cigarette butt, coins (GBP, USD, EURO), cotton reel, holly leaf, little wooden man, sharp metal pieces, metro ticket, nuts, plastic "O", polystyrene, rat poison (missing), seeds, slide, small rocks, specimen vial, sponge animal, sticks, teabag, wire caps, wooden block
2011–2012
Courtesy of the artist
Photography by Tom Little

In Derek Jarman's diary, he mentioned his assistant, Karl Lydon, a lot. Through some detective work that I've now forgotten, I got Karl's phone number and arranged to meet him so we could visit Derek Jarman's house together. I took my adult friend Janie for security. We drove the six hours to London and met Karl, who wore a black leather jacket; then, we drove down to the South Coast, to the nuclear landscape of Dungeness. I showed Karl my Jarman copies, in their tidy, plastic sleeves, and he laughed his head off. We spent the day together—me, asking him naive questions, and him, very seriously answering all of them. I remember taking a lot of photographs.

***

I left home at age 18 to go to Falmouth College of Art. I had a wonderful tutor, named Phil Naylor. He would go beachcombing, looking for little shards of blue and white pottery, and porcelain doll's arms that washed up on the beach. I'd never before met anyone who loved beachcombing as much as I did. It was on my one-year "Art Foundation" course that I felt that I had come home. I worked constantly, tried everything, and really felt like an artist. At the end of that year, I asked someone what the best art school was, and they told me Central St. Martins in London. I applied and got an interview. I went up by myself, got stuck in the tiny lift, with my black A1 portfolio wedged diagonally across it, and got a place there. That year, Jarvis Cocker was on the radio everywhere, singing about Central St. Martins in "Common People." That was probably why someone recommended I go there.

There are 8,178,800 more people living in London than in the seaside town of Penzance where I grew up. Aged 19, I moved to the city alone. A woman in the Central St. Martins housing office, when advising me where to live, said that if there was graffiti in a place that meant it was dangerous. There was graffiti everywhere. I was terrified.

I'd had a part-time job consistently since I was 13, usually waitressing, and in London, I had worked in a paper shop. We were the last generation to get a government grant to attend university, and the tuition was free. My parents helped with my rent while I was at art school, but otherwise I've been financially independent from the age of 18.

***

At St. Martin's I studied printmaking and immediately learned that I wasn't a printmaker. Finishing a print never felt satisfying to me. I wondered who the audience could be, how to find them, what would happen after that, etc. As students, we each had a studio and were pretty much left alone to make our work, so it didn't seem to matter that much. Occasionally, visiting tutors would come and ask us about what we were doing (making a pencil out of clay), and then leave again. I made stacks of tear-off prints that people could take home and, later, hundreds of sets of "fossilized teeth," made from small beach pebbles set in clay that I offered to 50 museums as an acquisition. They're still in the collections of the British Museum and the Natural History Museum as examples of objects mistaken for fossils.

In my second year at art college, we had to get work experience over the summer. I wasn't sure how to do work experience to be an artist. I wrote to my two favorite artists, Jimmie Durham and Mark Dion, and offered to be their assistant for a month on whatever they were working on. They both, astonishingly, wrote back and said yes.

Jimmie Durham was working in Berlin and invited me to fly out. To pay for the trip, I made a printed, limited-edition multiple. It was a pair of screenprinted, life-size spectacles that could be cut out and worn. Inside the lenses were scenes from Berlin, things I imagined I might see if I could afford to go. I sold them to everyone I knew for £25 each and funded the trip.

For a month I lived with Jimmie and his partner, Maria Theresa Alves, in a grand, old apartment behind the famous department store KaDeWe. Three things I remember from that time are:

Trying to raise money for Jimmie to commission a barge to collect stone from a quarry in Sweden, then purposefully sink halfway back across the Baltic. Our fundraising consisted of gluing small stones to cardboard, then Jimmie giving each stone a name.

A spider who lived in one of the plants on the windowsill and whose life we carefully observed.

The way Jimmie wrote essays: one draft, handwritten, slightly revised, looking up words as he went in an etymological dictionary.

***

Mark Dion met me off the train at the Lancaster train station. He had bought me a pair of wellington boots. He was working on creating a "tasting garden" with a team of local volunteers. We fought the knotweed that had invaded the walled garden by hand, for a month. In the evenings, we'd go to the pub. It was wonderful. After I left art school, I worked for Mark again—beachcombing the Thames foreshore, searching for illustrations of extinct pears in horticultural libraries, and looking for taxidermied flamingos in flea markets. Later, I was his regular assistant, translator, and babysitter whenever he traveled in Germany. He's been a great friend and generous mentor ever since.

***

After leaving art school at age 22, I was determined to work as an artist. My boyfriend, Hannes Ravic—a West German artist, tabloid photographer, and hunter-to-be—told me that Berlin was a cheap place to live. I moved there in 1999, ten years after reunification. On the corner of our block, you could still see remnants of the electric fence that ran behind the Berlin Wall. In the East, where we lived, many apartment blocks were open, so you could go up to the attic and walk the length of the street along the rooftops. There were also many abandoned apartments that had been left by people fleeing to the West. I felt absolutely in my element exploring these spaces alone. I remember finding fully furnished children's bedrooms that looked as if the children had just popped out, and closets still full of carefully stored fur coats.

With Jimmie Durham, the year before, I'd learnt to sing German nursery rhymes from a stern teacher who came once a week, but otherwise couldn't say much in German. I loved the process of beginning all over again, learning to communicate one word at a time. Being an outsider gave me a distance to my own experience from which I could observe what was happening at the same time as being part of it.

To make money, I waitressed and worked late-night shifts as a film projectionist. I had to project five films, all starting at the same time on different screens. I still have anxious dreams now, where I forget to start a film and leave 325 people sitting in the dark.

I started an artist-run gallery with friends and spent a lot of time working in my sketchbook. Many of the ideas I had then are the beginnings of things I'm still working on today. My friend, artist Guy Allott, and I started a magazine: *The One Day Magazine*. We didn't make many issues, but we did make ourselves laminated press passes that we used for years to get in free to concerts, museums, and art fairs across Europe and in New York. It never didn't work.

In Berlin, I made my first film, *Qaeda, quality, question, quickly, quickly, quiet*, an alphabetical rearrangement of President Bush's "axis of evil" State of the Union address. I had to buy a camera and computer to make it, and I learnt from a friend how to edit. I remember sitting at my kitchen table alone, for weeks, cutting up and naming thousands of clips. The first time I showed it at a small anarchist film festival in Berlin was excruciating. From that showing to about 15 people, it ended up traveling around the world. I experienced, for the first time, the generosity and infectious nature of the film world—the way things travel quickly and with apparent ease, and so different to my previous experiences of trying to show my artwork.

I'd started longing for home after four years in Berlin but couldn't make the decision whether to leave or stay. I applied on a whim to study documentary direction at the National Film and Television School, outside London, with my one (and only) film. And when I got a place, the decision was made.

***

My new home in London was a tiny houseboat, called Daisy. The cabin was 15 feet long and 6 feet wide, and I could just about stand up in it. In winter, when the Regent's Canal froze, the boat was stuck crooked for weeks, and onions would roll off the counter. I was woken in the mornings by coots nibbling weeds off the underside of the boat.

I imagined the life of a documentary-maker to have all the things I wished for and felt lacking in my art life: a structure, a career path, a daily rate, a collective endeavor. I had the idea that I was going to film school incognito, as an artist looking for tricks and tools from the film world to bring back into my own practice. My thesis on "Documentary Making in Alternative Media" was about an unexplored middle ground between the worlds of the artist and documentary maker; it included a magnetic arrow that could be moved around a portrait of a male voice choir and an interview with artist Harrell Fletcher.

After we graduated, my partner, James Price, and I made films. At first, we made short, experimental work for Channel 4 including the *People in Order* series (featuring one person of every age, from one to 100, banging a drum). Later, as the TV spots we were offered got longer, I quickly realized I didn't have the aptitude or interest in creating linear, developing narratives. I remember going into a meeting with a TV exec, who shouted at me, "WHERE IS YOUR PASSION [for television]??" I don't remember what I said, but I don't think it was the right answer.

***

I went back to Central St. Martins as a tutor and taught for three years on the "Art Foundation" course. The students were hard-working and passionate, for the most part. Some of them were also very wealthy. I remember a colleague saying that one of his student's excuse for being late was that she had lost her emeralds in the bath. I found, over time, that my main role was to help students understand that making work is not an external path to discover, but a reframing of the things they're already naturally engaged with and drawn to as material. One student was a beatbox busker at the weekends and, in class, was making symbolic drawings of trees. I still remember the moment he started using his voice to make art. I think, at the same time, I was also teaching myself this lesson.

***

When Google Maps was invented, James and I discovered that there is a tiny village in France named James, and a tiny village in Slovakia called Lenka. I'm always looking for signs of what to do next and have a great belief in serendipity, which spurs me into action more than anything else. We drew a 1247-kilometers-long, straight line on a map, between James and Lenka, that passed through five countries and the foothills of the Alps. We decided to travel the length of the line by bike.

We marked our starting point in James by knocking on villagers' doors and introducing ourselves: "This is James!" We met the mayor, who shook our hands and signed a declaration. For 30 days, we cycled through villages, fields, forests, vineyards, and industrial wasteland, along highways and the River Danube, and straight through the centre of Vienna. When we arrived in Lenka, a month later, I burst into tears at the sight of the sign. The mayor of Lenka greeted us enthusiastically; we were embraced by the villagers and treated like royalty. I wrote down the phone number of the public phone box in Lenka, in case of emergencies in the future.

***

I went to North Korea at the invitation of a composer I met because of the aforementioned independent travels of my film (he'd seen it somewhere and wrote to me). Another time, a musician, called Matthew Herbert (who'd been shown the film by a friend, who'd seen it at a festival in Israel), telephoned and said he'd like to make the soundtrack into a record. Now, it is played in nightclubs in Spain and is a ringtone in Japan. *People in Order* was once re-edited hundreds of times by a group of people who earnestly attributed magical powers to a 15-year-old boy in the film who was dressed as a wizard (he'd been on his way to a King Arthur re-enactment). The times when my work leaves my control and finds its own unexpected place in the world is one of the main reasons that I continue to make it. I wonder if (and hope) this is good practice for raising teenagers.

***

My friend, artist and writer Michael Crowe, and I used to meet up in the British Library in London to talk about ideas. One day, I was looking through his sketchbook and saw he'd written, "If I wrote a letter to everyone in the world, what would I say?" Coincidentally I'd written almost the exact same idea in my own sketchbook ("Write a letter to everyone in the world"). To mark the occasion, we decided then and there to start work. This became *Mysterious Letters*: our attempt to send a unique, handwritten letter to every household in the world.

Since 2009, we've written to nearly 3,000 households in entire towns, villages, quarters, and suburbs of Ireland, Switzerland, Germany, Austria, Denmark, France, and the US We usually temporarily move to the place we're writing to. We start with a person's name—Dear Frau Grünewald—then imagine what that (unknown) person might like to hear about. After two or three weeks of writing, we send all the letters at once and enjoy imagining the post(wo)man walking up and down every path, kindly finishing our project for us.

Mysterious Letters starts as an individual experience (Why did I get this? Who are Michael and Lenka? What does this mean? etc.) Then, word spreads as people pop into the shop, chat to the hairdresser, or take their letter to the pub to read to the bartender. We know these things, because sometimes people get in touch to tell us. But, mostly, we like the not-knowing about the thousands of things that might have occurred when each letter arrived.

The first iteration of *Mysterious Letters* was funded by us and by Bill Drummond. After that, Kickstarter was invented (thank goodness), and we have since been funded through two successful campaigns with them, as well as institutions who've hosted the project, including FRAC LePlateau in Paris, Kunsthalle St. Gallen in Switzerland, and Simultanhalle in Germany. We plan to continue writing and sending letters until we've written to everyone in the world, or we get too old to hold a pen, whichever comes first.

***

I had my first Skype interview applying for a visiting artist position at Alfred University, in upstate New York. The panel asked me what special equipment I'd need. I got nervous, completely forgot what I did, and told them I'd only need a pencil. I'm fairly sure that's why I got the job.

I loved the experience of living in that tiny town. For the first time in my life, I was asked quite seriously if I know the Queen. I spent time meeting Amish people, visiting estate sales and local history museums, and exploring the university archives. I found out about a campus museum from the 1800s that had once housed a collection of hundreds of thousands of objects that have since been lost or stolen. I declared a town-wide amnesty for the missing objects and, when that didn't work, collected things that fitted the descriptions of the lost artifacts, and temporarily recreated part of the museum. In London, my focus had been earning enough money to sustain my life. Being in Alfred was just what I needed to redress the balance and reconnect with my own work. At the end of my time there, I met Seth, a ceramic artist and my future husband.

***

In December 2008, I flew home to London. That New Year's Eve, during a long-distance telephone conversation with Seth about what the future might hold for us, I had a vision. In my mind's eye, as clear as anything, I saw the word "Pittsburgh." It was spelled out in three-dimensional letters and looked like it had been hastily constructed by a carpenter who usually made circus signs. Purely based on this vision, we decided to move to Pittsburgh and start a life together. Seth had previously spent a couple of days in the city at a conference and remembered that it was hilly. I'd never been there; I only knew the name because a dear friend had grown up there. Nine months later, on 09/09/1999, I immigrated to America.

At first we had no friends, jobs, or income and were constantly lost. We got married a couple of months after we arrived and slowly found work. Seth worked as a carpenter on film sets, and then later on other people's homes. I did graphic design, adjunct teaching, office work, and various other odd jobs. After two years, we were lucky enough to find a house for $15,000 which was in terrible condition but that we could afford. Thanks to Seth's vision and more than a year of his (and my mum's, and several friends,) very hard work, we now live there, on a hill in the center of Pittsburgh. In 2011, our son Otto was born, and two years later, our daughter Early.

***

Coming from the UK, I was shocked to discover how little support there is for parents in the US. Expensive healthcare, no federal maternal or paternal leave, no subsidized childcare, no financial support. We were a long way from our families, and our financial future was unknown. My friend tells me that, in Denmark, a woman will put the number of children she has on her professional CV, as being a mother has such a high status. In my experience, it is more normal to try to hide from your professional world the fact that you have kids, or to at least pretend that it has no effect on you and that you can continue to work "despite" being a mother.

During my first pregnancy, Dan Byers, then curator at the Carnegie Museum of Art in Pittsburgh, asked me to be part of a group exhibition at the museum. Our baby was due a few weeks before the show opened, and I experienced, for the first time, the strongly opposing pulls of the roles of artist and mother. I knew that everything in my life would soon change dramatically but couldn't imagine how, or what, this would mean for my work.

I found myself compulsively knitting. First, I knitted a baby jumper, then baby trousers, then a baby hat. Later, I realized that I was knitting the negative space of the baby I was trying to imagine, attempting to summon him up in wool.

***

These frustrations and uncertainties became the piece *Maternity Leave*. I proposed to the Carnegie Museum that, for the three-month duration of the exhibition, I would officially be on maternity leave from my work as an artist. My space would be completely empty, except for a pedestal displaying a plastic baby monitor that would broadcast a live feed of the sound in our baby's bedroom, two miles down the road. Visitors would hear the cries, coos, and nursery rhymes that we sang to Otto in real time, inside the museum.

An essential component of the work was that the museum agreed to publicly pay me the exact equivalent of the "maternity allowance," a government-funded benefit that freelance women in the UK receive for up to 39 weeks, during pregnancy and the early weeks of motherhood. This payment from the museum was both an essential, practical support for our family and a public manifestation of its lack in the US.

The mixing up of my professional and personal worlds was new territory for me, and beautifully absurd situations arose from it. We had to install a sign on our door to warn visitors that anything they said would be broadcast in a museum. Friends texted me from the exhibition to say they could hear Otto crying, and to ask if he was okay. I went to the gallery to give an artist talk, with Otto strapped to me, and then realized that the piece didn't function because we weren't at home.

For the three months of the show, I had the quite pleasant feeling that perhaps a religious person might recognize, of being constantly seen and witnessed. Once the live feed was switched off, I remember suddenly feeling very alone in my daily mothering.

***

Becoming parents drastically changed the way that we were able to work. I looked after Otto most of the time and, when he was napping, would work a little bit. Seth worked in his ceramic studio in odd moments but spent most of his time working hard on other people's houses for our living, and then working on ours in the evenings and on weekends. We were exhausted and not sleeping and wishing to be closer to our families.

Previously, I'd traveled to artist residencies and exhibition opportunities, and I remembered the inspiration I'd felt when all the everyday things were new and interesting. Now that I was a parent, traveling was tricky, and the residencies I found couldn't accommodate artists with families. I wondered how I might instead apply the framework of an artist residency to the wild new world that was unfolding at home, one that I usually felt entirely too tired to notice.

I imagined what the perfect residency at this time of my life would look like. It would have money that would buy me time to work; it would have a quiet and private space, as well as materials budget, peers, mentors, and exposure. It would require no traveling and, most importantly, it would give me a new, objective viewpoint on this most subjective of experiences. It would be called "An Artist Residency in Motherhood."

> Artist residencies are usually designed to take artists physically and mentally away from the routines and responsibilities of their everyday lives. An Artist Residency in Motherhood is different. Situated inside the traditionally "inhospitable" environment of a family home, it reframes parenthood as a valuable site, rather than an invisible labor for exploration and artistic production.
>
> As an artist-in-residence-in-motherhood, I aim to embrace the fragmented mental focus, exhaustion, nap-length studio time, and countless distractions of parenthood (as well as the absurd poetry of time spent with young

> children) as my working materials and situation, rather than obstacles to be overcome.
>
> —excerpted from *An Artist Residency in Motherhood Manifesto*

To realize the residency, I applied for and was delighted to receive a $10,000 grant from the Pittsburgh Foundation/Heinz Endowments. I later received additional funding from the Sustainable Arts Foundation, an amazing grant for artist/parents. This institutional support provided visibility, validation, accountability, and the means for me to publicly explore dual roles of artist and mother, rather than be forced by circumstance to prioritize one over the other.

The structure of the residency was simple: It was a manifesto, business cards (normal-sized for me, tiny for Otto), a site to explore (motherhood), a website to share my work, mentors, improvements to my studio, money to buy materials, and three mornings a week childcare for Otto. I worked every moment I could, and posted the work I made to the website.

***

The most important thing about being an artist-in-residence-in-motherhood, for me, was understanding that I was not making work about motherhood, but out of it.

I kept a studio diary, where I described things that were not-just mothering and not-yet art: Otto nibbling a graham cracker into the letter "P," or the things I took in a frenzied panic out of his mouth. This process helped me identify the obstacles I was facing; in naming them, they became my material to work with. Many projects sprang out of passing curiosities voiced in these notes. Over the two-year course of the residency, I made 32 works, from a proposal to obstructively childproof an art museum to a video that attempted to measure the exact distance I could be from Otto before I was compelled to run after him.

Many people began writing to me about wanting to be an Artist-in-Residence-in-Motherhood themselves. I decided to offer the residency as a conceptual framework to anyone who wants to interpret it according to their own situation. I made a website, which describes the steps I took to set up the residency and where anyone can download a free "Residency Set-Up Kit." People can also apply to a grant for artist/parents, called the Red Thread, or even learn how to begin their own grant!

The Red Thread was invented by writer Amy Krouse Rosenthal after a conversation we had about the difficulties mothers face in sustaining their creative practices. Amy offered to give me a check for $999 that I could use to sustain my creative work in whatever way I needed, just not to buy diapers. By accepting this gift that we called the "Red Thread," I agreed to pass the same amount of money along to another woman as soon as I was able. This could be weeks, months, or years later. When the time comes, the artist/mother who received the Red Thread will pass it along to someone else, and so on, and so on.

A Red Thread can be begun by anyone, and each separate thread continues indefinitely along its own timeline. Every time I'm invited to exhibit work from the Artist Residency in Motherhood, I invite the host institution to contribute to a fund to create a new Red Thread. I intend to start as many strands as possible.

***

Currently, our kids are in preschool for five mornings (Otto) and three mornings (Early) each week during the school semester. Seth is getting closer to one of his dreams of building his own small houses and is making extraordinary ceramic work in his studio. I look after Otto and Early most of the time, teach occasionally at Carnegie Mellon University, and work in my studio as much as possible. I have a small studio in the attic and a second beautiful studio down the street, inside an empty house owned by friends. I sell my work through my website, Instagram, and exhibitions. I make drawings using an old Smith-Corona typewriter, which I recently showed at testsite, Austin, curated by Veronica Roberts. I'm currently artist-in-residence at the Fabric Workshop and Museum in Philadelphia and am collaborating with artist Jon Rubin on a project in New York City.

Since the kids were little, Seth and I have had a weekend routine we call the McDowell Days. Saturday is Seth's McDowell

Day; Sunday is mine. On McDowell Day, we have no family responsibilities and can work all day and night if we want to. The name comes from hearing about the McDowell Colony, in which you get to make work in a cabin in the woods and someone leaves a basket of food at your door.

I run regularly at 5:30 am, the only time I can leave the house each day without thinking about who is looking after the kids. I meet an artist friend, Jenn Myers, each week at naptime. We write studio to-do lists and share them, which is inspiring and helps me focus on the things I've done, as well as all the things I haven't. And I keep a list of all the projects I will do, one day, when I have time. It's quite long.

***

It strikes me, writing this essay, that my story makes much more sense to me in retrospect than it ever did living it forwards. I will try to remember this in the future.

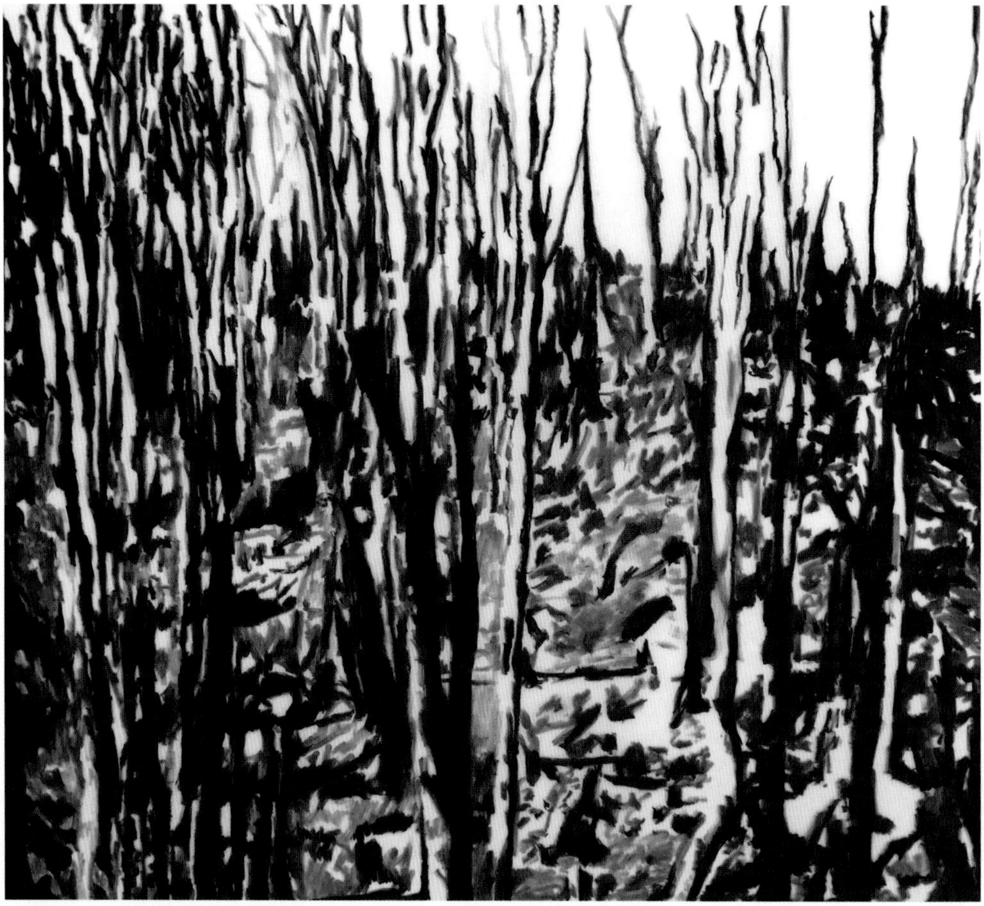

I got into art in 1987, during a year off from college. I was spending a lot of time in art museums and found much of the contemporary work puzzling. I remember one piece, in particular: *Brandt/Haffner* by Bertrand Lavier. It was just a small refrigerator standing on a safe. I had no idea why it was art, but I liked it. It seemed to hold a secret. It seemed to represent a kind of freedom.

So, I started making stuff. I took pictures, cut up the prints, and taped them back together. I shot video. I painted a terrible self-portrait on a mirror. I drew my left hand. I was hooked. When I returned to college, I changed my major to art and studied drawing, painting, silkscreen, photography, film and video, art history and theory.

In grad school at University of California San Diego (UCSD), my work shifted from painting and video to new media projects and participatory events. The most ambitious of these happenings, *Carpark*, was a collaboration with Nina Katchadourian and Steven Matheson. Over the course of a day in 1994, we sorted thousands of cars by color into the parking lots surrounding a community college, forming a giant color wheel on the suburban landscape. The college president got behind the project when he realized the colors would be visible from the air and he could take photojournalists over the campus in his private plane. We assembled a team of 50 volunteer "parking

Mark Tribe
Soylent Green 1
17"x19"
Charcoal on drafting film
2016
Courtesy of the artist

coordinators" and transformed the school into a temporary experiment in social aesthetics. That same year, I worked with a group of grad students on a complex virtual reality project. I had been monkeying around with the internet and decided to make a website for the project. The web was very new at that time (in 1994, there were fewer than 3,000 websites), and hardly anybody knew what it was, but I loved the idea that I could create a page and... zap! Anyone, anywhere in the world, could access it. I was sure that, within a few years, everyone would be using the web.

In my last year at UCSD, I got to know a visiting artist from Russia by the name of Gia Rigvava, and I applied for an ArtsLink grant to Moscow to collaborate with him. I also applied to a residency program in Berlin. The Berlin Wall had fallen a few years earlier, and the art world there was emerging from decades of isolation and starting to take off. I had visited my friend Olaf Westphalen there the previous summer and loved the city's dark energy. I got the grant to go to Russia, but I wasn't selected for the residency. I decided to move to Berlin anyway. I arrived in the spring of 1995, sublet Olav's apartment, and went on to Moscow a few weeks later. I slept on the Russian artist's couch for a month, and we produced a three-channel video installation at the Guelman Gallery, called *Bad Humor,* in which we told jokes through a simultaneous translator.

Then I returned to Berlin, lived off of savings for the summer, went to museums and galleries, and spent a lot of time online, trying to figure out how to make art on the web. I also started organizing participatory art events. I did one at a former beauty salon turned bar/art venue, called *Friseur*, and another at the Akademie der Künste. In retrospect, I was making what would later be referred to as relational art. But I was much more excited by the idea of the internet as a space for art making.

I went to an opening at Galerie Eigen + Art and met Eva Grubinger, an Austrian artist who was showing there and who, like me, was interested in new media. She later started C@C – Computer Aided Curating, the first online gallery for net-based art, and exhibited my first net art project, *Traces of a Constructed City*.

I was leaving a techno club one night, probably around 3 or 4 am, and came across a large metal cart—like a shopping cart on steroids. It was a thing of beauty, with enormous casters and great, chrome-plated racks, and I just couldn't leave it there. So, I start pushing it down the sidewalk on this dark, desolate street, and a guy walks up and immediately offers to help me get it home. Turns out, he's Erik Hobijn, an artist from Holland, and he tells me about his latest project—a giant, fire-breathing musical instrument called the Dante Organ—and how he worked with Mark Pauline of Survival Research Labs in San Francisco, who made incredible art machines out of found materials that he referred to as "obtanium," and... I realized that Erik should have the cart. So, we pushed it back to his studio, a few blocks away, and became fast friends.

A few weeks later, Erik invited me to drive with him and a few friends down to Ars Electronica, a media art festival in Linz, Austria. They were leaving right away, so I threw my laptop and a couple changes of clothes in a bag and jumped in his van. At Ars, I got my first look at the international art and technology scene. It was growing rapidly, with an influx of younger artists from varied backgrounds, and becoming less specialized and less isolated. I also met a young artist who helped me get a day job making web sites at a hip design firm, called Pixelpark, back in Berlin.

I went to Dutch Electronic Art Festival (DEAF, of course) in Rotterdam and saw many of the same people that had made the pilgrimage to Linz a few months earlier. At a panel on web design, the speakers recounted how their websites allowed visitors to participate by posting comments or, in one case, by building creatures in an artificial life system, and had been amazed how groups of people had formed around them. I had always thought of community as a local thing, but these web-based communities were defined by affinity rather than geography. It occurred to me that we—the globally dispersed but rapidly growing cohort of new media artists, curators, critics, scholars, arts administrators, and students—were an online community waiting to happen.

Over the next few weeks, I became obsessed with the idea of starting an online community for new media artists—an accessible and inclusive forum where we could exchange ideas and develop a critical framework for understanding the things we were making. I was turned off by the exclusiveness of galleries, museums, and mainstream art magazines, and wanted to create a more egalitarian space. I wanted to invert the hierarchies of the art world and, in doing so, to create a comprehensive online resource for the emerging field of new media art. I had always had a latent entrepreneurial impulse, a drive to start an enterprise of some kind. And I was not alone in believing that we were on the brink of tremendous changes, and that the internet was somehow enmeshed in those changes: simultaneously a catalyst of transformation and a symptom of larger historical forces. Artists are sensitive creatures; like animals, we can smell the storm before it hits.

At this point, I was sharing a coal-heated studio in Kreutzberg with my friend Olav. One chilly morning, I was sitting at my desk, shivering while the coal oven was warming up, and turned to one of the few books I'd taken with me from San Diego: *A Thousand Plateaus* by Gilles Deleuze and Felix Guattari. I flipped to the index, and my eyes landed on "rhizome," a botanical term for a kind of horizontal root that extends underground and sends up shoots. Deleuze and Guattari use the word as a metaphor for horizontally distributed, nonhierarchical networks. "Rhizome" seemed like the perfect name for a grassroots online community and, crucially, the internet domain name was still available.

I went home for the holidays and talked things over with my parents. My mother was an educational administrator who had also worked in politics, and my father was a law professor. They had paid my way through college, and I had gotten a full ride at UCSD, so I didn't have any student debt. My plan had been to work day jobs and make art, maybe one day to teach. Now, I wanted to quit my day job and put my art work on hold, so I could devote all my time to starting a website for artists. This was late 1995, and internet startups were still all but unheard of. Was I crazy? My parents didn't seem to think so, and they agreed to loan me some money, so I could get Rhizome off the ground. I went to a bookstore, bought a book for first-time entrepreneurs, and headed back to Berlin to start working on a business plan.

I had an MFA, not an MBA, and didn't know the first thing about starting a business, so I called a friend who was working at a thriving New York web agency and had started a not-so-successful nonprofit to distribute art films. He convinced me that I would be better able to raise money and attract great people if Rhizome were a dot-com, rather than a dot-org, and if it were based in New York. I finished the business plan and asked a friend, the brilliant designer Markus Weisbeck, to design the website. Another friend, Walter van der Cruijsen, agreed to host an email discussion list for free at his media lab in Amsterdam. In those days, email discussion lists, often called listservs, were one of the main platforms for online discussion. I had been collecting email addresses for a couple of years and, on April 1, 1996, I launched Rhizome by inviting everybody I knew to go to the website and subscribe to the email list. At first, I had to pester my friends to post, but pretty quickly the discussion started to take on its own momentum. The idea was to use the email list to feed content into a database that could be searched via the website, using names and keywords. I thought of it as *Artforum* meets AltaVista (the pre-Google search engine), a meritocratic space where anybody who was into new media art could join the conversation and tell the world about their work. A few weeks later, I moved to New York City to raise money and build a team.

It was a heady time in "Silicon Alley." It seemed like everyone I met was working on an internet startup. I met a Jamaican real estate developer who gave me free office space in exchange for helping him map all the dot-coms in the city, and started chasing after investors. I partnered with a guy who had just graduated from business school, and together we presented my business plan at a venture capital event where entrepreneurs pitched their ideas to potential investors. During a "breakout session," we met a couple of investment bankers who saw Rhizome as a way of building a new kind of stock photo agency: instead of supplying images, the new media artists in our network would provide gif animations and Java applets. We would store these in an online database and license them out to web designers, so they wouldn't have to make them themselves. We rewrote the business plan, created a new entity called StockObjects, and quickly the investors started to bite.

The next seven years were a wild ride. Rhizome grew into a thriving online community, complete with trolls, idealists, critics, and gadflies. In 1998, it became clear that the Rhizome artists weren't really contributing to StockObjects, so we spun it off as a nonprofit, and I went with it. I was much happier as director of a nonprofit arts organization than I was as CEO of a for-profit company. Within a few months of going nonprofit, Rhizome was awarded major grants from the Rockefeller Foundation and the National Endowment for the Arts. We also raised money from our far-flung community and were one of the first nonprofits to accept donations online. In 1999, we introduced several new programs, including an archive of new media art (now the largest of its kind) and an event series at The Kitchen. When the dot-com bubble burst in 2000, StockObjects went out of business. As the founder, I still had the largest equity stake, so I wound up holding the bag and went through the painful process of shutting down a company.

Rhizome continued to grow, but it was often a struggle, particularly financially. As a nonprofit organization, we were overly dependent on foundation grants and came close to running out of money several times. Twice we went into temporary hibernation, which meant keeping the website going while working from home. I remained deeply committed to Rhizome, and had come to think of it as a kind of social sculpture, and thus as a kind of artistic practice, but most of the work came down to fundraising and administration. It didn't really feel like making art. I was increasingly eager to step away but wasn't confident that Rhizome could survive a leadership transition. I had been trying for a few years to find an institutional partner, such as university or art museum, to provide Rhizome with greater stability. David Ross, who had directed the Whitney Museum and SFMOMA and who served on Rhizome's board, introduced me to Lisa Phillips, Director of the New Museum. Lisa agreed to host Rhizome as a kind of organization-in-residence. The deal was done in 2002, and I stepped down as Director of Rhizome. Our longtime Editor, Rachel Greene, took my place, and I joined the New Museum's board of trustees. Lisa and a number of New Museum trustees joined the Rhizome board, and the partnership has gone remarkably smoothly ever since.

I had announced my plans to step down a year earlier and started looking for teaching jobs. In 2003, I was able to transition directly from Rhizome to Columbia University's School of the Arts, where I directed the Digital Media Center, taught interdisciplinary graduate courses, and developed a proposal for a new MFA program in art and technology. That summer, I got married.

My job at Columbia involved a lot of administrative work, strategic planning, and hardball academic politics. It was interesting, but I was finding it hard to get my mojo back as an artist, so after about a year, I started looking for a regular faculty position that would allow me to focus on teaching and making art. My options were limited, geographically, because my wife was working as a magazine editor in New York. We also had a young daughter, so suddenly every moment was doubly precious.

In 2005, I was hired as an assistant professor at Brown University. I managed to squeeze my teaching schedule into three days a week and, for the next eight years, shuttled back and forth from New York to Providence. Splitting my life between two cities was hectic, but it had the advantage of providing a strong separation between my teaching job and my art work.

A curator with whom I'd crossed paths over the year invited me to co-write a book on new media art for Taschen. I was reluctant, because I was just getting back into to making art, but figured that, between the two of us, it would be doable. Then, my friend dropped out of the project, so I asked Reena Jana, an experienced journalist who'd written a column for Rhizome, to co-author the book with me. We wrote it over the summer, while I was between jobs, meeting every day at Columbia's Butler library. *New Media Art* has since been translated into several languages and appears on many syllabi. One thing I learned from the experience is that I'd definitely rather make art than write books.

By 2006, ten years after starting Rhizome, I had found my stride again as an artist and started work on *The Port Huron*

Project, a series of reenactments of Vietnam-era protest speeches. I didn't realize it at the time, but by staging participatory events in public spaces, I had, in a way, circled back to where I had started, before I got interested in new media. In 2008, my wife got pregnant again, developed complications, and had to spend five weeks in the hospital. Our daughter was born perfectly healthy, but my wife got very sick and eventually had to quit her magazine job. We finally figured out that our apartment was full of toxic black mold, had it removed, and gradually she started to get better. That was a very hard year.

The Port Huron Project got a lot of attention, and I rolled right into the next project, *The Dystopia Files*, an archive of video clips depicting interactions between police and protesters. Unfortunately, my colleagues at Brown weren't happy with the direction my work had taken: they had hired me to fill a position in digital art, and my new work wasn't particularly digital. Despite the fact that I was exhibiting internationally, had gotten grants from Creative Capital and NYFA, and published two books and numerous articles, I was denied tenure and had to go back on the job market again. It was a devastating rejection. I tried to remind myself that it was just a day job, but my wife was writing freelance, and we had two children, so I really needed a full-time position with health insurance.

Meanwhile, I continued to make art. In 2010, I collaborated with Chelsea Knight on *Posse Comitatus*, in which we filmed the training exercises of right-wing militia groups and translated them, with the help of choreographers, into dance. While I was running around in the woods filming guys in camouflage outfits as they fired automatic weapons, I developed an interest in landscape which led to two bodies of work: landscape videos shot on militia training grounds and landscape photographs shot in military video games.

Thanks in large part to an introduction made by David Ross, I was offered a job as Chair of the MFA Fine Arts Department at School of Visual Arts (SVA). In 2013, I replaced the founding chair, who had started the program some 30 years earlier. I spent my first year as chair listening and learning. In my second year, I started to make changes. One of my main goals is to make the program more diverse, both artistically and culturally. I also rewrote the curriculum to give students more flexibility, rethought our online presence, and made countless other changes. I'm now in my third year at SVA and am trying to strike a balance between my job and my art work, which, thankfully, is demanding more time and energy than ever as ideas for new projects, and opportunities to show them, come with increasing frequency.

This year, I am wrapping up a two-year project with the Coleman Center for the Arts that involves working with residents of York, Alabama to paint storefronts on their small, rural town's blighted main street. I've also started to draw again, for the first time in about 20 years: tracing landscapes from eco-disaster films. I'm interested in the idea of nature, and what counts as wilderness in a time when everything, even in the most remote places, is changing as a result of human activity. I recently began work on a new project in which I'm using ultra-high-definition video to record and preserve rapidly changing landscapes. I see myself working on this for several years.

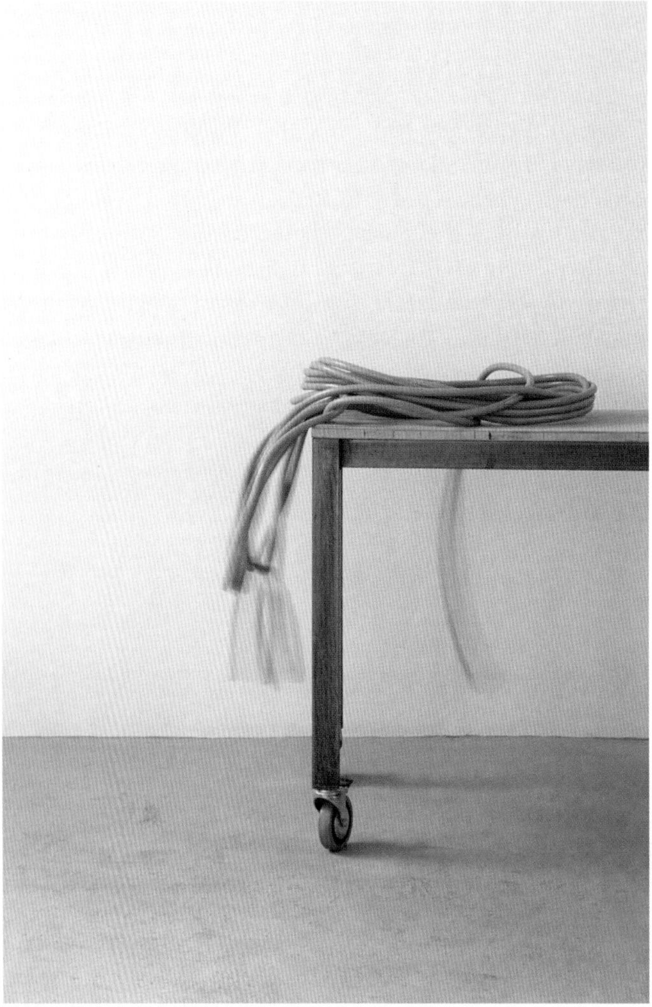

In my life, I have been a book trader, architect, sculptor, educator, and curator, and taken a journey through training and education. Different careers have connected—each part shaped who I am right now.

Raised in West Berlin, Germany to an English mother and an Eastern German, Italian-rooted father, I never felt that German myself. It was unusual, in those times in Europe, to come from a mixed national background, as both wars had left deep scars. Missing clear roots, I was free to look around, to dream myself into other places, another life.

My parents spoke English when they shared grown-up conversation, not wanting to be understood. Filling the gaps, I read the signs, gestures, intonation, and made up the missing words. Living in a foreign country, my mother did not always understand what was going on between people—their words, their interactions—especially, the rough Berlin humor left her puzzled, and that confusion affected me. Observing was an extremely important aspect for me, then a shy introverted girl. To perceive and recognize all these fine lines between what was going on among people made me feel safer, as I learned to comprehend a situation and another person.

My father was a painter who pointed us towards the visual world, with open senses. The one aspect he could share best was his enthusiasm about art—the visual, details and wonder, the process of making.

Martina Geccelli
Table-edge green hose
120cmx80cm
C-print
2012
Courtesy of the artist

Losing my mother during my teenage years, I matured rapidly. Life got tougher, less protected. At the age of 17, I moved out of my home and started an apprenticeship as a bookseller (which, in Germany, is considered a trained profession). This training offered me a long-term, secure income. In 1981, I took the step and went back to school into adult education (college) in order to gain the qualification for university entry. After two-and-a-half years in college, and working part-time as a bookseller, I applied for an architectural course at art school in Berlin.

During that time, I met my future mentor, the architect/artist Stefan Wewerka. His inquisitive and fearless approach towards creative expression was contagious. The study of architecture, for me, came out of a long cherished interest. It was while studying architecture that I fell for art. It was rather difficult to change careers, at first, working parallel on developing art projects and studying architecture. Working with that conflict, I finally was able, when joy and intense satisfaction in the making became persistent, to make decisions to pursue professional art as a career. I decided to leave Berlin to explore my curiosities.

First, I went to London, where I worked briefly for the architects Alison and Peter Smithson, followed by Trevor Horne Architects. While in London, I decided to move to Cologne in order to apply for art school at the Kunstakademie Düsseldorf, where I then studied sculpture.

Living in Cologne, I was studying and working at the same time. I could financially fall back to my old profession as a book trader and earn enough money for living. The trick was to keep my fixed costs low. That was foremost, concerning rent for home and studio, plus the bills. One learns skills, like home cooking with friends on a low, but tasty budget. Always having enjoyed having nice things, I found elegant secondhand clothes, collected designer items. I started sewing for myself, became quite self-sufficient—a hunter/gatherer.

Another helpful aspect was, way before Airbnb, when leaving town for a longer period, I would sublet my flat; so, paying rent did not become an issue. Of course, there were setbacks, but my debts never grew into the impossible.

Financing this lifestyle was manageable, as long as I got plenty of part-time work. Working long hours, at times, meant in exchange I could travel, or work in my studio undisturbed. At times, I could feel the financial strain. But I always felt lucky that I had professions to fall back on to earn a living. At times, that living was a bit improvised and not always reliable, but the jobs were good. Financial insecurity troubled me, but never to the degree that I gave up my artwork. Working like this was much better than being locked into an unloved job. I knew that, as I had experienced it previously.

My frequent traveling started when I fell in love with a man in Austria during a student exchange, followed by an Erasmus fellowship later. Arriving in a new country or new town, I explored the place with the camera. Taking photos, I first did not define as my "work"—photography just allowed me to observe the otherness of life—to hold on to it, and to a fresh view into things: architecture, streets, people, their marks left behind.

While in Austria, in 1994 to '95, I was working as a tutor at the Hochschule für Gestaltung, in Linz. I enjoyed working in education, as it did not remove me too far from my actual work, my sculpture. I liked working with young people, discussing art in general. Being in Austria opened new aspects of working as an artist, that there were different approaches.

During that time in Austria, I appreciated having a steady income and security. It came with a price, though: a full-time job! I felt locked in a catch-22 situation. There was not enough time for my own work, which was finally becoming established, and I wanted to focus more on that. During that time, I took part in two group shows in Linz, and a gallery in Muenster was interested in showing my work. In 1994, I worked in situ at the Offenes Kulturhaus in Linz, in order to work on a large sculpture, which was later presented in the gallery space.

How could I have it all? The inner tumult between safety, pension, living standard, and the freedom to experiment doing my artwork was an ongoing battle. The consequence was that I gave up my full-time job; I did not see myself living for long in a provincial town in Austria regardless. Leaving Linz, I returned to Cologne (Germany), where I had lived before. I was lucky to reestablish my old connections and continued working for an architectural practice part-time. Back to the juggling of time, work, and balancing my bank account, I worked flexible hours, more or less following the demands of either my bosses, or my bank account's needs. At times, one or the other became too much—the working time or experiencing an overdraft in my bank account. It wasn't ideal, as often I found myself trapped by anxieties caused by financial instability.

Added to the pressure, to make up for the stress, was my constant need to make *good* artwork—to develop my practice, to exhibit my work, to become successful. Somehow.

In 1996 came a year of a luxurious studio residency. My then gallery in Muenster, Galerie Stefan Rasche, recommended that I apply for a studio residency nearby, sponsored by the local government of North Rhine-Westphalia. This residency offers visual artists and writers an opportunity to live and work for up to a year in a rural setting outside Muenster. It was the first time since I was 17 that I did not need to work for my living.

Each artist had a studio cum living place within two old farmhouses. There were communal spaces for gatherings, workshops, and readings. Staying in the countryside, I enjoyed my free time. I felt relaxed, supported; I was focused, less stressed and, from this experience, I made new professional contacts. During that time I visited my boyfriend in London, back and forth, and we also travelled together to other cities and countries. Towards the end of the residency, in 1996, I decided to move to London. Just as my art career seemed to move forward, I decided again to interrupt that path in order to look for adventure—the evader. My escape was England, London, a very different cup of tea.

Arriving in London in 1997, I experienced difficulty getting part-time work in architecture. By then, I was 40 years old, which made architectural practices skeptical of my fees. Students were easily available and fully committed versus a person my age. Book trading is not a trained profession in the UK, and one earns less than is necessary to get by. Life was (and still is) expensive in London! For the first time in my life, I had to rely on my partner to support me. That continued, as we had a child soon after I moved to London, and then in 1998, we moved to the United States. My husband, who is a structural engineer, had the opportunity to open a new branch of his London office in New York City, working on larger-scale architectural projects.

That was an exciting step, as I knew and liked New York from earlier trips to the city. But it was very different from what I'd hoped for—due to being a new mum, my own professional opportunities had shrunk. I was needed somewhere else. In New York, all was new again—new country, new mum, new home. In the US, I was not eligible to receive income for my work.

Before I had moved to London, my approach to photography had changed. It grew to become a central part of my work. When traveling around Europe and the US, I was roaming urban areas, into unknown places, observing through the camera lens what situations I found. In documenting things, I could approach the new, the unknown.

While we were living in the US, my husband was invited to teach at several universities. We traveled to different cities in America, where I managed to step out briefly from my family life to explore various towns with my camera. Photography is how I read my work, me being the observer—from outside in, and out again. In observation and translation, one walks between the factual and the actual. It continues to be the theme of my work.

With a baby on board, my gender role kicked in, which was not something I'd ever planned for. It confused me; it angered me, but it also gave me new opportunities. Living in New York was, at most times, financially stable, as my husband's practice secured our income well. Staying stubborn, I did the housekeeping, child rearing, endless playground visits, and, at the same time, continued as much as possible with my own work. I enjoyed the time spent with my son. It is that other wonder—it's love, responsibility, dependency, and joy. As a working mother, one has to be well organized; routine is an important aspect, too. And it helped me get back to my artwork more quickly.

During year two in New York, in 2000, I received a studio residency through the Lower Manhattan Cultural Council (LMCC), which did me good and brought me closer to my own work again. New artist friends also helped me not to feel too isolated. My residency was in the World Trade Center–Tower One. I'd applied with a revised concept of my urban walks. I received access to emptied office spaces where tenants had left the space—that set the scene. *Suites*, my series on emptied office spaces, reflects the transformation of space when the people have left, leaving traces behind.

My work in *Suites* looks into the economic abyss of the regular, quick changeover in the financial world. Companies come and go—at times, leaving chaos behind. But it became different after 9/11. *Suites* was made during 2000 but by September 2001, the reading of the work had changed. By then, I had already left New York. My husband stayed on and experienced the changes, the outcry of patriotism which took over the atmosphere in the city. This made me feel distant; as a German, I've always felt skeptical and highly suspicious of patriotic outbreaks.

Returning to London for the summer in 2001, I felt lucky to have escaped that difficult time.

Back in London, I decided to receive some training in education. In the UK, the law was changing so that, in order to work in education, whether teaching in a school or university, one needed a certificate. To be able to get a regular income, I hoped to work in foundation-level studies at an art school. So, I went back to university to do a postgraduate degree in teaching art and design (PGCE). After my degree, I worked for a big educational organization. The educational work was ideal, as it was flexible. Unfortunately, with the government change in 2011, I lost my job. At times, I also felt torn between working at a job, parenting, and making art. As I could not find similar, flexible work again, I was once more relying mostly on my husband's income. That still is awkward for me, but I also see that I have put in work with my family. Me being there at all times gave my partner the freedom to focus on his own career. He could do all the traveling necessary for his work. Good or bad, that is where we were. Neither of us was planning for this.

Once one is over 50, it is harder to get interesting jobs. Enjoying organizing my days around my artwork and home tasks, I felt energized. I do not like to sell myself as endlessly young and overly dynamic. I feel I am experienced, interested, independent, lively, and not very young anymore. Something completely new grew out of that realization. The free time I gained opened up new opportunities. With my experience and interest in a particular art scene, I felt isolated in England. My specific interest focused on painting, sculpture, and photography of a non-representative nature of the sort that grew out of modernism and is non-narrative. Less interested in the more typical British approach favoring illustrative, narrative works, I was aiming to show artists who would meet my interests. What was missing in my life were professional contacts, likeminded professionals. So far, I had not found enough colleagues in London who were working in fields related to my work.

Knowing that it is always better to give, to offer, than to be on the expecting, receiving end, I became proactive. Lucky to have found a larger new studio space for myself, in 2013, I started within my studio an artist-led project space in North London, called RAUMX. RAUMX refers to the German word "Raum," that denotes both a room and a space at the same time. The letter X represents the unknown, the interchangeable factor. I have chosen the German word Raum, also, because for me it refers to a gap between what is on view in London and a broader European, modern outlook, inviting different points of views through exhibitions, which are not often on view.

Adding an art space to the vivid London art scene also demanded that I set something additional, or particular, against (or in contrast to) the typical gallery space. The big gallery giants, arriving from Europe or the US, flood the London market with big names. They make the market, but I feel they do not work on ideas or discussion, the livelihood of artists; nor are they interested in progress. Already established with their "stable" artists, these larger galleries simply try to gain more and more market presence. There are the big names with strong artists, no question, but it's also a big bluff. Their focus is on the trendy works, the '"fashion" and short-lived fireworks, which is something I am not interested in. I am interested in stimulating conversation—making an idea, an art work, the center of attention rather than its market value as an investment. Here I take an idealistic position: One can ask why, how, and why not? RAUMX should offer a space to look, think, and communicate outside the market. It should be a place that gives something to think about and look at and experience.

I was confident that, by stepping into this gap, I was supporting important artists and their art works. The purpose of RAUMX was and is to revive a discussion, to stir up our recently common understanding of what success means to an artist, as in making lots of money and having market presence. We all have to juggle in between, to make ends meet and survive. But an artist's life is also about quality, experience, and sharing. I look at success as an offering of serious work, strong ideas, sensual experiences. And that is what I could offer with RAUMX.

My intention for RAUMX was to open a space and give room for presenting works by other artists, ideas, and different work approaches than mine. In a bright room of my studio, I created a neutral exhibition space. There I have the freedom to show works of artists I am personally interested in. RAUMX, as a space, is multifunctional: it is a studio space for me and for artists in residence, and it is an exhibition space. At times, I need to rent out the studio space in order to fill the studio account again. I finance RAUMX myself: it is run on a tough, next-to-zero budget. Occasionally, I borrow some money from our family account. Financing this endeavor still needs sorting, and some sponsoring organized.

Knowing many artist-colleagues whose work I found interesting, I started contacting some of them to show work. Through word of mouth, RAUMX became quickly known, but without attracting the masses, as works shown here have been specialized, covering a small but fine area of non-representative art. Some invited artists also came to stay and work in situ for a while; it was exciting to meet new colleagues and see their work. And I establish more contacts all the time, either as people approach me or through new and old acquaintances. It is a snowball effect: through activities, one meets new people, which leads to new activities and contacts, which is followed by exchanging ideas.

As it is not the concept of RAUMX to have me be the sole curator, in 2015, I invited British painter Erin Lawlor to curate a painting show with me. In the painting show, *Suchness*, we were both interested in inviting international artists—American, Dutch, German, and British. This way, we could see the program as both inclusive and international. The principle continues, and showing mostly established artists with an international outlook remains important. Each invited artist brings new ideas, contacts, and perspectives.

As in my own practice, I am interested in presenting positions where the work itself is non-representational, not illustrative; rather, it stands for itself and asks the viewer to engage in the process of making, to extend one's sensual and spatial experiences. Having shown mainly painters so far, I will extend in 2016 into more sculpture and photography. Meanwhile, a small group of likeminded people has been established around the RAUMX project, who often enjoy coming to shows and dinner events.

The concept of RAUMX relies on an intimate setting, where people come, see, and talk, and exchange views with one another. Each show includes a professional dinner held on the premises. Through this process, one creates an atmosphere of discussion, new connections are established, and working relationships can develop into new ways of presenting art.

Being a curator and a colleague to other artists brings a completely new aspect to my own work. Curating works, I am asked to engage more deeply into someone else's vision. Through looking and talking, I experience more intensely what each work might ask for. There's a wholeness in these working processes that I can relate to my own work and use to approach freshly some ongoing questions. I feel freed to experiment with new art practices again, be they sculpture or works on paper.

Recently, I read a quote from a colleague stating that every artist should run a project space at some point in their life. That's because art is meant for the public. Art should be out there, and not only "curated" by the big galleries, by the market. Diverse positions should be visible, out in the open, to been seen and enjoyed. The market is and should be secondary. Interested as I am in contributing my personal view of artists work to the London art scene, I also like to add to the versatility of this city. Financially, running the space is like a pot with a hole. But so what? We are prepared to try to stuff the hole as long as it makes sense to keep the project going. RAUMX artists share most of the costs arising for each show.

I am glad I started this project. It helped me get out of my professional isolation. Still, I am cautious, not extravagant;

invited artists know the space's financial limitations, and that artists and curator alike have to work intensely together in order to reach the right audience. It works—and it works happily. I've learned a lot about running an art space, about the different work approaches of colleagues. Due to my position as a curator and initiator, I am now also enjoying conversations and collaborations with our invited artists.

RAUMX is asking for a fresh view into familiar aspects of art-making and presentation. Revision and experimentation will stay an essential part of the project. In making new contacts, the project space will continue to develop and extend my views and perspectives. In the long run, I am sure through these continued exchanges, the project will fertilize my own work and give me new opportunities as well. In fact, some are up on the horizon right now.

MATTHEW DELEGET

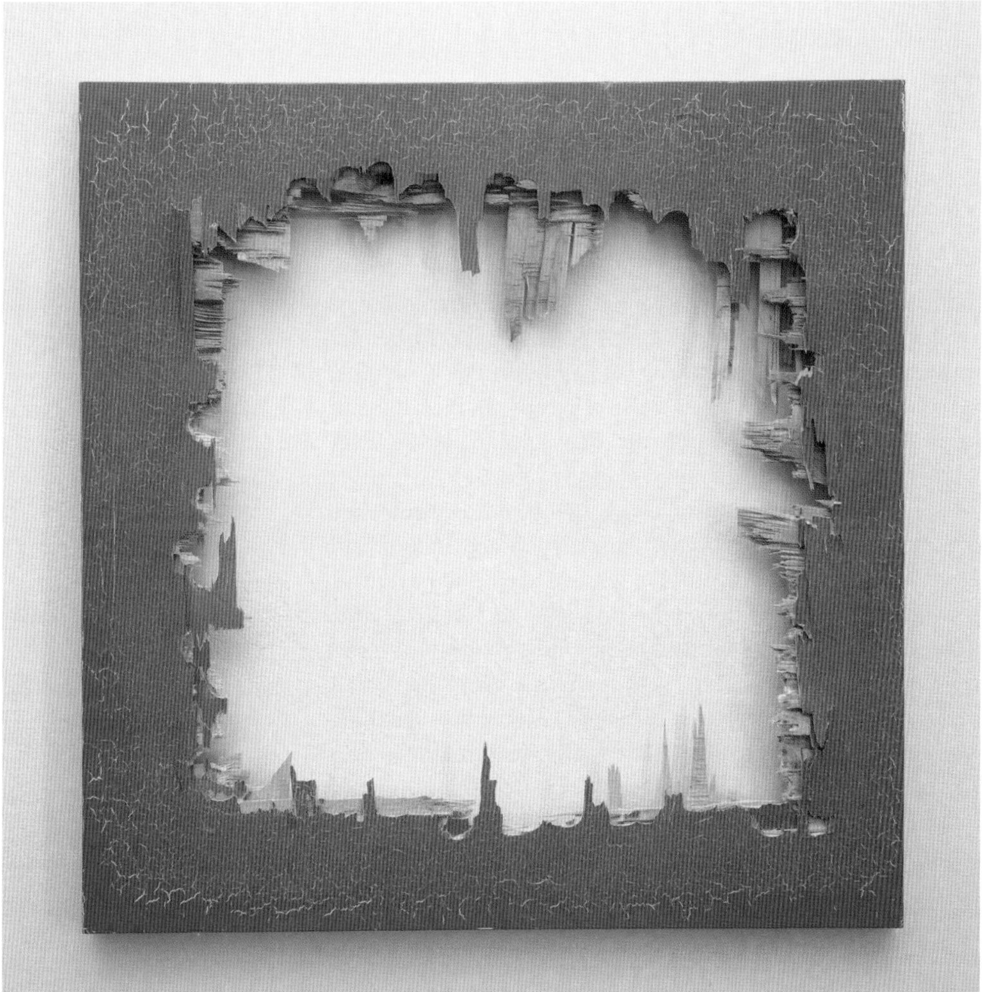

On March 5, 2009, my son Mateo was born. Aside from the day, at age seven, when I learned from my parents they were getting divorced, my son's birth was the single biggest day in my life, including in my career as an artist. It clearly marked the end of the first chapter of my career and the beginning of the roller coaster ride I currently find myself on.

I grew up in Highland, Indiana, a suburb on the south side of Chicago. In 1994, I moved to Brooklyn at age 22 to attend graduate school at Pratt Institute, where I spent the next three years completing an MFA in Painting and an MS in Theory, Criticism and History of Art, Design and Architecture. I did the degrees at the same time. I really didn't see any distinction between these two disciplines. In order to contribute anything at all to the artistic discourse, I knew I needed to have a deep understanding of the work and ideas that preceded me. At Pratt, I also met my amazing wife and life collaborator, artist Rossana Martinez. She was literally the girl next door and lived in the apartment adjacent to mine in the graduate dorms. She arrived at Pratt a year earlier from Puerto Rico to study sculpture and printmaking. I can't stress strongly enough how important Rossana has been and continues to be to me in literally every facet of my life. I must admit that it was absolutely love at first sight, and we moved in together almost immediately. We've collaborated on every aspect of our lives ever since. We see each other as partners and contribute to our household equally, both

Matthew Deleget
High Value Target
2014
Fluorescent orange enamel spray paint on wooden panel
24"x24"
Courtesy of the artist

in terms of housework and financial responsibility. This is a given for us, as we rely heavily on each other's contributions.

Rossana and I have both had regular jobs, in one capacity or another, since we were teenagers. This has included part-time, then full-time, and, for me, freelance work, ideally with a least a foothold in the arts or education fields. Although we do sell our artwork—in some years more work, in others less—we never expected our studio work to provide our livelihood. Yes, of course, that would be amazing. But due to the nature of the work we make (reductive, conceptual abstraction), it's just not realistic. After graduating from Pratt in 1997, I landed my first full-time job in the arts at the New York Foundation for the Arts (NYFA). I arrived there kind of through the back door. A friend of mine, artist Wendy Allen, asked me to fill in for her while she took maternity leave with her first daughter. I originally met Wendy working at Artnet, where I had worked part-time during graduate school as a researcher on their nascent auctions database (the first of its kind). After Wendy's time off from NYFA ended, she decided not to return to her job, and thus began my 12-year stint as a nonprofit arts administrator.

My starting salary at NYFA was $28,000, which was extremely modest, especially given the expense of living and working in New York City (NYC), but it didn't deter me. The job included other excellent benefits, such as health and dental insurance. More importantly, it was flexible and gave me a significant amount of time off, which I used to do my studio work. My tenure at NYFA, in retrospect, provided me with a once-in-a-lifetime education about sustaining my life as an artist in NYC. I also had the opportunity to work directly with two pioneering arts mentors, Ted Berger and Penelope Dannenberg, and to meet some of my now closest friends and colleagues in the art world.

My first job at NYFA was running their Visual Artist Information Hotline, a free live telephone service providing professional development and information resources to artists nationwide. During my first two-plus years, I spoke with at least 10,000 visual artists by phone and, later, email from all over the country. I took calls from every conceivable kind of visual artist in every conceivable kind of situation. My job was to research, identify, and advise them on everything from grants to health insurance to natural disaster relief. You name it, I responded to it and in real time. My job required me to be knowledgeable to at least some degree about everything.

After developing the hotline, I was promoted and charged with conceiving, building, and directing NYFA's new information and research department. This broadly encompassed all of the foundation's print, online, and in-person professional development services. Each year, my colleagues and I served tens of thousands of artists in all disciplines across the country. Possibly my proudest achievement there was conceiving and launching NYFA's Jobs in the Arts classifieds in 2002, which quickly became the employment engine for the arts and culture industry here in NYC and beyond.

As head of the department, I ended up directing a staff of about ten full- and part-time employees, all of whom were accomplished working artists, performers, and writers in their own right. Who better to advise artists than their colleagues in the trenches with them? I really saw it as a kind of dream team. As director, I also developed and oversaw an annual budget of well over $1 million, conceived and refined new programs, met with funders and wrote grant proposals, collaborated with other arts organizations nationwide, and so much more. I learned almost everything I now know about the arts industry at that job, including the importance of new ideas and innovation, the value of collaborating with creative individuals, and the need for hard work, nimbleness, and acceptance of perpetual change. All of this must be planned for deliberately and sustained over the long haul. I truly believe this experience primed me for the rest of my life as an artist.

When I was not working full-time at NYFA, I worked in my studio during nights and weekends. My studio was a dedicated room in the apartment that I shared with Rossana. I love working at home and, honestly, wish I had more space to do so now. As an artist, I tend to go to the studio and work when I have something to say, which can be unpredictable, because I usually don't find something to say while kicking materials around in the studio. I also tend to work in very short, intense bursts. I feel there's something virtuous about it. I don't think I could be in the studio for eight to ten hours a day. The isolation would make me crazy.

Right now, I think of myself as always in the studio, whether I'm there physically or not. I'm always thinking about my work, planning upcoming exhibitions in my head, writing down ideas on my cell phone, and making very fast, rough sketches on Post-it notes. I then source the materials I need for a specific piece and knock it out in the studio, usually very quickly. I'm decidedly unromantic about the creative process. Relative to other artists, particularly painters, my studio practice might appear somewhat erratic, but that's how it has evolved over the last 20 years. In the early 2000s, as the nature of my work changed—larger works, less than healthy materials—I needed to find a dedicated studio outside of my apartment. And as my studio time was so limited due to my full-time job, my studio needed to be as close to my apartment as possible. I was living in Carroll Gardens, Brooklyn at the time and found a great studio in an old industrial building within walking distance, in Gowanus, which overlooked the pastoral Gowanus canal, a Superfund site.

In 2009, after 12 years at NYFA, I followed in my friend Wendy's footsteps and planned to take a three-month paternity leave when my son was born. I grew up without seeing much of my father and was 100% committed to being present and hands-on with my son. That part, for me, was simply non-negotiable. When Mateo was born, it really flipped a switch in my brain and I knew in my heart that I simply couldn't go back, as much as I loved it, to working full-time at NYFA. With a heavy heart, I resigned from my job there. In retrospect, however, this was the best decision I've ever made in my life. It was also completely insane. It was 2009, after all, and the economy had just imploded, causing the Great Recession, from which this country is still recovering. Here I was, with a newborn son, no job or any prospect of one on the horizon for that matter, and in the middle of the worst financial crisis since my grandparents' generation. It was like a massive earthquake had just occurred, and I was, honestly, utterly overwhelmed by it. It was in the irrational fog of being a new, unemployed father that I decided to dive into a new venture and run MINUS SPACE full-time; it was an artist project I started with Rossana back in 2003. Our first regular exhibition, a group show called *Open House for Butterflies*, after the children's book of the same name, opened on July 31, just four months after my son was born and a month after I quit my job. I've been running the gallery full-time ever since.

My wife and I co-founded MINUS SPACE in our living room in Boerum Hill, Brooklyn in August 2003 as a platform for reductive art on the international level. After five years of exhibiting our work with some success after graduate school, which to some degree concerns the legacy of minimalism and conceptual art, we both felt that something was clearly missing. We felt there was a lack of real, genuine discourse, specifically artist-to-artist. A strong sense of community was also lacking, as well as a sense of greater meaning to what we were doing as emerging artists trying to get a toehold in NYC. Contextually, this was also a period of time when abstraction was at its nadir, in relation to the gallery scene and overall market. Then, you were hard-pressed to see new abstraction, let alone painting, which is my personal interest, on the walls of a gallery anywhere in the city. Many other artists we knew, who exhibited alongside us here in Brooklyn, felt the same way, and we decided to roll up our sleeves and do something about it. Rather than following the well-established route of opening some kind of exhibition space, which we felt wouldn't address our main concerns, we looked to the internet instead.

As a direct result of our day jobs—me again at NYFA and Rossana as an administrator in the Department of Art & Art Professions at New York University—we both had solid experience with conceiving, designing, and building web sites. I'll note here that the web, at that time, was not at all considered a serious space for art. Really, only a handful of arts organizations and individual artists had websites at the time, which were at best basic web pages or online newsletters. We felt, however, that the web presented a huge opportunity for what we wanted to accomplish, so we spent the summer of 2003 learning how to code in HTML and began to build MINUS SPACE online. Websites, at that time, were terribly labor-intensive and extremely expensive to build, so we knew we needed to do the work ourselves for it to come into fruition.

I want to stress that language was also a persistent problem for Rossana and me as emerging artists. We were often called "minimalists" in press releases, reviews, and in everyday conversation. We didn't see it that way, however. Although certainly part of our artistic heritage, minimalism really came out of the concerns of our parents' generation and was vastly different than our own. So, as we conceived MINUS SPACE, we dubbed a new term—reductive—and wrote language to define its scope.

In the very early days of MINUS SPACE, we simply invited a handful of artists we knew and admired from our immediate community in Brooklyn to participate in the project. We began with artists with whom we had forged deep, meaningful relationships during school, including both graduate students and faculty members, as well as other artists with whom we exhibited during our first few years out of school. We built profile pages for each of them featuring their work, information, and ideas. We posted news and other information on what we called our Log, which was an early incarnation of blogging. And we also published interviews with our artists, built a chronology of the development of reductive abstraction globally, curated exhibitions online (still a rarity today), and many other such things over the next three years. When we launched the site, we quite naively thought that it would never reach beyond the boundaries of Brooklyn. But very much to our surprise, it did. MINUS SPACE quickly took off, the moment the site went live, and artists from across the country and around the globe got in touch with us to participate. We gladly accepted. Artists were then followed by others interested in reductive art, such as art historians, curators, writers, and ultimately collectors. In retrospect, what we built was a social medium, a platform for reductive artists, our community of practice, our tribe.

We developed and ran the site for nearly three years, until it suddenly tipped in 2006. We began to receive email inquiries from people travelling to NYC who wanted to visit our "gallery," but couldn't find our street address on our website. No exaggeration, we received dozens of emails like this in 2006. We would, of course, write back saying MINUS SPACE was a website, not a physical space, but that we'd be delighted to meet up, get a cup of coffee, and share notes. That summer, we also travelled to Europe and saw firsthand the project spaces that several of our participating artists had created in their cities, including PS in Amsterdam, Hebel_121 in Basel, and CCNOA in Brussels. We returned home fully invigorated and immediately opened a project space of our own for temporary exhibitions. We decided to do it in our Gowanus, Brooklyn studio space.

To mount an exhibition, we simply moved all of our stuff to the side and turned it over to another artist with the specific mandate to do a project they weren't able to realize elsewhere. We'd mount a show or performance, send out an email announcement, and host a reception. Our exhibitions would sometimes last a few hours, a weekend, or maybe a couple of weeks, at most. After an exhibition finished, we turned the space back over into our studio again and continued working. In the end, we did about four projects each year with the goal of convening people together around an artist's work, sharing ideas, and building community. We envisioned it as a kind of utopian space, and we ran it in this manner until 2009, when our son was born.

Back in 2006, we also received our first invitation to curate a "MINUS SPACE" exhibition at another venue. This began a whole new area of exploration for us, which we still continue to today. Between Rossana and me, I generally take the lead on outside curatorial projects, and I've curated exhibition in collaboration with university galleries, museums, nonprofits, commercial galleries, and private collections, both here and abroad. The most recent project was a group exhibition in 2015, entitled *Breaking Pattern*, highlighting several generations of artists investigating and advancing the discourse around pattern, optical, and perceptual abstract painting. The show coincided with the 50th anniversary of the now legendary *Responsive Eye* exhibition at the Museum of Modern Art. *Breaking Pattern* originated at our gallery, but was greatly expanded for the Schneider Museum of Art at Southern Oregon University, our very first collaboration on the West Coast.

As I mentioned earlier, I dove into running MINUS SPACE full-time in July 2009 and launched a formal, year-round exhibition program. By "full-time," I mean a full-time work schedule, which was at least 40 hours a week, usually more, but with nowhere near a regular, let alone full-time salary with benefits. My salary during this time, and even now, is completely unpredictable and cobbled together from an array of sources, including arts consulting work, teaching, visiting artist residencies, curatorial fees, sales of my studio work, and, of course, sales from what is now our gallery. My income is usually pretty lean, with some years a little less so. As someone who is self-employed, every single day of my life involves hustling to find and secure regular work. It's relentless. And again, I have a family. As a younger artist, I could do without, but that's simply not an option anymore.

I will add that one terrific benefit to me was the Affordable Care Act, which continues to give me access to good, relatively inexpensive health insurance. My health is the second non-negotiable thing for me. In addition to my family, there are now many people depending on me to be in top form mentally and physically, and I'm really fortunate that my overall health is good. I'm literally knocking on wood with both hands as I write this. I eat well and exercise daily—swimming, running, and cross training. In fact, I actually do most of my strategic planning for my life, studio work, and the gallery while I'm exercising. My mind is usually incredibly clear and high on endorphins then. I've curated many exhibitions while running across the Brooklyn Bridge at night, and I've resolved major challenges with the gallery while swimming laps in the pool.

In 2011, we had the opportunity to move MINUS SPACE from our petite, 176-square-foot project space in Gowanus to a slightly larger one in Dumbo, Brooklyn. We moved to a slightly larger space yet again in 2013, and then again to our current ground-floor space at 16 Main Street in Dumbo in May 2015. With each successive move, four to date, we spent countless days planning, and, honestly, stressing to ensure sure we could sustain the additional overhead. Running a bricks-and-mortar space is so much more expensive than producing a website, and rent is a gallery's main expense. We do have an incredibly supportive partnership with our current landlord, Two Trees, which helps us keep our doors open. Our ultimate goal with the gallery is to be totally uncompromised in what we exhibit *and* to be self-sustaining, meaning the gallery will at least pay for itself and partly for us. Being uncompromised and self-sustaining are not mutually exclusive, but together they are an ongoing challenge, which regrettably produces some regular financial panic attacks. I will also stress here that Rossana and I are not people of wealth—we are middle-class at best here in NYC—and we do not have a financial backer for the gallery. We run it like your local coffee shop, as a true retail business.

Sustainability is something I think about every day. I ask myself: is what I do on a regular basis sustainable? I honestly don't have a clear answer for that. I do find, however, great personal meaning and satisfaction in what I do as an artist, writer, curator, teacher, and gallerist. Do I sometimes feel totally overwhelmed and exhausted by it? Yes, without question. But am I super lucky to do be able to do the things I feel so passionately about on an ongoing basis? Absolutely. At the end of every year, when we close up our studios and the gallery for the holidays, my wife and I dedicate time reflecting upon the past year. We look at our successes and our failures. We look at what worked and what didn't, what gave us satisfaction and what caused friction. We then spend time laying out a roadmap for the year ahead, which encompasses our studio work, the gallery, and our life as a whole. Each year, we also recommit our attention and energies to working smarter. It's simply not possible for us to work any harder at this point, nor is it sustainable for us, in the long run.

As I approach middle age, it's become increasingly clear to me that my time is not a renewable resource. I want to spend the best of me focused on the things that dovetail precisely with my core personal values and artistic beliefs. I am incredibly fortunate to have a strong, stable, and loving relationship with my wife and son. It is the cornerstone of my life in the arts. I also get to contribute in a small way each day to building a stronger artistic community, of which I am one small part. I don't think it's possible to be completely egoless as an artist, but I never think of myself as at the center of things. I am part of greater arts ecosystem, and the health of that system depends on what each of us contributes to it. I will also add that I love honest, hard work. Maybe it's the Midwesterner in me, but it gives me tremendous pleasure to get things done.

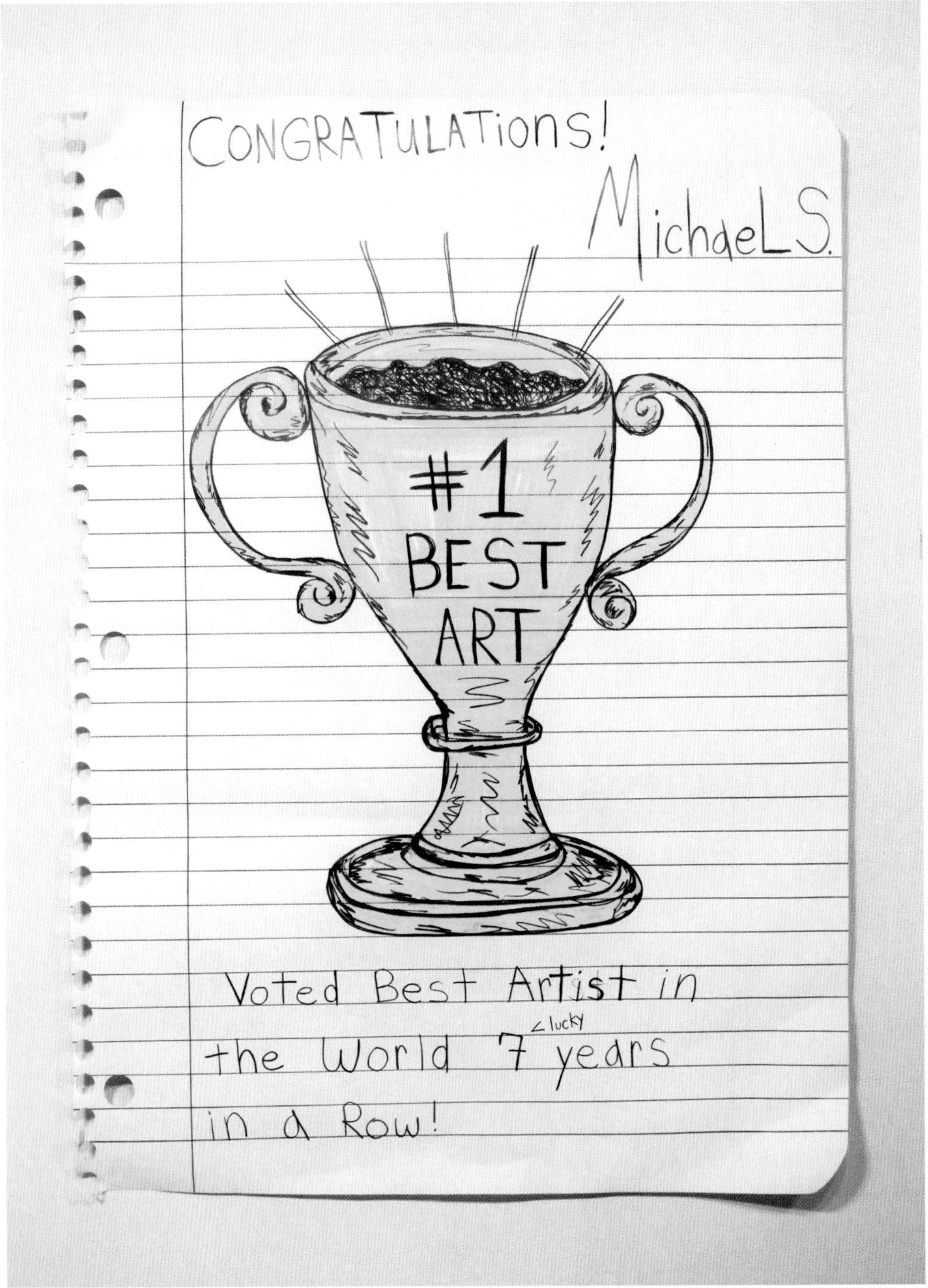
CONGRATULATIONS!
MichaeL S.
#1
BEST
ART
Voted Best Artist in
the World 7 lucky years
in a Row!

I believe that all good art is political, and this belief is what informs my work. As an artist working today, I feel it is my obligation to be knowledgeable about current events and to be active in my community. I do not want to simply make cultural and societal observations through art; I strive for it to also add to the greater cultural landscape. Art is not simply a stagnant decoration, but rather can activate change in the world. From Picasso's *Guernica* to Banksy's street art, art plays an important role in questioning governments and politicians who should be working in the people's best interest. Over the years, my work has tackled such hot-button issues as: the Iraq War, the Bush administration, the conflict in Syria, the Ferguson protests and race relations in America, income inequality, and the continuing gun violence in our society.

Politics has always played a significant role in my life. My grandmother was an elected county register in North Carolina. In 1964, she was one of the first women to hold public office in the state, which was unheard of at the time. She was the Polk County Register of Deeds for 27 years, until she retired. I have a vivid memory of her campaigning, yard signs, and election days from when I was very young. My father, too, always stressed the importance of knowing what was going on in the world around us. As a kid, we spent hours at the dinner table discussing the day's news and that interest stuck. Even today, the first thing I do every morning is read the paper, and then I spend most of

Michael Scoggins
Best Art
67"x51"
Graphite, marker, colored pencil on paper
2014
Courtesy of the artist

the day listening to NPR on the radio. My mother is a painter. She encouraged all three of her sons to use their imaginations and express themselves through drawing and painting. With my mother's artistic guidance and my father's political interests, my love for both art and politics comes to me as second nature. I'm truly equal parts of my parents, and so it only makes sense that I combined these two passions in my art-making practice.

During the lean years of graduate school, I bought a stack of cheap, spiral-bound notebooks at the drugstore and used them as sketchbooks. The sketches in those notebooks served as the basis for my paintings. At this time, my paintings primarily consisted of childlike war scenes, stick-figure soldiers battling across the picture plane. I was loosely addressing the war in Iraq and raising the question of what patriotism meant, and how American children are assimilated at an early age to believe the USA is superior to other nations. One day, I was looking back and forth, from the drawings on the lined notebook pages to the canvas resting on the easel. I found the sketches to be much more intriguing and honest than the painting, and something in my head clicked. I put the brushes away and began to use an enlarged notebook paper format as the foundation for my drawings.

With its blue lines and frayed edges, the spiral-bound notebook page is an object that is familiar to most people and inspires feelings of nostalgia. The image of the notebook paper places the viewer back in a youthful time, when life seems simpler. I started thinking about art and accessibility, and I decided that I wanted to create artwork that would challenge a larger and more diverse audience than just my immediate and extremely small, art-savvy crowd.

To forego painting in favor of drawing was scary yet exhilarating; I felt like I had just discovered a new dimension. I discovered that, for me, drawing was a much more democratic medium. I also wanted to examine the established hierarchies in the art world and to blur the barriers between high and low art forms. There is art and design all around us, and I began to look at mass-produced imagery, such as comics and political propaganda posters, for inspiration. These things are meant for wide distribution and mass consumption by the general public, and I wanted to use some of this familiar imagery and place it in a fine art context. Over time, I was able to create a unique visual language that spoke to a larger audience than did my previous work. Concepts became more important to me than materials. I started asking myself, "Why is there a need to paint, when drawing is a better way to communicate my thoughts?" I determined that I would use whatever materials were needed to best express my ideas and to allow those ideas to reach beyond the insulated art world. My art-making wasn't political in theme only, but was a political act, in and of itself.

Along with my drawings, I began using text, which was something I had always avoided in my paintings; after all, I was a VISUAL artist! I felt that if I couldn't express something through images, then I was failing. My attitude slowly started to evolve, and I began to see drawing and writing as the same lexicon. For me, language and drawing have a kind of strength that I feel painting lacks. There is a weight inherent in words that is missing in painting, because of painting's long, overshadowing history. Additionally, using text comes more naturally to me, which thus allows me to articulate my ideas more clearly. I felt that by addressing complex and controversial issues through language, I could disarm and inform the viewer at the same time. Some artists use writing to make didactic statements, but I see words as a way of empathizing with the reader. By discussing my own beliefs, ideas, and opinions in the honest and sincere way that text affords, I feel I can relate and convey concepts, rather than preach them.

Around the same time that I began using text, I also developed an alter ego in my works, named "Michael S." He is a younger, less reserved version of myself. By speaking through this character, I have more confidence to directly discuss controversial issues that I might shy away from otherwise. In the work, Michael S. discusses politics, war, race, gender, and other social issues in an uninhibited way that my adult self cannot. He has no internal filter, so he gets straight to the heart of the subject matter. Sometimes, he will take the opposing point of view from my own, in order to magnify vitriolic positions that border on the ridiculous. He can be funny, raw, politically incorrect, and is always tongue-in-cheek. There is a certain charm and honesty in his naivety that makes the message less convoluted.

In order to keep up with the demands of my life as an artist, I maintain a rigorous studio practice. My day consists of grabbing a coffee and heading to the studio around 10 am. I sit at my desk and read the morning news, then typically spend an hour or two taking notes and sketching out ideas. I, then, sweep my studio floor. This is a practice that I started a long time ago; it helps get the blood flowing and lets my mind focus on the day's tasks. Many of my days are spent writing emails and contacting galleries. A lot of time goes into documenting and inventorying work, filling out contracts, applying to residencies, setting up studio visits, or simply paying the bills. On an average day, if I'm lucky, I might get to draw for an hour or two. However, there are some days in the studio when I don't get to draw at all, because there are so many administrative tasks to be completed. It's a rare and welcomed luxury when I get to draw all day, uninterrupted.

When I talk to people outside the arts, they generally have no idea what I do or how I make a living. The first question they usually ask is, "What do you do to make money?" When I tell them I work full-time as an artist and make a living off of my art, I often receive a blank stare. I then explain how being a professional artist is a job, like any other, and talk about the daily process that I go through. Just like in my work, I feel that being transparent about my practice demystifies the profession and elevates its perceived legitimacy. I am the anomaly amongst many of my peers, in that I get to work in the studio every day. I know and admire many talented artists who work additional jobs while maintaining a vibrant studio life. For me, I have found the delicate balance between my art-making, my administrative workload, and my financial needs and responsibilities, and that balance enables me to be a full-time artist. Thus, to date, I have not felt the need to seek a job outside of the studio. But I never say never. This is a precarious and financially unpredictable line of work.

To reach a broader audience and allow more insight into the workings of my life as an artist, I have become active on various social media platforms. I originally started using these tools to document my daily routine, and I have found it's a great way to not only show the progress of my work, but also share my thoughts and experiences. I can discuss events and voice opinions as they take place, in real time, and show artwork that correlates to each situation. This allows art to have a political voice beyond the gallery walls. Using social media can help expand the conversation of what art is and as well as provide a journal of my daily grind. Studio life can be exciting and funny, but it can also be very mundane and isolating. I want to share the triumphs, but also the failures in order to give people a deeper insight into my process. I want to articulate my day-to-day, in order to deemphasize the gleam of celebrity and, in turn, champion the hard work and commitment to one's practice that it takes to be a professional artist. The use of these platforms has become part of the daily routine and a natural extension of sharing my process and progressing my ideas to a larger audience.

Curating exhibitions has become another outlet, where I can reach beyond my own studio practice to work with artists whom I respect and who I feel are making culturally significant artwork. I see curating as a way to draw connections between art and artists who work in many different formats, but may have similar underlying concepts and express my own thoughts. It's a way to expand the conversation through others artists' work. It's also an opportunity to showcase artists who deserve more attention than the art world is giving them and to group impactful artwork together to discuss ideas that are important to me. Curating exhibitions can create a new context for the works involved, and it allows me to bring artists together to collaborate, interact, and have a sense of community. I am thankful to have had the opportunity to work with so many wonderful artists, including my wife Alex Gingrow, Joe Nanashe, Ghost of a Dream, Amanda Tiller, Lindsey Landfried, Delanie Jenkins, Man Bartlett, David X Levine, Shanti Grumbine, Jessie Henson, Marta Buda, Allison Wade, Karen Mainenti, the late Robert Attanasio, and many, many more.

I have always felt that artists need to have a greater influence on the larger cultural landscape. I am continually looking for ways to advance my ideas and involvement, not only through the creation of art, but also by being an active and engaged member in my community. Art has the ability to move beyond the confines of itself and make a true impact on the larger world.

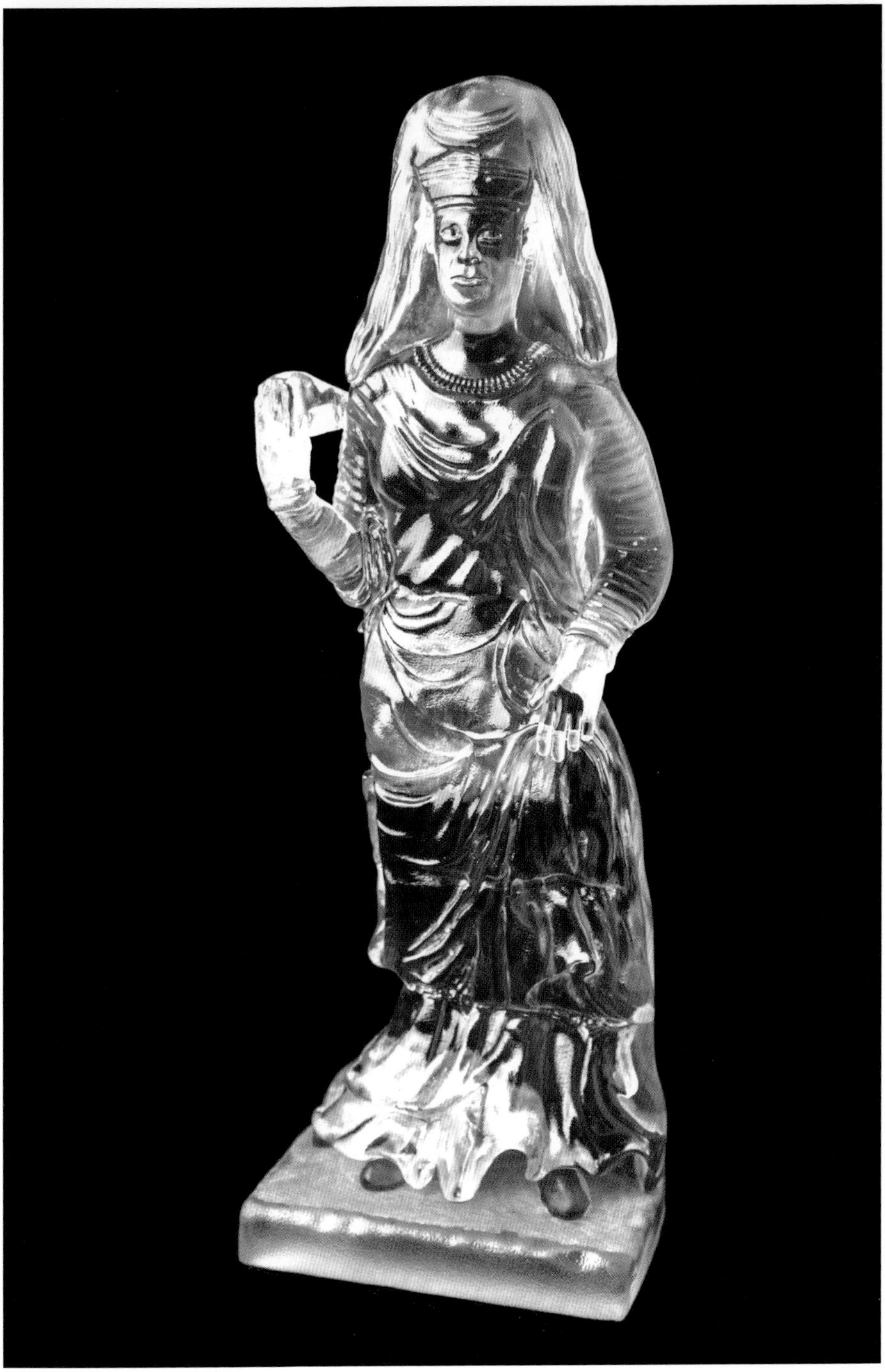

In 2005, I was a BA student majoring in Media Studies and Social Science at Tehran University. I was 20 years old and a geek: curious, motivated, and excited about learning, researching, reading, and exploring the world around me. I was in love with a class, called "Cyberstudies," strangely enough, taught by an Ayatollah with PhD degree from the United Kingdom.

Eleven years ago, on May 30, 2005, I wrote an email to a professor located in the US. I had met her at a conference in Iran some months before, and I was inspired by her research and talk at the conference. We had a brief conversation, as I walked her to the second floor of our school. This is the email. It changed my life in so many ways:

> *On 11/30/05 9:28 AM, "morehshin allahyari" wrote:*
> *Dear Lynn,*
>
> *This is Morehshin from Iran (Social Science Dept, University of Tehran). I don't know if you remember me. Probably you don't, because I know many students used to talk to you and get your email while you were in Iran.*
>
> *I told you about me and five of my friends doing research on six schoolgirls who got drowned three years ago. I wonder if you could send me some information about any journalist or*

Morehshin Allahyari
Material Speculation: ISIS-Ebu
4.5"x3"x12.25"
3D print, USB drive, memory card
2015–2016
Courtesy of the artist

media festivals. So we could translate our project and send it to them.

We are trying to publish the book in Iran. I got no idea if they would give us permission.

Anyway, I've sent a file with this email. I wrote this for a professor who teaches Psychology at Carleton University. I thought maybe you could also use it.

Sincerely,
Morehshin

A week after, Lynn wrote back:

12/08/05 at 11:39 AM
Hello Morehshin!

I'm so glad you wrote! I remember you well and enjoyed talking with you while in Iran. I found your research very interesting. The first thing that comes to mind for its presentation is a conference on media and religion that's taking place in Sweden this July: http://www.colorado.edu/journalism/mcm/mrc/mrc-conferences.htm. If you and/or some of your colleagues would be interested in attending, I could help find some funding for your travels and hotel while you're there. This would be a small conference – maybe 120 people – who would be very interested in meeting you and hearing your insights. The advantage of small conferences is that it is easier to get to know people well, and to find those who share your interests. Let me know if you'd like me to start trying to find funding and I'll work on that.

Thanks!
Lynn

That summer, I went to Sweden, where I presented a paper at the Religion, Media, and Culture Conference: the paper was on Iranian television and its biased presentation of religious and nonreligious women on national series and films. A year after, through Lynn and the Media, Film & Journalism Studies, as well as the Art Department at University of Denver (where she was a faculty), I was offered a full scholarship to study in the Digital Media Studies major, which was an amazing and exciting opportunity.

I was exhausted from living in Iran. I wanted to leave, to be somewhere where I didn't have to censor myself—my personal self, my political self, or my practice, which was mostly creative writing back then. I wanted to leave, not in search of a utopia or the American Dream, but in search of a place, a space where I could be myself without having to deal with so many layers of cultural and religious oppression. For me and the life I wanted to have, living in Iran felt limited. It felt like a loop, never growing outside of certain ways of thinking and being. I wanted to interrupt that, to break outside of it and to grow—to constantly grow.

My entrance into the art world has been through writing, literature, and cinema. That's what I spent most of my teenage years doing: going to a private creative writing class (since the age of 12 to 18), writing stories (and a 400-page novel that got published when I was 16 years old), reading books, and watching weird independent European movies that I would buy illegally from different movie stores in Tehran. (These were movies that had not gone through the Iranian Cultural Ministry censorship process, and so had scenes or content that were "un-Islamic" and, therefore, illegal.) Since the age of 16, until I left Iran (at the age of 22), I worked as an independent writer and journalist with different newspapers and art and cultural magazines in Iran.

I grew up in a family that was very liberal, nonreligious, and open-minded. My mother was a big influence on my love for literature. What I remember the most from my summers in Tehran is exchanging books with my mom, going to art openings and movies, and talking about poetry and Iranian and non-Iranian literature. My father was not into the art world, but he loved history and politics, so much of my conversation with him was around political events in Iran and beyond. My parents were both amazing supporters of my love and passion for art and writing. Regardless of the complications of life and rules in Iran, their attitudes toward life, and how they raised my sister and me, made living in Iran so much more tolerable and valuable. They both also agreed that it would be better and more productive for my sister and me to leave Iran after our bachelor's degree studies. My father specifically insisted that I would be much safer outside of Iran as an artist or writer. He felt that, if I didn't live in Iran, I would not need to worry so much about what I wrote; I wouldn't have to censor myself, so that I would not get into trouble, etc. (Iran is in the top five countries with the most imprisoned journalists and writers.)

So, I left. I arrived in Denver, Colorado on August 20, 2007, after a long process of waiting on FBI and a clearance check, and finally getting my student visa from the US embassy in Dubai. I had no friends, no family members, or relatives in Denver. I literally flew, by myself, to the other side of the world, going through a brutal process of "becoming an adult" in the matter of days. I wasn't alone in this experience. So many of my friends took the same path: going to "study abroad" but also, really, to leave Iran.

Prior to living in the US, I had traveled here and to many other countries. My mother was a flight attendant for 23 years at IraniAir, and through her job, my sister, my father, and I got to travel to different countries around the world. I grew up learning about other cultures—learning about people and understanding that there were always better things, better cities, and better lives and possibilities waiting for me/for us. I learned to be open-minded, not just about people and cultures but about how I made sense of options and choices and accidents. I think that's perhaps one of the most important things in my way of thinking about and through life—and to life as an artist.

I finished my MA studies at the University of Denver in 2009. By the end of the second year of my studies, I had learned an amazing amount of theory, history, and software. I also had started to develop a new perspective about what life meant in America—as an immigrant, as a woman of color, as a person from the Middle East in the post-9/11 era. I felt uncomfortable being constantly asked about my life in Iran, and with the things people were surprised by and wanted to know more about as soon as I opened my mouth and they heard my accent. Through these years of being a cultural ambassador, involuntarily, I learned about context and a constant redefinition of who I was and how I sustained my identity and my practice as an artist. That's something that, up to this day, I continue to challenge and interrupt. It's very much part of my way of growing and questioning and having a critical eye about my position in the world, and others' position in relationship to mine.

In 2009, I moved to Chicago with my partner, Andrew Blanton (also an artist and musician). We lived there for a year, and we continued to work on our art practice and art projects, creating art and curating/organizing shows and events. During the College Art Association (CAA) conference that year, I met with couple of professors from the University of North Texas (UNT) and talked to them about the MFA program they were starting in New Media Art. I told them that I felt like I had to move from Chicago and be somewhere else for a while. I also told them about all the things I was interested in learning and developing in my practice. Some months later, I was offered a full scholarship at the University of North Texas and a research assistant position with David Stout to help develop a research cluster, called Initiative for Advanced Research in Technology and the Arts (iARTA). I had talked with Stout in Chicago during his visit. If I accepted this offer, I was going to be the first MFA student in their program.

I remember not sleeping that night, imagining what life would be like in Texas—in Denton, Texas. The thought of living in Texas made me uncomfortable: as a person who had grown up in a huge city like Tehran with eight million population, as an Iranian, as an artist, as a liberal, as a feminist. Plus, UNT wasn't UCLA or USC or SAIC or any of those other fancy schools that I didn't have the money to pay for. (I couldn't get a student loan, because I was an international student.) I remember talking about this with Andrew for days and seeking advice from my former professors and mentors. I've always had mentors in my life: professors, older friends, and advocates. I put a great amount of my trust in sharing my life with them and seeking their thoughts and advice. That's one thing that has remained a constant element in my life since I was 13 years old. An email, specifically written to one of my mentors, helped greatly in making the decision. I asked about living in Texas and about the program, including whatever information I could gather about some of the professors that were at UNT, whom my mentor knew personally, etc.

I said yes to attend the MFA program at UNT and lived in Denton and Dallas for four years. I finished my MFA in New Media Art at the University of North Texas in 2012. Between 2012 and 2014, I started to teach at different universities in the Dallas/Fort Worth area, before moving to San Francisco, where I currently reside. We moved to San Francisco, because Andrew accepted a tenure-track position at San Jose State University. I decided to move with him and take a break from school and academia after 21 years. I wanted to focus more on my practice as a full-time artist. So, I started to apply for artist residencies. In 2015, I did a four-month residency at Pier9 Autodesk, followed by an artist residency at Carnegie Mellon's Studio for Creative Inquiry (with my collaborator of #Additivism project, Daniel Rourke, an artist and writer based in London). This summer Daniel and I will be in Berlin to be artists-in-residence at the Vilém Flusser Residency for Artistic Research, an annual award through the Transmediale festival for art and digital culture.

During the four years that I lived in Texas, my practice greatly formed and grew. I owe so much of that to the support I received and to my relationship with Andrew, as well the professors I worked closely with. But I also owe much to my friends in Texas, and an art community that was extremely generous and not competitive (in a very Southern, down-to-earth way). Living in Texas taught me a great amount about America, and that stereotypes about Texas weren't all true. It also taught me that, as an artist, there are so many ways to have a sustainable practice. There is no right answer for being successful and, for me, it has come down to so many personal and individual decisions, and ways of working and seeing the world. My experience there taught me that I don't have to live in New York City or Los Angeles to be "successful." In the internet age, I could still do an amazing job of putting my work out in the world, while traveling and participating in shows and conferences I got invited to. I used that as an opportunity to get to know other artists, curators, academics, and to also be known and respected by them for the work I did.

On the other hand, I don't think I have ever considered myself a "local" artist, based in one city. I find my practice to be more international and universal, in the way that my location has not had a big influence on its level of production or exposure. Maybe that's also because I am an artist in diaspora. I have travelled and moved so much, I don't necessarily have a "base" or "home." I make my work for an international audience. I want anyone, from any background and culture, to be able to connect to it.

Looking back at my life and my practice in the last nine years of my post-immigration life in the US, I think what I can be the most excited and proud of is the recipe I have come up with, which isn't necessarily the stereotypical recipe of "how to be a successful artist with a sustainable practice." I have taken things and left things, experimented with things and mixed things, in a way that I think works for me and what I need and want from my practice and its relationship to the political, social, and cultural circumstances of our time. Like so many new media artists, I don't really sell my work. I sustain myself by teaching or traveling around the world and by showing my work and giving artist talks. So much of my work falls into the art and activism category. That means the monetary aspect of the art world is not something that I make work for. That said, I stand for Working Artists and the Greater Economy (W.A.G.E.) and for artist fees, and I find that actually inseparable from being an activist. (Demanding to get paid as an artist for my labor and the work I do is, in and of itself, the way I think about my responsibility to existing in the capitalist economy as an artist and surviving.)

Since 2007, I have worked on projects with a focus on censorship, self-exile, and diasporic existence, virtual vs. physical, to expose in-betweens; I am, most recently, thinking about 3D printing as a radical tool for activism, poetic, and practical archiving. In all of these projects, I have used technology and looked for political and metaphoric ways to create a critical space that provokes difficult questions. So much of my thinking, about the work I do and my relationship to technology and activism, relates to my coming from a position that is not privileged. Growing up in Iran, and then carrying an Iranian passport after immigration, I have never had the option of not thinking about politics and religion and the non-binary world that I/we exist in. Politics is a reality that has been embedded in every single aspect of my life since birth. So, as an artist, I have never had the privilege of making work that is not critical of and concerned with these issues. It is all weaved together and connected.

My most recent work, *Material Speculation: ISIS* (2015–2016), is a creative research and activism project that inspects petro-political and poetic relationships between 3D printing, plastic, oil, techno-capitalism, and *jihad*. It's a 3D modeling and 3D printing project, focused on the reconstruction of 12 artifacts that were destroyed by ISIS in 2015. It creates a practical and political possibility for artifact archival, while also proposing 3D printing technology as a tool, both for resistance and documentation. In the last two years, I also have been working on a collaborative project with Daniel Rourke, called #Additivism (a portmanteau of "additive" and "activism"), embodying 3D print(er)/additive technologies through theoretical, creative, and practical means. In March 2015 we released *The 3D Additivist Manifesto*: "a call to push Additivist technologies to their absolute limits and beyond, into the realm of the speculative, the provocative, and the weird." We then opened up submissions to a radical "cookbook" of blueprints, designs, 3D print templates, and essays on the topics raised by our manifesto. During our residency at Transmediale, we will curate around 80 of the 120-plus submissions we received, alongside essays and speculative designs, which will be published as *The 3D Additivist Cookbook*. We are working with academic and artist-writers to support the critical framework for the *Cookbook*, including texts on environmental ethics; digital materiality and the politics of the open-source movement; the renewed contemporary significance of the artist manifesto, by the likes of the Accelerationist and Xenofeminist movements; and the potential of radical intervention in contemporary techno-capitalism. The *Cookbook* will position 3D printing and related technologies at the center of art and activism.

In so many ways—my personal and political life, the emails I have sent and received, the conversations I have had, and the places I have been and lived—my trust in what I know about myself and having the support of the people around me have all shaped a great amount of my practice. I see my life story, the narrative I have been telling here, as inseparable from how and why and in what ways I get to exist in the art world and make the kind of work that I make. In the complicated and non-binary world, there is no solution, no right or wrong. That's what I always remind myself and get to stand for (one day, I might look back at this text and want to interrupt even that).

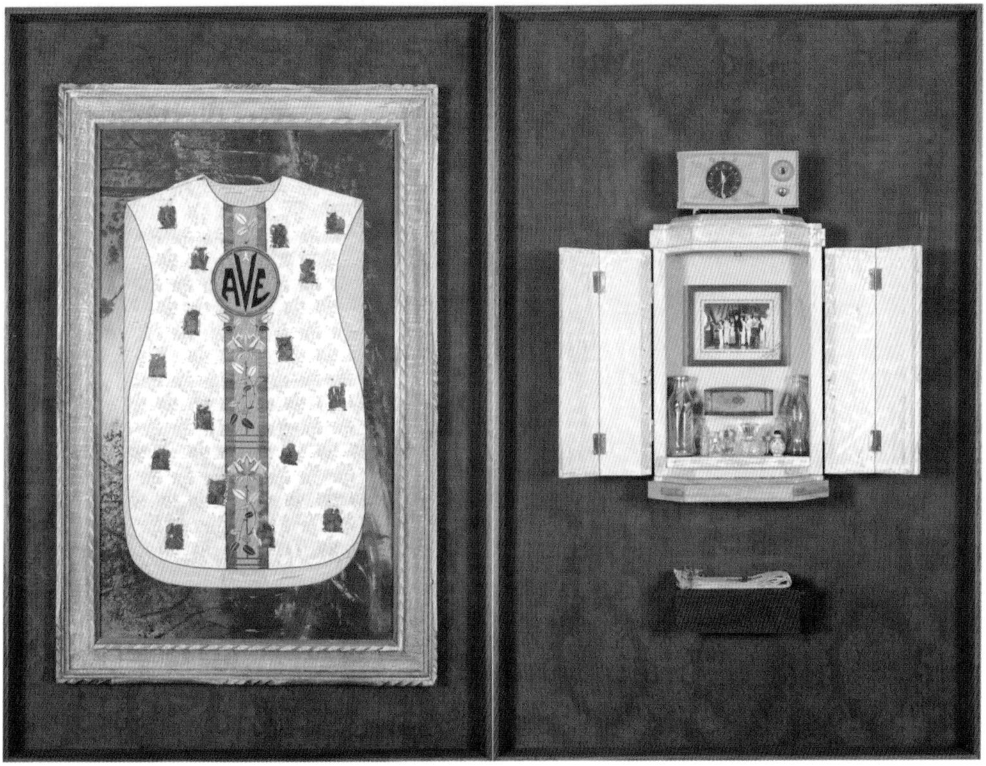
AVE

I come from a family of practicing architects—from my grandfather to my father and a brother—so drawing came as second nature to us. I used to do psychedelic posters during my teenage years, influenced by the hippie culture that was then popular. But I did not think much of it as art. After leaving the seminary where I took up my AB Philosophy degree, I went to the University of Santo Tomas in Manila to take up Fine Arts. When I decided to leave the seminary, after eight years of studies, in favor of the arts, my parents cried—not because I had deprived them of becoming proud parents of someone with religious vows, but because they felt sorry for me. They thought that artists were not capable of earning enough money to enjoy a comfortable and decent life. Of course, they were right to think that the Catholic Church is the richest religious institution in the world; becoming a priest comes with some form of financial security.

I started my art practice in the 1980s, during a very turbulent period in our country's political history. I married a schoolmate from art school who hailed from Bacolod City, an hour by plane south of Manila and the capital of the province of Negros Occidental. Despite aiming to build a career in Manila, I was persuaded by my in-laws to settle down in Bacolod when our first child was born in 1980, and to manage my wife's 60-hectare sugar farm, which she inherited. I never imagined myself

Norberto Roldan
My Brother and the Order of the Knights of the Moonshadows
72"x96"
Diptych, wall assemblage on two panels with old Roman chasuble, priest's maniple, vintage painting, old family photo, transistor radio, Buddhist altar, soft amulets, tin can, wooden box, assorted old bottles
2010
Courtesy of the artist

becoming a political activist, but being exposed to the history and realities of the semi-feudal system prevailing in this sugar-producing province easily turned me into one. Although I was born and grew up in the neighboring island of Panay, Negros was totally a different world to me. It was the country's sugar bowl, where sugar barons were born and ruled during the golden age of the Philippine sugar industry.

As a reluctant "sugar planter," I was exposed to the *hacienda* life, a capital-intensive plantation system devoted solely to sugar cultivation. Hence, as a mono-crop economy, the *hacienda* system, by its very nature, was never designed to be self-sufficient. Life on the farm periodically results in inhuman consequences, like hunger and abject poverty, for those at the other end of the very wide divide between the rich and the poor. I witnessed how sugar workers, historically referred to as *sakadas,* have been exploited through unfair labor practice. The *sakadas* have been enduring this injustice since the sugar industry began in the early 1900s. During the 1980s, as the island was wrangling with social unrest, the political upheaval against the dictator Ferdinand Marcos was gaining momentum nationwide. The insurgency mounted by the Communist Party of the Philippines/New Peoples Army (CCP/NPA) was at its peak. An armed revolution was practically unfolding in the countryside, with many far-flung villages in Negros declared as liberated zones by the revolutionary movement. This was a particular period in our history when one was expected to take sides.

Other than raising my young family, attending to the farm, and teaching at the local College of Fine Arts, I had always managed to do art together with a community of local artists. When the Concerned Artists of the Philippines (CAP) was organized in Manila in 1983 (an umbrella organization of politicized Filipino artists working across disciplines), it didn't take long for us to organize our own chapter during the same year. And so, I added to my expanding role, becoming the Chair of the Visual Arts Section of CAP-Negros. Together with other peoples' organizations from different sectors of society, this broad political coalition became the backbone of the protest movement against the dictatorship in Negros Occidental. That was how and when I became involved with both the mass movement and cultural activism.

As members of a progressive organization identified with the Left, our activities were always under government surveillance. We operated under constant threat from military harassment and persecution. It was the most fearful and challenging time to be both an artist and activist. Under the dictator, political activists—artists, writers, journalists, academics, students, religious leaders, and intellectuals who were identified as Marxist or left-leaning—were targeted as enemies of the state. During this autocratic regime, thousands of these perceived subversive elements were either incarcerated and tortured, or raped in the case of women, salvaged (summarily executed), or disappeared without a trace.

My practice is significantly informed by this personal experience. My work revolves around issues on class struggle, indigenous belief systems, war, history, and contemporary society. When I became involved with CAP-Negros, we were at the frontline of mass actions in Bacolod. Our work, comprising mainly of street art and murals produced for political rallies, was viewed by the reactionary public as nothing more than propaganda. After Cory Aquino assumed the presidency, following the People Power Revolution in 1986, I founded Black Artists in Asia with artists who were committed to pursue art with social relevance outside the ideological and organizational influence of the Left. This was followed by a two-year, self-imposed exile in Sydney, Australia (1987–89) that helped me completely disengage from being aligned with the national democratic movement. I never got back into farming in Negros after coming home from abroad. Instead, I resettled in Manila in 1992 to try to reclaim a career I once had an eye for.

Having worked for two years as an art director in an advertising agency while in Sydney opened doors for me in the lucrative creative industry. I eventually got a post as creative director in ABS-CBN Broadcasting Corporation, the largest media conglomerate in the Philippines. A day after the declaration of martial law in 1972, ABS-CBN was seized by the Marcos government. ABS-CBN's president, Eugenio Lopez Jr., was imprisoned and held without trial for five years, until he and his cellmate Sergio Osmeña III (now a Philippine senator) launched a daring jailbreak in 1977 and sought political asylum in the USA. The network was taken over by a Marcos crony, the political kingpin in Negros at the time, and it continued to operate under a different name. ABS-CBN was returned to its rightful owners shortly after Cory Aquino became president. It was a full-circle for me to get into ABS-CBN, a victim of the same martial law we all fought against. Behind the security of a corporate job that was my main source of income, I struggled to continue my practice as a visual artist.

Shortly after I retired from ABS-CBN, in 2000, I cofounded Green Papaya Art Projects. As an independent platform leaning towards more experimental practices, I and my cofounder Donna Miranda wanted to provide opportunities to young artists pursuing not only contemporary art, but also community and social engagements. I worked full-time as a freelance graphics designer to support Green Papaya and my family, while going to the University of the Philippines for my master's degree in Art Studies. And then, my third and youngest child was born in 2003. Serendipitously, that year I was recalled by a former boss to work again for ABS-CBN. Wanting to provide better financial security for my growing family, I accepted the job, even if it meant reporting to the broadcast center from 9 to 5 on weekdays. Those were exciting, yet very demanding, years; I actually surprised myself at how I was able to manage juggling those multiple roles. I finally decided to quit my corporate job in 2007 and started giving more time to Green Papaya and my art practice. Since then, I have been represented by a commercial gallery based in Singapore that takes care of my representation, mainly in Southeast Asia. Finally, my works started to find their way into private and public collections. I have also since organized a lean but committed team to manage Green Papaya's programs and day-to-day activities. My two older kids are now adults and financially independent, and my youngest kid has grown old enough to be on his own half of the time.

My long stay in the seminary and having spent a part of my life with sugar workers in the rural area fostered in me a keen fascination with Christian and folk religious rituals and objects.

My interest in exploring the myths and mysteries surrounding them has resulted in a body of work comprising medicine cabinets, assemblages, and installations. Working along this direction has helped me understand better the roots of Filipino spirituality. With this understanding came a clearer picture of the Filipinos' long struggle and resistance against colonial-imperialist interventions, both in the past and in the present. Some of my assemblages and installations contain real objects of Christian and pagan origins. Art-making, or magic as it is practiced in a rural setting, is integral in pagan rituals. Presided over by a *babaylan* (shaman), these rituals are traditionally part of survival and community gatherings. They contain a complex system of communication; beyond their aesthetic forms are layers of beliefs and meanings about the ancestral past. This knowledge is passed on from generation to generation.

I also became fascinated with anything old. I often wonder whether an old object ceases to really matter once it ends up in a trunk or in an attic. I collect stuff found in secondhand shops. Somehow, these objects acquire value as period novelties. I'm curious about old houses and their dismembered architectural details, old clothes and vintage fabric, liturgical vestments with their inlays and intricate embroideries, old boxes, bottles, Christian and pagan artifacts, personal mementos, and old sepia photographs. I'm constantly challenged by how to appropriate these objects in another context, to see how I can blur the past from the present, or break down disciplines that separate anthropology from contemporary art.

Having been involved in an intense political art movement in Negros, and being currently occupied with my own practice while running an independent platform, I can say that there is an intrinsic political element in all artists' works, whether the artist admits it or not. I think this element may or may not be signified in their works. I believe being engaged in a contemporary art practice carries with it some kind of political awareness, as one cannot deal with contemporary issues without dealing with the conflicts attached to them.

Looking back, I keep asking myself: Where and how have I pulled together all those precious hours to create art? I did it in between intense cultural and political work, in between rallies, in between teachings, and during the days that I did not have to drive to the sugar farm while I was in Negros. In between a regular job and a weekend job, I managed to curate and mount two Philippine group exhibitions, including my own solo show, while in Sydney. I did it after getting home from ABS-CBN, in between semesters in graduate school, in between projects and gigs in Green Papaya, on weekends, on holidays, and when my children were peacefully tucked into their beds at night. My marriage with my wife Mel, from Bacolod, has long been annulled, but we have remained good friends. Me and Donna, who is the mother of my youngest child, have also been separated but have remained as friends, and also as co-caretakers of Green Papaya's sustainability. Now I have more time for my art, and my two sons hang out with me, either in the studio or in Green Papaya, whenever we have something going on.

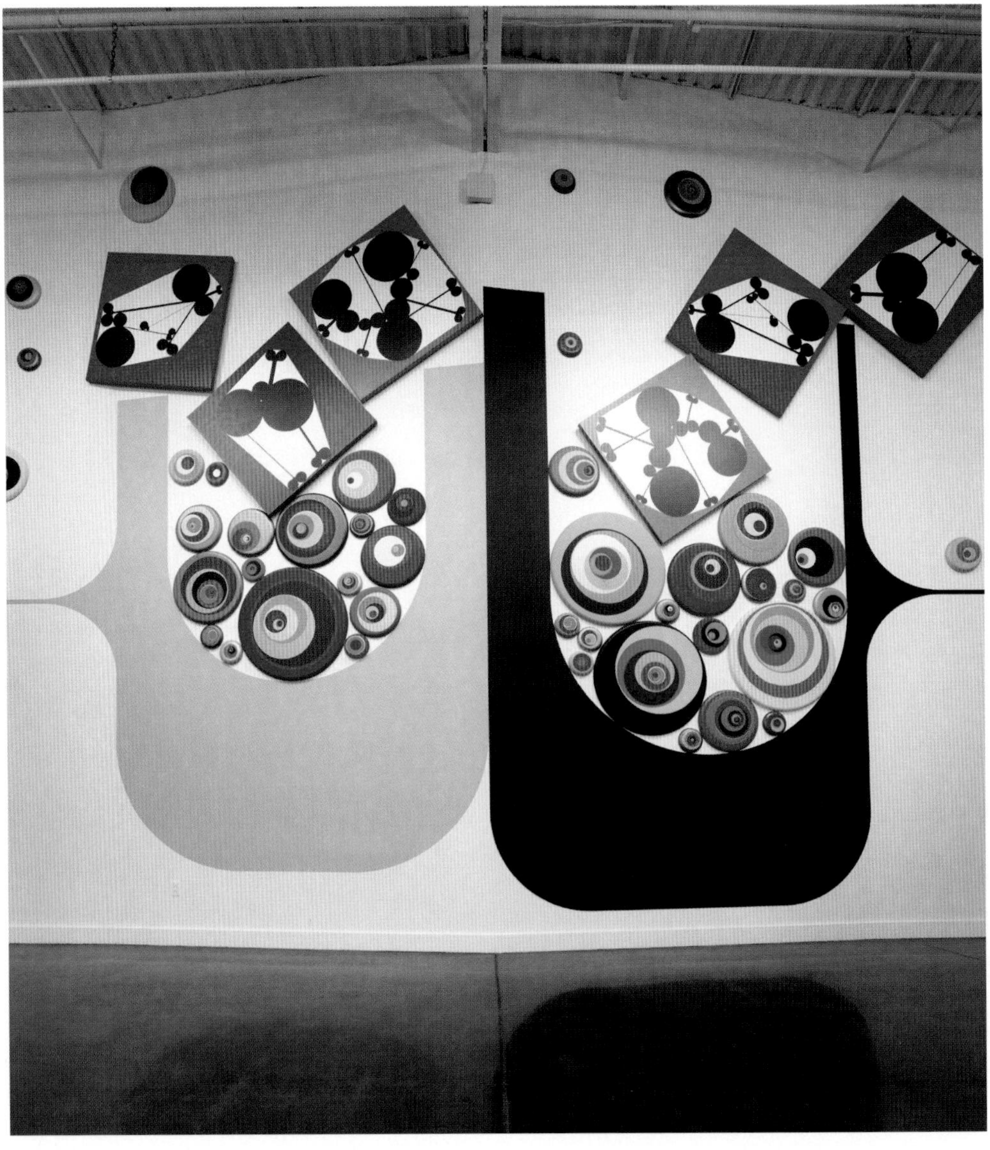

After graduating from high school, I found myself in a situation where I had to find somewhere to live and a job to support myself. I was on my own and did not know how I was going to be able to do it. Growing up in El Paso, Texas, a border city with Juarez, Mexico, the only thing I ever wanted to be was an artist. I knew I could not support myself being an artist. I wanted to go to college and study fine art, but, at the time, that was not an option either.

I always marveled at the advertisements of beautiful pencil renderings of models that The Popular, a local department store, would have in the newspaper. Illustration was something that really interested me. So, I thought maybe I could apprentice in the advertising department as a fashion illustrator. When I went to the store for the interview, they did not have any openings in the advertising department, but they did offer me a position in the visual merchandising department. I did not know anything about display, but I needed ~~the job~~, so I accepted the offer. I was designing display windows and store interiors. It was a very creative job. I couldn't believe there was such a job, being creative, making things, and actually getting paid for doing it. My heart was really into becoming an artist, so after working a full day at The Popular, I would go home, eat my dinner, and then I would draw and paint late into the evening. That pretty much has been my routine ever since high school. It was great

Paul Henry Ramirez
RATTLE
24'x67'x67'
Site-specific installation (detail).
Acrylic on convex canvas,
silkscreen on linen canvas, wall
painting, fired clay, window
film, furniture, and sound.
2016–17
Commissioned by the Grounds
For Sculpture
Courtesy of the artist
Photography by Ken Ek

working in a creative job and being rewarded for doing things I enjoyed.

I had this internal drive to create art. I did a lot of painting on my own and created a body of work that I wanted to share. I didn't want to wait, to go to college and graduate, before I could become an artist, so I decided to try to exhibit my paintings. I began to submit my artwork to juried exhibits and was fortunate to have my work recognized and accepted for several juried museum exhibitions. The recognition of my artwork in the juried exhibitions led to my work being introduced to José Diego Lizárraga, the director of the Instituto Nacional de Bellas Artes in Ciudad Juarez, Chihuahua, Mexico, and he graciously arranged to meet with me. I drove across the border to Juarez, Mexico to present my artwork to him, and he gave me my first solo museum exhibition. This was only several years after high school. It was really exhilarating to have a full body of my artwork shown in a museum for the first time.

A few years later, I co-founded and co-curated *Juntos 1985, The First Hispanic Invitational Art Exhibition*. El Paso was a city that was predominantly of Hispanic descent, so I wondered why there were not more Hispanic artists represented in the museums and galleries. That is when I decided to put together a Hispanic exhibition. This was the first ever bi-national exhibition in the region, and it brought together 20 artists from both sides of the United States and Mexico border. I titled the exhibition after my painting of the same name, *Juntos*, which means "together" in Spanish. It reflected the mission of uniting our two communities—El Paso, Texas and Cuidad Juarez, Mexico—into one historic exhibition. The imagery in my painting symbolizes two figures uniting, joining, and becoming one. The purpose of the exhibition was to encourage communication in the arts and showcase available artistic talent in the area. Some of the artists were already established, most notably Luis Jiménez Jr. and Manuel Gregorio Acosta; for many other artists, it was their first time exhibiting. It was after co-curating the second *Juntos Invitational Exhibition* that I moved to the East Coast, and other artists took over the *Juntos* exhibitions. It was a very educational experience to curate an art exhibition for the first time. It taught me a lot about curating, working with people and the press, and marketing. It was a wonderful exhibition, which brought the community together. I had never done this before; I just decided to do it, and did. And the act of doing it—getting involved with the community, working with different people and other artists, and helping other artists exhibit their artwork—was really exhilarating. In 1988, the *Juntos Invitational Exhibition* became The Juntos Art Association. The association has continued for over 30 years. It's awesome to realize that something which was started as a seed in 1985 has continued to help artists and the whole community for many years to follow. There was a lot of work involved, but it was a really fun time in my life.

Eventually I enrolled to take classes at the University of Texas at El Paso. After the first year at UTEP, I received a grant to study printmaking for the summer in Paris. I called a good friend who lived in New Jersey to tell him the exciting news. At the time, he was looking for a roommate and suggested I come live with him instead of going to Paris. I'd always wanted to live in New York City, so I took him up on his offer. It was one step closer to being there. I loved being on the East Coast and so close to New York. I decided to stay and quit my job in El Paso. My friend's family owned an import-export business. They loaded my clothes, canvases, and art supplies into the bed of my 1977, white Ford pickup, loaded my pickup into a large trailer truck, and shipped everything to the East Coast. I made a life for myself in New Jersey, continuing to do my art and working in visual merchandising.

It was in 1992, while I was taking an independent study class in painting, that my instructor, knowing I worked as a visual merchandiser, recommended that I visit this high-end fashion boutique on Fifth Avenue, called Henri Bendel. I went to see the store for myself and immediately fell in love with the opulent interiors, gilded chandeliers, Lalique windows, and all the most current beautiful fashions. As I walked around admiring the store, I ran into an employee dressing a mannequin, so I asked him if there were any job openings in the display department. He told me there was, so I applied for the position. After a couple interviews, I got the job, so I needed to find a place to live, with no time to waste. I was moving to New York City!

To afford to move and live in New York, I rented a small bedroom from an elderly lady whose apartment was within walking distance of my new job. It seemed like the ideal situation until the first morning, when I went out to get a coffee and newspaper. On my way back into the building, the doorman would not let me back in because I was not a tenant. It turned out, the lady was not allowed to sub-rent her bedroom and, unfortunately, she never told me. I had to move out immediately. I didn't know what to do. My first day of work at Henri Bendel was the next day. Luckily, my only friend in New York said I could stay with him while I searched for a new place to live. I quickly packed and moved everything to his apartment. After working with Henri Bendel for a few months, I was able to save enough money to rent my own apartment in Brooklyn.

When I first moved to New York City in 1992, I did not produce much artwork. It took some time to get settled into the new job and new home. The job was demanding on my time and energy, but was also very fun to be involved with the most cutting-edge fashions from designers, such as Karl Lagerfeld and Ann Demeulemeester. It was very exciting to be designing windows for Henri Bendel. Wednesday nights, we would change the windows and work late into the evening until they were completely finished. My first window display was to celebrate the first anniversary of Henri Bendel on Fifth Avenue and featured the fashions of Jean Paul Gaultier. There was an extravagant party with celebrities and supermodels. It was wonderful meeting Jean Paul Gaultier and seeing how thrilled he was about the windows I worked on, which featured his bridal gown with a 100-foot train. I wanted to do my very best at work and needed to dedicate myself fully to the job at Henri Bendel. I frequently brought design projects home with me over the weekend to prepare for the week ahead. It was okay, because it took several years before I became familiar with the New York City arts community. Eventually, I was able to spend more time on making my artwork, working at a full-time job during the day and spending my evenings in my studio, creating new artworks. It is inspiring to learn that many admirable artists, such as Andy Warhol, Robert Rauschenberg, James Rosenquist, and Jasper

Johns, also worked as window designers for a source of income, at the same time that they were creating their artwork.

There is a similar skill set I developed in visual merchandising that crosses over into my work practices for art installations. In the beginning stages of a new project, when I enter into a gallery or museum space, automatically I can visualize how to present my work, how the viewer might stop and view my work, and how they might take in the whole experience. I really take into account where the audience will enter the space and how they might move around in it, how they might see and feel and experience the whole environment. It's about creating a sensorial experience. There is also a similar skill set in office and studio work practices in the planning of an art installation, concerning timelines and deadlines, and preparations for a smooth installing process.

There could be some similarities in the collaborative process as well. Through my display jobs, I have had the opportunity to work with so many different people, creative people and non-creative people alike, from all levels of the visual department and all levels of store management. It has taught me a lot about working with people—how to give and take, and how to work together to make something fantastic happen—all having the same goal in mind, to create the very best experience that can possibly be imagined. Those collaborations have carried through into my collaborative practices for my installations, because I have learned to understand how to work with many different people with different inspirations, gallerists, museum directors, and curators, so that we can create and have the very best working experience in meeting all our goals.

Those first few years in New York City were a big adjustment, learning my way around the city, meeting new friends, and trying to figure out how to begin a new life and start my art career, all over again. I was not familiar with any of the opportunities for artists, so I had to research what was available. I was making new art but didn't know how or where to exhibit it. As I met new artist friends and became familiar with the arts community in the city, I discovered there were alternative gallery spaces available that gave artists opportunities to show their work. I decided to try to exhibit in as many alternative spaces and programs in NYC as I could. I had my first exhibitions at The Drawing Center in 1994, Franklin Furnace and Clock Tower Space in 1995, The Rotunda Gallery in 1997, and GEN Art in 1998. It was a great chance to show my art and meet lots of awesome creative people who also enjoyed the arts. And, fortunately, some art critics took notice of my work, too.

What was most rewarding, over the several years that I was learning my way around, was meeting a lot of great people and making a lot of nice friends. Without the mutual support with other artists, collectors, curators, and gallerists, the journey would not have been possible or nearly as fun or fulfilling. In the beginning, it really was the support of a few respected people who believed in my art that gave me the first opportunities to exhibit. Some of the early gallery highlights were meeting Annie Heron at Test Site and, subsequently, being part of the Ooze exhibit at Black and Heron Gallery, Renee Riccardo exhibiting my work at Arena Gallery, and being part of the Sauce Gallery's group exhibition.

Sauce Gallery was a Brooklyn-based gallery, curated and run by several artists. They would do studio visits and curate group exhibitions. One of the artist curators from Sauce, Natalie Moore, was so kind to introduce my work to Caren Golden, of Caren Golden Fine Art. Caren had just opened her gallery, above The Drawing Center on Wooster Street, a few years earlier. She came to my studio, was intrigued by my work, and took a few of my small paintings back to her gallery. Some important collectors saw the paintings and loved them. She gave me my first solo show, *Liquid Squeeze,* in 1997 and my next solo show, *Real Pretty Simple Innocent Paintings*, in 1998. We really worked well together. It was a great collaboration. We had tremendous success and basically grew our businesses together. It was a perfect fit. I kept really busy, producing new artwork, while still working full-time. She was really busy placing my work with wonderful collections and in wonderful museum exhibitions.

My first site-specific installations were created in 1994 and 1995 for exhibitions at The Drawing Center, Franklin Furnace and Clock Tower. Over the years, my site-specific installations evolved to include collaborations with other artists and designers to produce multisensory environmental experiences for the viewer. In 2002, I was invited to create the commissioned site-specific installation, *Space Addiction*, at the Whitney Museum at Phillip Morris. It provided me with one of the first occasions to collaborate with a furniture designer, and also a sound designer, So Takahashi, to create an immersive experience for the audience. When given the opportunity to create my site-specific installations, it is rewarding to be able to provide other creative people, artists and designers, with opportunities to showcase their work on a project. Shortly after that exhibit, I was commissioned to create *Elevatious Transcendsualistic*, an installation for the Tang Museum. For the first time, I collaborated on choreography and costumes. I collaborated with dance choreographer Deborah Fernandez on the dance performance, as well as with the costume designer, Kim Vanyo, on how I envisioned the costumes. Since then, we've had our second collaboration, for my installation, *BLACKOUT: A Centennial Commission*, at the Newark Museum in 2010, which included costumes, props, sound, and dance. My largest commissioned installation, *RATTLE*, opened at the Grounds For Sculpture in New Jersey in 2016, with painting, ceramic, furniture, window art, sound, and dance.

That is, basically, how it all started for me in New York. All the while, I was fortunate to have full-time employment doing visual merchandising in some of the most fashionable boutiques in NYC: Henri Bendel, Charivari, and Takashimaya. I was able to work to support myself as an artist and work on the art, at the same time. In those early days, I always had a job to support my artwork and needed to be creative to live within my budget. Looking back, it really was the love of creating that drove me. It never felt overwhelming because I enjoyed it so much.

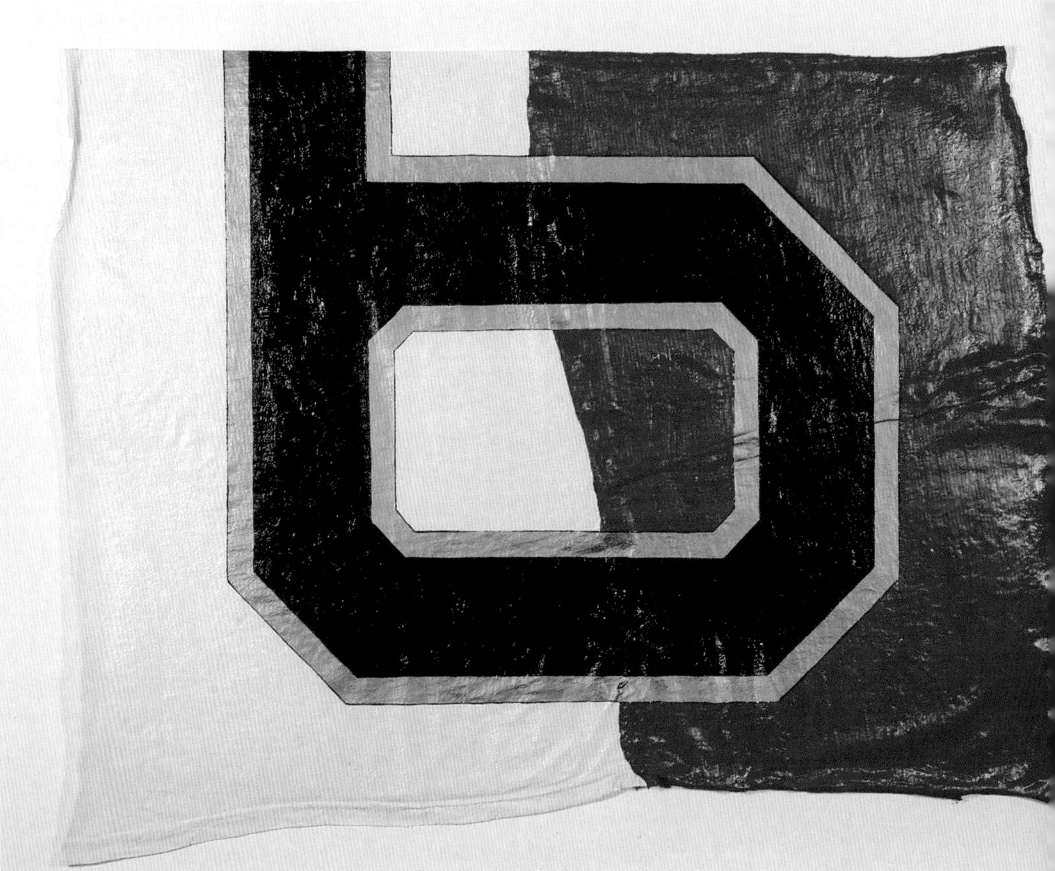

When I entered undergraduate school in Virginia, I wasn't entirely certain I wanted to be an artist. Having had four years of Spanish in high school and a semester in Santiago Chile, the idea of being a translator seemed very attractive. But a few weeks into university art classes with some fantastic teachers made the decision to be an artist easy. I've had several excellent teachers through high school and into college, and I'd like to thank them for opening new worlds and ideas. And to all the art teachers out there, thank you for instilling a deep curiosity in your students.

Right after graduation from college, I moved to Seattle to go to grad school. This was 1985, and we didn't have instant information about the rankings of colleges or their programs. I picked Seattle for several reasons; one obvious reason was it was as far away from Virginia as we were willing to go. I've lived here since then, making art, working day jobs, and for just over five years, showing art by others at my gallery, SEASON.

Seattle felt comfortable from the day I arrived. It was easy to get around and, considering the small town I grew up in, it felt big but manageable. I started working at an art supply store and quickly made friends and gained access to art events. I got representation in galleries, first in Portland, then Seattle, and eventually in New York. I've shown with and without contracts at numerous galleries, leaving some for my own reasons and leaving others at their request. Sometimes a gallery would close,

Robert Yoder
JAME6 Yacht
23"x29"
Oil on cotton t-shirts
2015
Courtesy of the artist
Photography by Mark Woods

or it would split, or it would just not be the right place for me to be. I admire loyalty between a dealer and an artist, but I also admire it when people make tough decisions that are better for everyone involved.

About ten years ago, I began working on and off with grad students at the University of Washington. It has been great seeing what a younger generation of artists are interested in and how some students change based on their surroundings and peer groups. With our interactions generally being studio visits, I get to talk freely about the situations they may find themselves in after graduation—how to price work, build a resume, approach a gallery, etc. It was after several of these studio visits that I realized there were young artists making interesting work which probably would never find a place in a Seattle gallery. The idea to have a reception and show their work to my friends and contacts took hold.

Having worked with many galleries, first as an artist and, later, as help at art fairs, running a gallery of my own seemed like a logical next step. The real impetus to open came during the financial crisis that started in 2008. With the crash of the stock market and the implosion of the housing bubble, luxury and discretionary shopping dried up. Galleries began showing Warhol—or friends of Warhol, or any permutation of Warhol—as a safe and sure sell. Lots of group shows by gallery artists also appeared on their calendars. Beyond how boring it all became, I thought these shows were taking a wrong approach, showing us something we already knew instead of showing us something new and exciting. Things seemed to be at rock bottom, especially out here where a whole new group of young collectors were suddenly erased. With nowhere to go and things at their worst, I opened SEASON.

Sometimes I think Seattle may be a benefit for artists, and sometimes I think it may be a block. General networking here is less likely to produce outstanding results, although many good things have happened to many artists. Seattle is seen as some sort of Wild West to many, and that may be an advantage at times as curators look outside of NY/LA/Chicago galleries for unknown artists. I know SEASON was once accepted to a fair because the producers wanted to broaden their geographical representation of galleries. And that is fine with me. This business is always about getting noticed, and I think that that one opportunity led to getting into bigger events. (Granted, all of this was based on the quality of the art and the proven ability of the gallery; all that was needed was the initial open door.)

It's been just over five years since SEASON opened, and it has been tough. Juggling my painting career with a day job has always been an effort—but that's what you do, because you have to. Add to that a low-maintenance gallery that disrupts your living arrangement, since the gallery is my living room and dining room. Suddenly, you realize you are working all the time. But that's okay: I enjoy working, and I really enjoy the work I get to do. Unfortunately, the switch from one job to the other is not always smooth or convenient. Right now, I need to work on wall labels for two fairs, and I have an unfinished painting I'd like to get to, as well as a few other things (laundry? grocery shopping?). It's really a jumbled mess when I think about it. No matter which job needs my attention, the other jobs are just as invasive and demanding. A friend suggested I get an intern for the gallery, which seems impractical and, frankly, very stupid. Why would anyone want to format labels or proofread a press release? How on earth could I ever pay someone to do that?

I was reminded today why I enjoy running a gallery. An artist posted a link to her show from three years ago, with a comment about how the catalog still brought new insights to her practice. I agree: the catalog author really dug deep and found relations and ideas that were barely surfacing at the time, but that have now fully blossomed. I feel I have an intuition (or maybe just crazy good luck) about making introductions that create deep and beneficial working relationships. For the first few years, each gallery show was calculated to be inclusive and equal: two artists, one male and one female; one local and one from out of town/state. This formula produced some interesting pairings, and I really enjoyed working out the combinations. My frustration came when, after doing this, I still heard the local drumbeat that women were not getting shows. Maybe I should have stressed the obvious facts about the shows I was producing. But like many things I do, I do my part of the work, and I expect others to do theirs.

I'm at a low spot in my studio these days. I struggle with the question of whether the world needs one more painting by me. I have a hard time feeling the use of it all when I see awards and accolades going to mediocre artists—or worse yet, when there is an appearance of a conflict of interest among organizations and winning artists. I feel like I need to crusade and call out these injustices, but part of me feels that, if I do, I'll just be seen as the upset artist, angry because he didn't win. Eventually, I just say fuck 'em. They are making a very ugly bed to lie down in, and I don't want to be associated with them. This, of course, comes at a cost when there is an opportunity to apply for funding but, due to some moral high horse I'm on, I feel I can't enter. I tell myself the same thing I tell my artists: that is, to just produce the best work you can. It is the only thing we have control of. Show opportunities and awards are granted for whatever reason, and since I have no control as to whether I get into this or that juried show, all I can do is make what I make and work harder to get it in front of an appreciative audience.

Just finding time to get in the studio is tricky. The day job keeps me standing and talking most all day, so by the evening, I just want to relax with my partner G, have dinner, and watch TV. I don't really like painting late at night; I prefer to work during the day. Maybe that habit came from when I supported myself purely on art sales—I enjoyed almost ten years at making art work and showing and having the freedom to have a full day in my studio. Then the recession hit and, practically overnight, people who were always going to openings and buying art and supporting museum shows just turned invisible. At the time, G had just quit his job, and I had just started a part-time job retail job. You could see art sales drying up pretty quick, and you could feel that things were going to be very different from there on. I still feel like G and I are digging ourselves out of some hole created by credit and wishful thinking, but things are fine, in reality. I love doing what I do. I just wish I could find more time to do it. I wish I could produce bigger results for my artists and for my own paintings.

SHARON BUTLER

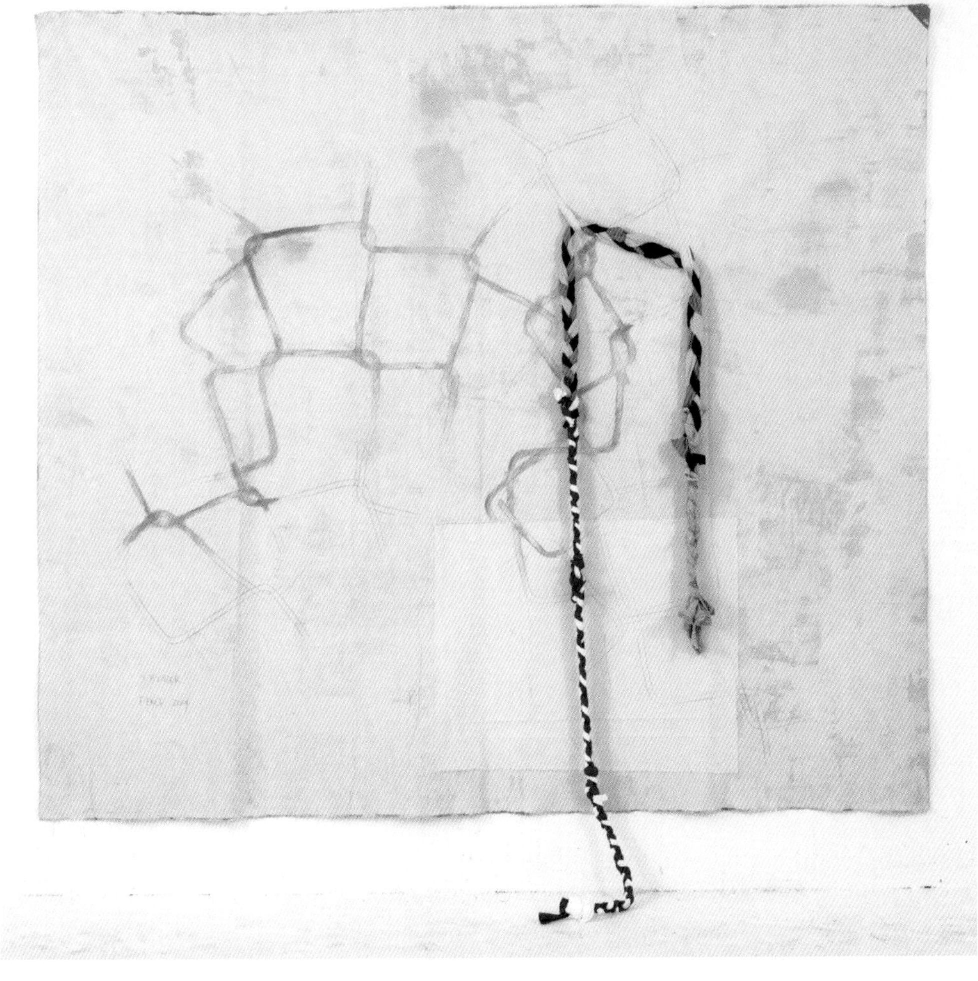

1. Imagine me, a small blond girl, with Chumley, a lanky, drooling Saint Bernard by my side, staring out a wall-sized plate glass window into the woods. The youngest of three daughters, I grew up in a beautiful, custom-designed modern home that my parents built in 1963. It was one of only three houses on the narrow, winding, dirt road, situated on a hill that overlooked the town's reservoir. My father didn't consider himself an artist, but he liked to make copies of abstract paintings (Mondrian, Picasso, Klee, Pollock) for the pristine white walls; inspired by Calder, he made aluminum sculptures and placed them throughout the woods. In the winter, they would gleam in the sunshine through the trees. My mother was a career woman in New York before they were married, and together, before he stopped drinking, they used to take us for weekend trips to the city to see plays, go to the ballet, and visit museums.

2. There weren't any other kids nearby, so growing up I had to amuse myself. I remember making odd projects from my favorite book, *How to Make Something From Nothing*, crafting small sculptures from candle wax, clipping and saving photographs from the Sunday newspapers (living halfway between New York and Boston, we got both the *Boston Globe* and the *New York Times*), and typing random

Sharon Butler
Fence
72"x90"
Pigment, binder, pencil, t-shirts, unstretched canvas
2014
Courtesy of the artist

phrases in iambic pentameter on a portable Olivetti typewriter. The isolation turned out to be good preparation for life in the studio.

3. I went to Tufts University, where I studied art history. I worked as a magazine designer and art director in Boston for several years after I graduated. At *Sail Magazine*, they paid for education, and after taking a couple night courses at Massachusetts College of Art (MassArt), I quit my job and enrolled in the BFA program to study painting. To support myself, I got a job as a guard at the Institute of Contemporary Art, where I sat in the galleries alone for hours. This is where I learned to love Robert Ryman.

4. Upon graduation from MassArt in 1987, I moved to New York City, where my then-boyfriend was a film student at Columbia. We sublet a small, furnished loft on the corner of Lafayette and Grand, upstairs from Rudolf Bass Power Tools, from an artist who had moved to Canada for a teaching job but kept the lease. I worked as a freelance paste-up artist at magazines like *Conde Nast Traveler*, *Vogue*, *Artforum*, and *National Lampoon*, barely making the $600 rent. I remember sitting at the table every morning, entering sweepstakes contests because winning one seemed more likely than getting a show or receiving a grant.

5. I never won a sweepstakes, but in 1990, I received a Pollock-Krasner grant. Naturally, my boyfriend and I broke up after a couple years (New York is hard on relationships), and when the recession hit, I went to graduate school at the University of Connecticut. They gave me a teaching assistantship that included a tuition waiver and a teaching stipend. I graduated, accepted a tenure-track position at Bergen Community College teaching Computer Graphics, and moved to Williamsburg in Brooklyn.

6. Up until that point, I was pretty much a loner, working in the studio and trying to grow my career through slide distribution rather than networking. The importance

of personal relationships didn't dawn on me until later. I wanted the same thing that every other young artist in New York wanted—gallery representation and critical acclaim—but I wasn't sure how to achieve these goals, so I spent most of my time painting. Eventually, a gallery in Soho run by a beautiful Chinese businesswoman, Zhang Zhang, saw my work in a huge group show in a nonprofit space and invited me to participate in a summer show. They sold my paintings, and the following year, they offered me a solo show. We discussed representation, and although it wasn't one of the galleries I would have preferred, I figured it was better than having no gallery at all. Michael Rees and Yigal Ozeri are two of the aritsts I remember who also showed with Zhang. I had several solo shows there, and after 9/11, she shut down and made plans to reopen in Chelsea when the art market improved, but she never did.

7. Looking back, it seems like a crazy decision, but during this period I married a guy who lived in my hometown—Mystic, Connecticut—and I began dividing my time between Mystic and New York. In 1998, anxious to teach beyond the community college level, I accepted a tenure-track position at SUNY Farmingdale, where my courses included Interactive Media, Typography, and Two-Dimensional Design. I also continued painting.

8. During a residency at Blue Mountain Center, an artists and writers' retreat housed in a huge lakeside lodge in the Adirondacks, I completed the first project I had undertaken that directly benefitted a group of artists, as opposed to myself alone. Every night at dinner, the writers, especially the poets, would talk about this or that competition, who won what, and so forth. When they turned to the subject of chapbooks, I was intrigued. Chapbooks are small books of poetry, generally no more than 40 pages. Poets submit their work to chapbook competitions, and acceptance is very selective and prestigious. The print runs are so minuscule, I wondered why the poets didn't just print their own. After all, anyone with a laptop and an inkjet printer—which I happened to have in my studio—could start their own

small press. Energized by the idea, in what my (second) husband has come to call my "manic mode," I offered to make a chapbook that included a poem from each of them. Using Rives BFK paper, a small elegant typeface (Goudy, as I recall), I printed and bound an edition that I distributed to the group. The poets, still somewhat discomfited by the idea of self-publishing, were amazed at how easy it was, and how "professional" it looked. Creating something for a group rather than for myself was a gratifying experience.

9. In 1999, my first husband and I had a baby. Between daycare expenses in the SUNY childcare center, loft rent, gas, ferry tickets between Long Island and Connecticut, and the mortgage on the place in Mystic, we were hemorrhaging cash. A series of bad decisions ensued. He didn't want to give up his used record store in Mystic and move to Brooklyn, so I quit my job at SUNY, gave up the loft, and moved to Mystic. After working as an adjunct for a semester at various nearby colleges, I accepted a one-year, full-time appointment in the Art department at Eastern Connecticut State University in Willimantic, Connecticut, an economically depressed mill town in the middle of one of the wealthiest states.

10. At Eastern, I taught Video Art, Computer Graphics, and other digital design courses, and the following year, they offered me a tenure-track position. With the responsibilities of the tenure track and a baby, I had to adapt my art practice to suit my new circumstances. As the quality of desktop video and animation improved, I gravitated towards digital projects, because I could work on them while I was teaching. With the encouragement of senior faculty members, I began developing strategies for integrating collaborative community projects with course content in ways that would benefit both the students and the community. Getting out of the studio and collaborating with other people expanded my view of what art making might be.

11. Mystic is home of the Mystic Seaport, which boasts ownership of the Charles W. Morgan, the last surviving 19th-century whaling ship. I grew up visiting the Seaport, thinking about whale ships and the whaling life. When I found a copy of *Moby-Dick* at a used bookstore, I began a series of projects based on the novel. *The Search for Moby Dicks* took me to Mexico and Europe, in search of establishments named for the novel's great white whale. The project culminated in a PowerPoint presentation about my search. For *Dickathon*, I worked with students animating Melville's text into a series of one-minute segments that we projected on the side of a building at the Fringe Festival in New Haven. In *Moby Dick, Used*, people donated copies of *Moby-Dick* (over 250 versions are listed in the Library of Congress) in exchange for limited-edition prints. My favorite contribution was a waterlogged paperback that someone used to keep on his sailboat. To put my new (non-painting) work in context, I curated my first show: a group exhibition called *Like Life* that included David Lloyd Brown, Jessica Schwind, Joselph Smolinski, Andrea Wollensak, and *Moby Dick, Used* at the Hygienic Gallery in New London.

12. In 2004, the divorce from my first husband left me without a studio, and I began writing. This seemed perfect: a conceptual practice that required no materials (other than a computer) and no studio space. Working on my MacBook, anywhere I wanted, was liberating. Sharing custody of my then five-year-old daughter Lena with my first husband was not.

13. In 2006, while on sabbatical leave, after I had earned (early) tenure and Lena had started school, I began painting again. My new husband Jonathan and I bought an old house in downtown Mystic, and I turned the spacious attic into a studio. Unexpectedly, my return to painting was also the catalyst for an enduring preoccupation with Web 2.0 tools and social media. Feeling out of touch with the painting world, after having worked mainly on digital and installation projects for several years, I began Googling "painting + museum, gallery, review" to find articles and

reviews about contemporary painting. I discovered art blogs like *Anaba, The Art Blog, Art Fag City, ArtVent, Big Red & Shiny, Chunky Monkey, Heart as Arena, Modern Art Notes, Newsgrist, Hrag Vartanian, Joanne Mattera Art Blog, Rhizome, C-Monster, Edward Winkleman*, and others (many no longer exist), and decided to make a digest of painting criticism. Thus, *Two Coats of Paint* began one afternoon in my faculty office as a simple Blogger template. With encouragement from fellow bloggers and the art community (and with help from Jonathan, a talented writer and editor) *Two Coats of Paint* has grown into its current form.

14. In the early days of blogging, art bloggers didn't get much love from the critical community, academia, or the art world in general. To gain some traction, Joanne Mattera and I formed an organization, called Art Bloggers @, and organized gatherings at the art fairs in Miami and New York. The idea was to raise bloggers' visibility and, we hoped, to increase their respectability. We assembled panels that included notable bloggers, such as Carol Diehl, Paddy Johnson, Carolina Miranda, Hrag Vartanian, and Ed Winkleman. Our first meeting took place one Miami morning, in a dark bar that stank of beer from the night before. A handful of people showed up, including talented artist (and early blogger) Amy Wilson. The next year, our events were standing room only, and now many fair organizers include bloggers on their rosters of official panel participants. I also began writing for *The Brooklyn Rail*. Publishing articles in an edited print journal burnished the blog's reputation and made *Two Coats of Paint* more respectable to the art and academic communities.

15. In 2012, Jonathan began working for the Obama administration, and I took a leave of absence from Eastern to join him in Washington, DC. Artsy hired me to write hundreds of artist profiles, and the blog flourished. Returning to Eastern the following fall, I realized that

my vision for their art program was out of sync with the parochial concept held by the rest of the art faculty. Rather than grind out my career working in a conservative program that would never embrace my ideas, I decided to leave.

16. I returned to New York, continued painting and blogging, and commuted to Brown University where I had been invited to teach a book arts course. The brainy, sophisticated, and quirky students there were delightful. Had I stayed at Eastern, I would never have had the opportunity to teach in an elite, private university like Brown. By necessity, after giving up my full-time position, my approach became more entrepreneurial, accepting short-term visiting artist invitations, writing assignments, and speaking engagements. No longer insulated from the art market with a university salary, I had to think more seriously about selling paintings as part of the new business model. I had solo shows at Pocket Utopia (New York, NY), Real Art Ways (Hartford, CT), and SUNY Westchester (Valhalla, NY).

17. During Bushwick Open Studios, instead of simply showing my own work, I invited artist Austin Thomas to curate an exhibition. I had met Austin at Pocket Utopia, one of the first gallery-salon spaces in Bushwick, where I had done a residency in January 2009. The exhibition included Margaret Atkinson, Guy C. Corriero, Lawrence Greenberg, and Edie Nadelhaft. I promoted the show on *Two Coats of Paint*, and it was included on many "must see" lists for the weekend. We all got more attention working together than we would have had we operated independently. Lawrence eventually opened Studio 10 at 56 Bogart Street, and Austin, after a two-year hiatus, reopened Pocket Utopia on the Lower East Side.

18. During my 2013 solo show at Pocket Utopia, instead of doing artist's talks about my own work, I invited people I admired to give presentations. One night Raphael Rubinstein read his poetry, and another night Gorky's Granddaughter (the ongoing video project of artists Christopher Joy and

Zachary Keeting) presented excerpts from their favorite studio visits. Naturally, I wanted people to come and see my paintings. But attracting them to the show by promoting these events established a larger intellectual context for the show, and a greater sense of inclusivity. People were there to see my work, to be sure, but they also came to participate in the art community. Staging these events with Austin, rather than simply asking people to come exclusively to hear me talk about my own work, turned out to be a satisfying experience for me, and I think a better one for those who attended. The gallery was jammed for both events. Kate Wadkins, a writer and obsessive 'zine publisher and collector, also came by one Sunday afternoon to talk about 'zines, an art form I've been interested in since I made the chapbook at Blue Mountain Center.

19. The blog has proven to be a means of staying current with contemporary painting, but it has also created a bridge to a wider community of artists. In 2013, the Creative Capital/Warhol Foundation Arts Writers Program gave me a generous grant for the blog, but after that, given the economic circumstances, I was uncertain whether to continue publishing. The blogosphere and social networking media have been colonized by large and well-funded organizations and corporate interests, making it increasingly difficult for independent voices to maintain a presence. Artists who once read blogs now turn to Facebook and Instagram to stay connected with one another. When I asked other artists, though, they seemed confident than the community at large would want *Two Coats* to continue publishing. In 2015, after turning to Brooklyn painter and gallerist Matthew Deleget for advice, I applied for fiscal sponsorship and launched my first fundraising campaign. More than 200 *Two Coats of Paint* readers contributed, so the blog continues. In 2017, we will celebrate its tenth anniversary.

20. As I write this, I am sitting in my studio at 55 Washington Street in DUMBO, at the foot of the Manhattan Bridge, listening to the B and D trains rumble by. After several years

moving from sublet to sublet, I was invited to participate in the Two Trees Cultural Space Subsidy Program, which means I get to keep this space for three years, at a rent that is considerably below market. Inspired to share my good fortune, in summer 2015 I introduced a short-term studio residency for artists who live outside the city. During the first eight months of this program, I have had four residents: Erin Wiersma (Manhattan, Kansas), Nancy Morrow (Manhattan, Kansas), Sue McNally (Newport, Rhode Island), and Gyan Shrosbree (Fairfield, Iowa). When I was living in Mystic, I would have jumped at the opportunity to set up in a NYC studio space and have visits with curators, dealers, and other artists, so I am pleased to be helping other artists to do this. I enjoy having the residents around, and I hope the conversations we have help move their work forward. I have also met some wonderful curators and writers through the residents.

21. My relationship with my daughter, Lena, who, at 12, chose to stay in Mystic with her father when I moved to DC, has gone through excruciatingly difficult periods, but continues to improve. She is now 17, a good student, and a gifted softball player, and we have begun to look at colleges. Her high school art teacher is showing her how to make a camera obscura, and how Vermeer painted. It was Lena who recommended the fascinating documentary *Tim's Vermeer* to me, and for Christmas, she gave me a beautiful faux stained-glass panel that she made herself. I still have the old house in Mystic, although I am trying to sell it, and I continue to spend part of each week there.

22. I love my life. I live primarily in New York, with a smart, handsome, extraordinarily thoughtful man, and I am often invited to give presentations about being an artist-entrepreneur or a culture producer to students and younger artists. I'm grateful to Leslie Bostrum, who invited me to teach at Brown University when I first left my tenured professorship at Eastern, and to Judith Thorpe of the University of Connecticut and Clint Jukkala of the Pennsylvania Academy of the Fine Arts, for continuing to

invite me to teach in their MFA programs. As I write, I am thrilled to have a solo show of new paintings on view at Theodore:Art, my favorite gallery in Brooklyn. A wonderful network of talented artists, writers, curators, collectors, gallerists, and friends sustains me, and I'm grateful that each of them has decided to make the art world a better place.

23. Over the years I've come to realize that, while working in the studio is primary, participating in the community and contributing to its enrichment and evolution is also important. The art world isn't really for loners; it's fundamentally built on personal relationships.

SHINIQUE SMITH

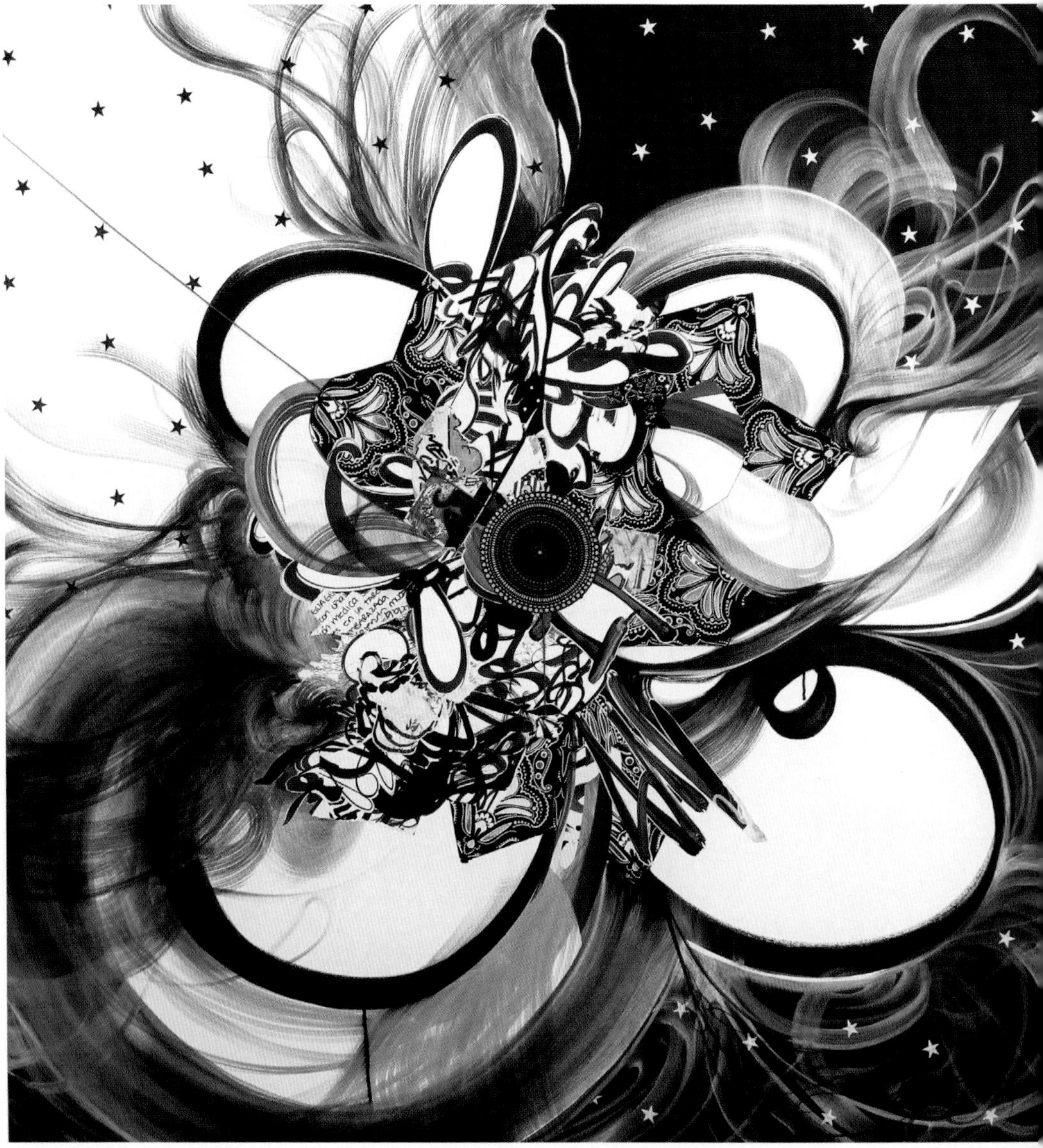

One thing I've learned is that clarity around how you see your work and how you value your work is the mark of a mature artist.

Being more mature and having love in my life have led to the conclusion that my health and happiness actually matter as much as being an artist. This has affected my life and work in unexpected and inspiring ways.

My path to living as an artist has been a curvy line. It began with my education. I attended the Baltimore School for the Arts for visual arts, and while there, I cut school and wrote graffiti, because at the time my friends were more exciting. After my second year, I was kindly asked to leave, as I "failed to conform to their standards." Entering my new school, it was discovered that I had enough credits to be a senior, so I took extra classes and graduated a year early. This school also happened to give me a full scholarship to attend Maryland Institute College of Art (MICA). One of my focuses in undergrad was video, and I was accepted to the School of Visual Arts (SVA) Film School. But I opted to stay at Maryland Institute College of Art (MICA), because I had a full scholarship and, after all, I was 16 years old when I entered college, so it was healthier to stay in my hometown. I don't regret that decision.

In 1992, I graduated with my BFA in General Fine Arts, a program which gave me the freedom to explore all media. At that time, I didn't want to pursue art anymore. I was burned

Shinique Smith
No Key, No Question
60"x60"x2"
Acrylic, ink, fabric and collage
on canvas over wood panel
2013
Courtesy of the Pamela Joyner/
Fred Guiffrida Collection

out from assignment-making and critiques. During my last semester, I interned as a wardrobe assistant on a feature film and found the world of film production much more appealing. I was young, and these freelance positions paid well. The Baltimore-Washington area was booming with productions at the time, and so assisting where I could on movies—in wardrobe, production, props, locations—became my thing. I loved film.

Following the path of working on movies led to working on commercials and television shows, which led me to Seattle, in 1993, to pursue production opportunities. There I joined the local union as a costumer and joined the board of 911 Media Arts Center, a nonprofit arts center that was at the forefront of new media in Seattle, providing access, education, and grant opportunities in video, audio, and web production. In the background, drawing and painting re-emerged as a private pursuit.

While it's a beautiful town, with liberal and active people, I found Seattle lacking diversity in the arts. In 1996, I founded a film and video festival screening the works of established and emerging Black filmmakers, called Flav'a Fest. I screened works by Cheryl Dunye, Isaac Julien, Thomas Allen Harris, Barbara McCullough, Kasi Lemmons, and Julie Dash, among others. There were open calls and lectures by filmmakers, such as Charles Burnett and Cauleen Smith, and I ran this for five years. Through that experience, I taught myself how to organize, engage the community, and fundraise for this annual four-day event. It was a labor of love, and the skills I acquired producing the festival were lasting and beneficial to other managerial positions I would hold in the future, including the management of my studio practice.

Above 911 Media Arts Center, which was my festival's hub, I noticed a curious older couple who lived next door. They were eccentric and kept to themselves. No one knew anything about him or her, except that they kept to themselves and owned a red, mint-condition Volkswagen bus that sat out front and was never driven.

One Saturday afternoon, I happened to stop into the Center and noticed the door to the couple's upstairs apartment was open, with a sign that said "estate sale." Upon entering, I was astonished to find each room filled to the ceiling with art: bronze sculptures and oil paintings hung salon-style; one small room with a small round table was filled with shoeboxes stuffed with drawings. The couple was Russian, I think? They were artists who had some success and recognition in the 1940s and '50s, as indicated by the catalogues from museum shows and collections in Spain and other places abroad. Everything had a Post-it-note price tag. All of the artwork, along with all the furniture and dishware, was up for sale by their children, or perhaps the landlord. They had passed away, surrounded by all their work—work that perhaps no one had seen. This struck me so profoundly, as I flipped through one of the shoeboxes of 100 small drawings.

These artists were prolific and good, and their legacy was being sold at an estate/ yard sale. I left suddenly; at the time, I felt I had to rebel against the sale, so I didn't purchase anything. I wish I had, so I could remember their names. It was at that moment that I subconsciously decided I did not want to live and die surrounded by my work.

I reflected on my life and what had brought me the most joy, and admitted that making art had been one of the things that fulfilled me in a sincere way. Also, I wanted to do good in the world and loved working with kids. So, the following year, I enrolled in an intensive Master of Arts in Teaching program with Tufts University and the former School of the Museum of Fine Arts (SMFA).

This experience was rewarding and eye-opening. I taught full-time as a full-time student. Working with teens was my concentration, and I count this as a pivotal time in my development, as a woman and an artist. I taught tenth-grade art and was allowed to create my own curriculum for an "Intro to Film Studies" course. I loved teaching but realized that I am not an authoritarian. Being in the position where I was obligated to discipline teenagers (I, myself, had been an unruly teen) felt like karmic debt for my behavior at my high school for the arts.

Teaching high school full-time was not the answer I had been looking for, however the knowledge acquired in that program was invaluable. In 2000, right before graduating, I saw an ad by the career development office for a summer artist residency in

Amsterdam hosted by an SMFA professor, and I jumped at the chance. It was the type of residency that you pay a fee to attend, so I used my last student loan funds to go make art that summer. At the time, the two-week residency was less than $2000 and included a small private apartment, a large shared studio, museum passes, a train ticket, and a shared hotel room in Paris for Bastille Day. It was amazing sharing a studio space with two young women artists who were fun and dedicated to art.

I woke up and could no longer deny that making art was my creative, intellectual and spiritual calling. The year 2000 was a transformative year, for the world and for me. I spent the year making several different bodies of work which were both figurative and abstract. I went back to my base, and I drew. Works on paper become paintings and, from work to work, my voice was growing. I decided to go back to MICA for my MFA.

The summer right before I entered the MFA program, I took myself to another artist residency in Venice that had just begun at a place primarily devoted to printmaking. Things were still cheaper then, as it was the year just before the euro was circulated. It also happened to be a Venice Biennale year, which I had not heard of until then. Outside my window in Campo San Maurizo, I started to notice there were new travellers dressed in all black amid the usual tourists. Suddenly, the city was flooded with the art world. One day, I was aimlessly exploring and absorbing Venetian architecture, when I ran into two African men who stood out in the landscape of new visitors for the art exhibits—they were smiling. We spoke to each other. One worked for an arts foundation and the other, Salah Hassan, had curated a new off-site show of works by African artists. They were on their way to the press conference, and they invited me to come along. I was not trying to network, but I enjoy meeting people who are creative wherever I go, so I joined them. This was a turning point for me, seeing these artists' works and meeting these Black international arts people. I felt I was part of something larger, on the fringes but part of the field that I wanted to have a dialogue with through my work.

Who knew that, when I decided to just go to Venice, there would be this show and these people? Following my intuition brought me to where I needed to be for creative and professional growth. Through those meetings came studio visits, and I was received a grant to have my first solo exhibit in Venice the following year. Intuition and proximity have played a huge role in the opportunities I've received and in the development of my work.

After Venice, two events brought me back to my birthplace—a broken heart and a job in the education department at the Walters Art Gallery in Baltimore. It's strange returning to the place you grew up and couldn't wait to leave. I didn't realize that it would have such an effect on my work. Returning to my roots and remembering my youth, reconnecting with my past, stimulated connections between all I had seen and experienced in between. These personal revelations kick-started a fresh investigation of the linear qualities of my work, and how that line related to the graffiti of my past.

When I began my MFA program at MICA, where I grew up in Baltimore, I entered knowing who I was and with the purpose of making art my professional life. I wasn't exactly certain what that meant, and no one has ever told me what that means. It is something I have defined for myself over the years, and the definition begins and ends with the work.

In school, I experimented with writing as a form of frenetic meditation; it was how I could connect my art practice with spirituality and aspects of popular culture. These ideas were explored through painting, drawing, video, and performance—using the wall, the floor, my voice, and my body through movement. I began thinking of space and meaning, about text and the power of writing, and I began building a body of works around those thoughts. Ultimately, my first-year work was what I sent to Venice for my first solo show.

My peers in school were diverse in age, experience, and arts education, and a few of them remain my closest confidants on art and life. We supported each other through dialogue and sharing things we read, artists we'd seen, and material techniques, and we continue to support each other in this way. Watching my fellow artists evolve their ideas and take risks, having an open dialogue with them about the challenges of growing a practice and supporting ourselves in the world, is one of the benefits of going to school or participating in a residency. I'm not so much interested in the kind of "group therapy" type of bonding people do when they commiserate about being overlooked. I'm drawn to more productive and enlightening conversations about how life affects art and vice versa, and how we are growing as human beings through the work. Being part of a community of artists, no matter our distance from each other, has remained a significant part of my survival as an artist.

Though I am grateful for those great friends and colleagues, there are also those who are more competitive—something I found out with my impending show in Venice. The critiques of my work became a little less generous. There were a few professors who were supportive, a few who were indifferent to all but their chosen favorites, and a few with whom I butted heads. There were many conflicting responses from one critique to the next: useful, indifferent, and also insulting at times. If I disagreed or was not ready to follow advice when it was given, it was OK, because I knew I was being true to the moment of my development and finding my own way. Graduating, I had a stronger voice; I also recognized that the voice which was most adverse was the most generous of them all.

Residencies have been milestones in my development as an artist, and I decided to go somewhere new to improve and meet new people every summer. The summer after my first year of grad school, I went to the Vermont Studio Center, where I was awarded my first fellowship for an artist residency. There, away from my usual materials and environment, I took risks and crossbred my work. I made installations of calligraphy on paper that became sculptural and began utilizing fabrics, like denim, as a surface. I used bleach and ballpoint pen to draw and write on denim, which reminded me of doodling on my jeans in class. These actions sparked memory and the contemplation of the poetry and meanings of cloth. This residency was particularly inspiring, as there were poets and writers in residence who had weekly readings, and established artists came to visit my studio. Those visits were a contrast to those from school, perhaps because these artists were free of institutional politics. It was amazing to come back to my last year of grad school with new ways of working and broader viewpoints.

Upon graduating, I was granted a summer residency at Skowhegan School of Painting and Sculpture, which is when I learned that having prestigious residencies on your resume was important—to show the world that you are serious, and that others have approved of you in some way. While at Skowhegan, I furthered the work, partied like everyone else, and applied to several studio residencies in New York, where I was accepted to the Lower Manhattan Cultural Council's Artist Residency (LMCC) for that fall.

When I returned home, I found that my lease had automatically renewed, and I couldn't get out of it without my landlord suing me for four months' rent. I could've stayed and waited to move until I sorted it out, or I could say "screw it" and go for the opportunity. I chose to go. I broke my lease and found a junior one-bedroom in Brooklyn that a friend from grad school had recommended. Arriving in New York the night of Halloween, I was almost broke, but I had some assistance from my mom, a small honorarium from the residency, and keys to an amazing studio with a view of the bridges in Manhattan. Intuition and proximity played a role, again, in being where I wanted and needed to be.

Being broke, the first concern is how to cover basic expenses and needs. That year, I worked for the Armory Show, which was a nice paycheck for 60 hours of work in ten days. Assisting in the Armory Show office, I got to see galleries; I was able to see who had paid for their booths on time, and who had good manners and who didn't, within a short period of time.

Through my residency at the LMCC, I had studio visits with curators and was asked to be in several shows. I said yes to everything! Internally, driven by the promise I'd made years before at the artists' estate sale in Seattle, I wanted the work to be seen and not gather dust. However, now I am more selective with my participation. After saying yes so much, I found that saying no is as important to nurturing the work and my health as an artist.

Art in General organized the first group show where my work was included. At the time, they accepted general submissions and curated by committee. Clifford Owens—an artist and friend whom I grew up with in Baltimore and someone I have always admired—was on the committee and saw the potential in my work. My first two years in New York, I was in almost 20 group shows—some great shows and some terrible, but each one helped me to develop my work, my exhibition resume, and exposure. These shows were accomplished while I worked to sustain my practice and myself.

I went to work for artist and friend, Kehinde Wiley, whom I had met one day while viewing an exhibition at the Studio Museum in Harlem. At first, he hired me as a painting assistant, and then promoted me to managing his studio. It was a great job, because I cared about the artist and the work. This allowed me to use the organizational and leadership skills I'd learned earlier but had not yet applied in my life as an artist. It gave me insight on how to manage my own studio through managing his. I feel grateful to have had this opportunity and so glad I moved to New York.

My first years were challenging, due to lack of resources. I began recycling and reworking things I had made before in my studio. I began to use whatever was available at the time to make art and began culling my own closet to stretch canvases. This was a moment of discovery, realizing that I could use fabric and its existing patterns and color, in lieu of paint. I created wall works that were stretched fabric, and many works on paper. Some materials were gifted via Materials for the Arts (a re-use center located in New York) and friends clearing their closets. As more bags of clothing appeared in my studio, it was clear to me that this was my most plentiful resource. The route I took between studio and home was often peppered and strewn with clothing and packages of recycling. I found these urban gestures beautiful and saw that there was a romance within the cycle of these things. The discoveries I made in the LMCC residency prompted me to make sculpture, a form I had not yet studied or explored.

Eventually, my calligraphic works and sculptures sparked the attention of curators who were engaged with inquiry and with supporting a broad community of artists. These curators were Franklin Sirmans, Dean Daederko, Edwin Ramoran, Koan Jeff

Baysa, Renee Ricardo, Sara Reisman, Chris Lew, and Christine Kim, who encouraged me to produce a monumentally scaled work from a sketch I'd shown her.

This was my first bale sculpture, and it garnered some attention in the *Frequency* exhibition at the Studio Museum in Harlem, in 2005. Being included in that show made a significant impact on my career, through the press and reviews it received, and from the interest of collectors and galleries it generated for all the artists involved. This led to my inclusion in other significant shows, like *UnMonumental: The Object in the 21st Century*, the inaugural exhibition of the New Museum, and *30 Americans* at the Rubell Family Collection in Miami.

These were exhilarating times in the studio, which I moved back into my apartment between residencies. Space is a highly sought after commodity in New York. I moved my studio eight times in nine years: from the residency at LMCC to an apartment to the Abrons Art Center to a series of Brooklyn spaces that I would never have known about had they not been recommended by friends. Studio recommendations are one of the many benefits of remaining connected to a community.

Through triumph and tribulation, no matter what "success" has yielded, these friendships have endured. Success is less about who you know and more about how you love, and who you share it with. Working and living in close proximity to a community of artists of my generation, like Jennie C. Jones, Luis Gispert, Jacob Hashimoto, Mickalene Thomas, Derrick Adams, David Antonio Cruz, Nicole Cherubini, EV Day, Wangechi Mutu, Marc Andre Robinson, Kalup Linzy, Chitra Ganesh, Katrín Sigurdardóttir, Mariam Ghani, Navin Norling, Thomas Chapman, Jeffrey Gibson, Rune Olsen, Liz Brown, Marcus Morales, and others was stimulating and encouraging. We would visit each other and share information, materials, tools, and ideas; we sometimes assisted each other with projects that were on deadline and too big to manage alone. Overall, just seeing glimpses of each other, working or passing on the street, confirmed the knowledge that I was not alone at the beginning of my journey. There was a free-flowing camaraderie and pride in knowing so many diverse, smart, creative, and independent artists and young curators.

Since moving to upstate New York, my husband, artist Gary Pennock, has been a central figure in my art and home life. Moving here displaced us from the community that we knew, and so we have relied on each other for intellectual and creative support. His skills with technology have been essential to my new works with dance and video. We have collaborated on sound, video editing, and creating my website; he has shared his knowledge for improving the organizational side of my studio. His keen commentary has been influential. This has been one of the most significant relationships of my life. Who knew you could find a kindred artistic spirit to evolve with? We have been fortunate to have each other out here in the country.

These relationships are the most important to the work. The artists and curators I have been grateful to know and call friend have been invaluable resources of inspiration, support, and love. Even at a distance, to see my peers striving and thriving, as part of our collective consciousness, is confirming, and I believe that we continue to inspire and celebrate each other.

No one ever taught me how to support myself as a professional artist, how gallery relationships or the art market work. I've learned some things from my friends along the way, and also by making mistakes.

Communication is a tool that I am constantly developing. In the beginning, communications with artists and curators were much easier than speaking with galleries. There were many things unspoken in developing gallery relationships. My friends have shared simple thoughts about perception—like, how having a solo show with a gallery can indicate, to the world and to that gallery, that you are now represented by them, even though the formal conversation about representation never took place. Who knew? Or, how essential it is to have assistance in the studio or administratively, at least with an intern, because it allows you to manage time better, and your studio production can be more fruitful.

After years of school, residencies, and living in New York, we have built a large network. Artists talk to each other. We share our knowledge and experiences. I feel it is part of my duty to share my experiences with galleries and institutions with peers who may ask—and many do in confidence. I've also recommended artists to galleries in the past, a couple of times before vetting the situation. One promising gallery relationship, in particular, turned quite negative, resulting in a legal settlement when I and some artists I had recommended found ourselves involved with a gallery that chose not to pay us. So, I am careful about involving artists in situations until I am certain it will be a beneficial and respectful relationship. I am open with them about my relationships, so that they can make informed decisions. The best gallery relationships I have had are with people who not only exhibit and sell the work, but also understand and honestly believe in the work and in me.

I have had the privilege of working with both small and high-profile galleries that have taught me how to value my work, and which value artists in general. These galleries have promoted and expanded the context of my work and have shown it alongside more established artists. Survey exhibitions have come from our shared efforts, and my work has flourished in those relationships. Over time, some galleries have closed, some I have outgrown, and a few I continue to grow with. I have found that, because of the time it takes to produce the work, it can be difficult to maintain multiple galleries and provide them all with new work. This is something I work on balancing, and why it is also important to work with people who understand my process. I think a relationship with a gallery is a true partnership and one that grows over time. It is not romantic, but it is like a marriage of sorts—where communication is key, and being single is better than being married for the wrong reasons.

Mistakes have been essential to my evolution. I've allowed myself to embrace failure in the artwork and in other things I was not prepared for professionally. I share my thoughts on pricing, and dealers share theirs, and we come to a consensus. Value is so tricky, and talking about money can sometimes feel uncomfortable. Over time, I have learned that the way one views money, in general, affects their ability to earn it. Through my experiences with galleries, I have learned that it is best for everyone involved if I am clear and confident in what I want and need within these varied situations. I have found that open communication is the foundation of great relationships. Luckily, I have had just a couple of bad experiences with galleries which were dishonest or simply didn't have imagination. These issues were momentary setbacks, and I strive not to let them affect my confidence, so that I continue to move forward despite hardship or success.

My grandmother always said: "Step by step, always forward never backward." I used to call her every day on my way to the studio, and her concern was comforting. My mother, husband, family, and friends are my bedrock, and still, I have had a hard time sometimes believing the good things people say. At times, in an effort to stay grounded and not drink the Kool-Aid, I have thwarted my own self-confidence; but I have also found that, sometimes, the good criticism is true. Accepting success, what is strong and good about the work, can be harder sometimes than accepting the negative criticisms. Ultimately, this is a constant battle that goes on in the studio, and it always comes back to the work.

When it comes down to it, my life and my art are interconnected. At this point in my life, if it is not about growth—creatively, financially, and personally—then why do it?

STEPHANIE SYJUCO

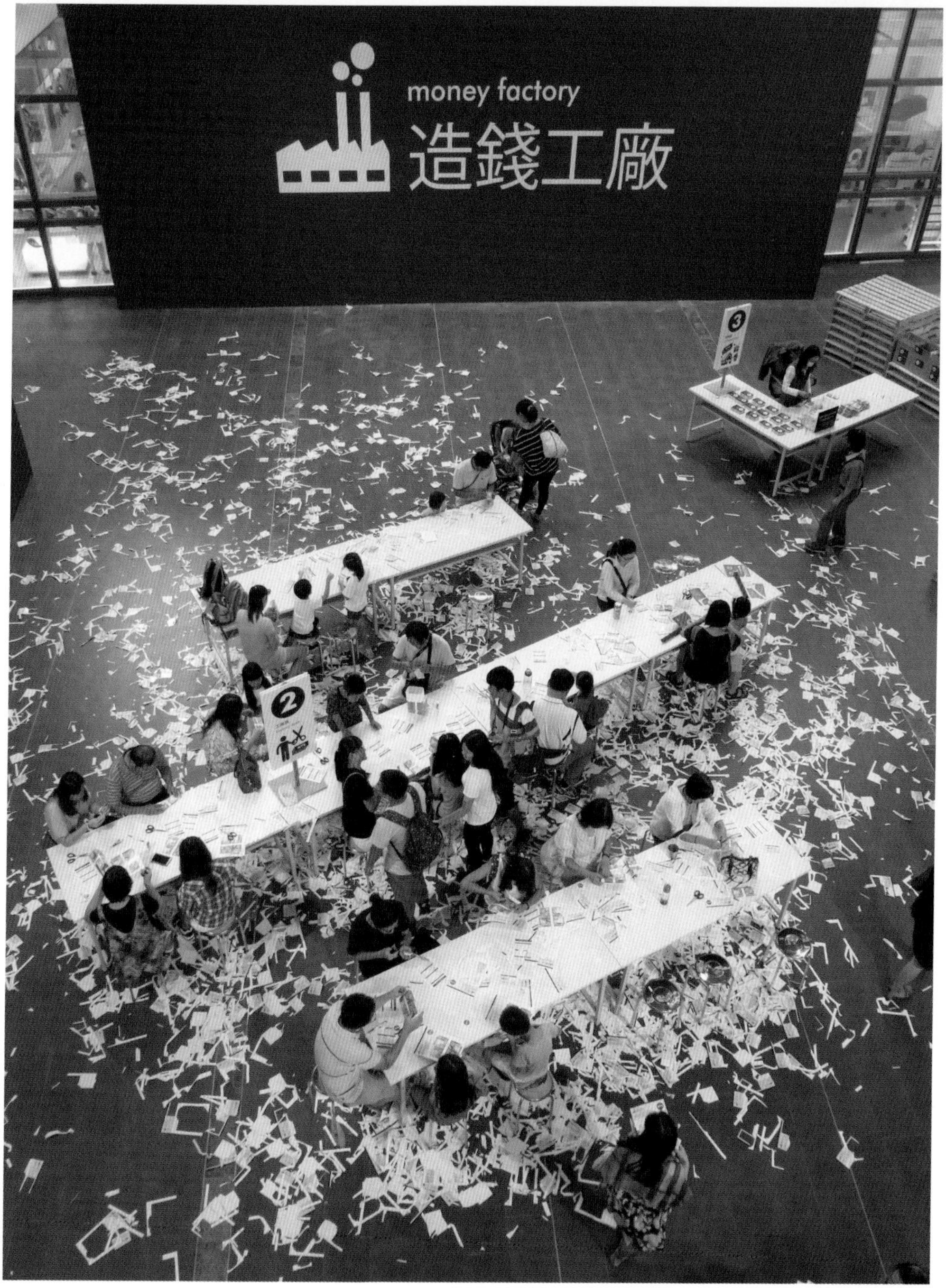

I make the type of work that can be difficult to fund but is intensely rewarding to produce. My projects range from large-scale participatory installations and online conceptual projects to publicly-sourced archives. In other words, my projects mostly fluctuate outside of the traditional commercial gallery model of art objects that can be bought and sold. Because of that, I've had to be resourceful in figuring out how to fund and produce the work; I rely mostly on grants and fellowships, commissions by exhibiting institutions (such as alternative spaces and museums), as well as any day job I might have at the time. I travel often, nationally and internationally, to produce and exhibit work. I've always been based in the San Francisco Bay Area, which has a thriving art community, but it has taken branching outside of the resources available here to meet the ambition and scope of what I want to make.

I've been a professional artist for over two decades now, and it has only been in the last five years that I think my career has hit a space where I feel more comfortable and satisfied about calling the shots on everything. Although I do apply for opportunities, I'm increasingly approached by others to be in exhibitions, present at speaking engagements, collaborate with organizations, or receive institutional commissions.

When I was 20 years old, I did a semester exchange program in New York City. I lived in SoHo when the galleries were all

Stephanie Syjuco
Money Factory: An Economic Reality Game
30'x100'
Activated "factory" production space, trading area, and bank vault display (three month duration). Commissioned for the Asian Art Biennial, Taichung, Taiwan.
2015
Courtesy of the artist and Ryan Lee Gallery, New York

still located there and worked as an artist assistant for sculptor Dennis Oppenheim, slogging it out in his messy fabrication shops. I also interned at White Columns Gallery, one of the preeminent emerging artist spaces at the time. Those experiences opened my eyes to an art scene that was ambitious, fast-paced, and oddly accessible when one was directly immersed in it. I went dumpster diving for bread, drank in bars I wasn't old enough to visit, and lived in unheated warehouses.

After returning back to San Francisco, that hunger and drive led to some initial success after a number of years, but it was definitely a burnout-inducing phase of my life. I started showing at a blue chip commercial gallery in the city and had moderate success in sales. But about seven years into all of it, I hit an incredibly disillusioned point, when it felt like I was just throwing large amounts of money, time, and energy into my studio but still economically treading water. The great irony was, by that time, I had already received several notable grants in the Bay Area: a Eureka Fleishhacker Award of $28,000 and an Artadia Award for $10,000. I was young, I was hip, and I was, it seemed, quite popular on the art scene. I had a commercial gallery that was dedicated to showing my work. I had been an artist-in-residence at the Headlands Center for the Arts in Sausalito. All these things "appeared" to be successful to the outside world. But although I was getting a certain amount of recognition, it wasn't translating into a livable and sustainable income. The money was all sporadic and would immediately get eaten by living expenses and exhibitions. I wasn't selling enough work to make a living, and that was taking its toll. Previously, I had been employed full-time as an exhibition designer at the Exploratorium Museum in San Francisco (a hands-on art and science museum), but I quit about five years into the job and decided to focus more on my studio work. So, I was working as a freelancer for mostly immigrant rights organizations and nonprofits, trying to toggle together an income. Hustling for odd jobs took a lot more time than I thought, and my studio practice started to lag. I remember attending a Creative Capital workshop, in which they were trying to coach young artists and discourage them from "dropping out;" it made a huge difference, just knowing that it wasn't only I who was struggling.

In 2003, I went back to school for an MFA at Stanford University, eight years after I finished undergraduate work. I went back, partly because I needed to break my own rut and jump start a new way of finding time to focus on my work, partly because I wanted to gain teaching experience, and also because Stanford has a tuition-free program and gives their graduate students a generous yearly stipend. The result is that I have zero debt from my education. I think this had a huge impact on my ability to spend that money investing in my practice right after graduate school. Plus, since the program encouraged each student to teach, I received a lot of hands-on experience in shaping classes and learning pedagogical approaches. Because of this direct experience, after graduating, I started getting random adjunct jobs at art schools in the Bay Area, including the California College of the Arts; Mills College; University of California, Berkeley; and the San Francisco Art Institute. But the shocking thing was, they all paid so low that I hit rock-bottom, with zero dollars in my bank account, when I was in my early 30s, just four years after graduate school.

I literally had no cash and thousands in credit card debt, due to my healthy studio habits. I was able to bail myself out, little by little, and with the advice of a fellow artist who was studying financial planning, I proceeded to create a systematic way to save and hold myself more accountable. She advised me to immediately pay off the credit card bills, not carry forward the interest, and to literally put aside 10% of all money I earned into a savings account that I couldn't touch. This would be my nest egg. That tactic was shockingly easier than I thought and helped raise my financial situation out of debt.

Another major way I saved finances was by saying "no" to so-called professional "opportunities" that actually drained money. In the past, I had said "yes" to almost everything, in an excessive attempt to get my artwork out into the world. That included any nonprofit requesting a work for their auction, random small shows, alternative space exhibitions where I was paying to ship out the work, etc., etc. By learning how to say "no" to these, I wound up being able to actually choose better what I wanted to participate in. I began seeking out the opportunities that provided artists some form of compensation and—voila!—I would actually get them.

This was the single most important decision I made: to stop shooting myself in the foot financially by taking on too many non-compensated art "opportunities." Since then, I have gotten used to being provided budgets from $500 to $40,000 on single exhibitions (with small nonprofit art spaces on the low end and museums, like SFMOMA, on the higher end). I walk away from offers of exhibitions which will drain me more than I can gain from them. It's a matter of conserving my limited resources and time, really.

Most of my projects are site-specific commissions, and I've built it in that I have to physically travel to the site to research and complete the work—from London to Manila to Istanbul. This has put me in touch with a wider art community around the world and has made me nimble about being able to do projects under different forms of pressure and with different communities. I've learned to be flexible and fast, to work well with others, and to think quickly about how to problem-solve on the spot.

The first big international break I got was a 2009 commission from Frieze Projects in London. On the invitation of the curator, I proposed a quite ambitious work that I, honestly, had no business actually proposing, because it literally was beyond anything I had ever done. *COPYSTAND: An Autonomous Manufacturing Zone* involved setting up a live production space within my own gallery booth, in which I would hire five young artists to bootleg and counterfeit other artworks being sold at the fair, and then sell them to the public at drastically discounted prices. It was a performative spectacle, with people buying and selling these insane knockoffs, me acting as "gallerist" and managing my hard-working counterfeiters, and fielding ridiculous amounts of press and the public. 35,000 people attended the fair in five days, and it felt like they all crowded into my booth. The project got on the front page of the *New York Times* "Arts and Leisure" section, as well as major coverage in international art journals. It hit a nerve contextually, because it was right after the 2008 stock market crash, and the art market was reeling from losses. No one knew if that year's Frieze Fair was going to boom or bust, and *COPYSTAND* appeared to be a provocative look at the economic fallout. The attention and project effort was literally overwhelming—a breakthrough piece that taught me a lesson in playing big and delivering big. I think it was partly my own naiveté about how the scale of these types of projects worked that made me bold enough to even propose it.

When I started believing that I deserved better and pursued better-paying opportunities, I received more back in terms of compensation and respect. In 2014, I applied for and received a Guggenheim Fellowship Award to fund an ambitious project, involving collaborating with international museum collections to do 3D scans of ceramic artifacts and digitally collide them to produce hybrid objects representing hidden legacies of colonialism. *Empire/Other* was initially supported by the FLACC Workplace for Visual Artists in Belgium, an arts residency that helps artists produce new work. Through their contacts and networking, I was able to meet with the museum curators and access their collections, as well as be provided with 3D modeling and scanning technicians to assist on the project. I'm extremely proud that this idea was supported by so many organizations, and I am still working on the project, since it is a long-term endeavor. But half the battle was just getting to a place where I could muster the guts to apply, write the proposal, and send it out, fingers crossed. I'm happy to report that my craziest projects—the ones I feel are more odd, or radical, in nature—are the ones that get the most attention and funding.

I spent a decade as an adjunct professor at almost five different art programs, and I know that's not unusual for many artist educators trying to make ends meet. After all that time cobbling together paychecks, with no health benefits and precarious scheduling, in 2013 I landed a tenure-track assistant professor position at UC Berkeley in Sculpture. There, I teach and develop coursework in social practice, sculpture, graduate studies, and professional practices, among others. I emigrated with my mother from the Philippines when I was a young child, and I remember growing up on welfare and being incredibly class-conscious. I know this feeling of economic alienation has influenced my consciousness about economic access and teaching at Berkeley. I actually do think that teaching at a public university is a political act in an era of privatized education and rising tuition costs; in some ways, doing so falls into line with themes that I address in my own artwork—mainly, working with and teaching others how to gain agency and a voice within a larger system of capitalism that seems overpowering or overwhelming.

In the design of coursework, I see myself as creating platforms for co-production and collaboration with the students, and we test out these ideas together in experimental forms. For instance, for one social practice class, the students were all sitting around, complaining about how they felt they weren't getting enough out of the Art department. I challenged them to create a better system, so we collaboratively set out to invent an "alternative art school embedded in an art department." ART SCHOOL X, as it was dubbed, was a semester-long project that forced the students to walk the walk of creating challenging content, activities, and discussions for themselves and their fellow students. What we took away from the experience was thrilling and a reality check—that educational systems are complicated, it's easier to say things than do them, and that overhauling pedagogy takes hard work. I wholeheartedly consider my students co-creators in the project and, since then, have implement similar tactics of co-creation in other classes. It seems natural to me, since many of my own projects involve collaboration and harnessing collective vision.

Incredibly, I just bought a house in Oakland, and as a single, female artist of color living in the ever-more-expensive San Francisco Bay Area, that is no small feat. I never thought I could own a house by myself—it's modest, but it's lovely and perfect for me. Being a professor is a huge part of how I am able to afford this stability. But it's at the price of now literally having two full-time jobs: that of a professor and a professional artist. There are many times that I have to make hard choices with my time about how to focus on each one.

What I've learned through the ups and downs of my art career is that it's imperative to advocate for and work towards sustainable models of art-making, for the sake of others moving forward with better knowledge. I lecture often about artist compensation from the standpoint of someone who has experienced the gamut, from precarious individual to well-funded collaborator. I create open-access archives of my grant and exhibition proposals, so that it demystifies the application process (you can even read a copy of my Guggenheim proposal, which I've posted publicly online). I'd rather foster a sense of cooperative knowledge-sharing as opposed to competition. It creates a healthier art community, and one that doesn't rely on keeping trade secrets or hiding information from fellow artists. We artists are a creative force, and we do much better when we consider ourselves to be collaborating on the ultimate project: a society and community that values what we produce. And this includes sharing the means to create that success.

STEVE LAMBERT

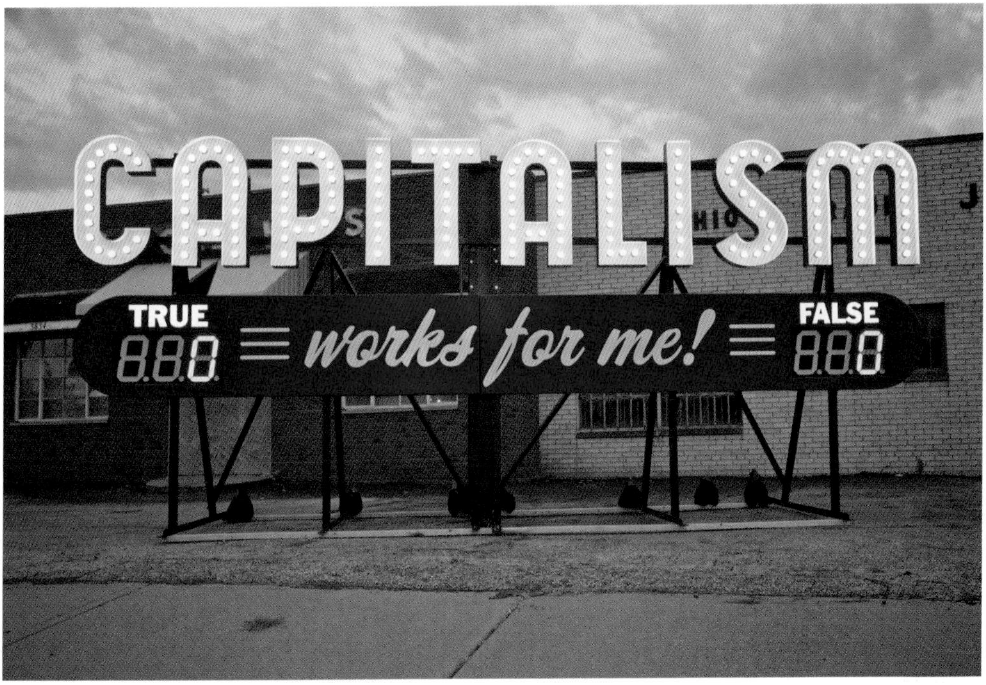

Compared against my artist peers, I'm not much of a museum goer—galleries tend to irritate me more than anything. I chose to be an artist because it gave me the most freedom. I'm able to make projects that reach everyday people and present ideas that, while perhaps unfamiliar or unusual, open up other possibilities for how our world can work. I'm an optimist, and I think we can do better. Of course, I can't make people do anything, nor would I want to, but I *can* create spaces where audiences see new opportunities and choose how to move forward.

An example: I built a scoreboard for capitalism. A traveling 20-foot-long, nine-foot-tall sign, reading "Capitalism Works For Me!" with a podium where people can vote "True" or "False." Nobody wants to talk to a stranger on the street about capitalism, so the voting process and the scoreboard are a ruse. The artwork's real purpose is to draw people into a space where they can evaluate the economic system—not on a global or national scale—but for themselves. "How is it working *for you?*" Many who have come across the installation in places like Tremont Farmer's Market in Cleveland or Times Square in New York City found themselves considering this specific question for the first time. But my bigger objective was creating an environment where the economic system, which so many see as the end of an evolution where all other alternatives have failed, can be up for judgment at all. Many see capitalism as the "least worst option" and say, "yes, it's flawed, but what else is there?"

Steve Lambert
Capitalism Works For Me! True/False
20'x9'x5'
Aluminum and electronics
2011
Courtesy of the artist, CC BY-NC-SA

My answer is that the alternatives to capitalism are infinite—so how do *you* think we could do better than capitalism?

Making art this way came naturally. First off, my dad was a Franciscan monk; my mom was a Dominican nun. Of course, they quit, but their reasons why, and what they did afterwards, were guiding influences for me.

My parents were both sent off to the church when they were young, later working for years in San Francisco's Mission district and Oakland in the early 1970s. They took to religious life for a mix of reasons, but mainly because they genuinely believed in the whole "serve your fellow man, help other people" liberation theology ideal. In fact, they realized they believed in that more than in the institution itself. So, they left. Falling in love helped, too.

With just a set of street clothes and a few hundred bucks, they needed new careers. My dad learned woodworking from his grandfather, so my mom put an ad in the classifieds. This became the family business for the next 30 years. My parents secretly hired addicts, vets, and immigrants for their furniture business. They visited the Redwood City V.A. Hospital, found vets in recovery, and sought out recent green card recipients from Central America, training them all to work in the business. Experience with woodworking was not a major hiring factor, as most of their employees had none. I grew up in the shop and remember lunches that probably looked from the outside like an outlaw motorcycle gang, or a group of Merle Haggard roadies on a break. It was me and grizzled, long-haired, cocaine addicted Vietnam vets, hunched over sandwiches with a guy who just arrived from Guatemala, learning English. My dad wouldn't look so out of place either. He was close to 300 pounds, bear-like, with a big beard, and—his church life aside—grew up fighting on the streets of Paterson, New Jersey and later, working, literally, as a cowboy and a picker in fields in Southern California. He could be intimidating when he needed to be, and was never fooled or manipulated by a guy on the crew who fell off the wagon. My parents had no problem firing employees who became unreliable, and they just as easily hired them back once they were clean again. Multiple times.

They didn't call the business "Second Chances," and they never revealed the pasts of their crew to the customers. It went unstated, irrelevant to their public face.

So, this was my initial context. My parents left the church, starting new lives at 35 with next to nothing, eventually having three kids, and starting a business where they hired people out of principle instead of practicality. We were financially unstable from the start, and it never really smoothed out, because the market for custom furniture was destroyed over the next 20 years by automation and globalization.

We were not a devout family. When I was 16, I asked why we never went to church. Bibles were around the house, but no one read them. My dad did wear his Franciscan robe—as a bath robe—until it became threadbare and fell apart. "Do you want to go to church? We could spend our Sunday doing all that, if you want," my father explained. "Or, we could spend our time actually helping people."

That was basically it: my parents' whole approach to their lives. Doing good wasn't something you did in a convent, or isolated to non-work hours, or designated to a Sunday. Values, ethics, and action were weaved into the everyday.

But doing good isn't very lucrative. We weren't always able to buy groceries or consistently have food in the house; the business was embezzled, and we regularly slept in the office, while my parents worked overnight and weekends. Eventually, the business folded coming out of the early '90s recession. But this helped my career later when, as an artist, I, too, had unstable income and little assurance of where I'd make money in the future. I saw how this made my artist friends anxious. For me, it wasn't ideal, but at least it was familiar.

Another thing that helped shape my practice as an artist: I was institutionalized.

When I was young, I was often told the future was wide open and full of possibility. But the means to that end was a strict and prescriptive path. Follow instructions, work hard in school, continue on to the best college possible, and from there, you're free to pursue your dreams! But be warned: not following this path will lead to limited options and likely failure. You can do whatever you want with your life, but you *have to* do all that first. The problem was, I couldn't stand school.

I was a good student. I was curious and wanted to do well; my grades were good, and I was liked by my teachers and fellow students. But over time, I wanted more than what my public high school could offer. For example, the few art classes offered were a joke; music was about rote performance rather than creation and composition; subjects like photography and film didn't exist. So, out of obligation, I set my desires aside and continued to push myself in areas that felt less and less relevant as I advanced: upper-level math, college-level history courses, marching band, track and field, and so on. I was disciplined. I endured as much as I could and tried to channel my frustration into improving the situation the ways I saw how. I sought out information on my own with the spare time I had and even tried to improve the school by running for, and becoming, class president. But this didn't change anything. Over time, my effort wore down to indifference, then to resentment. Yet every weekday I had to come back, continue to work hard, and I came to hate it.

All the details leading up to my being committed to a psychiatric hospital are not relevant here, but this antipathy with school was layered onto other issues, including a family health crisis and a death, severe migraine headaches, stress, and a lack of skills in coping or even speaking about my problems. It all collided. I was overwhelmed, in physical pain, severely depressed, and felt exhausted in every way. I'd run out of ideas and could feel myself self-destructing. I withdrew and internalized—I didn't tell anyone, because I didn't know how. There's a lot I'm leaving out, but it was bad. I needed it all to stop and felt, if I could die somehow, at least I could have relief.

Someone happened to ask me the right questions at a specific moment, and they caught a glimpse of what was happening inside. I was checked into a hospital later the same day on an involuntary hold—though, at that point, I was ready to volunteer. That intervention saved my life. Those months spent in treatment became a turning point. Over the next few years, I learned skills to manage stress in my life, but, more importantly,

I felt like I had narrowly cheated death. Doing what I was told had been a total failure. So, I could now, rightfully, say "fuck it all." I had license to reshape my life as I pleased.

I checked out of the hospital and took a state test to leave high school. I had no idea where I was headed, but whatever I did was sure to be better than before. The contrast was unreal. The outcome of my hospitalization was independence. I felt freed from constraints that had completely failed for me, released into an open space where I could choose for myself how to move forward. There were options, and I could make choices. It was the best possible outcome from a horribly painful situation, and I am still so grateful for it.

Today, I recognize the echo of these experiences in nearly every artwork I make. My work is about sharing liberation and agency. We don't have to accept our world as it is, the ways we're told we should navigate it, nor the costs and misery that come along with it, but which benefit so few. I don't want to make art that just points out problems. I want to go further than suggesting solutions. What I'm trying to do is offer the experience I had—to give people the feeling of liberation and power that I felt. The democratic ideal that we're not subject to culture; we can create it. And I trust they will go on and do so.

For me, it took me a while longer to figure things out. With my newfound freedom, I worked various odd jobs, traveled solo, drifted in and out of community college, and ended up taking a temp position at a title company, photocopying real estate documents. Around that time, a roommate who worked in the mailroom at the San Francisco Art Institute brought home the admissions paperwork I would need to apply to the school; he told me he'd take the completed forms in to work the next day.

Even though I had never been to a contemporary art museum prior to enrolling, I was accepted to the school and completed my degree. Because of my inexperience, as I sat through my art history classes, I learned the wrong lesson. In my art history textbook I saw in each image a definitive example of what art is. The paintings I saw defined the edges of what painters do. The sculptures I saw were examples of what sculpture is, and the weirder contemporary stuff were just updates to the definition.

I didn't relate to that artwork, or to those artists. They lived in eras I didn't live in and which I had no connection to. I was just some guy who grew up in San Mateo, California—and it was all a bit intimidating.

The mistake I made was seeing art history more as a dictionary instead of an encyclopedia: a list of rules that define what art is, rather than examples to browse showing unique people pursuing their practice. Later, it started to click: art history is *historical.* The work comes from one moment and place, with a conceptual approach specific to that time and those artists' life experiences and expertise. As I spent more time, I had another liberating realization: my art could be relevant to *me*, in my time, and a product of my experiences and knowledge. Art could be whatever I wanted.

And what I really wanted was to crush my landlords. I was living through the first dot-com boom in San Francisco. Rents were soaring, and there was lots of money to be made for unscrupulous property owners. I was fighting my second illegal eviction. The first, at a different apartment a couple years earlier, I had won against in a full jury trial. That experience gave me a crash course in San Francisco landlord-tenant law, so a couple years later, when I was served with another illegal eviction, I felt confident in simply following the steps I had before, this time without a lawyer. This led to a nerve-wracking day spent representing myself in San Francisco Superior Court and defending, rather poorly, pre-trial motions for my own court case against one of the city's top landlord attorneys.

Desperate for help, a friend referred me to the San Francisco Homeless Advocacy Project. Feeling a bit guilty I told the lawyer there "But I'm not homeless—is that OK?"

"If you lose, will you be homeless?"

"Yes." If I lost I'd have to vacate in three days "but, I dunno, I'd figure *something* out."

"But Steve, you *would be* homeless."

This was the terrifying fact I'd been ignoring since receiving the eviction notice. I had to admit, "Yeah, I guess I'd be homeless."

My life seemed split in two—learning about printmaking methods and Jacque Saussure at the Art Institute on Tuesdays and Thursdays, and filing high-stakes legal documents with the help of the Eviction Defense Collaborative and the Tenants Union during the rest of the week. Fighting for my home was urgent and real. In comparison, the world of studios, galleries, and museums felt abstract and insignificant in every way.

I contemplated becoming a lawyer. I didn't want to quit art, but all the people in my life who seemed to have the power to get things done we're lawyers. I even took the LSAT and considered law schools. Yet, when it came down to registering, I knew the law wasn't where my strengths lay. My skills were in the arts, I just hadn't figured out what to do with those skills, or how they even mattered against such daunting forces.

My creative practice made sense once I figured out how to connect my art practice to my reality. I started hanging around with the San Francisco Print Collective and worked in the Mission Cultural Center, using my printmaking skills to create and distribute political posters on the streets about gentrification and the real estate industry. I took over illegal advertising space and derelict billboards in my neighborhood and put art in its place. As I walked through my neighborhood, public spaces and the messages in it became something I had agency over instead of something I was subjected to.

I've never been an art lover. I love connecting with people, and learning and gaining some new understanding. But I only *like* art. Because art, for me, isn't the point. It's a means. Art can communicate profound ideas, and it can do it both beautifully and effectively, but I don't mistake the phone line for the conversation. The point is to connect with other people, to exchange ideas and have that mean something in the world. Specifically *how* it's done is just a matter of details.

Public space was the space most accessible to me and a direct venue to connect with the most people. My neighborhood was filled with murals, graffiti, and advertising billboards and posters. The contrast between the style and messages created by residents versus the advertising targeting us was stark. The fact that so much of the advertising was illegal just added to my frustration. Illegal advertising space became fair game in many of my projects. Around the city, marketing companies covered construction barrier walls with various posters for music, albums, and other products. I started painting over the ads—creating white walls—and organized art exhibitions for the sidewalk. These Budget Gallery shows were part garage sale, part block party, part art gallery, and we accepted work from anyone as long as they agreed it could be sold, stolen, or vandalized. Hundreds of artists from around the world responded to calls for "non-masterpieces" to be distributed to unsuspecting audiences. The gallery commission was arbitrary, optional, and determined by the artist, and we usually made just enough money at the end to buy burritos.

I continued my early career as an amateur, balancing my time making the best art I could while working at the highest paying day job I could tolerate. Figuring out how to keep money coming in is an ongoing challenge, and I've worked all kinds of jobs—parts manager at a Vespa shop, file clerk, undercover security agent, and bass player in a country and western band, to name a few—developing skills and experiences which still come in surprisingly handy.

I sought out institutional support for my art where I could. I was once awarded a grant, but I was never actually given the money, because the unclear legality of my work might "endanger the funders." It's a feather in my cap now, but at the time, I couldn't help but entirely doubt the feasibility of my career. I eventually won grants from the California Arts Council and, later, from the Creative Work Fund, which allowed me to turn more time and focus to major, longer-term projects.

As an artist, I've made money almost every way there is for artists to make money—teaching, grants, gallery sales, crowd-funding, and so on. And the hustle hasn't stopped. One place it at least eased a bit was during my Eyebeam fellowship. In the Eyebeam OpenLab my charge was to do R&D for the public domain. The fellowship brought me to the East Coast and gave me the freedom to do the work I thought most important, with less of a sense of dread about how I'd pay the bills. It was there that I worked on the *New York Times Special Edition*, a replica of the *Times* issue that hit the streets one week after the election of Barack Obama in 2008. With the help of dozens of writers and hundreds of volunteers, Jacques Servin from the Yes Men and I were able to distribute 80,000 copies of the paper around New York, each of which contained 14 pages of best-case-scenario news dated nine months in the future. The project and the ideas behind it quickly spread around the world on TV, newspapers, radio, through word-of-mouth, the project's website, and social media.

The stories weren't fantastical tales of an Obama presidency, the executive savior making unilateral decisions. Our newspaper was full of workable plans, grounded in reality, and told from a future where citizens demanded a better world and fought to achieve it. The project was a success beyond anything I'd imagined (in truth, we were working so hard on it, I'd only imagined as far as getting it done). But once the dust settled, Jacques and I were left wanting more. We'd helped to articulate a vision and plan for the future. But we didn't want to just inspire a dream, we wanted to make it real. For me, it came back to the reason my family didn't go to church. I wanted the work I did to have a more direct effect. I think Jacques felt similarly, and in the year that followed, we both started new projects to make that happen. The Yes Men started The Yes Lab, which teaches groups how to pull off Yes Men-style hoaxes; Stephen Duncombe and I created the Center for Artistic Activism as a research and training institute to help activists be more creative and artists to be more effective.

We're now about eight years into the Center for Artistic Activism. To date, we have led over 25 workshops with over 500 activists from three continents, nine countries, and dozens of states within the US. At each location, we teach activists the fundamentals of creative practice so they can design actions which communicate both the world they hope to achieve and how others can join them in moving toward it. We've worked on various issues, like Roma discrimination in Macedonia, transgender rights in Eastern Europe, gentrification in St. Petersburg, public health in Eastern Africa, and resegregation of schools in North Carolina.

While there are specific problems we work on, and concrete solutions the organizations we partner with are working towards, my bigger goals are much more ambitious. What many imagine "art" and "activism" to be both defines and *confines* the practice. Activists can be shortsighted in their vision and rely too heavily on what's worked in the past, not allowing themselves to dream of all that success might be, much less new and better ways to get there. Artists can lose their grounding and have their vision contaminated by the commercial art world; they often struggle to have an impact through poetic works that are illegible to non-art audiences, and with no effect on what's happening in the real world. Art and activism work best together, but it's a lot more convenient for the wealthy and powerful to pretend they're entirely separate fields.

I refuse to go along. I have to define my practice for myself, taking the best from art, activism, sociology, magic, psychology, martial arts, design, marketing, comedy, organizing, and whatever other practice I see working along the way. I have to scan all the possibilities, then create my own priorities and boundaries, and compile my own methods. Because when I haven't, it's been really bad.

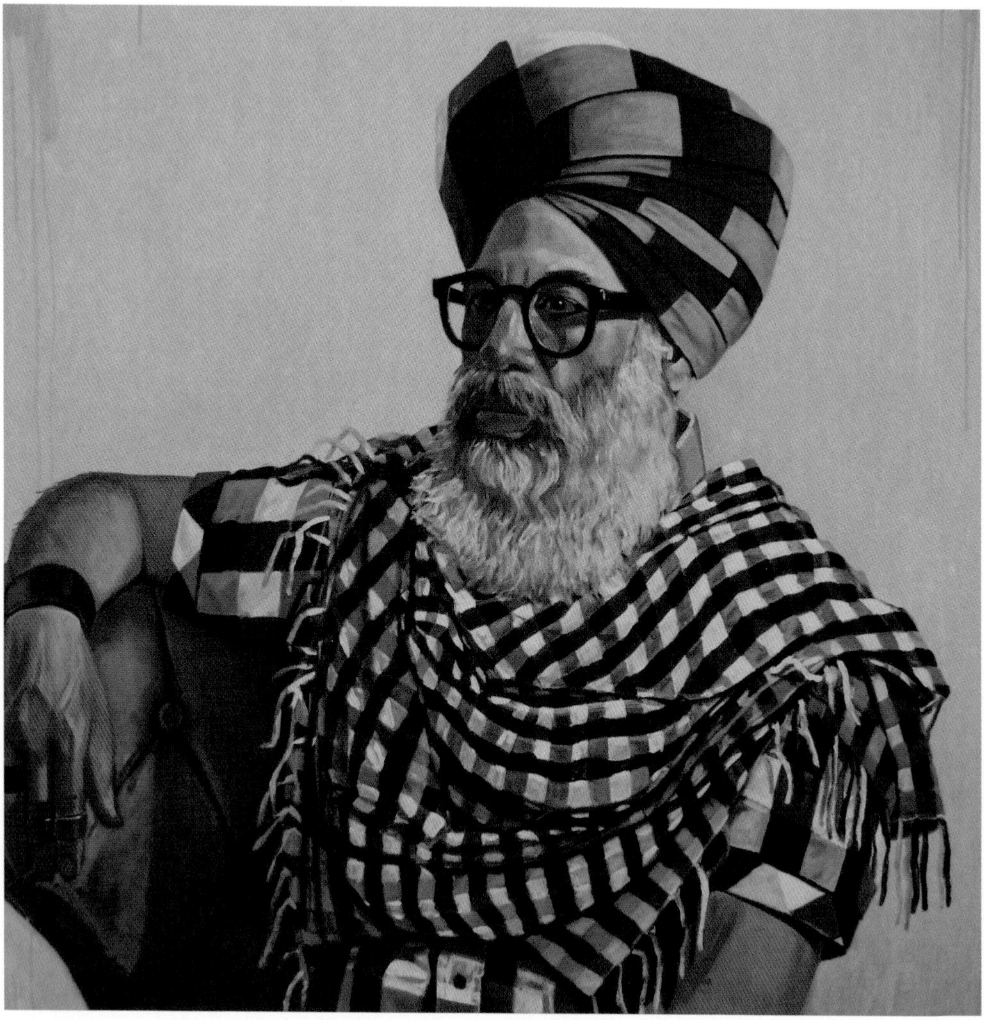

TIM: As a kid, I didn't know any artists. My introduction to an art-related job was my once-a-month elementary art teacher. I thought, "I want to do that." While teaching was a viable profession to me, I never realized I could make art as a career.

My dad served in the military, and so we moved several times. In fewer than four years, my family lived in Massachusetts, Texas, and Missouri. Culturally, we transitioned from a suburban community to a very rural, small town. I didn't know anything about museums; I first learned about and coveted paintings when my parents gave me a board game called "Masterpiece." I showed great interest in art from an early age; I was always drawing people. My high school art teacher took an interest in me and recognized my single-minded focus in art. The teacher, Mrs. Jobe, directed me to a good but small BFA program in the region.

—

ZOË: My dad was a career serviceman, a master sergeant 26 years in the Air Force. We lived in Florida, California, Japan, Maine, and Georgia. My dad retired when I was a senior in high school in Maine, and we lived off-base in a rented apartment. My brother and I had extra rooms that my mother assigned as our "studios." When I think back on this, it is clear that my mother thought it was important that my brother and I had designated spaces to create. My mother was an amazing educator; she specialized in teaching children with autism and

Tim Doud
Buffalo Check
40"x40"
Oil on panel
2014
Courtesy of the artist
Photography by Lee Stalsworth

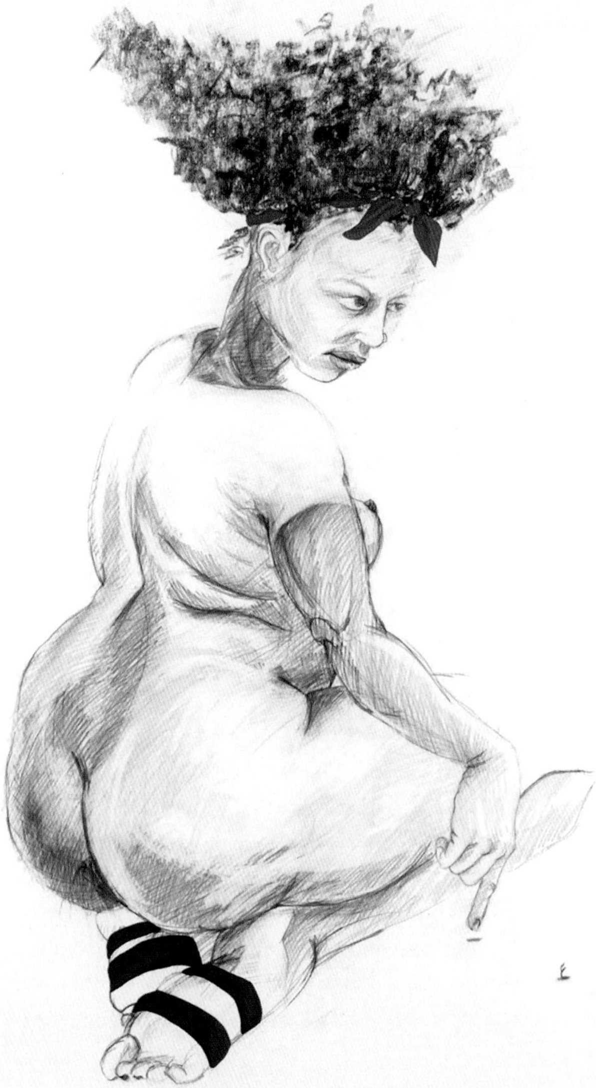

Down Syndrome. My frame of reference for education was that, as a Black woman, it was important that in addition to attending college, pursuing a master's degree was part of the equation. My mother had a master's of education. Though it wasn't expected that I follow in her professional footsteps in education, my family assumed I would get an MA....in something.

TIM: Neither of my parents attended college, but somehow it was always clear that I would. Moving helped me understand how other people live. I chose art as my undergraduate focus, but I dutifully pursued classes that would yield a profession—such as secondary education and graphic design. As I was only really interested in making art, I didn't go with any of the sensible options. I worked my way through college. I worked as a screenprinter for a sporting goods store and as a clerk in a liquor store. When I finished my undergraduate degree, I moved from Columbia, MO to Northern California where—long story—I ended up working as a wine buyer. Through all these moves and transitions, I maintained a studio and exhibited work. Eventually, I decided to pursue a career in art over a career in the wine business. I studied at the School of the Art Institute of Chicago (SAIC) with the intention of getting an MFA, so I could get a teaching job. (And, by the way, all of the paintings in the "Masterpiece" game that I played as a child are in the collection of the Art Institute of Chicago.)

ZOË: Unlike Tim, I never expected to teach. Most people attend graduate school to be able to teach at the university level, and I found that there are more artists with MFA degrees than there are teaching positions in academia. As an undergraduate at Tallahassee Community College and Florida State University, I had amazing mentors, Francios Baudoin d'Ajoux and the late Ed Love, who were instrumental in shaping my experiences in college and my trajectory as an artist. I applied to a small selection of universities and ended up in an MFA program at University of Texas at Austin. I chose it for a lot of reasons, but primarily because it was a three-year program, I fell in love with the city, and I felt an immediate connection with the faculty that I met when I toured the school.

Zoë Charlton
Cousins 1 (from Tallahassee Lassies series)
60"x40"
Graphite and gouache on paper
2008
Courtesy of the artist

TIM: I felt the same way about moving to Chicago. The prospect of working with Jim Nutt excited me, and artists I knew in San Francisco spoke highly of Susanna Coffey. Once I finished the MFA from SAIC, I worked at a liquor store again for about a year. After that year, an artist commissioned me to paint his portrait, allowing me to quit my wine sales job. I was hired to teach suburbanites in the northern suburbs of Chicago. These were among my first supporters and remain good friends. For the next four years, I concentrated on painting; I started exhibiting at artist-run spaces like Prairie Avenue Gallery, sold work, and continued receiving commissions. During this period, I also made sure to teach one or two adjunct classes, because I knew teaching was an important component to what I wanted to do.

I had great mentors in Chicago. Many people talk about Ray Yoshida, and all the reports about him are true: he invested in his students' art as much as he would invest in his own. He visited my studio throughout my time in Chicago and was one of the first collectors of my work. Phil Hanson, a significant Chicago artist and the chair of the painting program, offered me my first college-level job at SAIC. I'm paraphrasing here, but he emphasized the importance of teaching as a form of giving back. He saw my enthusiasm for teaching, and he also impressed on me that teaching is important work.

ZOË: I had three jobs after I graduated from UT Austin. I worked as an artist's assistant for Michael Ray Charles for around five hours a week and as a gallery preparator for 20 hours a week, which paid my health insurance. But the bulk of my hours came from two to three overnight shifts per week as a home health care aide, which paid the bills. In between jobs, I temped, as well as working a brief stint as an animator at Flat Black Studios. But, on average, I was working around 45-plus hours a week. Around my job hours, I worked (and lived) in my studio, which was a rented warehouse on the east side of Austin.

Two significant work experiences changed my trajectory. While working at Michael Ray Charles's studio one day, he casually suggested that I think about teaching. He said that I should consider the communities that would be important to engage for my lifestyle, and in my professional life, towards academia. Star Varner at Southwestern University offered me my first teaching job—a beginning drawing class. I wasn't so great! But teaching allowed me, for three months, to work my overnight job just once a week. Suddenly, I had all this time to spend in my studio! I did all this for a year after graduating, and it was clear that this lifestyle of a patchwork of jobs, for many reasons, was not sustainable for me. It was ridiculously exhausting.

Rick Delaney (my husband) and I moved to Missouri, where he held a tenure-track position for three years. I worked as adjunct faculty at a state school and at a private university during that time. When we decided it was time to leave, we had a huge choice: to move back to Austin or Houston, Texas, or for him to start looking at teaching jobs again elsewhere.

TIM: I didn't consider looking for a full-time job right away. I realized, after a few years as an adjunct at SAIC, that an institution like SAIC would not offer an adjunct with my experience more than one class, maybe two. As much as I loved teaching at SAIC, I could see that if I wanted a full-time position, I'd have to quit the adjunct job. While in Chicago, I exhibited in many venues that show emerging artists: Hyde Park Art Center, Contemporary Art Workshop and the Cultural Center in Chicago. I worked my way through the nonprofit spaces in Chicago and knew I needed access to new opportunities. I applied to the Space Program, a residency funded by the Marie Walsh Sharpe Art Foundation. The Space Program provides artists with a free workspace in New York City (NYC) for a year. I received the grant, deferred for a year, and moved to NYC. The move profoundly impacted my work. Even though New York City is a tough job market, I started teaching adults again at the 92nd Street Y, The New School and Cooper Union. After about five years living in NYC, I started looking for full-time teaching jobs. By then, I also started to exhibit my work in New York. I still took the odd job to pay my bills. A memorable one was assisting artist Yvonne Jacquette for a couple of days in her studio, mixing paint—my only experience assisting an artist. Around the same time, two schools offered me full-time teaching positions—one at Indiana University and one in upstate New York.

ZOË: Rick and I decided that it was my turn to apply for a full-time teaching job, so I submitted applications to a select handful of teaching positions in Florida and the Mid Atlantic. I had been out of school for about four years and was very active making work in my studio, and surprisingly excited about teaching. I really thought about where I wanted to live, because wherever that was, we decided that we were going to stay in the next place we moved to for a very long time. After growing up in the military and moving around so often, I wasn't too keen on how disruptive constantly uprooting would be on my studio practice. I paid attention to the demographic of the program's faculty (gender, race, age, and how long people had held their positions). I applied for five university teaching positions and one sabbatical replacement in Texas, Florida, and the Mid Atlantic. We also looked at opportunities for artists that existed in the cities of those schools, specifically to exhibit work, residency programs, and grants. Rick submitted a joint application for us at the Patterson Residency at the Creative Alliance, a live/work space in Baltimore, Maryland. I was offered an assistant professorship in the art department at American University in July 2003. Within a week of accepting the position at American University, Rick and I found out that we were selected as first-year residents at the Creative Alliance in Baltimore.

TIM: I decided to take a job that allowed me to stay in NYC. I was appointed to a two-year visiting assistant professor position at New York State College of Art and Design at Alfred University. I lived in half of a farmhouse in Hornell, NY, commuting with my dog, Buddy, three days a week and staying in Brooklyn the rest of the week. I didn't teach for a year after leaving that position; a colleague urged me to go on unemployment, and it became kind of a grant year to me, lots of time to work. I had my first solo shows and applied for tenure-track positions. My criteria was that I live in a big city with museums. I got a tenure-track assistant professor job at American University 11 years after receiving my MFA.

ZOË: The very first, unintentional collaboration between Tim and me was our hire at American University. We faced a unique situation: there was one position available. The chair at the time, Ron Haynie, found a way to hire us both and it made sense—Tim was a figurative painter, and I made figurative drawings. When we finally met, we decided that we needed to find a way to work together. We were very strategic about this—we made a pact.

TIM: We made a decision to be good colleagues. As colleagues, we have thought a lot about creative, collaborative, and co-working models. Our own working relationship developed, first, from collaboration by accident and necessity, and then, by collaboration through deliberation and intent.

ZOË: During our first semester and year, we had some real challenges. 1) The program seemed to exist on an island; 2) we found it difficult to find appropriate mentorship and a supportive community in the institution; and 3) we found it challenging to teach in a curriculum that didn't fully reflect the way we think about art-making. This wasn't just about pedagogy; this was also about the way that we live.

TIM: We are both married and came to our jobs with our husbands. We were both hired for our identities, a kind of academic retail: one gay, one person of color. The search committee chair kinda let me know this, which is a curious thing to disclose to a new colleague/employee. I was called in during part of the process and told that I would be promoted as a "gay" hire. I didn't know how to respond to that. So, I said, "Do I have to teach gay?" Zoë faced a similar quandary. During our first few years, the majority of our students were white, and in our first year, the graduate students requested that Zoë teach about race.

ZOË: Yeah, well, students wanted me to teach about blackness. So, I assigned a bunch of readings from authors that address whiteness...

TIM: ...and then, the crazy thing is Zoë had to miss that class for some sort of family emergency. So, I taught the class on whiteness. That was actually an unplanned collaborative teaching moment!

ZOË: That particular situation is a conversation about the ways in which diversity impacts both teaching and learning experiences. Because of our identities and our own experiences, we immediately recognized the lack of diversity in the classroom—from who teaches and studies in the art program to what information is presented in courses. The result of not experiencing diversity in academia limits the ways that people may expect you to teach or even behave.

TIM: We made decisions about being more inclusive in the classroom and in the program. We started giving our students readings in contemporary critical discourse—postmodernism from a non-Western point of view, gender and abstraction, and essays about reciprocity. We started working more with the visiting artist program at AU and invited artist that reflected our communities, or artists in extended fields in the arts that we found intriguing or didn't understand. It helps to work with someone who shares your perspective.

ZOË: Dwayne Butcher wrote an article for BMoreArt, called "Zoë and Tim Like Each Other." There's a rhythm and tone to our working relationship. Tim often initiates conversations, as it's in his personality—he has an enthusiasm and a willingness to immediately engage.

TIM: Zoë is typically more reserved in her approach, very social, diplomatic. Our different personalities complement each other in our work environment. But it doesn't mean that we don't have conflict.

ZOË: When I became Chair and Tim became Program Director, we had some serious philosophical and sometimes petty disagreements about our job responsibilities. Luckily for us, we both process ideas verbally, and we are rather long-winded. We take a day from campus, sit down and talk things through. We are colleagues who became friends.

TIM: The way we navigate our work life is complementary to that end, and conflicts between us don't happen that much; we have similar academic and professional goals. As a side note, our husbands don't think we actually listen to each other, ever, but we do...We just cycle back, 20 minutes later. We have seven concurrent conversations, and calendars, and a lot of understanding.

We also faced the challenge of figuring out what we could do at AU. We wanted to figure out how to navigate working in this institution, while acknowledging its history, and thinking about our own ambitions. It is also important to mention here that the full-time faculty does not rotate through a university as often as does the administration. Administrative staff changes frequently. While particular administrators may not understand our field, from the start we've had a lot of freedom. The college has never dictated our mission, curriculum, or programming.

ZOË: Early on, we received some impactful guidance. A senior colleague pulled us into his office and said something very significant to us. He said, "You need to make this the program that you want." But making a program your own is not straightforward; strong mentorship is also important. I knew I needed a mentor. But I had to have a strategy. 1) Find someone in your program and in the upper administration that you can talk with. 2) Attend administrative meetings or events in another program. 3) Find your counterpart at another institution. How does someone else at another school with a different set of rules and policies manage? How do they handle the teaching-service-research intensity?

At AU, it wasn't important for me to know who the best teachers were, but which faculty were really good at navigating academia. Hearing about their experiences transformed the way I thought about my job. I had a surprising ally who used to call me a PoMo as an insult, but he ended up being one of my best advocates.

TIM: There are limitations for a small arts program within a university. Art in a larger, liberal arts university is a tiny fragment of what they do, so you are working outside of the general system, and you have to recognize that. These challenges are why we are interested in working outside of the university, as well as inside of it. We recognize that as much as the university can support us, there are only so many resources the institution has to offer.

We want to help create a culture that supports change. Our program had a very particular relationship to painting, which could have been perceived as narrow. The faculty decided to make the graduate program non-discipline-specific. We like to think that some of these changes helped recruit faculty and attract students with diverse practices.

Our junior colleagues don't always agree with all the decisions that we make, just as we didn't agree with all the decisions that the people made before us. If you are aware of the cycle of things, you understand that change is inevitable, and you work to your strengths—we have different skill sets and interests. One of our colleagues started a Berlin program. We had nothing to do with organizing it, but we supported the development of the program. It is important to us that junior colleagues continue to shape the program.

ZOË: When we were junior faculty members, the department moved into a new building. It offered us many new opportunities—a huge museum space with a director who was amenable to collaboration, and facilities that appealed to prospective students. We thought, how do we work with what we have? We're in a great city with major cultural institutions filled with people who are very approachable and who are interested in engaging outside of their respective institutions. We also had students who were really hungry. They wanted something beyond the university. The bottom line: we wanted to feel connected in the community and to help our program hold a place of relevance in the city.

TIM: I commuted from NYC twice a week to maintain my studio there, and Zoë was commuting from Baltimore to DC five days a week. During my commute, we talked a lot about programming and decided to co-direct the Studio Art program at AU. We also wanted to move programming into the greater DC metropolitan area and bring the regional art community into AU more directly. We approached some local galleries and curators and asked if they would curate our students' work into a small series of exhibitions. We proposed a series of projects to Jack Rasmussen, the director of the AU Art Museum, for which local art institutions, galleries, and nonprofits would curate shows in the AU Art Museum and participate in the AU Studio Art program's visiting artist program.

ZOË: I was an artist-in-residence at the Hirshhorn Museum. When the residency ended, we began cultivating a relationship with Milena Kalinovska (the previous Director of Public Programs and Education at the Hirshhorn) to share visiting artists. Tim and I met with her each semester, which led to cohosted Hirshhorn artist talks. This program added an amazing array of artists to our roster of visiting artists, like Doug Aiken, Marina Abramovic, and Jake Chapman.

TIM: The DC art world is not so large. As we met more people, we began to think differently about community engagement. We capitalized on our relationships with people at their respective institutions and, if we didn't know people, we asked for a meeting.

ZOË: In academia, institutions can be "tribal," but we were motivated to cultivate relationships with faculty at colleges and universities in the DC metro area. We decided to curate an exhibition for the American University Museum in 2014. We visited one or two faculty at each of the major academic institutions in the DC metro area, including James Madison University, Maryland Institute College of Art, Towson, Howard, George Washington University, George Mason, and Bowie State University. The result was an exhibition was called *The Neighbors*. It was really exciting.

TIM: We made allies at various schools. We now have colleagues where we can share information, resources, opportunities; we have shared visiting artists. We also contacted arts organizations, such as the Hamiltonian (where we both serve as mentors), the Phillips Collection, and the African Art Museum (Smithsonian) to cohost artist visits.

ZOË: We worked with Nudashank, The Contemporary (with Sue Spade), and collaborated with individuals in the DC community. Dr. Darryl Atwell, a DC art collector, has partnered with the Studio Art program for more than five years; he initiated the *Kinetic: Conversations in Contemporary Art Series* held annually at AU. Our collaboration with him is a great example of the layered relationships we have with artists and art professionals in the city.

TIM: Bringing local organizations into programming at AU benefits the students and makes our curriculum more relevant. Before moving to DC, I met Victoria Reis, cofounder of Transformer, a small not nonprofit with a national reputation. From 2014 to 2016, we collaborated with Transformer to host panels on the shifting landscapes of artist-run and nonprofit art spaces, bring residency programs into the museum and our programming as visiting entities, such as Elsewhere Museum/ Residency (Greensboro, NC), Pelican Bomb (New Orleans), ThreeWalls (Chicago), and The Design Studio 4 Social Intervention (Boston, MA). The American University Museum is committed to showing the work of Washington artists, as well as hosting traveling exhibitions. We also advocated for a more direct connection to what happens in a Studio Art program.

ZOË: Through all of this, we've learned from other successful models of what can happen in and outside of academia.

TIM: Individually, we've profited in our careers from being part of institutions: Marie Walsh Sharpe, Skowhegan, Creative Alliance, Art 342. All of these places had a powerful impact on our careers, and we wanted to bring that part of our trajectories to our students.

ZOË: We emphasize to our students that, to be on an island, to be separated from community is not the way of the art world, or even of the creative instinct. Participation is key. As much as we were bringing people and opportunities into AU, we had to get our people out into other areas through trips, studio visits—the things that all schools do—to see the different ways people build their careers.

TIM: Our students ended up taking collaboration into new ways: Former students Tori Greisling, Camden Place, Dan Perkins, and Sam Scharf founded a curatorial project named Delicious Spectacle. Their project/gallery was on the first floor of our colleague Isabela Manalo's row house. Isabel Manalo founded *The Studio Visit*, an online blog that she uses to share the work of artists that she knows or artists she is interested in meeting.

ZOË: Community-building extended into our pedagogies and the way we teach. Tim and I both teach an MFA Thesis course in the fall semester. It's historically been taught as two distinct classes. We had students that would benefit from interacting with each other in a structured way. We scheduled the thesis courses at the same time, in essence, to team teach.

TIM: Instead of asking permission, we just did it. We now teach the entire grad program together. It's much more dynamic. And way much more work. We and all the students are working extra hours. Most of our students don't come from art schools; they come from small regional universities. So, when they come to us, they're open, and it's amazing to see their work progress.

We even started a joint art collection. We have acquired four works, two by former students. It may sound funny, but we will likely build a collection together. The collections stems from the location of our adjacent studios, and there are politics behind that story.

ZOË: A few years ago, I had an opportunity to relocate. Part of my renegotiations to remain at AU included a studio space. Tim had a studio in Brooklyn, and the university wanted him to reside in DC. We had two other colleagues who held administrative/leadership roles in the program, who had studio spaces on campus. In multiple conversations with the dean, and to acknowledge the informal studio arrangements that were made with the other faculty, it was decided that all full-time, tenured/tenure-track faculty would receive studio spaces. This was unprecedented at our school, and highly unusual in DC. What this said to me was: when you are working in a community, it's in your best interest to be an advocate for your colleagues. People I know at other universities complain about contentious relationships with their colleagues. We just don't have a community like that in our program. Though we're not without our share of drama, we've worked really hard to get along and be supportive, which is important in a small program.

TIM: All the faculty have studios in an "office" suite that used to be an architectural firm housed off the main campus. The unexpected thing that happens when one has a neighbor is you spend lots of time with them. Zoë and I became engaged with each other's practices in ways that we did not anticipate. Through the years, we saw that there was overlap. Without realizing it, we were both working on tangential projects or using processes that were not a part of our primary bodies of work or that didn't widely exhibit. Zoë has always made small sketches and collages in preparation for larger work, as well as video and animations. However, those smaller pieces eventually found their way into her main body of work.

We were using some of the same props with our figurative works, and we rely on the signifying components of those props, and on textiles, in general. We had similarly themed works, albeit distinctly different subjects.

ZOË: Tim was making small paintings that looked like abstractions, but he had never shown them. Our peripheral work made its way into two-person exhibitions we did with one another. We wanted to see how our common areas of interest would read in the context of an exhibition. This context-making was a way to extend the micro conversations that occur between our individual practices and in our content, broadening the possibilities of the read, simply through associations.

TIM: Isabel Manalo, founder of *The Studio Visit*, invited us to show work in Berlin. She gave us the opportunity to show anything we wanted. Most recently, we exhibited work together at RandallScottProjects in Baltimore—while we each made our own work, we essentially made the work together.

We'd been thinking about how people have made opportunities for us, and how much we want to create opportunities for people *outside* of academic institutions. There's a wonderful kind of condition in academia and even in the museums that is built around a particular kind of structure. We wanted to see what would happen if we didn't have that structure or its parameters. We developed a plan for project space while we were sitting in a cafe in Minneapolis.

ZOË: We are fascinated by artists who we consider "opportunity-makers" for other artists. We're inspired by The Studio Visit Berlin/DC; project spaces like Marginal Utility in Philly, PA; the Suburban and the Poor Farm in Wisconsin; Generous Art in Austin, TX; smaller spaces like The Bindery in St. Paul; and communities such as Project Row Houses and artist-run spaces Terrain and Devening Projects in Chicago. We wanted to continue our push beyond the university and start a project space for artists to make work outside of their standard practice. We opened a project space in Baltimore called ‘sindikit, housed within the Oliver Street Studios in the North Arts & Entertainment District.

'sindikit is two-room project space. We are interested in artists with practices with which we are largely unfamiliar. We like the idea of supporting the local art community by connecting people in the region with people outside of the region. It's about context building.

TIM: 'sindikit is our new collaborative venture. We have several ways that this will work: we are inviting artists to make and show work that they consider outside of their general practice, that they'd consider experimental, or that they'd simply like to "test out." We've even come up with a set of parameters for artists we'd like to invite to do a project but who have a more singular practice. We've made a commitment to do this project for a certain amount of time, and that's really good for us. We feel confident that 'sindikit will lead us to places in our collaboration that are foreign and challenging.

ZOË: It has also allowed us to think more broadly about our relationship to community. I've been commuting between Baltimore and DC for more than ten years. It's been very interesting to see the differences in the ways that artists are supported in each city. Baltimore is very artist-friendly, yet it faces challenges regarding the kind of work that is supported in exhibitions and grants, particularly by artists of color. DC has an established museum culture that overshadows smaller organizations. Increasing real estate prices make studio space for artists difficult to come by, and there are few artist-run spaces. Even with these challenges, both cities have vital, albeit different art scenes. Artist-organized events and programs, like the Transmodern Festival and Y-LEAD, make Baltimore an amazing place to live and work. We want to contribute meaningfully to the city's cultural landscape with 'sindikit.

TIM: Baltimore is an urban city, and it has a really big art school, and both aspects provide a great deal of energy. It also has the infrastructure: lots of old warehouses that allow artists to live and work cheaply. We couldn't have opened the same kind of space in DC. It is significant to join a community that has supported many artist-run spaces. I was a big fan of Freddy and have been a long admirer of Guest Spot@Reinstitute and Area 405.

'sindikit is funded by us. It gives us a way to act on ideas that have, until now, only existed in theory. We teach, we engage with ideas in the classroom and in our individual practices, we prod other artists and our students to build and contribute to the communities they want to engage.

ZOË: As a collaborative pursuit, 'sindikit combines our mutual interests in creating opportunities, sharing our resources, and our enthusiasms about how artists think and what they do. We feel strongly that this is what we should be doing with our time together. What's really inspiring is when other people participate and are as excited as we are. That's when real collaboration starts and our pursuits come full circle.

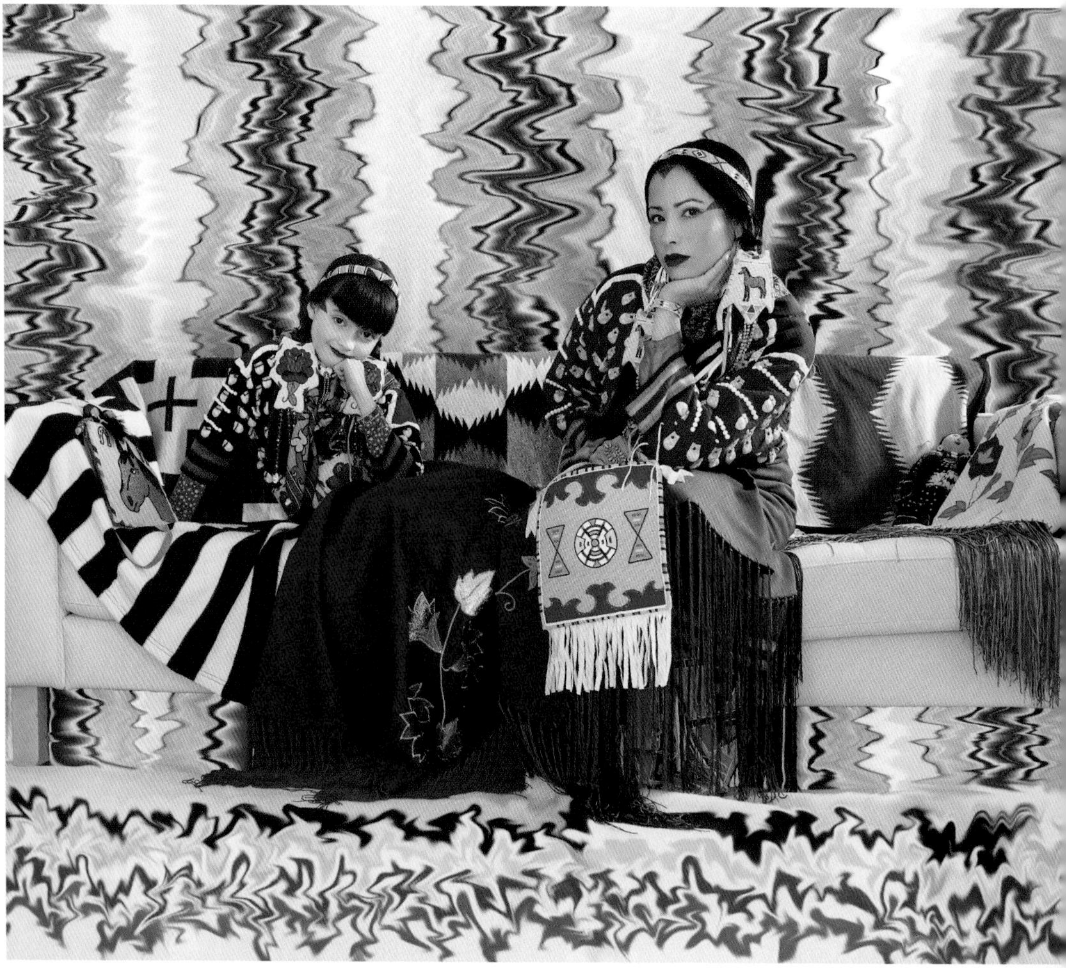

I have a deep connection with the land of my ancestors on the Crow Indian reservation, the homeland of my people, *Apsáalooke*. Located in south central Montana and encompassing almost two-and-a-half-million acres, the Crow reservation includes three mountain ranges, two rivers, numerous creeks, grazing, and farm lands. Within its borders are six towns, clusters of individual country homes, and ranches; the nearest large city is Billings, ten miles from the closest reservation border and 100 miles from the farthest. This is my childhood home, the backdrop of my inspiration, where, of necessity, I spent hours on its roads driving to school or work or social visits. I still smell the smoke of the sweat lodges in the evenings, hear the drums of a sun dance half a mile away, see rows of jeans hanging out to dry on a wire fence, and recall slowing my horse through town to check out who was playing basketball along the curb.

Although the reservation is big, there is an intimate sense of belonging to its history: its people, your clan, your family. Clans are matrilineal: my mom, Molly, is *baashcihile* (white), so I am of the *Ashkaamne (Piegan)* clan, my grandmother's clan. My father is Wallace Red Star Jr.; his father is of the *Ashiiooshe* (Sore Lip) clan. The *Ashkaamne* clan proclaims respect and ownership of my dad's accomplishments, including being one of the first Crows to reclaim family land from over-grazing and make it a working ranch. Every Crow also has a teasing clan, whose purpose is to discipline in a teasing or humorous manner,

Wendy Red Star
Apsáalooke Feminist #4
41"x34"
Digital print on Museo Silver
Rag photo paper
2016
Courtesy of the artist

to keep one's ego in check, and to remind individuals to not take themselves too seriously.

My teasing clan is the *Ashiiooshe,* and it is because of this ingrained humor that comes innately to Crow tribal members that I often view situations from skewed angles and make light of difficult situations, finding the bright to the dark. Wit comes so naturally to my practice and can be seen in various forms of mimicry, like in the *White Squaw* series (2014), where I posed as the main fictional book character Rebecca Caldwell, a.k.a "White Squaw," a half white-half Indian woman, the product of a rape of her white mother, Hannah, by an Oglala brave. This book series, consisting of 24 books of fiction featuring graphic hypersexualization of Native women and grossly dehumanizing acts towards Native men, was written in the early 1980s to mid-90s. I collected all 24 books from various used stores, scanning all the covers and keeping all the original titles, subtext, and pulp fiction-style illustration, replacing only the main character's image with my own wearing various "Native American" Halloween costumes. I did this to own the word "squaw," a derogatory term towards Native women.

My grandmother, Amy Bright Wings, with the support of my parents, made sure that my sister and I participated in Crow cultural traditions. She provided me with a traditional elk tooth dress, a shawl, beaded belt, and moccasins—all objects that I have since integrated into my artwork and a tradition I have passed to my own daughter. Through traditional Crow practices of learning, I soaked up as much of my grandmother's knowledge as I could by watching her continually making. Although she never actually directly showed me how to make traditional Crow regalia, I learned through the process of immersion. I am grateful that my mother recognized the uniqueness of my cultural upbringing, so rooted as it was in the land and landscape of my father's family. My parents' combined sensibilities fostered my early awareness about being *Apsáalooke* and not being *Apsáalooke*, about being somehow and somewhere *between*. This sensibility is the bedrock of my art-making practice, and my childhood memories spent growing up on the Crow reservation are a constant source of creative inspiration and what draw me back during the summer months. I doubt I would be an artist without this deep and ongoing connection to my people.

My first big move off the reservation was to attend Montana State University in Bozeman. Feeling fearless, I majored in fine art and took Native Studies courses. For one of my first big projects, I brought in lodge poles and placed various stages of the Crow-style tipis around campus—over popular pathways where students would have to walk through them, across from a dorm, and a full tipi enclosed with canvas where students sought sanctuary. This project culminated with my team of tipis taking a stand on the 50-yard line of the MSU - Bozeman football stadium. They declared that the land upon which they stood originally belonged to the *Apsáalooke* people until it was taken away in the mid- to late 1800s, and that the *Apsáalooke* people were still there, and had never left. This was my first significant artwork that flowed from my heart, and it set the stage for providing me strength to overcome obstacles and challenges through my art practice.

It was in graduate school in 2004 at UCLA where, working with the incredible professor Nancy Rubins, I learned of the importance of generosity in the art world. Nancy invited me to participate in the group exhibition *J'en rêve at the Fondation Cartier pour l'Art Contemporain* in Paris. This incredible experience, and Nancy's belief and trust in me as an artist, taught me that art could not only provide life changing experiences, but that they were made sweeter when shared with other artists and creators. As I reflect, I often crave the fearlessness of my time at Montana State University, where I was just discovering my power and visual voice. I had no frame of reference concerning art history or the contemporary art scene. I was simply inspired to turn my ideas about history and identity into visual statements too large to be ignored. I miss the immersion in academic learning that came in graduate school, as I began reading art theory and exploring my place—and if I had one—in the art world.

Yet those days were also full of doubt. I was the only Native artist making reference to Native experiences, and I knew that others were afraid of honestly critiquing my work. They feared their ignorance about Native people, and they feared offending me as a *Native* artist, rather than just as an artist. I wanted to be treated like the other students and get feedback on my art; I wanted to talk about the aesthetics of the work, not politics. I felt caught between the realities of my lived experience, my desire to honor my people and land, and my desire also to push myself as a visual artist and find my unique creative language.

It was during this time that I created *The Four Seasons*. The works were born partly out of this sense of isolation, a longing for home, and of the necessity to point out misconceptions about Native people using some of the humor of my teasing clans. People will often ask me why I choose humor for sensitive topics, such as the portrayal of Native peoples in popular culture. Humor is healing, healing is power, and power overcomes obstacles.

After graduate school, real life began, and it was a true test to sustaining my art practice. I taught at three different institutions in Portland, Oregon and offered foundational art courses and contemporary Indigenous art seminars, yet I only earned $15,000 a year. I was passionate about teaching, enjoyed my students, and discovered that building courses from scratch gave me a creative outlet. While teaching at Portland State University (PSU), I created a blog on Tumblr, entitled *Contemporary North American Indigenous Artists*. My students interviewed Native artists in the US and Canada, and each post highlighted an artist and included a detailed interview, images, and information for public resource. By creating this blog with my students, I gained access to a network of artists with whom I remain in contact and who I have included in exhibitions. In spite of how challenging teaching was, in terms of time and being underpaid, it extended my knowledge of how I could be a creator and artist through technology and make a connection with a broad network of artists through social media.

2012 to 2013 was full of crushing life changes and stress: divorce, child custody battles, and my father's battle with cancer caused me to completely stop making art. I moved back to Montana with the goal of caring for my dad, giving my young daughter Beatrice a connection to her Crow people, and working as park manager for Chief Plenty Coups State Park. I was truly honored to be a part of Chief Plenty Coups legacy (he was the last official primary Crow chief) and to take care of his property. The job was a wonderful way to reconnect to my community, and it was also a way to support my father, my hero, through the most difficult time of his life. During this time I often felt I might not continue as an artist, but I persevered. In my sorrow, I felt embraced by my tribe and my many Crow friends, and ultimately the experience helped me further in my journey toward my independent life as a creator.

I returned to Portland after just a year away to provide stability for my daughter and for her to be in close proximity to both her parents. From the beginning, Beatrice has been a primary source of inspiration in my art: within a few months of her birth, I learned to sew. I wanted to dress her in sophisticated outfits, like blazers and colorful frocks—things I could not find in typical children's stores. Little did I know that I would fall in love with sewing and fabric and find a talent for it. Sewing is now an important part of my practice, which has allowed me to further explore new avenues of art-making beyond the sculpture and photo-based work I had been producing.

Beatrice and I had also begun to collaborate in my art practice. Our collaboration happened organically, beginning in 2014 when I handed her a stack of 8.5" x 11" photocopies of Crow chief delegation portraits to play with. I was two weeks away from opening a solo exhibition at the Portland Art Museum on the 1880 Crow Peace Delegation, and I still needed a few pieces to help solidify the show. Beatrice returned to my workstation with a beautiful, vibrantly colored drawing on top of one of the chief's portraits. Her interpretation on top of the Crow chief's images was a stamp of cultural ownership. This was what I needed to finish the show; she represented the future generation, and I was inspired to include 20 more of Beatrice's drawings over the Crow chief delegation photographs. Since then, she and I have continued to work on various museum-based projects, and I treasure this time of collaboration with her. Not only does Beatrice help with input in each project, she often decides which exhibitions she wants to participate in. Watching her articulate our projects, and her enthusiasm to explain them to the public, is nothing short of amazing. My hope is that we will continue to collaborate as long as she is comfortable and excited to work together.

As a Native person, I have witnessed the lack of inclusion for Native artists, in particular, in the contemporary art world, many of whom struggle for inclusion in important exhibitions, let alone to find gallery representation. Also troubling is a prevailing but antiquated expectation of what Native art should be, whether from the 19th century or the 21st. This leaves many Native artists feeling segregated into categories of "traditional" work and without a place in the contemporary art world.

As a way of addressing this problem, over the last two years, I have curated two contemporary Native art exhibitions: one in 2014 at Bumbershoot, an annual international music and arts festival in Seattle, and the second in 2016 at Weber State University in Utah. The Native artists in each exhibition represented both the US and Canada and work in media ranging from video, performance, painting, digital media, photography, sculpture, and experimental installations. As an artist curator and a friend of the artists in the exhibitions, I found the experience to be engaging and challenging, with a fine balance of business and friendship with each artist. The gratification of curating these exhibitions greatly outweighed the stress, however, especially when seeing how each artist was so excited to show their work alongside their peers' and have it shown to a broad audience. The unique opportunity to aid other indigenous artists through opportunities that have been granted to me has been immensely fulfilling, and I look forward to continuing to explore this process in the future.

2016 marks the first year that I currently sustain my practice with a combination of lecturing at various institutions around the country, special workshops, and selling my artwork. Selling my artwork is a new experience, as well as working with commercial galleries. My exhibition record is mainly museum-based, and the pressure to make more commercial work is new. I am learning to navigate by making a variety of work that makes me happy and that the gallery can sell. The lows of sustaining my practice are that nothing is guaranteed, and I never know when an opportunity will come my way. I work very hard to get my artwork out to various institutions, which helps me meet potential people and resources for my next project, lecture, or sale. The positives of having a full-time art career is being my own boss, making work that I believe in and that inspires and informs my new work, and investing in the best that I can be. At times it seems indulgent, but I can't think of a better career then one where I am pushing myself to explore new ideas and have the support of people and institutions to see these ideas through.

WILLIAM POWHIDA

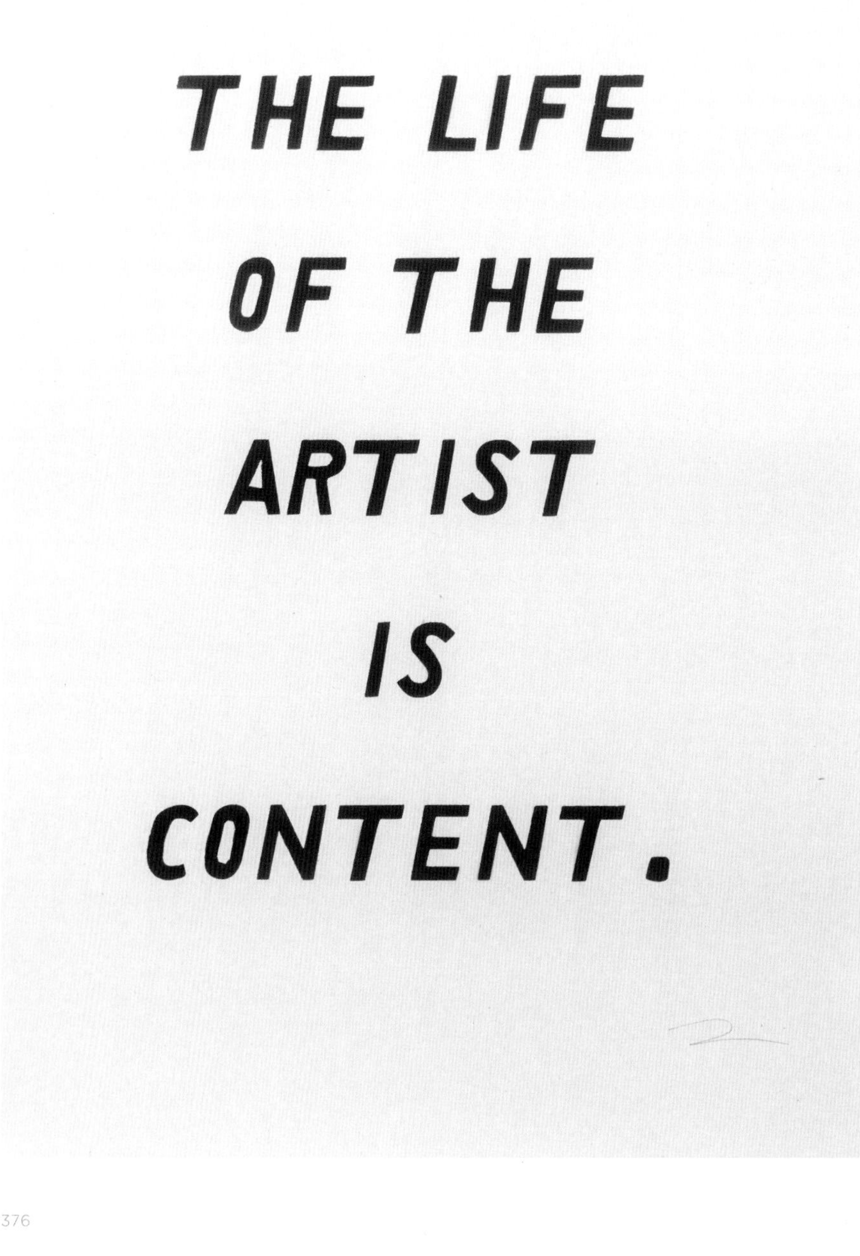

Hi. I'm the artist William Powhida and author of the character "William Powhida." The biography of the artist, and how artists' lifestyles are depicted in the media, has been a subject of my artistic practice since 2004. In paintings, like *The Bastard* (2007) and *Ganek Acquires Powhida* (2007), I have fictionalized my life and experience in an attempt to satirize the way biography becomes part of the mythology that helps create extraordinary value in the art market. In my artist talks, I often mention the infamous *New York Magazine* cover story "Warhol's Children" about the lives of Dash Snow (deceased), Dan Colen, and Ryan McGinley, as well as "The Salesman," a *New Yorker* profile of the dealer Leo Koenig, as material sources for the paintings.

In December of 2009, I was profiled in the *New York Times* by writer Damien Cave, who had recently returned to the US after serving as the Bureau Chief in Baghdad for five years. A print I made in 2007, *Market Crash*, which imagined a stock market crash bursting the art market bubble, left an impression on Mr. Cave when he saw it at the 2008 Aqua Art Fair in Miami. In between 2007 and the time of Damien's profile, I found myself embroiled in a controversy over a drawing I made for *The Brooklyn Rail* called *How the New Museum Committed Suicide with Banality* (2009). The show detailed the New Museum's decision to show a trustee's private collection of blue chip art by established artists at an institution that had been founded to bring under-presented and emerging art to a public audience.

William Powhida
You Statement (Unnumbered)
11"x15"
Acrylic on paper
2015
Courtesy of the artist and
Charlie James Gallery

The editorial drawing, which may very well be a career-defining work for me, was printed on the cover of the November/December issue of *The Brooklyn Rail* and helped shape the contentious public debate about the increasing overlap between the market and nonprofit museums.

I imagine the controversy was one of the reasons Mr. Cave reached out to my former gallery, Schroeder Romero, a year after he had read *Market Crash* in a small Miami art fair. The strange thing was, *Market Crash* pre-dated the very real stock market crash of 2008, but unlike the drawing, the crash did not drag the art market down with it like the 1989 market crash did. Even in 2009, in the wake of the financial crisis, the art market barely hiccupped as the wider economy plunged into recession. In 2009, the art fairs carried on as usual in Miami with some frayed nerves and lowered expectations, but the festive atmosphere celebrating art was in full swing. It was against this backdrop that I met Mr. Cave at the Pulse Art Fair to discuss my life and background as an artist for his piece, titled "Tweaking the Big-Money Art World on Its Own Turf," in December of 2009.

Mr. Powhida is not comfortable in this world. He was reared in upstate New York by a single mother who paid the bills with a government job, and he has earned his own living for the past decade as an art teacher in some of the toughest public high schools in Brooklyn. He said his artwork brought in only about $50,000 over the past three years, and that he was still repaying his undergraduate loans from Syracuse University.

The profile was published on the Monday morning after the art fairs ended and greeted art dealers flying home to New York. These biographical details were central to supporting the credibility of my ongoing criticism of the art market's displays of wealth and privilege, in contrast with the grim reality of the ongoing occupations of Iraq and Afghanistan and the financial crisis. The differences between the art world and the world have always seemed absurd to me, and I have often responded in kind.

The slippage between the way I perceive things and the way they might actually be has been fertile territory for my work, but since late December of 2009, I have found myself living in that space somewhere between the dissolute character "William Powhida" and the "socially-responsible public high school teacher" that is described on my Wikipedia page. This duality has deeply informed my experience as an artist living and working in Brooklyn with my wife, artist Kristen Jensen. While my work makes visible many of the class distinctions in the art world, from the emerging gallery to the blue chip mega gallery, I have only hinted at my life as a public high school teacher in a few drawings from 2004–05.

Teaching, in one form or the other, has been the primary source of income for my wife and me since I began working at Bushwick High School in the fall of 1999. I also explained to Mr. Cave that, while I had earned about $50,000 from the sales of my work, there was also a gap between what I had sold and what I had been paid for. He suggested to me that it wouldn't be in anyone's interest to tell that story in the profile. In many ways, my teaching and my business relationship with Schroeder Romero have been two areas I've never made the subject of any works. Teaching low-income black and brown students was public service, not content for satire or parody. In 2007, after selling a number of works at my first solo show with Schroeder Romero, I decided to switch to teaching part-time at the school I had helped co-found, Brooklyn Preparatory. Unfortunately, I ended up being paid intermittently for sales Schroeder Romero made over the course of several years, in money and studio space, which made my decision to go part-time much more challenging than I imagined it would be.

My financial dealings with Schroeder Romero were difficult and put a strain on my relationship with my dealers, two women I love, Lisa Schroeder and Sara Jo Romero. I maintained a studio at Lisa's former Williamsburg gallery space from 2008 until 2013, and she provided an enormous amount of emotional support for me, personally. It was a difficult decision, but I left the gallery in early 2011 to work with Postmasters Gallery, in part, because I valued my friendships with Lisa and Sara Jo Romero more than any money between us. By 2013, I had been paid what I was owed by the gallery. It just took a lot longer than I imagined it would. People say that the art world is a business like no other, and I agree, having experienced the painful difficulties that can arise when life, art, and business become so closely intertwined with matters of survival. Still, it left me with a deep skepticism about the gallery system where 30% of galleries operate at a loss and another 30% earn between 0 and 10% profit. Basically, 60% of commercial galleries lose money or barely break even.[1]

In the winter of 2014, I left public education and took a job as the artistic co-director of the New York Studio Residency Program. It is a program for art school students to study in the city for a semester. It is a ¾-time position that supports my wife and me, along with the income I earn from art sales. The most striking difference in my daily life is the population of students I teach. I now work with mostly white, middle- and working-class students from across the country and Canada—a near inversion of the classrooms I had taught in for nearly 15 years. It was not an unfamiliar transition, as it mirrored my experience of leaving a low-income school for the very white art worlds of New York. This general sense of dislocation and inversion along racial and class lines had become a routine experience for me. I think it fueled a constant, low-level sense of outrage about the rest of the inequities that I observed in the art world. I was confronted on a daily basis with the racial and class segregation of people in New York, five days a week, at work. I wondered how, in a city of such vast wealth and progressive values, both the its public schools and its art world could be so regressively structured around inequality.

Even as I avoided bringing my experience as a teacher into my work, I also did not discuss my art with my coworkers or students. Occasionally, a fellow teacher would say something like "Nice piece in *New York Magazine*," or a student would say "Mr. Powhida has a Wikipedia page!" On one occasion, a piece, titled *YOU*, had to be delivered to the school, since I couldn't make it over to the studio to receive it. The painting is composed entirely of the word "FUCK." What I didn't know is that the gallery which shipped it had put a printed image of the work on the outside of the box. My colleagues made me open it up for them at our grade team meeting, and thankfully, the English teacher said, "It's like a Lenny Bruce piece!" At work, what I did as an artist didn't matter to my colleagues. It was incredibly hard work that constantly challenged me as an educator, and I have an enormous amount of respect for the students and the teachers. The job often made the goings-on in the art world seem trivial and ridiculous.

Instead of reacting respectfully and deferring to the value system of the art world, I responded with outrageous and satirical attacks on its apparent indifference and even disdain for the struggles of the poor and working-class through numerous individual and collaborative projects. The class consciousness that runs through all my work might be attributed to growing up with a "single mother who paid the bills working a government job." This biographical detail elided the fact that I am also a third-generation artist. Both my mother and grandmother are artists whose struggle with social norms and patriarchal expectations informed my perspective on art.

I should also add that I come from a downwardly mobile family. My grandfather's family were Dutch immigrants who colonized Brooklyn, literally. Remsen Avenue is named after my ancestor Rem Vanderbeek, who had nine sons. At some point, my great-great grandfather moved north, and my grandfather ended up in Hudson Falls, New York. His wife, Elizabeth (Betty) Hawkins, turned out to be an artist. As a kid, it didn't seem unusual to have a 20-foot-tall abstract sculpture of a nude woman by the dock at their lake house. I grew up surrounded by my grandmother's Picasso-influenced sculptures and paintings at her homes and ours. Unfortunately for my mother, Nancy, *her* mother never practiced her art in front of her family. It was not socially acceptable for Betty to be a wife, mother, and artist in the small town of Hudson Falls in the 1940s and 50s. I don't think she ever felt it was socially acceptable, and her art always remained a separate aspiration.

My mother did not come to study art until she was in her thirties, years after I was born. She says she wondered why I spent so much time drawing obsessively as early as three or four, and it made her curious enough to take a class at the local high school. She never looked back and has earned three art degrees over the course of three decades. If I saw art in my grandparents' homes, my mother made the practice of it a central part of my life. I spent many evenings in middle school wandering through the art studios at Skidmore College, where I would eventually take figure drawing on Wednesday nights. My male high school friends would ask incredulously, "Wait, you draw naked women?! Where do I sign up for that?" Thankfully, none of them actually tried, because they would not have had the discipline to observe a body for three hours. I have to admit, that despite the many horrors of high school, my friend Seth and I were encouraged by our friends to make art. Making art did not mark us as outsiders, and it was probably odd that the alpha males wanted to paint and draw, while drinking beer in our basements. As much as I remember wanting to escape the conservative culture of upstate New York, I have to admit there was a lot of support from unusual sources.

When I explained to my mother and grandmother that I wanted to study art in college, they were both resistant. They wanted me to study law and become a judge like my grandfather. Eventually, they both relented after I switched my major to painting in my sophomore year at Syracuse University. My grandmother's permission came in the form of her beloved Picasso book, her manual for *Modern Art* held together with duct tape. My mother continued to worry, rightly, about how I would support myself as an artist and tried to make the decision to major in painting as difficult as she could. She didn't want me to enter into the field lightly, knowing some of the difficulties and struggles of being an artist herself. I think my decision to study at Syracuse helped put her at ease, since it remained a possibility for her that I was at a university and could go to law school later if I failed completely as an artist.

I think it's important for me to explain this, because I am not some outsider with a working-class grudge against the art world's elitism. I grew up with many privileges, from weeks of summer camp to weekend art classes, often paid for by my grandparents who, themselves, came from old family money. While there was always tension from my grandparents' tacit disapproval of my mother's choices, they provided an economic safety net for us. That didn't change the fact that my mother worked incredibly hard as a state rehabilitation counselor, artist, and single mother to support us, my brother and me, but there was always a little family money to avert disaster. I have a memory of my mother coming to pick me up at the mall in an aging, bumblebee-colored Chevy Citation spewing a cloud of smoke behind it. It was burning a quart of oil a day. Before the engine failed completely, my grandparents bought her a new car when she had no money. Being without a reliable car in upstate New York is a severe limitation and, without my grandparent's support, I don't quite know how we would've ever managed. I think my mother would have had to abandon her own art practice entirely, and I might have not developed mine. It is more correct to say that I was reared by two female artists who introduced art into my life at a very young age, despite the powerful social constraints that limited their own ability to be artists. That is a personal history I think about often when confronting the hierarchies and values of the art world, particularly who is permitted to call themselves an artist.

It's questions like that which have motivated many of my choices as an artist, particularly the work I have done with other artists and activists following the controversy around the New Museum and the public attention it brought into my life. That implications and opportunities that developed out of that debate began a bifurcation of my artistic practice, between satire and a more earnest engagement with the issues that I think continue to polarize the art world and society.

In 2010, artist Jennifer Dalton and I worked together with her art dealer Edward Winkleman on a project called *#class*. Together, we transformed Winkleman Gallery into an open platform for discussing the status of contemporary art as a luxury commodity for the ruling class. The project did away with my satirical public persona (mostly), shifting my role into that of a collaborator and co-moderator with Jennifer for a month-long series of performances and contentious discussions that challenged our own assumptions about who art was for. Over the course of a month, we met five days a week with artists, critics, collectors, curators, art dealers, and the public to discuss topics that addressed a central question "Is contemporary art a luxury commodity for the wealthy that limits the possibility of ownership, understanding, and access based on class, education and geography? If so, why exactly is that a problem?" The project, in retrospect, is probably the cultural contribution I would like to be remembered for, rather than the New Museum drawing. The project put a great deal of media attention on the way the art market was changing the art world, and I am extremely proud of the way that attention was shared with so many other artists, critics, and curators. *#class* was the first place I heard about Working Artists and the Greater Economy (W.A.G.E), and it proved to be the starting point for Ben A. Davis's excellent book, *9.5 Theses on Art and Class*.

The following year, I did two projects that I think fully reflect the growing schism between my satirical practice and my social and political concerns. During the summer of 2011, I presented a show called *POWHIDA* at Marlborough Gallery, where I placed an actor in the Chelsea Gallery for a two-week show that largely began and ended with the spectacle of the opening. The show received comic levels of media attention, ranging from scathing attacks in *Artforum* to an appreciative review in the *New York Times*. This all occurred while I was doing a community-based residency in Sheboygan, Wisconsin, working with the public on a collaborative drawing based on shared pop culture memories. It marks a moment for me where the character "William Powhida" became an autonomous entity, embodied by the performer Rick Dacey who improvised the performance from a daily script I wrote; but the project existed almost purely as a mediated spectacle in the press.

That fall, I opened *Derivatives*, a show organized around a large-scale drawing of Matt Taibbi's book *Griftopia*, which I finished alone in the studio as the Occupy Wall Street (OWS) movement erupted in Zuccotti Park. OWS introduced the concept of income inequality and the slogan "We are the 99%" into the social and political lexicon. At the time, I felt the extreme limitations of the political efficacy of an isolated, individual artistic practice. I wanted to abandon the studio and join the occupiers in the park to share my outrage at the concentration of wealth in the hands of the 1%. Instead, I finished my solo show for Postmasters.

Eventually, in the winter of 2012, I joined the Occupy Wall Street working group Arts and Labor for about six months before the various factions splintered off into separate working groups. The most important part of the experience was developing relationships with people working in the arts who shared similar concerns about our labor and working conditions in an age of historically unprecedented levels of wealth and income inequality. That experience and working with groups like W.A.G.E reflect the shift in my creative life that is dedicated to social and political organization. This has involved different ways of working creatively, both collectively and individually, that have reciprocally informed my studio work.

I have arrived at a place in my creative life, as an artist, educator, critic, and organizer, where I can see the value of the intersection between the symbolic value of art, which exists outside of the cycles of social relevancy, and the pragmatic value of social and political engagement. I am glad that I finished drawing *Griftopia* in the studio while Occupy broke out. The drawing has been touring the UK for the last three years as part of a show called *Show Me the Money: Image of Finance, 1700 - Present*, which points to the way art can leap through time and spaces that would be impossible for me as person. Conversely, I am incredibly aware of the time that I have, and the different ways I can be useful, as an artist. I recently finished some designs for an activist network protesting our mayor's plans for "affordable development" in New York City, which is enduring a housing and workspace crisis that is hitting low-income and working-class people the hardest, particularly people of color. I do agree with Mr. Cave that I am not comfortable in the "art world," and I would add that I am not comfortable in the world as it is.

1. Resch, Magnus. *Management of Art Galleries* (Hatje Cantz, 2015), 30. This is the only useful piece of information in Magnus Resch's book; *Management of Art Galleries* is an odious plan for a corporate gallery model. It is a useless book that I wouldn't recommend to anyone thinking about opening a gallery. The figures I cite are from Resch's survey of 8,000 galleries in the US, UK, and Germany, and the 16% of them that responded to his questions about gallery profitability. He should publish his research findings for free on the internet as a public apology for the rest of the book.

CONCLUSION

Chen Tamir

Currently based in Tel Aviv, I've witnessed the many recent lashes against artistic freedom over the past two years in Israel—which include government ministries defunding controversial plays or institutions, redirecting funding for political gain, and blatantly censoring works or artists. It is all too easy to link censorship episodes to the fiery tinder that sparked the early onslaught of fascist or dictatorial regimes, as several have done recently, but what we should look at is how these scenes play out in *democratic* societies rather than totalitarian ones. We are far from the threats of totalitarian regimes taking hold as they did in the 1930s in Europe; much more likely are shifts towards nationalistic, neo-liberal limitations to freedom of expression via democratic means, making the history of the individual artist grant program of the National Endowment for the Arts (NEA) an important precedent from which to take lessons.

The following summary of the NEA's individual grants program is based largely on Michael Brenson's *Visionaries and Outcasts*,[1] a wonderful, in-depth study of the changing tropes of the artist in American society.

The NEA was founded in 1965 under Lyndon Johnson—it was not John F. Kennedy, as many believe, but Johnson who saw how Kennedy's support for the arts gained him favor. Johnson was also trying to get support from East Coast liberals for the Vietnam War, since he was about to deploy more troops. He also had some understanding of how the arts were important in "marketing" the US after WWII. Abstract Expressionism, and modern art in general, was reviled before WWII, but after the war it became a symbol of a new world, led by the US. It symbolized individuality and democracy. It was paraded around the world; international exhibitions were funded by government money—the State Department!—and showed the world a strong new America, where freedom of speech reigned and where they let artists make works that look like drippy goop. That these works were all about individual interpretation fit perfectly with the ideals of democracy being paraded around the world. Subjectivity was the new connoisseurship, and what mattered one's own viewpoint and what *they* saw in the work.

In 1965, there were still traces of the Communist witch-hunts in the 1950s, whose victims included many artists. But despite that, the rhetoric of the Cold War championed independence and free expression as paramount American values. America was about anti-ideology, complete freedom. And even though some artists were persecuted as Communists, artists generally epitomized the notion of individualism and freedom in a country which founding metanarrative is having been built by outsiders: pioneers, cowboys, and puritan renegades.

The artist was considered an outsider as well—an introspective person who was independent from mainstream life, who had a sensitivity and spiritualism that was akin to religion and nature but not part of organized religion (and therefore had no power). This meant that the artist was built of a stronger moral fiber and answered to higher beings that befit a secular democratic nation. Because America was putting more and more emphasis on conformity and consumerism, the artists' estrangement from society was crucial for his or her integrity and insight.

The 1960s also saw a culture boom in the US, particularly mass media and popular culture—especially through TV and consumerism. Some worried about the moral and spiritual nature of Americans. The artist served as a foil to such consumerism. Within this milieu, the NEA was born, funding organizations in all the arts and pioneering the important individual artist grant program, giving money directly to artists via a peer review process. These grants were important, not just in terms of commissioning new work. They legitimized an artist's work to their peers and were proof to puritan parents that making art wasn't a waste of time—that being an artist was important. It was a service to society.

Over three short decades, the world changed radically—and America changed with it. Global paradigms shifted in many ways. The Cold War was over, and there was no longer a need for art as political propaganda. America didn't need art as self-analysis or as a moral and cultural compass. There was no longer competition to the American, capitalist ideology. And in any case, artists were certainly not the ones to serve as moral examples anymore. Whereas in the 1960s the artist was special, enlightened, led a meaningful ethical life, and embodied humanitarian values, the 1970s and 1980s saw a significant increase in the Christian fundamentalist movement, whose adherents saw themselves as leaders in social and moral values.

Similarly, technology and science were no longer seen as menacing. There was no need to question them. There was blind belief in them—as there was in the market. The economy was seen as an "invisible hand" that should be surrendered to without question. And, by then, art itself was no longer seen as separate and pure, but very much a part of a huge, booming art market. The image of the artist was no longer that of an idealist starving in a studio. These were rock stars in SoHo lofts, doing cocaine and selling artwork for exorbitant prices. They didn't need grants, certainly not from the taxpayer. The belief was that if people wanted art, they should pay for it.

At the US Senate on May 18, 1989, Republican Senator Alfonse D'Amato dramatically ripped up a book with a photo of Andres Serrano's *Piss Christ* on the cover. Senator D'Amato was joined by Senator Jesse Helms in publically denouncing the work of art. The infamous photograph of a crucifix submerged in the artist's urine was shown at a group show of artists who were awarded grants from the Southeastern Center for Contemporary Art in North Carolina, which receives operational funding from the NEA as an institution.

Senators D'Amato and Helms didn't hear about this show by accident. A group called the American Family Association vehemently attacked the exhibition as "immoral" and "anti-Christian." They sent out newsletters with names and addresses of congressmen and senators, urging people to demand of them the firing of NEA officials.

Alongside this hysteria was the fight against a large retrospective of Robert Mapplethorpe's work that was supposed to open on July 1 at the Corcoran Gallery in Washington DC. The traveling show was organized by the ICA Philadelphia, which received $30,000 from the NEA for the exhibition.

The Mapplethorpe exhibition was canceled, and many artists and arts groups protested, lobbied, and formed anti-censorship organizations. All this intensified attacks on the NEA, with politicians calling to cut their budget and insert new regulations that would limit or end NEA subcontracts to arts organizations.

At the height of the AIDS crisis, when openly gay and lesbian artists were making work about their bodies and their identities, it came to performance art being debated on a national level. The infamous NEA Four—Karen Finley, Tim Miller, John Fleck, and Holly Hughes—had their grants from the NEA vetoed in 1990 by John Frohnmayer, the NEA's newly appointed director. Continuing to buckle under the pressure, the NEA stopped the individual artist program the next year. However, it had not been the individual artist program that had funded any of the controversial exhibitions! The Mapplethorpe and Serrano exhibitions had been funded by institutional grants that remained intact. And the NEA Four had been awarded money from the theatre grants, not the visual arts. Regardless, the NEA discontinued its individual artist program. The neo-liberal rationale was that the system would let funding "trickle down" from institutions to artists, effectively proving that America, though still wanting art, just didn't want artists.

A similar scenario is playing out around me as I write. Over the past two years, the arts in Israel have been increasingly threatened by censorship and draconian government funding proposals.[2] The calls for and instances of censorship have been both top-down (from government officials banning books, plays, or artworks) and grassroots (by private citizens calling for the removal of artworks). But in all cases, the crux of the matter is the money trail and whether tax revenue should be used when it comes to politically charged artworks. Even the Minister of Culture has been campaigning for a "Freedom of

Funding" bill that would grant her ministry the "freedom" to fund projects and institutions as it sees fit. She's also enacting steps within the framework of the "Loyalty in Culture" bill to sway funding toward individuals and institutions that agree to program or perform in the occupied territories, and away from anyone who does not sign a legal statement attesting to their readiness to do so.

Although these developments sound like something out of George Orwell's *1984*, they are taking place through democratic mechanisms. And this is precisely why there is a fundamental principle to opposing the manipulation of public funding. We do need more public funding, but not the kind that comes with strings attached or that's used to curry political favor or push forth propaganda.

The alternative to public funding, consistent and significant private funding for the arts, is a challenge in Israel considering the lack of philanthropic attitudes in the country, where the vast majority of private support comes from the US or parts of Europe. There simply is not a strong enough philanthropic culture within Israel for arts to make up for the public sector, and the situation is even worse in many other countries where the private sector scarcely exists.

Even if institutions in Israel manage to secure private funding, the meaning of such a framework is different in principle. If an Israeli organization presents politically challenging work, or invites a Palestinian or Arab artist or organization to collaborate with them, it carries a different meaning as an official, state-supported organization than it would in a privately funded one. This example only illustrates the importance of public support for the arts around the world. That we as a society chose to value freedom of expression and creativity—even dissenting voices—is to manifest democracy.

And today, it can sometimes be hard to distinguish how to do that. The fine line between austerity and censorship is not always clear. Over the past several years, many European countries have scaled back their funding for the arts as more right-wing governments were put in place. The Netherlands, for example, cut 25% of its art budget and nearly decimated mid-level arts organizations. In more nationalistic governments, like in Hungary for example, the austerity measures went hand-in-hand with an antagonism to freedom of expression that can be seen in other countries as well, like Poland and Russia.

Though the tactics may have changed, the basic argument remains the same. "You can do whatever you want, just not with public funding—not in public institutions." "You can be gay, but keep it in the bedroom, we don't want to see it." "You can have abortions, we just don't want them to happen through our healthcare system." We cannot let ourselves get confused by this rhetoric. We have to ensure democratic and open systems for the arts. We need to fight for a healthy cultural ecosystem that can provide a true platform for what artists have to say. Otherwise, artists become a puppet controlled by someone else. They no longer function as a mirror of our societies. They no longer raise questions about the world we live in. If in a democracy, the government serves the people and must demonstrate its loyalty to them; in fascism, individual citizens must demonstrate allegiance to their government, and nowhere is that more easily done than through the platform that art provides. We see the dangers of this very clearly in the budding McCarthyism taking place in Israel. But beyond Israel, or even the US, we must constantly ensure that, as the mouthpieces of a society, artists have an essential right to freedom of expression. They are the canaries in the coalmine: if they can't be free to make artwork or speak their minds, we'll be next.

1. Brenson, Michael. *Visionaries and Outcasts: The NEA, Congress, and the Place of the Visual Artist in America* (The New Press, New York. 2001)
2. These developments are outlined in detail in a text I originally published on Guggenheim.org. Some of the following content first appeared there. (https://www.guggenheim.org/blogs/map/censorship-in-israel) © 2016 The Solomon R. Guggenheim Museum, New York. Used by permission.

CONCLUSION

Courtney Fink

It's not often that I'm asked to explain the value of the work I do supporting artists. Maybe that's why it seems like such an existential proposition to discuss my personal reasons for that work.

Have you ever asked yourself what value artists bring to you? To the world? Is it that artists help us see a vital piece of our existence? That they create a shared sense of humanity and remind us what we have in common? Yes and no. While dreaming about the more visceral ways artists and art affect us is one way of looking at their value, there is something more practical at play when the work of supporting artists becomes your purpose. Artists improve my life and, by extension, the world. Yes, I mean *the world*. Coming to that realization was a moment of clarity for me, and one that has led me to try to help other people understand how this is true as well.

The things I have done and do in my life have laid down the groundwork for talking about value. Simply put, I work to support artists and, by extension, organizations that are focused on artists. Of course, it's not really that simple, but my efforts all boil down to that. Specifically, I am supportive of visual artists whose work is experimental, engaged with the world, and at the vanguard of new ideas. I want to ensure artists are able to develop new ways of thinking and that they have a supportive space—community, city, region, and larger culture—in which to do so. I make spaces, opportunities, and systems to this end, primarily through working at several artist-focused organizations, including a long-time stint as Executive Director of a not-for-profit organization, Southern Exposure, in San Francisco. I pioneered a re-granting initiative to support independent arts organizers that has now become a national effort across the US; I have also collaborated to found and run a new, nationwide network of these organizations, called Common Field.

Through more than 20 years of trying to make stuff happen—sometimes meeting with great success, and other times with failure—I've come to understand that, through this work, we're trying to manifest a deeper set of values. We're trying to return public participation and autonomy to culture producers who have been edged out by a focus on capital. We are attempting to create much-needed, non-commercial spaces of experimentation and contemplation. These efforts form an essential foundation which builds value and culture around risk-taking rather than money, with the central goal of supporting artists whose work aims to have impact far beyond the space of the gallery.

Smaller scale does not mean smaller impact. Operating from a nimble position allows for the creation of new models and highly participatory strategies that would not otherwise be possible. Working at a smaller scale allows for more direct connection to people and communities. This is where real dialogue and contact happens, where new forms of culture are developed, and where people truly can come together. This kind of work builds bridges between artists and communities. Often, the public doesn't know how to reach artists; likewise, artists don't readily know how to find or communicate well with the public. Often, arts organizations are in a position to bridge those gaps.

In turn, connecting the public to artists in an intimate and direct way builds culture. The value of such engaged arts practices, while well understood by those within the field, is not widely appreciated more broadly, because these practices often exist in opposition to commercial and capital culture. Additionally, the impact of these artists' work is very difficult to measure and can take many years to realize. Engaged artists and small organizations build social, artistic, and financial value, but it's often many years after a project has been realized. If you follow the trajectory of a project, the full value of its impact is often attributed far from where the galvanizing work began. Sometimes, those impacts are linked to larger institutions and commercial entities which are increasingly eager to absorb ideas whose genesis is in the work of artists and small organizations. But the ground level is where things start.

Especially now, at a time of great change in cities across the US, when issues of equity and affordability present tangible challenges for artists, it has become crystal clear that spaces for artists and the public to come together are essential. Even more, it's imperative to better educate the population about how critical artists are in their communities—from ensuring cultural hubs can remain sustainable to artists and organizations' work improving the changing social landscape.

It all comes back to our measures of value. The real work is amplifying the value of artists to society. The advocacy and organizing work involved in that is to ensure artists are valued, understood, and supported. Instead, too often these efforts are challenged by the fact that our field is threatened and destabilized. But if you don't experiment and take risks, you don't move things forward. Not all risks work out, but you have to be willing to try.

Experimentation and risk-taking are common values of smaller arts organizations. The culture created by small organizations is similar to the culture made by artists who engage with the world. I see their work and practices as intertwined, as related forms. Like artists who work beyond the space of the institution and in the public realm, so, too, do small organizations engage directly with the world. I champion organizations that are focused on artists, in particular, because at their core, they have resiliency, ingenuity, perseverance, and willpower. These are the organizations which have helped to reshape and redefine the social function of art. They are on the frontlines of ensuring artists get the support they need and have resources to do their work.

This organizational layer of the creative ecosystem is large. It is artist-driven, in flux, nimble, and exists in many forms, scales, and models. So much culture is built on the foundation small arts organizations have established and the precedents they have set for risk capital. Artists, historically, have created this field of work. And this work exists in line with the cultural production made by artists who work outside of the commercial and institutional realm, who impact and affect social movements, field building, activism, and organizing.

The value collectively made by this field of small organizations, and by the artists who have established them, has paved the way for artists as cultural producers. Hand in hand, the value that they all build together has established a new way of working, a new role for artists in the world, and a new form of thinking about what art can truly be.

CONCLUSION

Deana Haggag

In 2011, I moved to Baltimore shortly after returning to the United States from Egypt, where I was living when the Mubarak regime was overthrown. It was one of many uprisings in the region that hurled Cairo and the rest of the "Arab Spring" into a global 24-hour news cycle that aired endlessly across the world. Today, I am still in Baltimore. It has been over five years since I arrived here and almost one year to the day since Freddie Gray died in police custody, once again situating me in the incredibly abstracted and meta experience of living in a city under media siege.

I have chosen very deliberately to embrace my times. My work in the arts feeds off current events—so much so, that I literally work for an organization called The Contemporary. I spend countless hours consuming the news and considering "the current," because it moves me to remember that I am one person amongst many in the world and that things are always happening. And yet I have learned, through a very privileged lens, that nothing forces you to examine "the current" like living within the speculative confines of a news narrative. I've also learned that giving oneself up entirely to the realities of "the current" can be a threat to the spirit.

In both Baltimore and Cairo, I found myself repeatedly asking why the global media's narrative was so different from what was actually happening on the ground. I underestimated certain media tactics used to blur truth and entertainment. Like many, I became too familiar with the infinite ways in which a thing can be exploited. It was mind-boggling and so very disappointing. I watched violence be assigned to bodies who did not author it and communities be taken advantage of to increase ratings. I witnessed, first-hand, the trail of destruction left behind by a media circus that did not care about those places to begin with. I watched a lot of people feel lied to and betrayed—first by their governments, and then by the media that swore it would help them.

Despite this darkness, in both cities, across two continents, two languages, and with the distance of five years between both uprisings, I watched artists and cultural workers act to fix it. They were like first responders, working hard to fill in the media gaps and respect their communities. I watched them tell the truth. I believe that this is because art helps create free human beings. And thus, the most free, the most likely to question the status quo, the most fearless are the artists.

I have the honor of watching artists do incredible things all the time. They work to upset rape culture and honor sexual assault survivors, like the members of FORCE (a collective based in Baltimore and organized by artists Hannah Brancato and Rebecca Nagle). Some, like New York-based artists Eric Gottesman and Hank Willis Thomas, have founded Super PACs to improve political dialogue. They examine the violence forced upon trans communities, like in the performance, video, and sculpture work of LA-based artist Cassils. Their efforts challenge incarceration and the prison industrial complex, like in the public works of Chicago-based artist Maria Gaspar. They remind the world that, no matter how hard it tries to make it not so, black women are still here and resisting, like in Philadelphia-based artist Ei Jane's *#NotYetDead* series. And there are so many others.

But what I witnessed in Cairo in 2011 and again in Baltimore in 2015 went deeper for me. It helped me better understand what it is that makes the arts so indispensable to our collective humanity. In those places, at those times, I watched artists respond with a kind of urgency that other sectors couldn't quite keep up with. I watched artists make space for the stories that needed to be told, so solutions could actually be found. They were responsive and responsible. I watched artists organize massive marches and peaceful protests that brought thousands of people together across race, religion, age, and socioeconomics. They also supplied food and water to those who needed it, hosted programs for young people and the elderly who were often overlooked or targeted during times of unrest, and brought people together for discussions over exhibitions and performances in ways that made space for dialogue and healing. I watched artists rail against the infrastructures of power that let their cities suffer. I watched artists be fearless and empathetic in ways the world really needs in times of crisis. Again, I watched them tell the truth.

As an arts professional and a person who has happily done this work for as long as I have been able, I need no justification for the value of the arts. I exist in a community and live a life that constantly reminds me that the arts are necessary. It is a part of my every day. But as the director and chief fundraising officer of an arts nonprofit organization, I am directly responsible for its overall survival. This comes with being asked regularly to defend the arts solely on the basis of its economic impact. It took me a while to get used to this, not because I don't think it's important, but because I value the arts in ways that I believe infinitely transcend financial productivity. Alas, I can't control our capitalist expectations any more than I can control the media. I am, at times, a pragmatist. And so, I tout that, in Baltimore alone, artists and art organizations create over 9,500 jobs, pump $388 million into our economy, and generate $33.9 million in tax revenue.[1] Nationally, the arts generate about $135.2 billion in economic activity, including supporting 4.13 million full-time jobs and earning $22.3 billion in revenue to local, state, and federal governments each year.[2] These are dazzling numbers and ones that I am always armed with, because I know that they are the mightiest tool I carry.

It took me many years, but I have finally and begrudgingly accepted that the revenues earned by the arts will always be their most convincing justification. However, I still can't help but wonder: at what point does the sector's intrinsic value outweigh its economic impact? In other words, what do we need to exist as whole and healthy people on this planet?

I have spent a lot of time thinking about this question: what is the value of the arts? It may be helpful to know that I am not an artist. I have been a faithful arts administrator and organizer for many years but have never had the impulse or skills to hack it as an artist. I say this so that we can properly frame my devotion to this field. I chose, very willingly, to spend my life in this sector. I owe this decision to many artists, some I've met and some I never will, but all of whom taught me that there are other ways of looking at the world, other ways that it can be.

But perhaps the single most important thing I have seen artists do is tell the truth. I will never forget the first time I heard Devin Allen speak. It was just a few weeks after his photographs of the Baltimore Uprising went viral and landed him on the cover of *Time* magazine. At the time, he was 26 years old and had been making work as a self-taught photographer for some while. He was poised and gracious, and he spoke plainly and honestly about growing up in West Baltimore. He was frank about being disappointed in the media and feeling relieved that his story, the people's story, could actually get out there. He was not shy about the enormity of his luck or circumstance, about how much being on the cover of *Time* had changed his life, even in just those few short weeks. In a media cycle that only showed the wreckage, Devin showed the causes and inequities that led to that wreckage, the people affected by it all, and the communities that were still in strong spirits despite unfathomable systemic disadvantages. He showed the world the truth about Baltimore, contrary to so many other trending narratives.

I remember sitting in the audience listening to Devin and feeling overwhelmed by my gratitude. I remember thinking about all the conversations I had had in those Baltimore weeks and in the weeks I was in Cairo. I remember how little authorship people in both cities had over their own stories. And then here was this artist, one among many, who deliberately sought to change that. Devin went out into the streets of his city and used his camera to tell the truth. He told the truth, and he won. And in his winning, I won; Baltimore won. We all won. I remember feeling so thankful for this young artist and for what he had done for this city, and to *Time* magazine for helping this artist help us all. I remember laughing to myself, because my gratitude for *Time* magazine stood in such sharp and ironic contrast to all my other media frustrations. It was a lot to take in.

Living in a city under media siege is a humbling experience. It is a strong reminder of the misery that comes with feeling voiceless and a testament to the power of the truth. It is a time when you are looking desperately for community, catharsis, and confirmation that someone out there is listening. I am grateful for the artists who led us to those places and who made sure we were heard. I know we couldn't have done it without them.

1. Americans for the Arts. Arts & Economic Prosperity IV, "The Economic Impact of Nonprofit Arts and Culture Organizations and Their Audiences in the City of Baltimore" (http://aftadc.brinkster.net/AEPIV/MD_CityOfBaltimore_AEP4_SummaryOfFindings.pdf). Accessed August 17, 2016.

2. Americans for the Arts. Arts & Economic Prosperity IV, "The Economic Impact of Nonprofit Arts and Culture Organizations and Their Audiences" (http://www.americansforthearts.org/sites/default/files/pdf/information_services/research/services/economic_impact/aepiv/NationalStatisticalReport.pdf). Accessed August 17, 2016.

ACKNOWLEDGMENTS

It takes a village to be an artist. I certainly could not have produced this book without great assistance, partnership, leadership, mentorship, and referrals from many people.

First and foremost, I'd like to express my heartfelt gratitude to all of the artist-contributors who had the courage to share their truth, personal stories, and models of how they sustain their lives. I'm honored to have had this experience with each of them and will always remain tremendously inspired by them all. I am immensely grateful that they chose to take this journey with me and to be part of this important community of culture producers.

Hrag Vartanian is an exceptional thought leader, and he is changing the face of art criticism today. I have never met a more accessible, open, and genuine critic, writer, and curator. I'd like to thank him for his commitment to continually showing the public how important artists and the arts are in the world. In addition, I am grateful for our public exchanges, endless conversations, and always having the opportunity to learn from him by just being in his company.

Chen Tamir, Courtney Fink, and Deana Haggag are all community builders who are tireless advocates for artists. Their words of wisdom chart important paths that help artists thrive. I am indebted to them for their participation and wonderful contributions to this book.

To all of the photographers who considerately contributed images of the artists' works that were selected for this book: thank you very much!

Many thanks to our copyeditor, Susannah Schouweiler, who worked diligently, smartly, and efficiently. A special thanks goes out to Jillian Steinhauer for connecting us.

Because I wanted to work with artists and thought leaders who I didn't necessarily know, I reached out to the following friends and colleagues for their advice and referrals: Sharon Butler, Matthew Deleget, Gina Fairley, Jason Ferguson, Patrick Heide, Julia Kunin, Dylan Neuwirth, Jennifer Phelps, Harry Philbrick, Veronica Roberts, Austin Thomas, and Hrag Vartanian. Without their recommendations, many of the contributors in this book would not have been included.

Thank you to my mentors, who have taught me so much about public policy and the vital role that nonprofits play in the visual arts ecosystem: Matthew Deleget, Linda Essig, Ruby Lerner, Kelley Lindquist, Shervone Neckles-Ortiz, Heather Pontonio, Alyson Pou, Jason Schupbach, Kate Schutta, Steven Tepper, Darren Walker and Laura Zabel. They have all created openings for me to grow my advocacy for artists.

Lots of hugs and kisses are directed to Laura Skoler, Bill Schwinghammer, and Tony Long for being my New York family and home away from home. Thank you so much for your endless and generous support of me. I couldn't do any of the work I do without you!

A book is a powerful platform for conversation. I cannot express enough gratitude to all of the donors who have helped support my book tours. Without their assistance, we would never have been able to use the *Living and Sustaining* series to connect and cross-pollinate artists throughout the country and abroad. My hope is that this book continues to inspire building communities of artists for years to come.

Finally, thank you to my love, my husband, and project manager in everything I do in my life, Vinson Valega.